D0571469

INSIDE
RETAIL
SALES PROMOTION
AND
ADVERTISING

HARRY SPITZER
Senior Instructor, UCLA Extension
Vice-President, Southern California Broadcasters Association
Los Angeles, California

F. RICHARD SCHWARTZ
Vice-President, Marketing and Sales Promotion,
Liberty House, Oakland, California

i

Sponsoring Editor: Earl Shepherd
Project Editor: Beena Kamlani
Designer: Michel Craig
Production Manager: Jeanie Berke
Compositor: Progressive Typographers
Printer: R. R. Donnelley & Sons Company
Binder: R. R. Donnelley & Sons Company
Art Studio: Vantage Art, Inc.

INSIDE RETAIL SALES PROMOTION AND ADVERTISING

Library of Congress Cataloging in Publication Data
Spitzer, Harry, 1916–
    Inside retail sales promotion and advertising.

    Bibliography: p.
    Includes index.
    1. Advertising. 2. Retail trade. 3. Sales promotion. I. Schwartz, F. Richard, 1931–   II. Title.
HF5823.S75   658.8′2   82-971
ISBN 0-06-046383-X   AACR2

Contents

About the Authors

HARRY SPITZER *has been a teacher of advertising almost from the day of his graduation from the University of Georgia's Henry W. Grady School of Journalism in Athens, Georgia. While advancing his career in advertising and retailing, he taught classes and lectured at his alma mater, at Georgia Tech, Georgia State College, Florida State University, the University of Miami, the University of Buffalo, Pasadena City College, UCLA, and the University of Southern California. He is currently on the staff at UCLA extension, teaching courses in retail advertising and supervising and teaching classes in the business of radio broadcasting. His background of over twenty years in advertising and sales promotion positions has served as preamble to his full-time post as sales director for the Southern California Broadcasters Association, where he is vice-president, responsible for the development of new business for the radio industry, primarily from the retail sector. In this capacity he counsels, advises, and instructs retail organizations in the development of efficient advertising campaigns. His career includes stints with Rich's, At-*

lanta, Georgia; Richard's, Miami, Florida; Sattler's, Buffalo, New York; and Zodys, Los Angeles, California. He received his retail executive training in the Macy's organization in Atlanta, Davison-Paxon Company. He operated his own advertising agency in 1971–1972. He holds a bachelor of arts degree in journalism/advertising (ABJ), class of 1947. Spitzer lives with his family in Encino, California.

F. RICHARD SCHWARTZ, vice-president, marketing and sales promotion, Liberty House, California, is a graduate of the University of North Carolina with a B.S. in marketing. He attended New York University Graduate School of Retailing and has been a frequent speaker at the National Retail Merchants Association meetings in New York and other annual meetings around the country. He began his retail career in Bloomingdale's where he received his executive training. He eventually became assistant to the home furnishings vice-president. He was retail merchandising manager for the Celanese Corporation before joining Hochschild/Kohn Department Stores in Baltimore, Maryland, as a buyer of cosmetics. He was subsequently promoted to sales promotion director. He also served as vice-president and sales promotion director for Gimbel's in Pittsburgh and May Company, California, with total responsibility for the media planning and operations of these major retail organizations. While a resident of Los Angeles, he taught a course in retail buying at Los Angeles Valley College. He lives with his family in Orinda, California.

Preface

The authors acknowledge the existence of several texts on the subject of retail advertising, sales promotion, and advertising design and copywriting. There are many books on retail marketing and merchandising. We are also aware that these subjects are usually presented as separate and distinct at most schools. The possibility certainly exists that the student may study one aspect of retailing without ever coming in contact with the other.

In the real world, merchandising and advertising are so closely intertwined that neither can operate without the other. In the large, complex department store, it is imperative that merchandising and buying personnel have a thorough working knowledge of advertising. It is equally imperative that advertising personnel be knowledgeable about retail buying and selling. In the chain store operation, even those of considerable size, advertising and merchandising responsibilities are most frequently combined at a relatively high executive level. In the smaller retail establishment, the entrepreneur wears all the hats. The separation of advertising from buying and merchandising is unrealistic. This book will show

how these two facets of retailing work together, how they interrelate, and how one depends on the other to achieve results.

Rapidly changing patterns in buying trends, fashion acceptance, and life-styles in the last two decades have created a greater need for linking the buying, selling, and advertising functions more closely. The store manager, the department store merchandise buyer, must have in mind not only who will buy the merchandise, but how to best communicate with that customer. The advertising person must, in turn, understand what retail merchandising is all about.

This book is designed to provide practical insight into the current workings of the retail business, with emphasis on the interrelation of the buying/advertising/selling functions. We have updated basic retail operating procedures and principles from our combined experience in merchandising, advertising, and sales promotion positions with major retail organizations.

The book is intended to serve the needs of a number of persons interested in careers in retailing: the student; people presently engaged in some phase of retailing; the newcomer to the field seeking more understanding of the sales promotion function; the store junior executive or department head interested in advancement; store managers who want and need more information about the advertising and sales promotion process; entrepreneurs or individual store owners who need to operate their own promotion programs; and the retail advertising persons who needs to know how to cope and perform successfully within the restrictions and patterns of the broader picture.

The book also provides the store management viewpoint toward advertising and sales promotion. The advertising and sales promotion person who deals constantly with retail store buyers and merchandise managers needs to know how "the other side" functions in order to produce effective advertising.

In this book, merchandising is perceived within the broad spectrum of the total retail environment. Fashion is not restricted to apparel, but we have chosen ready-to-wear for many of our references, since most people readily understand fashion apparel in retailing. Fashion includes apparel for men, women, and children, of course. But fashion is everywhere in our lives today—in home furnishings, furniture, kitchen appliances, refrigerators, carpeting, bedspreads—the entire gamut of merchandise sold at retail (and often at discount) prices. Our chief thrust is to explain and demonstrate how advertising and promotion, properly planned and executed, play a major role in the successful retail operation. We investigate new and developing means of communicating with the elusive, fickle customer, who has ever-changing moods and tastes, newly evolving life-styles, and a high degree of mobility. We present retail sales promotion and advertising as a means of increasing store sales and customer traffic through the investment and proper use of promotional dollars, and thereby increasing net profits.

At the conclusion of each chapter there are questions for discussion and class assignment, many requiring practical application of text material. Illustrations throughout the book endeavor to highlight specific items. Appendix material, compiled from several sources, features glossaries, forms, systems and check lists to make the book usable to the student as well as the retailer.

Acknowledgments

The authors have learned much and received help and assistance from many people and many sources during their retail careers. After years of using facts and ideas acquired from research, observation, practice, and personal contacts, the ability to separate original from research material becomes extremely difficult. Our special thanks to Liberty House, Oakland, Ca., and to The Broadway, Bullock's, Robinson's and May Company, all of Los Angeles, Ca., for their generous contributions of illustrative material which add immeasurably to the text. To those we do not credit directly, we here say "thank you" and reflect with gratitude on what we have learned from so many people along the way.

Perhaps this book can serve as a learning experience—and as an inspiration to those who read it to continue their education and growth in the field of retailing.

Chapter 1
Introduction to the Retail Experience

THE INFLUENCE OF FASHION

From the time the earliest cavewoman checked her reflection in a shimmering jungle pool up to the present day, the job of dressing the woman has been the function of fashion. Today that function includes the job of dressing both men and women, of clothing their children, of designing their kitchens, their homes, of fashionably furnishing the workplace and their places of recreation.

Reaching the buyer with a fashion merchandising offering—the right item at the right time at the right price, combined with the proper styling, color, and texture—is the function of merchandising.

Reaching that person with your fashion story—reaching as many potential buyers as possible for the lowest practical cost—is the function of fashion advertising and sales promotion.

Reaching that person—to determine what, when, how much, and at what price your merchandise will be bought, and determining the ways to reach that person despite the influences of changing life-styles—is the increasingly important role of fashion marketing.

1

The world has moved too fast and too far in recent years for the jack-of-all-trades fashion retailer to re-invent the wheel each time a new problem is encountered. Today the successful retailer must rely on outside sources. The tools are there: the systems; the talent; the information. It is necessary only to put it all together to create an individualized, distinctive fashion operation to serve a specific portion of the consumer public better than the competition.

The influences on fashion have changed over the centuries, but they have always been there. In early times, class distinctions were obvious because royalty and the wealthy wore clothes; slaves were naked. Catherine of Russia dictated what her subjects could wear. Henry VIII accented his broad shoulders with his massive costumes and his daughter, Elizabeth I, wore thick neck ruffles to hide a long, scrawny neck. These personal whims were reflected in the approved fashions of the day and were adopted by the people. In a sense, Henry and his daughter were fashion setters. In more recent times, we have seen the influence of the French designer Coco Chanel, creator of the classic Chanel jacket, who made the little black dress the perpetual memorial to her lost love; of the Duke of Windsor's necktie knot, which many men emulated; of Van Dyke's beard; of Al Smith's derby hat; of the Beatles' haircut; of Jackie Kennedy's pillbox hats and little white gloves. The 1960s youth culture blue jeans have become high fashion, with designers like Calvin Klein and Gloria Vanderbilt building million-dollar businesses on this one item alone.

One consistent influence on fashion over the centuries has also been politics and life-styles. The French Revolution dictated equality in dress as a sign of political change. The drabness and uniformity of dress in Communist societies today confirms the theory of the relationship of fashion and life-style. In the United States today, to be dressed fashionably, to drive a fashionable car, to live in a fashionable home or apartment is a source of comfort, of security, of pleasure, and of social acceptance.

The influencers of fashion are always with us. It is the alert, perceptive merchant who can spot the trends, recognize the signs of consumer acceptance, and take a position on a style. That merchant becomes the community's fashion leader. The stars of television, movies, the stage, rock stars, sports personalities, political leaders, business and industrial executives, their spouses, their activities, their life-styles—all play their part in the fashion cycle.

THE FASHION CYCLE

The fashion cycle is a predictable pattern that has shown remarkable consistency throughout history. Over the 200 years of Amer-

ican history, for example, three basic women's skirt forms have repeated themselves in sequence over the years. The skirt, the
foundation of costume silhouette, has passed through times when
the hoop, the bustle, and the sheath were the accepted popular
shape. The length of the skirt has varied from the floor to the knee,
stopping at different levels according to current dictates. It has
been said that skirt lengths rise in bad economic times and go down
during periods of prosperity, but this has not been totally true in
recent times.

Women's pants were first a fashion "shocker" worn by only a
fashionable few, then a necessity for the women factory workers of
World War II defense plants, but not a staple in the wardrobe of
every woman. Constant change in the styling of the pants—from
bell bottom to pencil slim to "baggies," in a variety of fabrics and
colors—now follow the cycle of fashion along with every other
fashion trend.

Consider too the way men's fashions have changed in recent
years—from the broad shoulders and tightly cuffed trousers of
the 1940s to the narrow-lapeled, slim-tailored suits of the 1980s—
with changes from wide to narrow (and back again) from season to
season.

That "predictable" sequence is often interrupted by social and
economic forces, by wars, conflicts affecting trade and commerce,
and the availability of goods for manufacture and sale. World War
II, social and political upheaval, and rapidly changing life-styles
have perhaps forever interrupted the patterns of the past. Changes
happen more quickly, more often, and for unpredictable reasons.
The result is chaotic market conditions, problems of manufacture
and distribution with which fashion retailers two decades ago
never had to contend.

In practical terms, today's retailers are concerned with a much
shorter time span. Their forecast periods are limited to one, or at
most two, seasons ahead. Their projections may include only three
months, and perhaps nine months. They are more concerned with
consumer acceptance of the current fashions than with the long-
range problems of deciding which styles will be more important in
five years, or even next year.

The fashion cycle itself (Figure 1.1), the life and death path
through which each new fashion idea passes, is basically what it always was, although the time factor is highly accelerated. It begins
with the *introduction* or creation of a new fashion idea or item. The
item may be new in itself, or an adaptation or new version of a formerly popular style. Then comes the *acceptance* of the new fashion
by style leaders, society's tastemakers. Acceptance leads to adop-
tion of the style at the manufacturing level, which assures its distri-

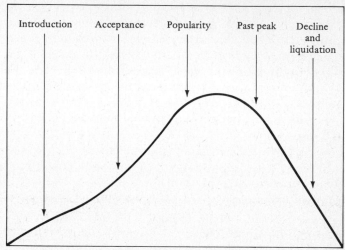

Figure 1.1 The fashion cycle. Each new style passes through the sequence from introduction to acceptance, reaches and passes its peak of popularity, then goes from past peak of popularity into decline and liquidation. The accelerating pace of today's communications affects the retailing world as well. And as a result, the fashion cycle spins more rapidly.

bution to high-fashion stores throughout the country. As time goes by and sales continue, acceptance becomes *popularity*, and the style reaches the general public. It is at this stage that mass merchandisers—Sears, Penney's, Ward's, and the like—take the spotlight. Heavy demand results in mass production and distribution to all kinds of fashion retail stores. The final phase, after the style has passed its peak of popularity, is *decline* and *liquidation.* At this stage, markdowns are taken to reduce prices and move the no longer desirable styles out of the stores' stocks through clearance and sale events.

A major influence in the introduction and reporting of new fashion ideas is *Women's Wear Daily,* a Fairchild publication, subscribed to by most retailers and manufacturers. It is the "bible" of the fashion industry—reporting, communicating, and interpreting fashion at the fiber, fabric, manufacturer, and retailer levels. Many store buyers are influenced by what they read in *WWD* (as it is known in the trade), but rely more often on the market information they receive from their resident buying offices. The competition to be first with the "next great fashion idea" sometimes gets too much attention. Fashion predictions do not always work out: The consumer is the ultimate judge of what new fashion will be accepted.

Successful fashion executives are able to recognize which stage of the fashion cycle an item is in at any given time. They have the instinct, the "feel" for when it is time to move to a new style with conviction and assurance or when it is time to withdraw and unload existing stocks. The ability to know when and how to move can spell the difference between a profitable purchase and a purchase that will end up as a heavy markdown.

The problem of developing this instinct becomes more of a challenge as the duration of the fashion cycle is shortened—from the acceptance of a style for several years to acceptance for a single season, or even a number of weeks in some instances. It is easy to understand that the period of introduction of a new fashion is shrinking rapidly with the help of mass communication and mass media.

A style with little previous acceptance, seen on a national network television show, in a particularly enhancing setting, by an audience of 40 million people, can become overnight a fashion item of national interest. Major TV productions, striving for maximum audience interest, mount their presentations with the assistance of nationally known designers who showcase their fashions under ideal conditions. There are benefits to both parties—the availability of the newest fashions for the TV show personalities and tremendous publicity for the designer.

The retailing adage pictures the ideal as the "right item at the right time at the right price." The more successful operator adds a fourth "right"—the right quantities. This implies merchandising skills that predict when it is time to make a move and maximize sales potential while an item still has acceptability with the buying public.

Sales or clearance merchandise is often created by guessing wrong, by holding merchandise past its peak selling period, by buying too much of a given style or color, by waiting too long to take planned markdowns. The merchant must read the consumer correctly, gauging the extent of initial wants as well as noting when the customer is tiring of the style and does not want to see it any more.

A fine retail store can be seen as an extension of the personality of the store's leadership. Consequently, there is much variation in successful store operation. Timing decisions on merchandise movement is often dictated by the fashion image the store is projecting. A high-fashion store would want to phase out a style as soon as it began to gain popular appeal. A popular-priced store that follows the trends carefully and from a safe distance would tend to bring in merchandise that had been tested sufficiently through sampling or on-floor activity to warrant heavy buying support. And it would keep the items in stock for a longer period of time.

The mass merchandiser is always on the alert, picking up the sure winners copied by manufacturers and offering them at lower prices to the buying public in large assortments of sizes and colors. At season's end, the mass merchandiser or discounter cuts prices until the racks and counters are cleared. At this point, the once bright-and-shiny new fashion item has run its course.

FASHION EXECUTIVES AS MARKETERS

Successful fashion executives today are also marketing experts. They run their organizations from the consumer's point of view. Their ancestors, the single-store, one-person operators, did not know they were marketing people, but they were. They knew their clientele's needs. They had intimate knowledge of the consumers in their market area. Merchandising reflected customers' needs and wants in fashion, and advertising informed them of the new fashions being offered for sale in the establishment. Today's fashion executives handle their jobs in a much more scientific manner. They have research tools and data not even dreamed of by their predecessors.

Positioning the Store

Today's retailers must first determine the demographic characteristics of their market area. Surveys and research projects can give them that data, broken out by age, sex, income, marital status, lifestyle, hobbies, and the like. Specific groups or combinations of groups are then selected as targets for the store. This determination is worked out after considering such factors as strengths and weaknesses of the organization, its reputation in the market area, economic conditions and future potential, and competitive strengths and weaknesses (Figure 1.2).

Once established, this decision, called *positioning*, serves as the guideline for all other merchandising and operational decisions. Now store management can determine at what level of fashion it will operate—what merchandise lines the store will carry to achieve this level; what brand names they will stock for prestige purposes; what price points they wish to set; what selling techniques will be employed; what supporting services will be offered.

Every aspect of the store's operation is then blueprinted, in

Figure 1.2 Johnny Hart's "B.C." cartoon characters deliver unique comments on advertising and other elements of American life-styles. (SOURCE: By permission of Johnny Hart and Field Enterprises, Inc.)

writing, as a policy statement from which all other decisions are made. It includes the information needed to marshal the store's total resources—finances, people, physical space, advertising philosophy, and merchandise mix—in the directions the store has set to achieve maximum sales and profits.

In many cases, especially when starting a new business in an established shopping center or retail shopping area, the retailer will find that the demographic characteristics of the market have been predetermined by the existing stores, their personalities and merchandising presentations. Consumers' acceptance or rejection of the available retailers is the clue the newcomer seeks in order to position the new store to serve unfilled needs and wants. There are also customers the existing stores do not reach. This presents an opportunity for a specialized new store, catering to larger sized women, to racquetball enthusiasts, to bridal and wedding fashions, or to some other segment not being covered.

The store establishes itself in terms of fashion status, customer service, sales goals, and how it plans to make money. Within the framework of the positioning policy, each department in the store sets to work planning its portion of the total effort. The complicated planning process involves anticipated sales and sales trends, markup and markdown levels, gross margin dollars, return-on-investment, and expenses. Within the smaller store—the independent, the chain—each category is planned to contribute to the store's acceptance, to its sales, to its profit.

Written, fixed policy assures consistency and continuity throughout the store, and in every branch outlet of the chain store. The picture the store reflects to its buying public is its "image." Stores often are not perceived by their customers as they would like to be, but what consumers think you are is more important than what your management says you are. A majority of consumers buy from the store they visit first on a shopping trip, and the decision to visit a store for specific merchandise is based on a previously held image of that store. The impression you have given the public from the appearance and decor of your store, the attitude and genuine helpfulness of your sales staff, the merchandise you carry, the advertising that may have brought them to the store, and the satisfaction they have received from dealing with your store all have combined to project your image, your personality, to customers and potential customers.

Chain stores in the fashion field have successfully established niches in the minds of the buying public through consistent presentation of fashion merchandise within style and price lines their customers know and accept. A Mervyn's in Anaheim is the same as a Mervyn's in San Francisco. A Kinney's Shoe Store is identical, whether in New York or Los Angeles. A Kmart store attracts the same type of customer wherever the store is located.

Physical appearance and size, and consequently the merchandise assortment, may vary from city to city—and major chains such as Sears and Penney's have A, B, and C classes of stores—but the "image" is usually consistent in every store.

Planning Is the Key

The ability to plan, organize and control a multifaceted fashion organization in a multitude of locations across the country has helped certain groups grow rapidly while others have been left behind. To achieve their goals, the well-organized fashion operations have turned to the scientific approach in all phases of their businesses (Figure 1.3).

Planning is mandatory. In many areas of fashion retailing, computers allow management to keep a constant check on everything that is happening. Computerized cash terminals feed instant information on the movement of merchandise—by type, by brand, by style, by size, by color. Fashion items on the ascendance are spotted quickly, reordered immediately, shipped more rapidly and reach the selling floor more swiftly than ever before possible. There is constant checking against planned goals—sales, markdowns, operating expenses. Control is the secret to financial success and to greater profits.

Many retailers still operate in the traditional ways, suspicious and perhaps afraid of computers. But they are resisting the inevita-

Figure 1.3   Finalized retail sales promotion and advertising calendar, distributed to all key executives in pocket-size form for handy reference. (SOURCE: By permission of May Company, Los Angeles.)

ble. The next generations of retailers will have grown up with the computer, will be comfortable with it, and will make use of its great potential.

In recent years, failures in retailing can be traced to companies that failed to bring in professional management or to upgrade management with the skills and techniques to handle rapid growth. Failure is not restricted to large organizations. The small fashion retailer, with limited capital and family or small staff operation, is failure prone too, unless the retailer is aware of the tools and methodology available today and has the desire and willingness to grow in today's highly intense, rapidly changing fashion world.

Lessons from Large and Small Operations

Small retailers can learn from the success or failure of bigger counterparts. There are errors of omission. There is the need for a firm, workable plan and the determination to stick with it. There is the need to develop and recruit talent at whatever level required, as well as the need for merchandising and financial advice and counsel.

And some of the larger retailers have much to learn from the small entrepreneur. The large-store executive must be a fine administrator—the job demands it. This skill is so necessary that top management positions often are held by administrators who are not merchants, who do not have customer rapport. But when the decision-making retailer is too distant from the customer, or has no understanding or "feel" for customers' needs, trouble follows.

Independent retailers have challenging decisions facing them now and in the near future. Should they move into the new shopping complex or remain in their currently successful free-standing location? The profit squeeze has been tightening in recent years, yet there is still a profit. Is it wiser to move to the shopping center, with its attendant increased overhead, promotional expenses, and perhaps lower profits? If they do move to the new center, will they be able to hang on for the two or three years it usually takes a shopping center to establish itself?

The resident buying office is a most important source of information for the independent retailer. These service organizations, located in major market areas like New York, Dallas, and Los Angeles, provide noncompeting retail stores with representation and market information and service. They limit their operations to specific categories of merchandise and align themselves with retail stores of similar size and merchandising requirements. The constant flow of information from the buying office is the chief source of market data for most small retail operations.

The lessons of the fashion chains are also there to be learned, to be adapted to the special needs and problems of the independent retailer. The chains have originated inventory management techniques to improve turnover and, consequently, profits. Information on classifications, assortments, price line planning and reporting, size and color mix, and controls can be obtained and integrated into any size operation.

The fashion chains have learned to narrow their focus by limiting the kinds of merchandise they sell, and from this concentration have developed specialized management systems to turn over stocks faster and boost gross profit margins. The successful store becomes the prototype for new stores repeating floor and fixture plans, merchandise mixes, displays, and advertising formats. Result: a greater return for investment dollars and a higher profit percentage ratio to sales.

Nothing, however, replaces the overriding need to achieve accurate insight into the needs and wants of consumers in the market area. Whether these needs are ascertained by instinct or by diligent application of sophisticated information systems, they *must* be ascertained. Independent retail store owners have this insight because they have been in business in a given location for years. But does that alert them to the rapidly accelerating rate of change in taste and acceptance?

What used to require years of planning is now accomplished in months. What used to take months happens in weeks. Computers and information systems have telescoped time into shorter and shorter periods. There is more information, available more quickly. Decisions must be made faster. The fashion executive must be capable of recognizing and seizing opportunities, and must act quickly and decisively to maximize the benefit to the company.

HERE COMES THE FUTURE

The future? Forecasters see a cashless society, shopping in a mechanized world, with the television set as the catalog of the air. There will be, they say, automation for the sale of convenience goods—household needs, toiletries, sundries, and such—from 7-day, 24-hour vending machines operated by credit card via optical scanners. Some stores with their own credit card charge systems have started to accept bank credit cards, such as Visa and MasterCard, as an added convenience for shoppers. Quality standardization and labeling will simplify purchasing decisions (Figure 1.4).

The growth of even larger retail giants is forecast. Vertical control from textiles to manufacture to sale at retail will become more common. Catalog buying, aided by TV, will mushroom. There are predictions that video discs and other electronic devices will replace the mail order catalog of today. They will show a continuous display of merchandise-in-use presentations. Direct mail special-

*". . . Well, the way our holiday sales are limping along no one can
accuse you guys of over-commercializing Christmas."*

Figure 1.4   Christmas shopping time is the best and worst time of year
for retailing.

ization has just begun to scratch the possibilities of target marketing.

But what about fashion? Fashion will always be special. It will
probably always require the personal, individual involvement of
the customer with the retailer. It will be a very long time before the
retail customer is willing to give up the ability to see, to touch, to
handle, to try on fashion apparel.

Despite the resurgence of downtown shopping centers, rede-
velopment of blighted areas and other major happenings that will
affect retailing generally, the fashion customer will always go to the
store to shop for fashion. The individual taste for style, shape, color,
texture, and fit can only be satisfied in person, in a store, in a fitting
room, in front of a mirror.

Fashion tastes and fashion leadership may come from new
sources—from space travel, from new life-styles, from new
methods of communication—but the link between the consumer
and the fashion merchant will remain. As long as the retailer can
"read" the customer, can bring to the selling floor the fashions the

customer desires and will buy, *that* fashion cycle will never be broken.

But there will be changes, and stores of the future will prepare themselves. There will be, for example, increased drive-in shopping, improved transportation with federal and state help, more night and Sunday shopping. As suburbs grow, as downtowns are "born again," the communications media will have to keep pace. The ability of fashion retailers to reach potential customers will become increasingly difficult. Communicating with a highly mobile, uninterested, and distracted consumer will be the special province of the sales promotion expert in the store. The basic principles will not change. Getting the attention of consumers long enough to deliver a convincing selling message that will move them to action will remain the vital premise of all advertising.

As department stores continue to move farther and farther away from home base (the downtown store), as shopping centers continue to grow and flourish (still the most efficient method of retail distribution yet devised) and as communications problems mount (in terms of reaching target audiences), the interrelation of marketing, merchandising, advertising, and promotion will become more and more apparent. Our purpose in writing a book that combines the merchandising function with the advertising–promotion function, a text that is both descriptive and prescriptive, is to help the retailers of tomorrow meet these challenges.

QUESTIONS FOR DISCUSSION AND CLASS ASSIGNMENTS

1. Research recent fashion predictions that failed to receive popular acceptance. Discuss reasons why this may have happened.
2. Name prominent people in your community who are fashion leaders or influences. Are the fashion leadership stores in your city reflective of fashions reported in major metropolitan newspapers? Discuss.
3. Trace a recent fashion item (apparel or home furnishing) through its life cycle. Discuss whether it was a successful item.
4. Select three local stores and describe their positioning policy statements as evidenced in their advertising.
5. Discuss the advantages and disadvantages of operating a retail store in a shopping center versus a store located on a main downtown thoroughfare.
6. Discuss how the increased use of data processing and computerized information contributes to the profitable operation of retail stores.
7. Interview local merchants and report on special services they receive from their resident buying offices.
8. Is it a valid assumption that customer in-person shopping for fashion merchandise will never be replaced by automated devices? Discuss.

9. Describe how a new retail fashion store could position itself in a market through modern research methods.
10. Interview a local national chain store manager and report on the effectiveness of advertising and sales promotion communications between branch stores and headquarters. Does the manager have the opportunity to submit regional or local input? Discuss possible improvements in the system.

Chapter 2
Retail Sales Promotion:
The Preplanning Stage

SALES PROMOTION: OBJECTIVES AND DEFINITIONS

Most experts agree on the basic objectives of fashion advertising and sales promotion. Their importance will vary for each individual store or company, and so will the emphasis in its advertising and sales promotion approach. However, whatever is done in any phase of sales promotion, through whatever medium, communicates something about the store—and the message must be consistent.

Fashion sales promotion and advertising is designed for these purposes:

1. To communicate the total character of the store to its market.
2. To stimulate and maintain a steady flow of customer traffic.
3. To sell advertised merchandise immediately, or in a few days.
4. To establish the store as a headquarters for fashion, for price, for selection, or for any combination of these.

The traditional merchant's approach to advertising consists of running an ad on Thursday and looking for immediate sales action on Friday or Saturday. It does not always work that way. All ads cannot be immediate response ads. No store depends on or could afford to depend on the sales of advertised items for the major portion of its daily business; advertising does not always guarantee a marked increase in sales. This kind of store traffic could be a direct route to financial disaster. The high percentage of advertising cost in relation to sales would be prohibitive.

Most stores develop a fairly predictable daily traffic flow and sales pattern that accounts for 80 to 85 percent of weekly business. Rarely can a store trace more than 10 to 15 percent of its sales to direct response to advertising. Many retailers, especially those with limited advertising funds, seek direct response from all their advertising and are often disappointed. A recent survey conducted by the Newspaper Advertising Bureau, involving many of the country's major retailers, confirmed the 10 to 15 percent direct response averages. John Wanamaker, one of the pioneers of modern retailing, has been credited with the statement that half of his advertising was wasted, but he could never figure out which half it was. Retailers today still face the same dilemma.

The small retailer located in a regional or specialty shopping center has a special problem in allocating advertising dollars. In many cases, a substantial share of the sales promotion budget is committed to the center's promotion program through the store's lease arrangement. Whatever remains after that obligation has been met is usually reserved for price promotions. The merchant picks an item with a strong price incentive and hopes the customers who respond to that item will be exposed to everything else in the store when they get there.

A sound, effective advertising plan requires the establishment of clearly defined goals set far in advance of actual sales periods. The larger the store or chain of stores, the farther ahead the planning takes place. In fashion retailing, the usual practice is to plan the full year ahead in broad strokes, then in two six-month periods, spring (February through July) and fall (August through January). Within this half-year planning there is constant rechecking or revising as the actual month and week approach. The volatility of the fashion business requires flexibility, and the advertising program must retain this pliability to meet the retailer's needs.

What Advertising and Sales Promotion Mean

Advertising and sales promotion are not interchangeable terms. *Advertising* is defined by Edwards and Brown as "any paid-for form of

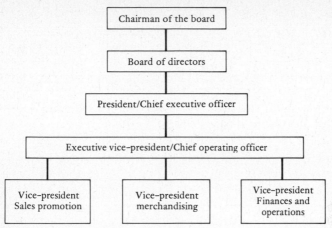

Figure 2.1 Basic department store organization plan. All stores are not structured as shown, but most stores provide for someone to handle these basic functions. Responsibilities of the chief operating officer and the chief executive officer are interchangeable among the president, chairman, and executive vice-president, as the organization desires. There is no one way of structuring the chain of command.

non-personal presentation of the facts about goods, services or ideas to a group." *Sales promotion* involves the coordination of all store activities that contribute to sales, including advertising, display (window and interior), publicity, public relations, and customer services. Anything a customer sees or hears can be considered part of sales promotion (Figure 2.1).

Advertising is an important part of sales promotion, but only a part. It should not, and cannot, stand alone, for to have advertising work best—and successfully—it must have the full support and cooperation of every section of the store (Figure 2.2). The only advertising that does the complete selling job is direct advertising, where the customer responds to the ad by filling out a coupon or writing a letter, enclosing a check or a charge account number—in effect, completing the sale. Direct advertising includes mail order coupons in newspaper and magazine ads, preprinted rotogravure or full-color newspaper supplements, and statement enclosures inserted in charge customers' monthly billing. Direct response by phone or mail to radio and television is effective in some merchandise categories.

Advertising adds an important part to the sales function by motivating the customer to visit the store, or at least phone or write to get additional information in order to make a buying decision. The balance of the sales function is the responsibility of the other sales

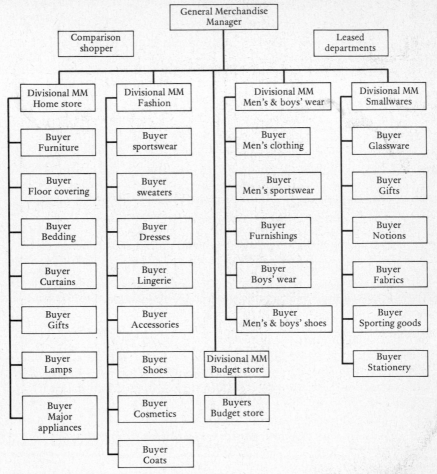

Figure 2.2 Basic merchandise division organization plan. Medium-sized department store plan grouping major merchandise divisions in traditional alignments. Many variations and combinations are possible from this basic plan.

promotion sections. Let us dissect some of the terminology of advertising and sales promotion so that the elements can be stated clearly.

Advertising is distinctly different from *publicity* because advertising is paid for by the store and the publicity is "free." Newspaper or magazine space, radio or television time is paid-for advertising. Publicity in any medium is run as news or a happening of general interest. It includes stories about new merchandise in the store that editors of newspaper, radio, or TV news shows feel is worthy of coverage. This type of publicity is run without charge to the retailer. In some media, regular advertisers receive more than their "fair" share of free publicity than nonadvertisers, partly because the larger advertisers generate more news, partly because even editorial people are somewhat aware of the need to keep large advertisers "happy." There are occasions when the store creates newsworthy events such as fashion shows, the arrival of new fashion merchandise, personal appearances by celebrities or fashion designers, new store openings, and so on, and the media deem it deserving of publicity.

Advertising is communication between store and customer—presenting information about the store and its merchandise to interest, involve, and motivate the customer to immediate or eventual action. Advertising is always directed *to a group*, which distinguishes it from *personal selling*. It must be pointed out that although advertising is addressed to hundreds or even thousands of people simultaneously, each message must be directed to individuals within the group to be effective. Groups do not buy fashion; individuals do. The aim of advertising is to single out those most likely to buy from within the group and deliver the message to them.

Defining sales promotion becomes simpler once we have clarified advertising. The organizational chart of a typical department store sales promotion division (Figure 2.3) shows the various functions that operate under the guidance and control of the sales promotion director. Some stores use the title publicity director or marketing director to indicate the scope of that individual's responsibility.

Sales promotion includes *display* (often called visual merchandising in larger stores), which is the presentation of the merchandise itself. This includes window display, as well as interior display within the store or in specific departments. The display director or visual merchandise manager heads this area.

Some retailers look at *internal advertising* as a separate medium (after newspaper, direct mail, broadcast, and outdoor) with the express purpose of maximizing store traffic. There are three levels of internal advertising: (1) the *stage*—a heavy grouping to tell a specific story; (2) *Major*—a highlight presentation in a traffic location; (3) the *top*—spotlighting a fashion idea on a counter top. In all three types a king-sized photo showing the merchandise in use and a descriptive sign always accompany the display of the actual merchandise. Keeping in mind the statistic that only 15 percent of a store's merchandise is advertised, internal advertising's job is to present as much of the remaining 85 percent as possible.

Sales promotion includes *public relations* defined as the job of

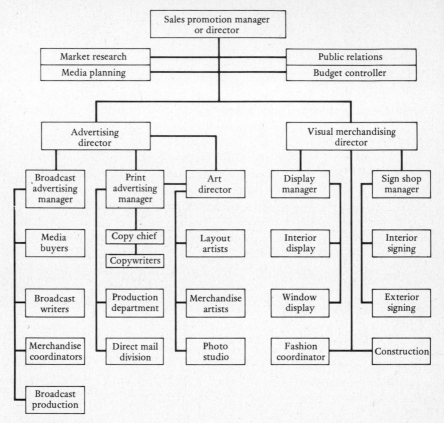

Figure 2.3 Basic sales promotion division plan. Most sales promotion functions are covered in this plan, which lends itself to various other combinations.

enhancing the image the community has of the store. It is the sum of the way business is done: the merchandise and brand names carried; the attitudes and actions of salespeople and executives; and customer services and policies. It is the effort to improve the way in which the public perceives the store, not, necessarily, the way the store sees itself. Sales promotion executives usually cannot change store policies and operations, but these are elements of concern to them.

Sales promotion includes *customer services*—credit policies, return and exchange policies, delivery schedules, and anything the store does or does not do to make the customer welcome, comfortable, and satisfied.

Sales promotion includes *fashion promotion*. When fashion is all the store sells, the fashion director could be the advertising or sales promotion director. The responsibilities are the same: to be sure that all communication with the buying public reflects the store's fashion image. The fashion impression delivered by newspaper ads, direct mail pieces, statement enclosures, window and floor displays, radio and television commercials must all mirror the fashion personality of the store.

The Role of Fashion Sales Promotion

The essence of good sales promotion is the coordination and combination of as many of the sales promotion elements as possible to attain maximum results from the expenditure of promotional dollars.

Imagine this routine situation: When advertising is placed for a special sales event, the information first reaches the customer via newspaper, direct mail, or radio or TV commercial. In the store, the customer is reminded or made aware of the event by the window display or a special display at the store entrance. In the department, a fashion display again shows the merchandise, the sign repeats the sale theme, and a salesperson appears wearing a ribbon or tag inscribed with the final reminder. The sequence has established a favorable selling opportunity. Now the salesperson and the merchandise take over to complete the sale. Customer service assures satisfaction with the purchase. End of transaction. Chalk up another friend and potential repeat customer for the store.

Many stores utilize this idea of combining and mixing for maximum results. Advertising alone can stimulate sales. So can good window or departmental displays of merchandise. Using both advertising *and* display creates a synergistic effect that greatly increases results. The Radio Advertising Bureau's major ARMS II Study quoted many examples of advertising synergism. In one instance, a $15,000 weekly newspaper budget reached 43.8 percent of the target audience 1.8 times. When the budget was split evenly between newspaper and radio, the combined effort reached 58.5 percent of the target audience 3.1 times—a distinct strengthening of the advertising's impact.

This mixing of elements is an accepted practice in advertising media decisions. The combined action of advertising media (newspaper with radio; direct mail with newspaper; TV with radio and newspaper) results in geometrically greater results from the combination than from the sums of the individual media used separately.

PREPLANNING AND BUDGETING

It has been said that most small retailers would rather be good followers than bad leaders. They would rather buy and sell only those items that had proved themselves as "wanted items" by customers or by their competition before they commit and stock them in their stores. They hesitate to be the first to advertise a new dress or sportswear fashion for fear it might be a mistake. They watch their competitors' stores closely—check their ads, their windows, their floor traffic—and wind up imitating the other stores to such an extent that all the stores tend to look alike and carry the same merchandise, thus creating confusion in the minds of the public.

It is important to keep abreast of competition, but that is not the only guideline to be followed. Look at the fashion advertising in your local newspapers. Their look-alike quality is the result of too much "me-too-ism" in the retail fashion business.

Controlling Advertising and Sales Costs

Sound planning is the bulwark of good business practice. Good sales promotion planning is essential for retail success. Of all the expenses encountered in the operation of a fashion store, the two largest and *most controllable* are advertising and sales help. Controllable in the bookkeeping sense, that is, because if the money is not spent on advertising or salespeople, it is retained in the store's possession. The fallacy in that thinking, of course, is that a store *must* have salespeople to sell fashion merchandise and *must* advertise and promote to tell people what it has for sale, to bring traffic to the store, and to keep the store growing.

Without these twin factors, both of which are elements of sales promotion, no store can succeed and grow. Advertising and salespeople are not simply expenses; they are *investments* designed to increase profits by developing audiences for the merchandise the salespeople can sell. In this sense, of course, we refer to salespeople who sell, not those who are posted to watch the store, to look out for shoplifters, or to point the way to the fitting rooms. Salespeople who assist customers and do more than write saleschecks are assets to sales promotion.

Some retailers might say "I don't advertise," or "My merchandise sells itself." Not completely true. The mere presence of a sign in front of a store is advertising. The occasional sale announcement mailed to a customer list is advertising. The "me-too" sale ad in a shopping center supplement is advertising, too. It is not what we would recommend as the best way to spend advertising dollars, but every store does it to some degree.

Because of the shortage of skilled salespeople and the apparent nonexistence of salespeople in many stores, most fashion merchandise must sell itself. Store designers are constantly challenged to develop attractive, functional, self-service fixtures. For example,

Revlon "gravity feed" cosmetic sales islands provide highly productive merchandise displays and self-service fixtures, including a mechanism that automatically replenishes stock in the display unit as customers make purchases. Any fashion item that does not require assistance to assure proper fit and a completed sale can be sold through self-selection via advertising, display, and signs. It has been estimated that if well-trained salespeople were available, their services could add 30 percent or more in additional sales volume to a well-run store.

The cutting or elimination of advertising when business is slow can be a shortsighted bookkeeping device to save expenses. Curtailing promotion when sales plans are not being met makes some sense, but eliminating advertising entirely rarely does. Sound planning lets management budget salespeople and advertising in tandem with sales patterns for greatest efficiency.

The stop-and-go pattern of advertising, spending when business is good and cutting down when business is slow, is a wasteful device. A basic principle of efficient advertising is *continuity*. The more a store advertises, the greater the results. There is a cumulative effect, like a snowball rolling downhill; advertising picks up speed and audience as it goes along. Advertisers who drop out in off seasons have to spend a portion of their money to rebuild the audience that was lost while they were not advertising. It is like the gasoline you waste warming up a cold auto engine. Compare the better mileage you get when you drive your car steadily and smoothly on the open highway against the lower miles-per-gallon in stop-and-go city driving. In the same way, consistent advertisers get more mileage from their advertising budgets and a cumulative buildup from continuous promotional efforts.

Elements of the Sales Promotion Budget

Included in the sales promotion budget are all the expenses charged directly to the sales promotion division:

- Salaries
- Sales promotion media
    - Newspapers
    - Radio and television
    - Direct mail
    - Display and visual merchandising
    - Exhibits and shows
    - Supplies and production materials
- Fashion director's activities
- Administrative supplies (not media connected)

- Outside services purchased
    Freelance art, copy, photos
    Ad agency, other nonstaff functions
- Miscellaneous
    Travel, professional fees
    Nonbudget promotion expenses

In the strict sense, charging only sales-promotion-related expenses to sales promotion, some recurring charges may not be included in the list. In a large department store, if the fashion promotion function is under the direction of the merchandising manager, those expenses would be charged to the fashion division. Some stores have the fashion director reporting directly to the store president, and fashion expenses are budgeted as the president sees fit. For our purposes, we could list fashion direction as either a function of merchandising or sales promotion, since their activities are so intertwined. Where the operational costs are listed is strictly a bookkeeping decision.

Budgeting Methods

There are two basic methods of appropriating sales promotion funds. Many stores allocate a straight percentage of sales—based on last year's sales or this year's planned sales—and let it go at that (Figure 2.4). Others determine, in planning their total operation, what their goals are for the season and how much sales promotion money it will take to achieve those goals. A third method is a combination of the two.

The *percent-of-sales* method is widely used because it is easy to calculate and assures a reasonable control of advertising costs in relation to sales. The figures are arrived at in various ways. National averages for fashion stores place the advertising percentage at from 3.5 to 5 percent of sales. Regional figures vary based on special conditions, such as climate and economic factors. Local market figures vary based on local conditions, such as growth patterns, sales trends in the area, population movements, and so on.

The straight percentage method can be dangerous because it limits activity from the start, inhibiting the aggressive buyer and promoter from operating at full potential. Stores that budget based on last year's figures put the tightest clamps on their promotional people. Stores that set their advertising base on planned sales for the incoming year are more optimistic and are taking into consideration more of the positive factors in planning a sound budget. Sometimes, however, these stores will plan higher sales, but hold

	U.S. Average	Sales $ Last year	Sales % By month	Adv. $ Last year	Adv. % By month	Planned sales $	Planned sales %	Planned adv. $	Planned adv. %
Feb.	5.8								
Mar.	7.5								
Apr.	7.6								
May	7.9								
June	7.6								
Jul.	6.6								
Aug.	7.5								
Sept.	8.0								
Oct.	8.8								
Nov.	10.1								
Dec.	16.2								
Jan.	6.4								
Total	100%								

Figure 2.4   Sales and advertising plan. Sound planning includes making a detailed sales and advertising history before projecting sales and advertising figures for the coming year.

promotion expenditures to last year's dollar figure—a device to "cut" advertising to a minimum cost factor. These stores are nonbelievers. To them, advertising is a necessary evil to which they must allocate funds. They usually do not understand how advertising and promotion work, but advertise mainly because the competition advertises. This attitude is counterproductive and creates poor results.

Using the second method of planning advertising and sales promotion budgets, called the *cost-of-goal* method, management establishes the store's sales and profit goals for the year, then decides how much money it will take to reach those goals. The percent-of-sales information is not ignored, but the total budgets are checked for comparison purposes only. This keeps the aggressive store from getting too far out of line, from increasing sales volume at a reduced profit.

The managers of a well-run store always refer to statistical data on stores with similar merchandise, and of similar size and type, as a matter of good business tactics. These figures are available through trade associations, media research, or the store's own history. The key decision is fixing the budget figures somewhere between what the store should spend to achieve its goals and what the store can reasonably spend and still show the required profit. The percent-of-sales method is like an edict handed down from on high, with promotional budgets assigned by merchandise divisions, by department, and by classification. This assures each aspect of merchandising getting some advertising, and is a fair method from that viewpoint. It does not allow, however, for sufficient flexibility in the total promotional effort.

Once advertising dollars are assigned to a department, that department will usually spend the money. Rarely can buyers or merchandising managers willingly be talked out of advertising budgets because another department makes an opportunistic purchase of merchandise and the money is needed to run an unscheduled ad. "For the good of the store" does not carry much weight in situations where each buyer's compensation is based on performance.

The budget allocation method that establishes objectives and then sets advertising plans is usually developed by the "buildup" process—analyzing the needs and objectives of each part of the store and then melding the individual goals and plans into a total store package. The buildup is from department level to division level to total store. The technique will vary from store to store and may take various routes to the target, but all stores, small or large, must adopt most of the principles and procedures to achieve a reasonable, workable, controllable promotion budget.

Beginning the Planning Process

The initial planning meeting is held at least four to five months before the start of any season. The larger the organization, the greater the number of stores in the chain, the greater the distance of the stores from headquarters—all add time to the planning process. Large-scale catalog operations, like Sears, could be a year or two into advance planning, in comparison to the independent fashion retailer who works from month to month.

Let us take as an example a department store with a strong fashion division. We can discuss the planning phases, keeping in mind that all the elements in the planning operation apply to stores of any size. The kickoff to the six-month plan for the fall season would take place in early March. For the spring season, it would take place in September. The aim would be to conclude spring planning by November 1, clearing the deck for full concentration on late fall ⌐¹ Christmas business in the store. Fall planning should be pped up by Memorial Day, before summer vacations and heavy e activities begin.

In attendance at the initial planning meeting are all divisional merchandise managers, all buyers, and all sales supporting department heads. The fashion and fashion accessories managers, the fashion director, the advertising and display managers, and the public relations director should attend. At this gathering of the people who manage all phases of the store, the chief executive officer, president, or chairman of the board sets the keynote for the coming season. Included are broad statements of policy; economic conditions and forecast; and any major expansion, improvement, or remodeling plans that might affect the total store picture. Overall goals and projections for the organization are outlined and timetables for each department's portion of the package are announced.

These long-range and far-reaching meetings are best held away from the store. The local hotel or motel conference room, a quality restaurant, or the store's own eating facility after hours could be a proper setting for the kickoff meeting. The tone of the meeting should be positive and optimistic, and the group should adjourn on a high note, all charged up and ready to attack the coming season with enthusiasm.

The divisional merchandise manager for the fashion division then meets with the buying staff and the fashion director to determine how the fashion division's operations and plans should fit into the projections for the entire store. In a fashion specialty store, this division *is* the store. If the general plan is to increase store sales by 10 percent, the fashion division decides on broad plans to accomplish, and perhaps exceed that goal. Major promotions are discussed, such as an international fashion show, a fashion forecast series of newspaper ads, a series of television fashion commercials, a radio campaign to reach more young adult customers. Tentative target dates and degrees of emphasis are agreed upon, and the buyers then disperse to work on their individual department plans.

Assuming that each buyer buys for a single department or category of merchandise, let us trace a buyer's activities, step by step, in planning merchandise activities for the fall season. (Keep in mind that the advertising plan follows the merchandising plan.) Sales performances and trends in the department are checked and studied. Since sales records are kept in great detail, past performance information is readily at hand. To evaluate sales results, other sources should also be checked. Information is available through trade publications, through industry reports, from sales statistics, from manufacturers. Comparisons should be made with local sources to check against direct competition in the marketplace. In fashion chains, comparisons from store to store and from region to region provide yardsticks for study.

The buyer has, of course, kept track of the results of the department's advertising from the previous season. Good practice is to keep a paste-up book with each ad mounted and sales results recorded. This should be done on a regular and consistent basis, and as soon as the information is available. Memories are short and unreliable. All results of promotions should be kept, in writing, to ensure that the successful ones are repeated and the unsuccessful ones are not repeated.

Watching the Competition

A record book and advertising results obtained by observation or by comparison shoppers should also be kept on competitors' advertising and promotions. In most cases, they will also repeat last year's successes and usually with similar timing. The decision to clash head on with a competitive push or plan around it can be made more effectively at long range. Close up, in the heat of the moment, emotion sometimes overwhelms calmer, earlier judgment.

If a competitor is planning to open a store on a certain date, it might be unwise to plan to launch a major campaign or promotion at the same time. It is said that a store's grand opening is the toughest kind of event to compete with, because the excitement and curiosity are difficult to resist, even by the most loyal customers. Better, perhaps, to hold your event a week earlier or a week later to give your promotion a clear field and a chance for maximum results. Too often the retailer, determined not to budge in the face of stiff competition, allows pride to overcome good judgment, causing the failure or limited success of an otherwise excellent promotion.

Checking the Percentages

Suppose we look at the fashion sportswear department for a closer examination of the planning process. The department is planning for the fall season. Checking the chart, which shows the sales percentages of the year's total business achieved each month (see Table 2.1), we find that 8.0 percent of the year's sales occur in August, 8.6 percent in September, 8.8 percent in October, 9.2 percent in November, 15.9 percent in December, and 5.1 percent in January. Table 2.2 shows the percentages of each month's sales by departments in relation to the total store. This indicates how important each department's sales are to the total volume. We see that 55.6 percent of the year's sales in sportswear are registered in the fall season. The spring season, therefore, brings in 44.4 percent of the store's sportswear sales. These figures, from the Newspaper Advertising Bureau's Planbook, are five-year averages and provide a fairly stable base from which to begin planning.

The next checkpoint should be regional sales history. It would stand to reason that stores in warmer and rural parts of the country would tend to show stronger sales figures in sportswear in the spring season than the national figures might indicate. States like Florida and regions like Southern California, with their balmy weather, have higher sales all year in clothes for outdoor activities, and regional sales figures confirm this. Stores in cold climates, where ski activities and other winter sports are popular, would show stronger heavy weight sportswear sales in the winter months.

Buyers must be aware of conditions that might affect sales in comparing sales statistics. Sales figures are available through sales tax records, trade publications, and newspaper and broadcast associations, which provide this information as a service to their advertisers and prospective advertisers. In larger cities, city and county sales are accessible for the buyer's study. It helps to know the total amount of business being done in your market area, for then you can estimate what percentage of the total area's sales you are achieving at your store. The buyer also uses these figures, checking them month by month, to see if the store is in line with, better than, or worse than the sales trends in that market. Table 2.3 shows how the national figures might vary from the sales pattern of the regional or local market areas.

Researching Your Own History

The next step in the planning procedure is to contrast your sales history with your advertising history. Tables 2.4 and 2.5 show the percentages of the year's advertising lineage used each month by fashion departments. Have you been spending your advertising and promotion budget with regard for your sales pattern? Have you been advertising heavily when sales are going well and cutting back when sales slow down? Or have you been doing the reverse— holding back on advertising when business is rolling along and spending heavily when things are tough?

Neither pattern is recommended, although both can be found every day in the retail world. Proper timing—advertising and promoting when customers are ready to buy—will bring in maximum sales results. The better approach is to plan your advertising at a slightly higher percentage when sales are down and slightly lower than the sales percentage when sales are up.

To get a clearer picture of the sales and advertising patterns, let us compare our sportswear department's figures from a *hypotheti-*

Table 2.1 MERCHANDISE SALES TRENDS[1]

MERCHANDISE	PERCENTAGES OF YEAR'S TOTAL SALES DONE EACH MONTH												FIVE-YEAR AVERAGE
	JAN.	FEB.	MAR.	APR.	MAY	JUNE	JULY	AUG.	SEPT.	OCT.	NOV.	DEC.	
Apparel and accessories— total	5.9	5.7	8.4	8.4	8.2	7.0	6.1	7.6	8.7	9.2	9.7	15.1	100%
Aprons, housedresses and uniforms	6.1	6.2	8.1	9.8	12.3	9.9	7.8	7.1	7.7	7.3	7.4	10.3	100
Blouses, skirts and sportswear	5.1	5.0	6.6	7.6	8.8	8.7	7.7	8.0	8.6	8.8	9.2	15.9	100
Corsets and brassieres	7.7	6.3	8.2	8.5	8.9	9.5	7.9	7.7	8.3	8.6	7.8	10.6	100
Furs	8.4	6.0	6.1	6.1	4.3	2.4	4.1	9.0	7.9	12.4	13.1	20.2	100
Handbags and small leather goods	4.2	5.0	7.6	8.1	8.6	7.2	5.3	5.8	8.3	8.6	9.9	21.4	100
Handkerchiefs	4.9	5.6	6.1	6.3	7.4	6.2	5.1	5.4	5.7	7.0	11.1	29.2	100
Infants' wear (incl. infants' furniture)	5.3	5.5	8.6	7.9	6.2	5.9	5.9	8.4	9.2	9.3	11.3	16.5	100
Juniors' and girls' wear	4.2	4.9	9.3	8.5	7.4	6.4	6.1	10.3	8.9	8.9	10.1	15.0	100
Juniors' coats, suits and dresses	4.6	5.2	9.6	9.3	8.6	7.0	6.3	9.1	8.7	8.8	9.3	13.5	100
Girls' wear	3.7	4.6	9.1	7.6	6.1	5.8	5.8	11.7	9.0	8.9	11.1	16.6	100
Millinery	5.0	6.0	13.6	11.8	6.3	4.6	3.7	6.2	11.1	11.7	9.6	10.4	100
Neckwear and scarves	4.6	5.3	7.5	7.7	8.2	7.4	5.9	6.3	8.1	9.6	10.1	19.3	100
Underwear, slips and negligees	5.3	5.2	6.0	6.5	8.7	7.4	6.5	6.2	6.3	7.4	10.8	23.7	100

Knit underwear	6.2	5.4	6.1	6.5	9.6	7.5	6.4	6.4	6.5	7.5	10.1	21.8	100
Silk and muslin underwear, slips and nightgowns	5.1	5.2	6.1	6.7	8.8	7.9	6.8	6.1	6.1	7.3	10.2	23.7	100
Negligees, robes, lounging apparel	4.1	5.0	5.9	6.2	8.5	6.6	5.5	5.4	5.8	7.1	12.1	27.8	100
Women's and children's gloves	5.4	4.8	7.7	7.9	5.8	4.1	2.6	3.5	6.5	11.0	13.9	26.8	100
Women's and children's hosiery	7.1	7.0	8.4	7.9	8.0	6.4	5.2	6.3	8.5	9.1	9.7	16.4	100
Women's and children's shoes	6.1	5.8	9.4	9.5	8.4	7.6	6.1	7.8	9.9	9.4	8.6	11.4	100
Children's shoes	4.8	5.3	10.1	10.3	5.9	6.9	5.9	11.7	10.7	7.5	8.5	12.4	100
Women's shoes	6.1	5.7	9.3	9.6	8.5	7.9	6.3	7.1	9.8	9.8	8.6	11.3	100
Women's and misses' coats and suits	9.7	7.2	10.6	8.8	4.7	2.8	3.5	7.0	9.3	12.2	12.0	12.2	100
Coats	10.4	7.1	10.1	8.2	4.0	2.3	3.2	7.3	8.8	12.2	13.2	13.2	100
Suits	6.7	8.5	13.7	12.1	7.0	4.5	4.7	7.0	10.3	10.1	7.0	8.4	100
Women's and misses' dresses	5.9	6.0	9.0	10.0	11.1	8.4	6.6	7.4	9.2	9.0	7.8	9.6	100
Inexpensive dresses	5.7	5.7	8.7	10.0	11.2	8.9	6.8	7.3	9.1	8.9	7.6	10.1	100
Better dresses	6.0	6.4	9.1	10.1	10.2	8.0	6.6	7.8	9.4	9.1	8.0	9.3	100

SOURCE: Newspaper Advertising Bureau Planbook, 1981. Used by permission.
[1] Five-year averages of percentages of the year's total sales done each month, for women's, misses' and children's apparel and accessories. **Boldface** indicates months when the department or item did 8.3% or better of its annual volume. (If sales were constant across the year, each month would account for approximately 8.3%.)

Table 2.2 SALES BY DEPARTMENT[1]

MERCHANDISE	PERCENTAGES OF MONTH'S TOTAL SALES DONE BY DEPARTMENTS												FIVE-YEAR AVERAGE
	JAN.	FEB.	MAR.	APR.	MAY	JUNE	JULY	AUG.	SEPT.	OCT.	NOV.	DEC.	
Aprons, housedresses and uniforms	3.9	4.1	3.7	4.3	5.6	5.2	4.8	3.4	3.4	3.0	2.9	2.5	3.8%
Blouses, skirts and sportswear	12.4	12.6	11.2	12.8	15.2	17.5	17.8	15.0	14.0	13.5	13.4	14.9	14.1
Children's shoes	1.4	1.5	2.0	1.9	1.2	1.6	1.5	2.5	2.0	1.3	1.5	1.3	1.5
Corsets and brassieres	7.4	6.4	5.7	5.8	6.2	7.7	7.3	5.7	5.4	5.3	4.5	3.9	5.7
Furs	3.2	2.4	1.6	1.7	1.2	0.8	1.5	2.3	2.1	3.0	3.1	3.0	2.3
Girls' wear	3.7	4.7	6.4	5.3	4.4	4.8	5.7	9.1	6.2	5.6	6.7	6.0	6.1
Handbags and small leather goods	3.0	3.6	3.8	4.0	4.5	4.1	3.6	3.2	4.0	3.8	4.3	5.9	4.1
Handkerchiefs	0.5	0.7	0.5	0.5	0.5	0.5	0.5	0.5	0.4	0.5	0.7	1.2	0.6
Infants' wear (incl. infants' furniture)	6.3	6.8	7.2	6.3	5.2	5.9	6.8	7.8	7.5	7.2	8.1	7.6	7.0
Juniors' coats, suits and dresses	4.9	5.6	6.9	6.8	6.4	6.1	6.3	7.5	6.2	6.0	5.9	5.5	6.1
Knit underwear	3.3	3.1	2.3	2.5	3.6	3.3	3.4	2.8	2.3	2.7	3.4	4.6	3.1
Millinery	2.0	2.4	3.7	3.2	1.8	1.5	1.4	1.9	3.0	2.9	2.3	1.5	2.2
Negligees, robes and lounging apparel	1.2	1.5	1.3	1.3	1.8	1.6	1.7	1.2	1.2	1.3	2.3	3.2	1.8

Silk and muslin underwear, slips and nightgowns	3.3	3.4	2.7	3.0	3.9	**4.1**	**4.1**	3.0	2.7	2.9	**4.0**	**5.9**	3.8
Women's and children's gloves	1.9	1.6	1.8	1.8	1.4	1.1	0.9	1.0	1.5	**2.4**	**2.8**	**3.6**	2.0
Women's and children's hosiery	**5.5**	**5.6**	4.6	4.3	4.4	4.2	4.0	3.9	4.4	4.5	4.5	**5.1**	4.6
Women's and misses' better dresses	**5.9**	**6.4**	6.3	6.8	**7.2**	**6.4**	**5.9**	**5.9**	**6.2**	**5.6**	4.7	4.0	5.7
Women's and misses' coats	**10.8**	**7.4**	**7.2**	5.8	3.0	2.1	3.3	5.7	**6.5**	**8.5**	**8.5**	5.3	6.1
Women's and misses' inexpensive dresses	6.7	6.8	7.4	8.2	**9.8**	**8.7**	**7.5**	6.5	**7.4**	6.7	5.4	4.6	7.0
Women's and misses' neckwear and scarves	2.2	2.6	2.4	2.6	2.7	**3.0**	2.7	2.3	2.6	**2.9**	**2.8**	**3.6**	2.8
Women's and misses' suits	**2.0**	**2.5**	**2.7**	**2.3**	1.5	1.1	1.3	1.5	**2.1**	**2.0**	1.2	0.9	1.7
Women's shoes	**8.5**	**8.3**	**8.6**	**8.8**	**8.5**	**8.7**	**8.0**	7.3	**8.9**	**8.4**	7.0	5.9	7.9
Apparel and accessories— total	100	100	100	100	100	100	100	100	100	100	100	100	100%
Accessories—total	46.5	**47.4**	**46.6**	46.0	45.7	**47.4**	45.9	43.1	46.0	46.1	**48.3**	**53.2**	47.3
Apparel—total	**53.5**	52.6	**53.4**	**54.0**	52.6	**54.1**	**56.9**	**54.0**	**53.9**	51.7	46.8	**54.3**	52.7

SOURCE: Newspaper Advertising Bureau Planbook, 1981. Used by permission.
[1] **Boldface** indicates months when the department or item contributed the same or a bigger percentage of this division's total volume than it did during the year as a whole (as shown in last right column).

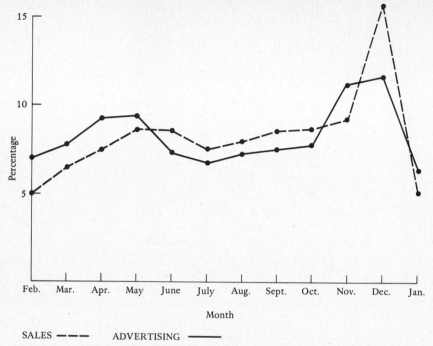

SALES ――― ADVERTISING ―――

Figure 2.5 Unbalanced sales and advertising chart. Plotting sales and advertising percentages by months shows imbalance between when people buy and when advertising dollars are spent. Not a recommended pattern.

cal last year performance, using as our statistics the averages listed in the Newspaper Advertising Bureau's Planbook (Table 2.6). We see that the annual sales volume for the department was $1,000,000 and that the advertising expenditure, $50,000, represented 5 percent of sales, a little out of line with industry standards. If we chart these figures on a grid, we see some interesting relationships between sales and advertising (Figure 2.5). There seem to be sharp

Table 2.3 SALES PATTERNS FOR REGIONAL OR LOCAL MARKET AREAS

SPORTSWEAR	NATIONAL	REGIONAL	LOCAL
August	8.0	7.8	7.9
September	8.6	8.2	8.3
October	8.8	8.6	8.7
November	9.2	9.2	9.0
December	15.9	14.9	15.5
January	5.1	6.5	6.6
	55.6%	55.2%	56.0%

Table 2.4 PERCENTAGES OF ADVERTISING LINAGE USED BY FASHION DEPARTMENTS[1]

ITEM	JAN.	FEB.	MAR.	APR.	MAY	JUNE	JULY	AUG.	SEPT.	OCT.	NOV.	DEC.	TOTAL
Coats and jackets	8.0	8.1	8.3	4.4	3.0	3.0	5.7	**8.7**	**8.5**	**13.4**	**16.2**	**12.7**	100%
Cosmetics	6.8	6.0	7.2	**9.6**	**10.9**	6.4	4.8	6.4	7.5	**9.0**	**10.2**	**15.2**	100
Dresses	6.5	**8.3**	**11.6**	**11.8**	**11.3**	**8.3**	5.8	6.9	7.6	6.5	**8.7**	6.7	100
Fine jewelry	3.2	7.0	5.7	**9.3**	**11.4**	**9.0**	3.7	3.7	3.7	6.7	**15.1**	**21.5**	100
Fur coats	**12.6**	**9.6**	7.9	4.5	3.3	1.8	6.3	**9.0**	7.3	**8.5**	**13.9**	**15.3**	100
Girdles and bras	7.2	4.9	**10.0**	**8.3**	**10.2**	**12.6**	4.6	5.5	**8.7**	7.4	7.5	**13.0**	100
Handbags	4.4	7.7	**11.6**	**10.0**	**13.1**	5.4	4.6	7.4	7.3	6.2	**10.2**	**12.1**	100
Hosiery	**10.5**	7.3	**10.6**	**11.9**	7.4	4.7	4.2	**8.8**	**11.3**	8.1	**9.6**	5.6	100
Junior dresses	3.6	6.1	**11.5**	**14.3**	**12.5**	**8.6**	6.5	**13.1**	5.6	5.5	7.3	5.4	100
Lingerie, sleepwear and robes	5.2	6.0	5.7	8.1	**13.5**	5.1	4.9	4.9	6.0	7.9	**15.1**	**17.6**	100
Pants and shorts	6.1	7.2	**8.6**	**10.7**	**10.3**	**9.1**	7.9	**8.4**	7.3	6.9	**8.5**	**9.0**	100
Shoes	6.8	6.9	**10.3**	**10.6**	**8.5**	7.1	6.7	8.1	7.8	**8.4**	**9.7**	**9.1**	100
Skirts	5.2	**9.2**	**15.6**	**13.2**	**9.9**	8.2	7.0	4.8	3.8	4.3	**11.2**	7.6	100
Sweaters and knittops	6.9	5.7	5.3	7.5	7.1	6.3	6.7	6.6	**9.3**	**10.2**	**13.9**	**14.5**	100
Swimsuits and beachwear	7.0	4.2	6.6	**15.1**	**15.0**	**18.9**	**23.4**	1.8	0.6	0.2	2.0	5.2	100
Woven blouses and skirts	5.8	8.1	**9.9**	**9.5**	**10.9**	6.7	6.1	7.0	6.1	6.5	**11.5**	**11.9**	100

SOURCE: Newspaper Advertising Bureau, 1981. Used by permission.
[1] **Boldface** indicates months when the item got 8.3% or more of the year's advertising devoted to it. (If advertising were constant across the year, approximately 8.3% of the year's advertising would be used each month.)

35

Table 2.5 PERCENTAGES OF ADVERTISING LINAGE USED

	MONTH				
ITEM	JAN.	FEB.	MAR.	APR.	MAY
Pants and shorts	6.1	7.2	8.6	10.7	10.3
Sweaters and tops	6.9	5.7	5.3	7.5	7.1
Blouses and skirts	5.8	8.1	9.9	9.5	10.9
Averages	6.3	7.0	7.9	9.2	9.4

SOURCE: Newspaper Advertising Bureau, 1981. Used by permission.
[1] Combining figures from sweaters and knit tops, pants and shorts, and

differences between the percentages of advertising spent by month and the percentage of sales volume generated for those months. But everything is not wrong; let us look at these discrepancies, or seeming discrepancies.

The First Half—Spring

Most retail fiscal calendars begin the year in February, not January, although some retail organizations have not switched to the 4–5–4 or 4–4–5 accounting systems (see Retail Accounting Calendar, Appendix 12) devised to provide comparable 13-week periods for retail statistics. For most stores, January is primarily a clearance month as well as the month of many traditional sales events—white sales, notions sales, bra sales, home furnishings events, and certain national brand cosmetic sales. They are usually launched right after

Table 2.6 ADVERTISING AND SALES COMPARISON

MONTH	SALES LAST YEAR	PERCENTAGE, LAST YEAR'S SALES	ADVERTISING LAST YEAR	PERCENTAGE, LAST YEAR'S ADVERTISING
February	$ 50,000	5.0%	$ 3,500	7.0%
March	66,000	6.6	3,950	7.9
April	76,000	7.6	4,600	9.2
May	88,000	8.8	4,700	9.4
June	87,000	8.7	3,700	7.4
July	77,000	7.7	3,450	6.9
August	80,000	8.0	3,650	7.3
September	86,000	8.6	3,800	7.6
October	88,000	8.8	3,950	7.9
November	92,000	9.2	5,650	11.3
December	159,000	15.9	5,900	11.8
uary	51,000	5.1	3,150	6.3
Total	$1,000,000	100.0%	$50,000	100.0%

BY SPORTSWEAR DEPARTMENTS[1]

			MONTH			
JUNE	JULY	AUG.	SEPT.	OCT.	NOV.	DEC.
9.1	7.9	8.4	7.3	6.9	8.5	9.0
6.3	6.7	6.6	9.3	10.2	13.9	14.5
6.7	6.1	7.0	6.1	6.5	11.5	11.9
7.4	6.9	7.3	7.6	7.9	11.3	11.8

blouses and skirts to give average advertising expenditures.

Christmas and carry through the month of January. For fashion stores, January is an opportunity to bring in new goods, to perk up customers' postholiday spirits with fashion excitement and interest. Fashion leader stores introduce these new season items during the preceding November and December, taking advantage of the "natural" Christmas traffic. Many retailers limit their January activities to the clearance-sale pattern to sell off as much of existing stocks as possible so that inventories are at their lowest levels for tax purposes.

Once the new fiscal year begins, however, new spring merchandise starts to appear on the selling floor. The mobility of the Easter date has a direct effect on the sale of spring fashions in many parts of the country, and may affect the total spring season. It can cause problems in merchandising and advertising planning for the retailer, especially when the date shifts two or three weeks from year to year. If Easter is late in the season, fashion buying starts later. If Easter is early, the buying season is earlier—and often shorter in duration.

In major retail organizations, the sales promotion calendar is adjusted to offset the fluctuations in buying patterns that result from the customers' perception of the "natural" time to buy spring fashions. The shift in emphasis was especially apparent in the 1977–1978 seasons. Easter Sunday moved from April 10 in 1977 to March 26 in 1978—in effect starting the spring and Easter shopping period *three weeks early*.

To avoid upheavals in sales planning, many retailers think of March and April as a combined 9-week period during which Easter must fall, shifting other promotions around during that time while adjusting planned sales and advertising dollars to fit the calendar. We've called this hybrid sales period "Marpril" for easier handling. Figure 2.6 shows how the sales promotion calendar can attack the problem of the changing date of Easter.

With this in mind, spending 6.7 percent of the year's advertising to get 5 percent of the year's sales in February looks like a major

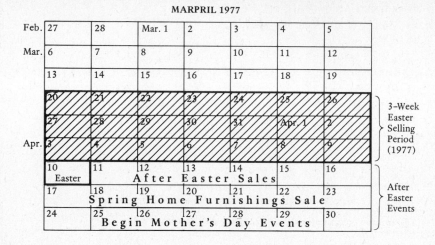

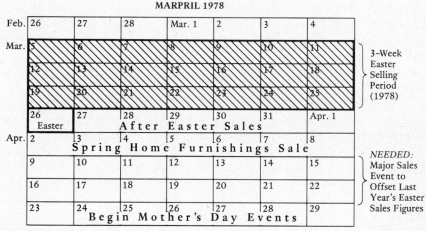

Figure 2.6 The Marpril plan. Combining sales and advertising figures of March and April to create a nine-week period for planning purposes to adjust for changing date of Easter and its effect on spring sales and advertising patterns.

error. It also looks wrong to spend 8.6 percent of the budget in March to get 6.6 percent in sales. Possibly, but we must weigh the problem of launching the new season when we have been dormant since December against the lack of direct sales results from consumers who have not yet begun to think about spring clothes. Some consideration must be given to "startup" time and to planting the idea of coming to the store to get the customer in the mood to buy. These factors should influence advertising decisions.

Advertising percentages are still higher than sales in April, but by May they come closer together. In June, however, sales stay at a higher level and advertising drops down—8.7 percent sales to 7.4 percent advertising. At the height of the summer fashion buying season, with warm weather throughout most of the country, and vacations and outdoor activities booming, sportswear is also booming, naturally. Many retailers spend less than normal percent-to-sales on advertising and roll with the tide of sales. In July, the summer season is ending and the first half of the year is coming to a close. Inventory time again, and again the flow of new fashion merchandise, and new items to be advertised, is slowed. Clearances and end-of-season promotions are run with limited advertising dollars, but sales (at reduced markup) bring in store traffic.

The Second Half—Fall

August brings with it the traditional back-to-school promotions and the introduction of new fall fashions. A higher percentage of advertising is required to tell the public all the fashion news. Our table shows 7.3 percent of the year's ad budget being spent to achieve 8.0 percent of the year's sales! Another mistake? Hard to say. Most fashion retailers want to "shoot the works" as soon as possible in the new season.

On the other hand, since 25.4 percent of the year's fashion business is done during August, September, and October, the allocation of 22.8 percent of the advertising budget to this period might be out of line. An upward month-by-month adjustment could be the answer.

November and December are the two highest-volume months of the year in all retail departments. November is basically a poor sales month, but picks up sharply in volume after Thanksgiving Day. In some categories, like toys and jewelry and other gift items, 50 percent or more of the year's sales happen in that two-month period. In fashion, sales range from 20 to 40 percent in most departments. That certainly justifies over 23.1 percent of the advertising budget being spent at that time, but perhaps the timing of the expenditures could be better balanced. A better plan would dictate spending more dollars earlier.

January, as noted, usually the last month of the fiscal year, is basically a clearance month, with some opportunity for fashion promotion. Traditional year-end sale events dot the promotional calendar in January, starting with the most important after-Christmas clearance and sales. This major sales event was established to take advantage of the "natural" traffic coming back to the store after Christmas to return or exchange gifts. By offering sale-priced mer-

Table 2.7 ADVERTISING EXPENDITURES AND SALES

MONTH	ACTUAL SALES LAST YEAR (BY MONTH)	ACTUAL ADVERTISING, LAST YEAR	PLANNED ADVERTISING THIS YEAR (ASSUMING SAME $ SALES PLAN)
February	5.0%	7.0%	6.0%
March	6.6	7.9	7.5
April	7.6	9.2	8.0
May	8.8	9.4	8.5
June	8.7	7.4	8.0
July	7.7	6.9	7.5
Spring totals	44.4%	47.8%	45.5%
August	8.0%	7.3%	9.5%
September	8.6	7.6	8.8
October	8.8	7.9	9.5
November	9.2	11.3	10.2
December	15.9	11.8	10.5
January	5.1	6.3	6.0
Fall totals	55.6%	52.2%	54.5%

chandise and seasonal promotional events, the store has a chance of converting that traffic into sales dollars and possibly corraling Christmas bonus money received too late to be spent before the holiday.

Now that we have discussed some of the reasons why sales and advertising percentages do not always jell, let's look at an advertising plan that takes into consideration some of the elements we've talked about. Assuming the same sales volume figures as last year (per the NAB Planbook), we can adjust the spending of the advertising and promotion money more in line with sales trends (Table 2.7). Let's see how these figures look on a chart (Figure 2.7). There is a much closer relationship between sales and advertising with this plan. We have scheduled 45.5 percent of the year's advertising budget to match the 44.4 percent of the year's sales planned for the spring season. Last year we spent 47.8 percent in the same period —by most standards, too high a percentage. For the fall season, we plan to spend 54.5 percent of our ad budget to gain 55.6 percent in sales. Last year's 52.2 percent looks too low, indicating that some sales opportunities might have been lost through lack of advertising dollars.

Within this seasonal adjustment, we shifted the amounts of money to spend monthly. Less budget is allocated to February and March. It is still a higher percentage than sales might indicate, but not as far out of line as last year and still providing for adequate pro-

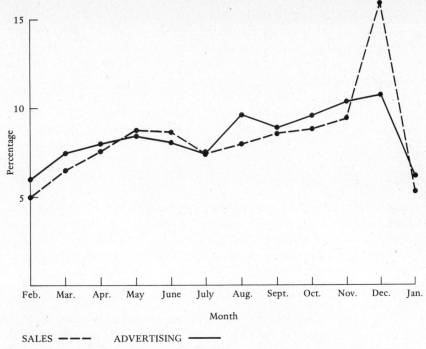

SALES — — —   ADVERTISING ———

Figure 2.7   Balanced sales and advertising chart. Better relationship of advertising expenditures to sales trends makes ad expenditures more realistic. Advertising percentages are slightly higher than sales in poor months and lower than sales in good months. A more realistic approach to ad budgeting.

motion in April, May, and June, when the fashion sportswear season is reaching its peak. More money is allocated to July to add impact to the traditional summer clearance sales and to help clear the shelves and racks for incoming fall fashions. Adjustments made for the fall season include a shifting of funds to build up August, September, and October (9.5 percent versus 7.3 in August, and 8.8 and 9.5 vs. 7.6 and 7.9 in September and October). Now, 27.8 percent of the advertising budget is planned to produce 25.4 percent in sales in those three months and to launch the fall season in a bigger way.

Our planning more advertising dollars in fall than in spring allows us to build into the Christmas season more smoothly. We have spread our advertising punch to ensure a good start to the season, with a stronger impact in October and November, and emphasis increasing as we approach Christmas. Even though December is the best month of the year, representing almost 16 percent of annual sales in our hypothetical department or store, it would be bad planning to wait until December to promote and to spend 16 percent of the budget, when customers are probably going to buy, with or without promotion. What a store has done all year to satisfy its clientele and to attract new customers will show up in sales figures in December, but the store cannot wait until then to start looking for business. Additional funds have also been set aside for January, to promote historical January events more aggressively and to establish a reserve fund to advertise end-of-year closeout opportunities.

Planning for Emergencies

A common practice in some stores includes placing 10 percent or so of the total year's budget in reserve for emergencies or unexpected promotional opportunities. In a business as volatile as fashion, a contingency budget is recommended. It allows management to act quickly when circumstances dictate a fast decision to buy, ship, advertise, and sell without disrupting ongoing plans. As noted, it causes problems when the store wants to run an unplanned promotion and lack of advertising dollars means some buyer's planned advertising is canceled to provide funds for the new, unexpected promotion.

Figure 2.4 showed a simplified form for following the procedure of researching your own store sales and advertising history as a basis for determining this year's plan. From the department's records, the buyer lists the sales figures for the past year, month by month. The percentage for each month is figured by dividing the year's sales into each month's sales. The same thing is done with advertising and promotion costs, listing the dollars spent last year, month by month, then dividing the year's total into each month's expenditures to determine each month's percentage. Now the buyer can look at the store's own track record and check it against national, regional, or local statistics.

Before projecting sales plans for the coming year, consideration must be given to many factors that affect sales, and consequently advertising and sales promotion. Here are some of them:

1. *Economic Conditions.* Is the population in your market area increasing or decreasing? Are new homes being built at an accelerated rate? Is the ethnic mix changing? Are incomes rising or falling? Are new industries and businesses planned? What is the employment picture? How is inflation affecting consumer spendable incomes? Are you aware of any demographic changes in population?

2. *Your Store's Growth.* Are new stores being planned to open during the next fiscal year? Are existing stores, or fashion depart-

ments, being remodeled or expanded? Are changes in store policy and procedures going to affect the fashion operation? Will store plans create problems that will affect sales?

3. *Competitor Activities.* Are your competitors opening new stores, expanding, remodeling? Are they advertising and promoting more aggressively than before? Have they brought in new executive personnel that might provide stiffer competition than before? Has their fashion image improved so that they represent a current or future threat to your business? Are you losing your position in the market? Are you keeping up with trends?

4. *Merchandising Events.* Should you repeat last year's events? Are there new fashion promotions to be added? How many fashion shows should you include? What increased sales and advertising efforts will require the greatest share of the budget? Will each promotion activity enhance your fashion image and store profits?

When all factors are considered, each buyer includes the department's individual needs, wants, and problems before arriving at a sales projection for the season to be submitted to the merchandise manager for approval. The buyer establishes sales goals and then requests advertising and sales promotion funds to accomplish sales objectives.

The buyer's request for more promotion dollars than department sales might warrant could be based on several factors:

1. The buyer feels that the location of the department in store requires more advertising to bring customers to the selling floor ("Nobody knows I'm back there behind the lingerie department!"). This argument of a bad location is often used by stores not in "good traffic locations" or on the wrong end of shopping centers away from the "hot" stores.

2. Additional money may be needed to make the public aware of new departments, expanded or remodeled departments, or new categories of merchandise being added. (In many cases, cooperative advertising is available from manufacturers to promote new products.)

3. New and aggressive competition has come into the market since the last budget period, or new competition is coming.

4. Management decisions to stress price and value in fashion promotions this coming season might require larger newspaper ads, heavier radio and TV schedules, and more fashion shows than last year.

5. There is more news in sportswear fashion this coming season and the store must demonstrate its fashion leadership by advertising the new trends first and better than anyone else.

The aggressive fashion buyer knows how to appeal to management's self-interest when seeking to acquire additional advertising money. This also applies to asking for extra floor space, sales help, window display, new fixtures, or markdown money. Buyers find they can get all the "extras" as long as they maintain and improve their contributions to sales volume and profits. When sales and/or profits start to slip, it's a different story.

At the divisional merchandising manager level, each fashion department has been working concurrently on six-month plans. Each buyer has conferred with the divisional manager on individual department plans, objectives, and problems. General agreements on basics are sought at this stage of the planning process. The talks cover past performances, trends, and projections. Suggestions and recommendations are made, added, or rejected.

Finally, a composite picture of the fashion division emerges from the individual plans, and the divisional manager begins preliminary discussions with top management. Again the give-and-take between store principals and division heads resolves major differences of opinion, with management relying on the experience and knowledge of the store's executives for the final decision and responsibility for success.

Our discussion of sales promotion planning so far has emphasized the merchandise planning aspect. We have done this deliberately. We want to leave no doubt that merchandise decisions lead the way to a majority of advertising and sales promotion decisions. Advertising must be a mirror of a store's fashion image. Good advertising and promotion enhances that image and makes more people aware of it (Figure 2.8).

While the buying and merchandising staffs have been developing their sales plans for the coming season, the sales promotion division has been hard at work. Classified in many major department stores as a "sales supporting" division, sales promotion develops its own six-month plan in conjunction with and paralleling the step-by-step pattern of the merchandising division. In Chapter 3 we will cover the planning of the advertising and sales promotion budget; now we will look at another promotion tool, cooperative advertising.

CO-OP ADVERTISING

Three basic types of cooperative advertising programs affect retail ad budgets. The *traditional* co-op program, where the manufacturer or supplier sets up an advertising allowance for retailers based on the size of the retailer's past or current purchases, is the best known. Each time the retailer runs an ad that promotes the

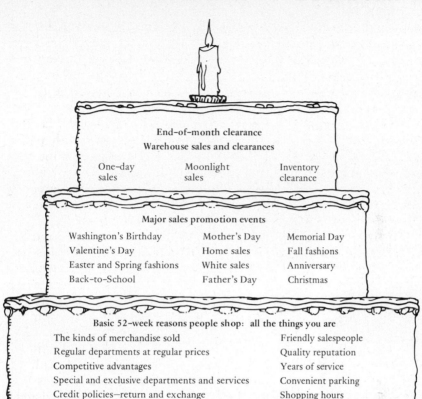

End-of-month clearance

Warehouse sales and clearances

One-day	Moonlight	Inventory
sales	sales	clearance

Major sales promotion events

Washington's Birthday	Mother's Day	Memorial Day
Valentine's Day	Home sales	Fall fashions
Easter and Spring fashions	White sales	Anniversary
Back-to-School	Father's Day	Christmas

Basic 52-week reasons people shop: all the things you are

The kinds of merchandise sold	Friendly salespeople
Regular departments at regular prices	Quality reputation
Competitive advantages	Years of service
Special and exclusive departments and services	Convenient parking
Credit policies—return and exchange	Shopping hours

Figure 2.8 The three-layer cake theory of sales promotion. A visual approach to sales promotion built on a blend of compatible ingredients. The base of the cake represents the basics of a retail business, 85 percent of which comes from day-in, day-out elements. The second layer of the advertising recipe is the traditional promotional events common to most stores. These are the seasonal sales and events. The top layer, the icing on the cake, is the short-term, special sales and events unique to the store. The theory is that the special activities, the "icing," are more productive when all three levels of promotion are utilized. A continuing stream of "sale-sale-sale" does not produce as successful results as a full slice of promotional cake would.

manufacturer's product, the retailer bills the manufacturer for a portion of the ad cost. This arrangement could be a 50/50 deal, with the vendor and the retailer sharing the cost of the ad equally. Depending on the program, the manufacturer could pay as much as 100 percent of the ad. Reimbursement by the manufacturer is made in cash after the retailer has submitted proof of performance indicating that all conditions of the co-op program have been fulfilled (see Table 2.8).

Table 2.8 SAMPLE CO-OP ADVERTISING PROGRAMS

MFG/BRAND	PRODUCT(S)	PROGRAM/ MARKETS	ACCRUAL BASED ON	PARTICI- PATION	OTHER MEDIA	REMARKS/ EXP. DATE	HOW TO GET PAID
3M Household and Hardware Products Division 3M Center St. Paul, MN 55101 612/733–1110 retail	"Micropore" Brand— Cold Weather Dusk Masks	All	5% of net purchases	100%	Radio, TV, shoppers, penny-savers, flyers, circulars, and/or handbills	Ad must be at least 2 column inches, or a cents-off coupon All ads must prominently feature the product brand name, illustration, and price No competitive mdse	Retailers purchasing from wholesaler/distributor must include invoice Send claim with full-page tear-sheet by March 31, 1981, to: ACB, Inc., c/o 3M, P.O. Box 8121, Chicago, IL 60680

| Fieldcrest Mills, Inc.
60 West 40th St.
New York, NY 10018
212/398–9500
retail | St. Mary's sheets and towels | All | 3% of net purchases | 56% | Catalogs, radio, TV | 100% color on 1% of net purchases
Prominently feature St. Mary's name in headline or subhead
Name must be in boldface of at least one point larger than body copy
Use of logo preferred but not required
First-quality mdse only | Send full-page tear-sheet within 60 days of date of ad to: St. Mary's Co-op Adv. Dept. c/o ACB, Inc., P.O. Box 8335, Columbus, OH 43201 |

SOURCE: Newspaper Advertising Bureau. Used by permission.

The *promotion allowance* co-op program is a common practice in the food business. The retailer features the manufacturer's product or products in a price promotion during a specified period. The size of the payment to the retailer depends on the size of the order, not necessarily the size of the ad campaign. The purpose of this type of co-op is to build maximum store support through in-store display, price promotion, window signs, and inclusion in the store's advertising.

Dealer support co-op programs, popular with manufacturers and their ad agencies because it is more controllable, are growing. Instead of set allowances or billing procedures between retailer and supplier, the program is handled completely by the supplier. Under this plan, if the retailer orders established minimum amounts of merchandise, the manufacturer will create and place advertising for the retailer. The ads will be designed in the retailer's style to look like the store's regular advertising. The complicated billing procedure, with its affidavits of proof of performance, is thus eliminated.

The growth in popularity of the dealer support programs can be traced to the problems that have developed in the allowance system: keeping up with the accrued allowances; being sure the ads run during the specified time period; dealing with media to deliver the affidavits of performance so that the vendor can be billed before the deadline; and bookkeeping disputes on both sides of the program when figures do not agree.

Cooperative advertising became a fact of retail advertising life when manufacturers decided to ensure that their merchandise would be advertised by the store that carried their products. It bridged the gap between national advertising programs designed to develop customer demand for specific products and retailer ad programs designed to tell customers where to buy those products. By offering to share the costs of the ad, the suppliers increased the chances of their products appearing over the logos of local stores. If there is advertising, more merchandise will be sold, and presumably both store and supplier will be happy. Often, the presence of a more generous advertising allowance can swing the buyer's decision to buy from manufacturer A to manufacturer B, assuming equality or similarity in product, price, and other considerations. The danger in this type of decision, called "buying ads instead of buying merchandise," is the possibility of stocking the shelves with secondary line merchandise that may still be sitting on those shelves after the ad has run. Good merchants buy the right merchandise, negotiating price, delivery date, payment terms, and so on, and *then* work on advertising allowances (see Figure 2.9).

Gather co-op program information using a form like this

Co-Op Advertising Information Request

Date: *February 1, 1980*

Manufacturer's Name: *Nordstrom Manufacturing Co.*

Home Office Address: *1435 Sanders St.*
Bell City, Ohio 06512
Attn. National Sales Manager

I am budgeting a yearly advertising program for my store. In order to take advantage of any Co-op Advertising allowances offered by vendors supplying me, I would appreciate your filling out the following information and returning it to me by *March 15, 1980*

Thank you for your help.

Cordially, *Frank W. Wilson*
Frank's Appliance Store
Lebanon, Missouri 61202

1
Does your company offer a co-op ad allowance that I qualify for?   YES ☒   NO ☐

2
If answer to question #1 is YES, and your company has a printed Co-op Program, simply send the program and answer only those questions NOT covered in your printed plan. If NO, please return the entire form to me in the enclosed envelope.

3
What is the basis of accrual of co-op funds? (Example: 3% of net purchases, 5% of net purchases, unlimited, or 50¢ per unit, etc.)

10% of your purchases

4
What is the time period that the accrual is based on? (Example: based on last calendar year's purchases)

This year's purchases

5
How much ad allowances, based on my purchases, have I available to spend?
Dollar figure: *$1,500.00*

6
Please stipulate whether your Co-op Program is on a 50/50—75/25—100% paid, or a fixed line rate basis.

100% paid

7
What are the time limits in which the Co-op ads must appear in the paper, to insure your company's participation?
March 1st thru August 31st

8
What "proof of performance" does your co-op plan require? (Example: tear sheet, newspaper invoice, store invoice, etc.)

A tear sheet and duplicate net invoice from your newspaper

9
How soon after an ad appears must we submit "proof of performance" to your company and whom do we mail it to in order to get paid? *30 Days*

1435 Sanders St., Bell City, Ohio 06512
Attn. Co-op Auditing Dept. - Nordstrom Mfg. Co.

10
What requirements does your company have in order for us to comply with their co-op plan. (Example: ads must use illustrations of product, registry symbols, product logo, (your policy on competing products in same ad, etc.)

Logo and trademark - a picture

11
Are there any restrictions in your co-op plan regarding newspaper classified advertising?
No! As long as a picture of our product and our logo appear in the newspaper ad

If your company has a printed Co-Op Plan and/or retail kit, will you please enclose it with this form and mail to me today.

This form has been completed by
Name *Thomas C. Nordstrom*
Title *National Sales Mgr.*
Phone *614-222-3156*

Frank W. Wilson
Retailer authorized signature

Figure 2.9 The NAB Planbook suggests this form as a method of gathering information from manufacturers and other sources of co-op funds. (SOURCE: By permission of the Newspaper Advertising Bureau.)

Stanley Marcus, chairman emeritus of Neiman-Marcus, the legendary Texas retail chain, in his book *Quest for the Best*, supports this idea, stating: "Often, the best is kicked out because goods that are not necessarily the best have money for co-op advertising, whereas the better make either doesn't believe in it or doesn't have the funds to do it." In one of the country's best department stores, store policy once forbade the advertising manager from running more than 20 percent of the store's ads with co-op funds. The premise behind this rule was the belief in the public's reliance on the store to inform them of the importance of its merchandise by the amount of advertising it devoted to the items. If, for example, a department had budgeted a quarter-page of newspaper space for a specific item, but because there was a 50/50 co-op allowance devoted a half-page to that item (still only costing the department half the cost), the public would get the impression that the item was more important than an item of similar value in a quarter-page space on the same page. There are more factors involved in the success of an ad than size, but it is a strong indication of what the store considers important.

This kind of attitude is impractical in today's competitive market. Manufacturers, almost without exception, have some type of co-op plan to encourage buyers to sign the order form for their merchandise. Where the cost of the program is shared (50/50 or 75/25), the store must be convinced to spend its share to be sure the ads run (Figure 2.10).

Many hundreds of thousands of dollars in co-op funds are never spent each year because retailers neglect or choose not to participate in the programs. At the start of each season, manufacturers set aside a portion of gross sales in anticipation of claims that will be forthcoming from retail customers later in the season. Retailers who do not choose to match funds with their suppliers never claim their allowances. The unused portion of these funds eventually reverts to the manufacturers' bank accounts.

In some instances, larger advertising allowances are available if the retailer advertises in the vendor's preferred media. Some co-op contracts specify that the manufacturer will pay for 100 percent of the ad if it runs in a daily newspaper, but only 75 percent if it is on television and only 50 percent if it is on radio (Table 2.9). This assures that the advertising will appear in a newspaper, for given the choice, most retailers would rather run a "free" ad than pay for part of one. More and more, however, the choice of media is left to the retailer, who generally is better informed about the media in the area, knows which medium can most probably reach the target

Calculate Co-op Money

Cooperative advertising control sheet

Company _Jones Camera Co._

Product(s) _35 mm still cameras,_
lenses, accessories

Co-op terms _5% of net purchases_
50/50 participation

Accrual period _Jan. 1 – Dec. 31_

Sales representative _Jim Roberts_
_(914) 557-1883_

Reimbursement requirements _Claim must be submitted_
within 45 days after insertion

Send to _Co-op Dept._
Jones Camera Co.
44 Short St., Anytown, U.S.A. 00388

Planned $ merchandise purchases	$ available for co-op	Date & size of ad	Co-op $ spent	Date invoice & tear sheets submitted	Date re-imbursement received	Balance of co-op $ available
12,000	600	6/12 40 col. in.	120	6/30	7/28	480
		11/12 50 col. in	150	11/28	12/28	330
		12/15 110 col. in	330	12/30	1/21	0

Summary of planned allocation of co-op funds for year ending _Dec. 31, 1980_

JAN	FEB	MAR	APR	MAY	JUNE	JULY	AUG	SEPT	OCT	NOV	DEC
					40"					50"	110"

NOTES:
June, November and December are months
when camera sales are greatest.

Figure 2.10 NAB's suggested form for calculating co-op funds. Reimbursement requirements are listed and there is control of monies earned and where and when spent. (SOURCE: By permission of the Newspaper Advertising Bureau.)

Table 2.9 SAMPLE RADIO CO-OP CONTRACTS

Excello Shirt Company
Division of Kayser-Roth Corporation
1221 Avenue of the Americas
New York, NY 10020
Contact: Chris Esposito, (212) 391–2500.
Products: Excello sport and dress shirts
Allowance: 2/3–1/3 up to 5% of net shipments.
Radio: Spots must be devoted exclusively to Excello merchandise and feature first-quality, regularly priced goods.
Co-op Year: July 1–June 30. Unused accruals are cancelled at year's end.
Billing: Dealer submits copies of scripts, receipted station invoices, and notarized affidavits of performance within 30 days of broadcast to above. Dealer will be reimbursed via a credit memo.

Farah Manufacturing Company
Men's Wear Division
P.O. Box 9519
El Paso, TX 79985
Contact: Frank Maccarrone, (915) 591–4444.
Products: Farah slacks, shirts and casual wear for men.
Allowance: 65–35 to 5% of net purchases during current year and last quarter of previous year combined. Allowance is to be used for menswear only, not combined with boyswear. Ask about special incentive program for new dealers.
Radio: Dealer copy okay. Spots to prominently feature Farah name and be exclusively devoted to menswear. Spots featuring noncompetitive brands will be prorated.
Co-op Year: Calendar. All advertising must run during this period.
Billing: Dealer submits copies of scripts, receipted station invoices, and affidavits of performance within 60 days of broadcast to above, att: Co-op Dept.

SOURCE: Radio Advertising Bureau, *Co-op Money Book,* 1980.

audience, and can negotiate a better price at the retail level than the manufacturer can from afar.

A good nationwide co-op program can give a manufacturer the effect of a national advertising campaign while taking advantage of the stores' lower retail rate. Many of the larger stores establish their own co-op rate schedule, which includes the cost of producing the co-op ad. Some vendors balk at this kind of charge, but the major department stores have no trouble collecting. Smaller retailers, with less buying clout, can be restricted to the letter of the co-op contract. The key legal limit to co-op is the Federal Trade Commission's ruling on cooperative advertising which specifies that manufacturers and their agents (distributors, regional managers) must make all co-op programs available to all retailers on an equable basis.

Some vendors get around the co-op rate established by individual stores by researching the media in each of the major markets and setting up fixed rates for each medium used in that market without regard for the rates any local store pays. This can lead to constant disputes between bookkeepers, and a serious disruption in vendor-retailer relations. The dealer support programs we mentioned are an outgrowth of these disputes about who pays what and have led to the elimination of retailer-controlled co-op programs by some manufacturers.

Proof of performance requirements vary by the medium used. For newspaper ads, the store furnishes the vendor with two tearsheets (copies of the ad torn from the day's newspaper) showing that the ad had been published, along with the store's invoice for the cost of the ad (Figure 2.11). In direct mail, a copy of the book, two tearsheets, and a notarized copy of the Post Office delivery slip showing the number of pieces delivered is usually required. For radio and television, excerpts from the stations' logs (kept meticulously by Federal Trade Commission ruling) with notarized copies of the script and/or the tape that was broadcast, plus a notarized affidavit of performance signed by the general manager of the station verifying that the schedule ran as indicated, are needed. The Association of National Advertisers, in cooperation with the Radio Advertising Bureau and the Television Bureau of Advertising, has developed a format for this type of broadcast document that is widely accepted throughout the country. Standardization of invoices from radio and TV stations makes invoicing and billing of manufacturers by retailers easier and less cumbersome for all concerned (see Figure 2.12).

The prime benefit of a co-op program is that it enlists the dealer or retailer as the manufacturer's partner in moving merchandise to the consumer. Manufacturers want to sell their products. Dealers want to make the sales in their territories. Retailers want the products bought in their stores. Properly administered, and creatively planned and executed, co-op advertising can be productive for all three, and can mean extra exposure in advertising media as well as additional sales for suppliers and retailers.

ANOTHER LOOK AT TRADITIONAL PLANNING

Before we leave the preplanning stage, however, one final word about traditional retail sales and advertising planning. As we have shown, there is a long-established pattern of year-to-year, season-to-season planning that focuses on beating last year's, last month's, last week's, even yesterday's results. This pattern is impossible to

Collect co-op money using a form like this

Cooperative
Advertising Claim

To:

Co-op Auditing Dept.
Nordstrom Manufacturing Co.
1435 Sanders St.
Bell City, Ohio 06512

We submit the following cooperative advertising claim in accordance with the terms of your cooperative advertising program. Proof of advertising is enclosed in the form of duplicate bills and newspaper tear sheets.

From:

Frank's Appliance Store
185 Madison St.
Lebanon, Missouri
61202

Your prompt issuance of a credit or a check covering payment of this claim is expected and will enable us to continue and extend use of your cooperative advertising program.

Newspaper	Date of Advertisement	Space Used	Net Rate	Total Cost	Vendor's Co-op Cost
Lebanon Daily Record	*April 15, 1980*	*80 inches*	*$5.00 per inch*	*$400.00*	*$400.00*

I certify that the above is billed at my exact LOWEST NET RATE, computed after all normally earned discounts and expected rebates—and that the amount billed does not include (1) production costs, (2) special or preferred position premiums. If any further discounts, or rebates, other than those already computed, are earned by us for space used, your share will be promptly refunded.

Date _*May 3, 1980*_

Signature _*Frank W. Wilson*_

Figure 2.11   NAB's suggested invoice form for retailers requesting reimbursement from vendors for co-op ads after publication. Tearsheets of the published ads are sent with the invoice. Radio and television bureaus offer similar assistance to advertisers. (SOURCE: By permission of the Newspaper Advertising Bureau.)

break. All figures in the business world compare this year with last year, and so on. This applies to sales figures, advertising expenditures, salespeoples' costs, and of course profits and losses. The pattern is traditional because it works. It is possible the tradition

ANA/RAB FORM FOR SCRIPT (IF TAPE IS USED, PREPARE SCRIPT FROM TAPE)

W___ | ANA/RAB RADIO "TEAR-SHEET"
FORM AT BOTTOM OF SCRIPT PERMITS KNOWING HOW MANY TIMES THIS SCRIPT RAN, AT WHAT COST.

Client:				For:	
		Begin:		End:	Date:

HERE'S NEWS FOR YOU HANDY HOMEOWNERS. IF YOU'D LIKE TO LEARN HOW TO PUT UP A BEAUTIFUL NEW ARMSTRONG CEILING IN YOUR HOME, COME TO ACE LUMBER THIS SATURDAY AT 10 A.M. ACE LUMBER IS HOLDING A HOME IMPROVE-MENT CLINIC. IT WILL TEACH YOU EVERYTHING YOU NEED TO KNOW. YOU'LL LEARN HOW EASY IT IS TO INSTALL ARMSTRONG CEILING TILE IN BASEMENTS, ATTICS, OR ANY ROOM IN YOUR HOME. YOU'LL SEE HOW TO CUT AND FIT BORDER TILES AND HOW TO DO A NEAT JOB AROUND LIGHTING FIXTURES. YOU'LL ACTUALLY INSTALL PRACTICE CEILING TILES YOURSELF. ACE LUMBER IS HEADQUARTERS FOR ALL THE NEW AND EXCLUSIVE ARMSTRONG CEILING DESIGNS, SO IF YOU'RE PLANNING TO REMODEL OR REDECORATE YOUR HOME, IT WILL PAY YOU TO ATTEND THIS CEILING CLINIC. AND THERE'S NO OBLIGA-TION TO BUY A SINGLE THING. WRITE IT DOWN. THE PLACE IS ACE LUMBER. THE TIME IS THIS SATURDAY AT 10 A.M.

▼ (STAMP OR PRINT THIS FORM ON THE BOTTOM OF YOUR SCRIPT PAPER)

STATION DOCUMENTATION STATEMENT APPROVED BY THE CO-OPERATIVE ADVERTISING COMMITTEE OF THE ASSOCIATION OF NATIONAL ADVERTISERS

This announcement was broadcast _____ times, as entered in the station's program log. The times this announcement was broadcast were billed to this station's client on our invoice(s) number/dated _____ at his earned rate of:

$_____each for _____announcements, for a total of $_____
$_____each for _____announcements, for a total of $_____
$_____each for _____announcements, for a total of $_____

_____
Signature of station official

_____   _____   _____
(Notarize above)   Typed name and title   Station

Figure 2.12   Radio co-op procedure form created by the Radio Advertising Bureau and the Association of National Advertisers to provide a "tearsheet" equivalent for radio co-op documentation. This form is to be used when local advertiser has provided the radio script. In addition to the certification of schedule, this form lets the vendor know what was said about the merchandise. (SOURCE: By permission of the Radio Advertising Bureau. Copyright RAB.)

emerged because the typically conservative retailer dared not vary from the familiar, "safe" pathway. And those retailers still in business and operating at a satisfactory profit may be right.

Periodically, it is sound business policy to step back and take a look at where you have been (more than one year back) and a look to where you might be heading (more than one year ahead). It is wise to reexamine every facet of your business, of your sales and sales promotion activities. Do not repeat this year just because you did something last year. Question every expenditure. Dissect every phase of your fashion buying and selling procedures. Call it—to borrow a phrase from government—zero-base planning. It means taking nothing for granted. It means keeping an open mind instead of being trapped by tradition. It means starting from scratch in the new year instead of just padding last year's figures so they will look good in the plan. It means avoiding preconceptions, ignoring sacred cows, taking a fresh look at everything. Question, examine, compare, review—throw away the book and start from scratch.

Fashion changes from year to year, season to season. Fashion retailers often do not change or adjust fast enough to keep up; habits drag them down. Zero-base planning does not mean discarding everything you have done before. But it makes sure you do not do things again *just because* you have done them before.

When the composite six-month planning is completed and approved by store management, it is *not* cast in concrete. It is not followed literally, point by point. It does, however, provide a firm guide to the direction the company plans to take for the season. In practical terms, the plan undergoes constant review. Each three-month period is checked before the start of the next quarter to be sure all elements of the plan—sales and expenditures—are in line. If sales are ahead of or behind plan, an adjustment might be in order. If advertising expense is on target but sales have slipped, a change in the next period's ad plan might be made. Again, with tight controls, each month's progress is reviewed before the start of the new month to be sure no changes ought to be made before the month begins.

Constant attention to sales and expenses, trends and patterns, is maintained to avoid surprises at the end of the quarter or the end of the season. Figures are continuously updated and projected to the end of the month, quarter, and season. Eternal vigilance, the watchword of the U.S. Coast Guard, might have originated in retailing.

QUESTIONS FOR DISCUSSION AND CLASS ASSIGNMENTS

1. Visit a local department store during a special event (Easter, back-to-school). See how many sales promotion tools are used. Describe and evaluate your findings.
2. Bring in examples of stores using the synergistic effect of two or more advertising media during a promotion.
3. Which budgeting method—percent-of-sales or cost-of-goal—do you think is better? Discuss. Give reasons to support your position.
4. Using the Newspaper Advertising Planbook, trace and chart the patterns of a Linens and Domestics Department's sales and advertising statistics. Discuss the good or bad aspects of the resultant pattern.
5. Research a local men's store's advertising. Clip all newspaper ads which indicate the store uses cooperative advertising from manufacturers.
6. Visit a local fashion store and compile a list of national manufacturers' merchandise on display that would indicate the availability of co-op advertising allowances.
7. Visit a local department store advertising department and compare its organizational plan and procedures with the model illustrated in this chapter. Discuss the differences and comment.
8. Should the sales promotion or marketing director of a store be responsible to the general merchandise manager or to the general manager of the store? Give reasons for your position.
9. Develop a sales and advertising plan for a medium-size specialty store in your area using Figure 2.4 as a guide.
10. Develop a six-month advertising and sales plan for the fall season for a full-scale men's furnishings store in your area.
11. Discuss the pros and cons of a store using all the cooperative advertising available to it from its national manufacturers. What factors should be considered in making this decision?
12. Are there any dangers for the retailer who depends on cooperative advertising as the basis for the store's advertising program? Discuss.

Chapter 3
Retail Sales Promotion:
The Budgeting Stage

THE ROLE OF SALES PROMOTION

While each department in the fashion division is developing its
sales plan for the coming season, the sales promotion director and
the fashion director are working along parallel lines. They meet
with the buyer in each merchandise category to plan in broad
strokes the basic departmental fashion events, the themes, the
monthly budgets, and the advertising strategies that will best present the department's merchandise story.

Under discussion at this stage are the timing of the major fashion campaigns, the fashion shows, window and departmental displays, trunk showings, and any special promotions that can be
anticipated and scheduled. The timing differs from department to
department. Buying and selling patterns are studied. The promotion manager pencils in tentative dates for designer personal appearances, and tie-ins with storewide promotional events. After
consultation with each buying and merchandising executive, the
sales promotion manager has acquired the necessary overview of

the store's merchandising objectives and goals for the season. Now the advertising and promotion people can formulate preliminary plans with recommendations to implement the merchandising sales goals.

The key role of the sales promotion division, including the roles of the advertising manager and of the fashion director (bearing in mind that one person could be wearing all three hats in a smaller retail operation) is to create a framework that will encompass all aspects of the store's total program. The final program should be structured to include these elements:

- Sound planning to achieve a proper balance in the store's promotional presentations.
- Defining the audience to assure that all promotional efforts are aimed at prime customer targets.
- Accurate timing to schedule fashion events, advertising, and special events at the peak of customer interest to attain maximum results.
- Media selection to determine the advertising vehicles that offer the best opportunities for reaching the customer target audiences with the store's messages.
- Merchandise planning to include the products the store will be asking customers to buy.
- Advertising technique to develop distinctive methods of presenting the merchandise stories to the target audiences.

To say it more succinctly, the overall plan must tell *whom* we are trying to reach, *what* we will advertise and promote, *when* we will advertise or promote, *where* we will say what we have to say, *how* we will say it, and *how* we will arrange our advertising and sales promotion budget to provide every facet of our business with a proportionate or fair share of exposure to the buying public.

You may detect a similarity in this approach to the credo of the newspaper journalist, who must include the "who-what-where-when-and-how" in the lead paragraph of every well-written news story. The parallel is not accidental, if we agree that advertising fashion means advertising *news*. If it is not news, then it probably is not fashion either. This should be kept in mind, particularly in selecting the items to be advertised.

Advertising old or passé fashion merchandise could mean wasting advertising money. Some retailers, when advertising, offer only items that have been reduced in price to make the ad more attractive to customers. *Why* the items are reduced in price could mean the retailer is offering real value or is advertising a mistake. A mistake in fashion advertising could be an item out of style, an unwanted color, a late season overstocked item, or other less than desirable merchandise.

A balanced advertising program would include about 40 percent of the merchandise at regular price and 60 percent at reduced or "sale" prices. Market research departments of major newspapers report advertising usage by retail clients as a service and a guide to all. The *Los Angeles Times* publishes a detailed Advertising Appraisal report that tallies the full-run advertising by major clients, classified by type of ad. This affords advertisers a chance to compare their advertising against that of competitors while determining if their proportion of regular price versus sale advertising accurately reflects the store's merchandise philosophy.

The January 1980 *Times* Advertising Appraisal shows the varying percentages of trend and image advertising, regular price, storewide sales events, and departmental sales (Table 3.1). Trend and image ads display merchandise coming into fashion; regular price ads promote seasonal fashions, assortments, and selection. Storewide sales and departmental sales events offer merchandise at reduced prices. The degree to which each kind of advertising appears reveals an interesting picture of each store's personality.

Bullock's, a full line department store, spent 47.9 percent of its advertising linage on image/trend and regular price advertising and 52.1 percent on storewide and departmental sales, a good balance. May Company, a more promotion-oriented department store, spent 63.1 percent of its advertising on sale ads and only 36.9 percent on regular price and image-building ads. May Company's direct competitor, The Broadway, was 59.2 percent sale and 40.8 percent regular price, although Broadway's trend/image percentage was 32.4 percent to May Company's 24.9 percent, indicating an attempt to portray a stronger fashion leadership role in its advertising.

The heavily promotional stores—Sears, Penney's, and Ward's—accurately reflect their merchandise policies by spending 97.9, 94.5, and 95.6 percent, respectively, of their ad budgets on sale ads.

The specialty department stores, according to the same *Times* Advertising Appraisal, take the opposite tack to reflect their philosophies of fashion leadership. Bullock's Wilshire, the specialty store division of the Bullock's group, spends 66.4 percent of its ad linage on trend/image ads, plus 13.0 percent on regular price ads. Only 20.6 percent goes to sale ads. Both Neiman-Marcus and Saks Fifth Avenue spend 80 percent of their newspaper space on trend/image ads—which should be expected from these high-fashion, trend-setting leaders.

An added element in this "mix" of regular price versus off-price advertising is the influence of cooperative advertising money.

Table 3.1 KINDS OF ADVERTISING, LOS ANGELES RETAIL STORES, 1980

	TREND/ IMAGE	REGULAR PRICE	PERCENTAGE OF TOTAL	STOREWIDE SALES	DEPARTMENT SALES	PERCENTAGE OF TOTAL
DEPARTMENT STORES						
Broadway	32.4%	8.4%	40.8%	20.8%	38.4%	59.2%
Bullock's	37.7	10.2	47.9	19.1	33.0	52.1
May Company	24.9	12.0	36.9	28.7	34.4	63.1
Robinson's	45.6	3.9	49.5	18.9	31.6	50.5
PROMOTIONAL DEPARTMENT STORES						
Montgomery Ward	2.5%	1.9%	4.4%	57.0%	38.6%	95.6%
Sears Roebuck	1.5	.6	2.1	34.7	63.2	97.9
JC Penney	2.7	2.8	5.5	55.5	39.0	94.5
SPECIALTY DEPARTMENT STORES						
Bullock's Wilshire	66.4%	13.0%	79.4%	13.6%	7.0%	20.6%
Joseph Magnin	54.9	3.7	58.6	19.9	21.5	41.4
Neiman-Marcus	80.0	.8	80.8	3.8	15.4	19.2
Saks Fifth Avenue	80.0	1.6	81.6	5.7	12.7	18.4

SOURCE: Los Angeles Times Advertising Appraisal, 1980. Used by permission.

In many cases, co-op ads, by agreement with the vendor's contract, must advertise the merchandise at regular price. In some instances, the co-op plan will allow for sale-priced advertising.

The premise of advertising off-price merchandise is to use the strong appeal of savings to attract customers. Once in the store, the customers are exposed to all its other attractions—its full line of merchandise, attractive displays, inviting decor, helpful salespeople, and so on. If all conditions are right, the increase in traffic will result in increased sales of regular-priced goods as well as the advertised items.

THE ELEMENTS OF SALES PROMOTION

Just as the buyers and merchandisers turn to records of previous years' activities, so do sales promotion and advertising executives. For the purpose of having guidelines to follow, the sales promotion manager must be aware of industry parameters in the budgeting of sales promotion dollars. Information is available from trade associations, industry publications, other stores in the chain, regional sales and advertising statistics, media research, and other sources.

As in merchandise sales planning, this information provides a backdrop against which promotion managers can "bounce" their own history, local data, and related information in establishing ground rules for sales promotion budgets.

The National Retail Merchants Association (NRMA) provides excellent planning materials for its members. Nonmembers can buy NRMA materials, but at a higher price. From the 1979 edition of their Merchandising Planbook and Sales Promotion Calendar, we show the breakdown of "How the Publicity Dollar Is Spent" compiled from national department store statistics (Figure 3.1).

Newspaper Advertising

Well over 50 percent of the entire budget is spent on print advertising. It has always been this way. Remember that there was nothing but print available to the advertiser until the advent of radio in the 1920s. It is said that when Gutenberg invented movable type and the printed word became possible, a retailer was standing by, waiting for a proof of that week's ad. Far-fetched, of course, but newspaper advertising always has, and probably always will be, the main thrust of most retailers' advertising.

In every market there are newspapers. Every city, every town of any size, has at least one daily, semiweekly, or weekly newspaper. There are paid circulation newspapers, home-delivered or sold

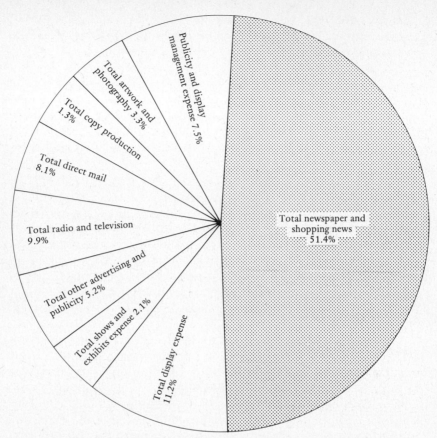

Figure 3.1 How the sales promotion dollar is spent. Chart from the NRMA Planbook shows the distribution of advertising expenditures by expense category, averaging figures from all United States department stores. Total in 1977 was 3.83 percent of net sales spent on sales promotion. (SOURCE: By permission, 1978 Edition (1977 results) FOR, published by The Financial Executives Division, National Retail Merchants Association, New York.)

at newsstands; controlled circulation newspapers or shoppers, delivered free to the doorsteps or driveways of homes throughout every neighborhood; "pennysavers" or classified ad "free delivery" papers that offer a variety of service ads in limited circulation areas. In some markets, ethnic and foreign language newspapers can be important and deserve consideration.

Over the past ten years, the total number of newspapers in America has been reduced through mergers, failures, and continually spiraling production costs. Since 1960, almost 50 metropolitan-area newspapers have folded—five in New York City alone.

(*Los Angeles Times*, April 7, 1978). Despite this, newspapers still continue to gross the largest share of all the advertising money spent in the United States. As the retailer's "best friend," the newspaper continues to garner the lion's share of the retailer's advertising dollar even though the generations of shoppers born since World War II are more electronic-media-oriented than their parents. As cities have expanded into the suburbs, newspaper growth has not kept pace. Big-city papers, large and prosperous as they are, reach smaller and smaller percentages of the total market as time goes on.

But retailers are comfortable with newspaper advertising—it has worked for them over the years, and the existence of some sort of regularly printed publication in every market assures the retailer of one place to spend an advertising budget with confidence and security. The inroads made on this long-standing advertising habit of retailers by television and radio will be discussed more thoroughly in the media selection chapters; suffice it to say at this point that most retailers would give up any other kind of advertising before giving up print advertising.

Direct Advertising

Direct advertising, or direct mail, means printed material distributed directly to the groups of people with whom the fashion retailer wants to communicate. Whether mailed to the store's charge account customers, or hand delivered by a door-to-door service, the retailer can control the cost of every piece of direct advertising. It is an excellent sales tool, flexible, versatile, and specific, but constantly rising in costs and suffering from erratic postal delivery service. Many stores advertise by mail in preference to newspaper, especially small retailers with limited budgets.

Some stores buy specially selected demographic lists to augment their own mailing lists—for example, a list of high-income doctors and lawyers to whom a special promotion on custom-made clothing can be sent, or a list of new home buyers to promote a home decorating service. The technique is expensive, because the retailer pays a good price for the one-time use of the list and must also invest in a suitable high-quality, costly mailing piece.

Broadcast Advertising

Broadcast advertising, both radio and television, is becoming increasingly important to retailers. The ability of radio to reach young people, whose reading habits are not the same as those of their elders, has prodded conservative retailers to the awareness that many potential customers are never reached by newspaper advertising. The spectacular growth of television and the availability of color, along with sound and motion, has made that medium very attractive. To show fashion on live models in realistic situations is a sales tool no retailer will resist for long, although high costs, in both production and air time, have kept many retailers from using this powerful medium.

Radio is now gaining stature in the eyes of retailers who, along with others, wrote off radio when television appeared. Modern radio, offering specific demographic segments of the market, preselected by people's tastes in listening, has added a strong marketing weapon to the promotion manager's arsenal. As a supportive medium, backing up newspaper or TV promotions, or on its own, radio has shown the ability to produce results for many items and sales events. It is said that anything that can be imagined can be advertised on radio.

Despite the growth of broadcast advertising in the total mix of media used by department stores and fashion stores, the percentage of the promotion budget allocated to radio and television is still relatively small—around 10 percent. The use of broadcast is increasing more rapidly in some markets than in others, and as more retailers make the commitment to broadcast, the tide should turn more rapidly. But retailers, being traditionalists and conservative by nature, are slow to change.

Using national budget figures, we note that the cost of advertising production is generally only 4.6 percent of total sales promotion expenditures. This figure may seem small to one accustomed to the higher production costs of television or fine-quality direct mail. Part of the explanation stems from the traditional role the newspaper has always played in retail advertising. There is no production cost in newspaper advertising—at least so it seems. At most papers, the cost of production is included in the cost of the space purchased —it is in the line charge. It is not free, of course; (there really *is* no free lunch). It is built into the cost of the space. This includes engravings, typesetting, proofs, pickup and delivery service, and so on. The retailer has received these services without apparent charge for such a long period of time that it has reflected negatively on the quality of retail ads produced in any medium other than newspaper. There is some resistance to spending production money on professional-quality radio or television advertising. The retailer questions the fees, residuals, and commissions charged by advertising agencies. Although these may be legitimate charges, the thought of paying for production when it came "in the price of the goods" for so many decades is still a bitter pill to swallow.

Salaries

A critical portion of the total sales promotion budget is spent on salaries, usually less than 10 percent. Again, it has been traditional for retail stores to pay their advertising and sales promotion staffs less than handsome salaries. To many the jobs are considered training for neophytes in the advertising business, and not enough effort is made to develop and hold good people. This attitude, which fortunately is being changed by more far-sighted retail managements, results in constant turnover in advertising and promotion personnel. Only the top person in the sales promotion organization warrants a salary comparable to similar positions in manufacturing or in ad agencies. Result: difficulty in maintaining quality standards in advertising and promotion, with consequent loss of effectiveness.

Display

The display department, often called the visual merchandising department (if its responsibilities warrant the title), also commands around 10 percent of the total budget. The fashion area of a department store snares the lion's share of that budget because of the visual impact of fashion and its overall contribution to the image of the store. In a fashion specialty store, the percentage could run considerably higher, and should be a major sales promotion expense.

Other Advertising

The category of sales promotion expense called "Other Advertising and Publicity," which accounts for more than 5 percent of the budget, could include items such as outdoor posters, car cards, painted bulletin boards, theater program ads, balloons, and souvenir-type advertising. This is a catch-all category to which we charge advertising and sales promotion activities that do not fall into traditional slots for bookkeeping purposes. This is also a good place to hide a reserve of promotional dollars for unexpected events or unanticipated increases in media costs or special projects.

Special Events

As you can see, the "Shows, Exhibits, etc." category of sales promotion expense is a tiny portion of the budget in the total department store picture. In a specialty shop or fashion chain, it could be the entire budget. Here we find the funds for fashion shows, for models, scenery, music, programs, and all other costs not included elsewhere. If not planned as part of the regular advertising pro-

**ɂ 3.2 SAMPLE PROMOTION BUDGET BREAKDOWN FOR A
CAL DEPARTMENT STORE**

t (newspapers, shopping news, circulars, inserts, statement enclosures, catalogs, and other direct mail) including production costs	$1,505,000	(43%)
Broadcast (radio and television) including production costs	1,050,000	(30%)
Special Events (shows, publicity, and public relations)	105,000	(3%)
Displays and Signs	350,000	(10%)
Sales Promotion Management	315,000	(9%)
All Other ("kitty" and miscellaneous)	175,000	(5%)
Totals	$3,500,000	(100%)

gram, the cost of advertising the fashion show could be charged to this account too. Good, long-range planning anticipates as much as possible, eliminates surprises, and allows sufficient time for the sales promotion staff to perform to its full capabilities. Table 3.2 shows a budget breakdown for a department store.

ADVERTISING MIRRORS THE STORE

Effective advertising is a true reflection of the store. If your store is highly promotional, offering fashion at discount prices, you cannot run high-fashion ads in the newspaper. The customer just won't believe you. Your advertising should be a mirror of all the things you are—your merchandise, your brand names, your service, your sales staff. As a first step in planning a balanced sales promotion program, get to know yourself, your store, your policies, your attitudes, your merchandising philosophy.

There are stores that advertise regularly, some that advertise occasionally, some that do not advertise at all. Within each type of advertising, the seasonal pattern and the acceptance pattern of the merchandise are superimposed. The *seasonal pattern* of when people buy tells you what items should be advertised and when. The store buyer is very important in this phase of the advertising planning because the selection of the right merchandise, from a timing and season viewpoint, is the buyer's decision. The fashion leadership store's advertising will often precede actual buying by several weeks, planting the idea of the new fashions in the minds of customers well in advance of competitors and establishing its fashion position in customers' minds.

The *acceptance pattern* helps determine the type of advertising or promotion the store will run. When introducing new or exclusive fashions, the advertising takes a prestigious approach to establish fashion authority and leadership for the store. At the height of the season, when the merchandise is in demand by more customers, the advertising, somewhat promotional, talks about selection and assortments. Of course, the items are at regular prices. As the season wanes, prices are reduced to empty overloaded racks and shelves of merchandise, and the ads talk of "special savings" and "reductions from stock." The final phase of the acceptance curve is the season end. Here we see the "special purchases" from manufacturers' overstocked showrooms and clearances from stocks. It is now clearance time, and the advertising says so. (See our earlier discussion of the fashion cycle in Chapter 1).

Presenting a Balanced Picture

The problem is establishing a workable advertising plan and budget that allows for all the contingencies while presenting to the buying public a balanced picture of the store's fashion image. What percentage of the budget should go to introductory, prestige ads? How much should be spent to tell the world the store is first with the newsiest fashions? What share of the budget should be for best-selling items at regular prices? What should be set aside for clearances and special purchases? These decisions are made jointly with the merchandise staff.

The responsibility of the advertising and promotion manager includes keeping these various types of advertising in perspective so they present a true picture of the store. Every buyer wants to achieve the greatest return in sales volume from every ad. No one can blame the buyer for this attitude. Store management may not question how a department managed a successful, profitable season as long as it was a successful, profitable season. The advertising manager must resist the desire of the buyer to run nothing but off-price ads to ensure direct results. In the long run, a store or department that runs only "sale" or off-price promotions gains a reputation for being a "schlock" or bargain-type operation. Eventually that store will get response to its ads only when the items advertised are off-price. This could become a problem, because it will become very difficult to get response from customers to regular price or fashion leadership ads. Why come in and buy at regular price, when the customer has been "trained" by the advertising program to wait a bit and pick up the merchandise at a reduced price?

The advertising or fashion director must allocate a specific portion of the store's total budget for image or personality ads. Many stores call these *institutional* ads, schedule them with reluctance, and expect, and get, no appreciable response when they run. Many buyers balk at supplying the ad department with merchandise for these "nonproductive" ads. They feel they are wasteful. They miss the point that the image-making ads, whether they inspire immediate store traffic or not, lay the foundation for future sales results. These ads inform and educate the public, and as a fashion leader, it is the store's duty to do this.

In the same vein, a definite percentage of the budget must be set aside for "trend" advertising and promotion. These are the ads that tell the public the store has the newest, the latest, the most popular fashions in stock right now.

Thanks to the information and guidance supplied by the fashion director, the store buyers have received sufficient advance notice about the fashion trends for the coming season. Purchases have been made, and the merchandise has been shipped and is on the selling floor when the ads are published or broadcast.

Advertising at Regular Price

A substantial chunk of the advertising budget should be set aside for the regular-price ads that are run at the height of the season. These are the ads that bring in the bulk of the store's traffic. They are the fashion brand name ads, with the "right" items. Talk to any merchant; these are the most profitable ads, with the merchandise at full markup, and with the best selections and assortments of the season. These are also the ads for which manufacturers share in the cost as part of their co-op program.

Regular-price ads assure customers of the best chance of finding the styles and colors they want, in their sizes. With full selections of merchandise to choose from, the customer has the best opportunity of making a satisfactory transaction. The retailer knows that a purchase, once made, is never assured until the customer keeps the merchandise.

Returns from unhappy or dissatisfied customers play havoc with sales results from ads. This may not sound like the advertising manager's responsibility, but anything that inhibits sales results is the advertiser's business. For example, if sales results from a promotion are poor because the merchandise happens not to fit properly, and customers return items to the store for that reason, the result reported to the ad department may not show an accurate count. All it may record is the number of units sold. If the number of units sold is low, when that ad is evaluated at a later date, the poor score may be attributed to the ad copy, the artwork, the photo, the timing, or some other element of the ad, when the fault was actually in the merchandise. This may happen in many stores where incomplete information is reported. After all, buyers, being basically human, would hesitate to report the true cause of the flop in this hypothetical instance. Sometimes there is insufficient merchandise in the store to back up the ad. In these cases, the customer might not find the right size, color, or fabric, with a resultant low sales score for the ad.

Regular-price advertising produces the bread-and-butter results that a fashion operation must have to be successful in its promotional program. Heavy store traffic produced by effective advertising can improve gross profit performance remarkably.

The success of the regular price advertising portion of the ad program impinges directly on the success of the off-price advertising of the store. Sales advertising that runs in the latter stages of the fashion cycle will be more productive if the store has built a solid foundation of customer acceptance with consistent regular-price ads. Regular customers have developed the habit of reading these ads, have responded to them, and have received satisfaction from their purchases. It is only logical that they will respond to the store's off-price advertising because they have learned from past performances that the advertising is truthful and believable. Off-price advertising can only be an extension of the sound relationship a store has established with its clientele.

It follows, then, that the advertising and sales promotion director, in scheduling a proper balance of each type of advertising, must work closely with the merchandise division. The proportion of off-price to regular-price advertising, and trend to image-enhancing, is determined by an objective evaluation of the true personality of the store. The highly promotional store runs a higher percentage of off-price ads, special promotions, and manufacturers' overstocks. The nonpromotional, fashion leader store runs more image and trend ads. The semipromotional, middle-of-the-road store runs a more balanced program, with a planned percentage of each type of ad reflecting the merchandising policies of the store (Table 3.1).

Retailers have always watched the competition closely, sometimes too closely. Retailers tend to copy their competition in many areas. The thinking goes something like this: "They're smart merchants. They must know what they're doing. Maybe they know something we don't know. Let's do it their way." This is sometimes called the *copy cat theory of merchandising*. In the advertising phase of the business, it is called "the grass is always greener in the other store's ads." Research is good, and necessary. But letting your competition dictate your policy is wrong. Use competitive activity as a factor to be considered in making decisions, but not as the only path to follow.

All media (newspapers, magazines, broadcast) can furnish the retailer with some information on competitive activity in its medium. Some stores feel they must be No. 1 in everything—operate the most stores, out-advertise everyone, run bigger sales—and smart media salespeople cater to this attitude. If this attitude is deliberate, and planned to achieve the image of "the biggest and the best," fine. If, however, the attempt to achieve this objective is not financially sound, or stems from the ego needs of store management, it could backfire and lead to an unhealthy, overpromotional balance in the store's operation. Stores have failed and closed because of overexpansion before the organization was capable of handling a multiplicity of branch stores. Stores have overpromoted—at the expense of the profit picture—and lost money. And stores have failed because they were underpromoted.

Proper balance is the answer. What is right for your store may not necessarily be right for your competitor. You are what you are—the composite of all the things that make your store a successful store. These are the stories—the merchandising philosophies, the service policies, the salespeople's friendliness—that should be told in your advertising and promotion. The right proportion of sale advertising to regular-price, image to trend, will emerge as a natural result of your analysis of what makes your store tick. Use the research, investigate the market, watch your competition—but, in the words of Shakespeare's Polonius, "To thine own self be true"—and you can't go wrong.

Defining the Store's Market

The sales promotion manager, the fashion director, and the merchandise manager, working as a team, must define the customer audience for the store. Back in the days of sole proprietorships and prior to World War II, when the department store was a single store, the experienced owner or manager knew instinctively who the customers were. They were able to see them, talk to them, find out what they liked or disliked. They could sense, with this firsthand knowledge, when changes were in order. A look at the fashion racks at the end of a busy day would indicate quickly which items customers were buying. There was little need for research, for market analysis.

When multistore organizations began to flourish in the 1950s, and locations farther and farther from home base became the retail trend, the need arose for a formalized feedback system to keep management and decision makers abreast of store activity. Whether the store established a research and marketing division, hired a research marketing firm as consultant, or used the talents of existing personnel, it needed to collect the facts about its market and potential buying public to ensure the greatest return on its advertising investment.

The marketing research program, an integral part of the modern retail operation, exists in all fashion retailing. It may not be formalized, but it must be there for the retailer to function properly in today's competitive world. Through proper market research, the retailer can more closely identify the audience for the store's fashions and can tailor merchandise purchases to their specific needs. And, from an advertising and sales promotion viewpoint, the audience must be identified before media plans can be made to reach that audience.

The research program will reveal the demographic characteristics of the store's audience. *Demographics* are the data relative to the composition of a specific group of people. Demographic categories include age, sex, income, occupation, education, ethnic background. The demographic data of greatest concern to fashion retailers include the age-sex-income data, but much more information is needed. A close examination would indicate the composition of the store's customers and its relationship to the market as a whole.

These data will help identify the prime audience and define the target for the store's advertising. Important information is gathered, such as customers' attitude toward the store's merchandise (shoddy, good quality, very current), their reactions to the store's merchandise mix (I can't find my size in the styles I like), their impressions of the advertising (love their ads!), their shopping behavior (after work), their shopping experiences (such polite salespeople!).

There are many experienced marketing research firms in the retail field today, specializing in helping stores develop programs that will satisfy the needs of specific consumer segments in the markets they serve. Life-styles vary within demographic breakouts by age, sex, income. The way people live to a great extent indicates their merchandise needs. Retailers who understand these life-style patterns can cater to them more accurately, make fewer mistakes, and increase net profits.

Consider the contrasting life-styles of these two families, both married, both adults working, combined incomes of $30,000: The Joneses have two young children, drive a compact American-made car, own a camper for recreation, and live in a heavily mortgaged house in the suburbs. The Smiths have no children, rent an apartment on the bay, drive twin foreign-made sport cars to work, and spend their weekends on their fiberglass sailboat. Same basic demographics, but two entirely different ways of life. Result: different needs in clothing, home furnishings, recreation equipment, food. The retailer needs to know *who* the customers are. The sales promotion department must know *how* to reach them, so it must know *who* they are, *where* they are, and *how* they live.

Many stores are developing excellent customer profiles right in the store. The detailed information can be gathered at the checkout terminal—the electronic device that has replaced the old-fashioned cash register. *Can* be gathered, that is, if the capabilities of these terminals are understood and used. Whenever a sale is registered in these highly sophisticated terminals, information can be fed to computers to record details of the customer's shopping habits. It may take an entire generation of retailers comfortable with these computer-brained terminals to fully utilize the capabilities of the systems. Even now, charge card records reveal to the alert retailer the clothing sizes of all members of the family, prices of merchandise bought, brand name preferences, frequency of visits, regularity of payments, and many other bits of information.

The availability of customer profile information can be an invaluable tool for the sales promotion planner. Its information could result in interesting advertising decisions. Just suppose that, in a period of slow business, the store decided to cut down on the cost of the traditional fall fashion catalog. A quick decision could mean that the catalog would be smaller, with fewer pages of merchandise, but the buyers would not like that because it would mean some departments would be eliminated. It could mean printing on cheaper paper to save on paper costs and perhaps lower the cost of postage, but the store's image would suffer if the quality image was not maintained. The sales promotion manager studies the charge account records and decides to trim the *number* of catalogs printed and distributed. This is achieved by deleting from a mailing list all customers who have not made a purchase in the past six months or who have not paid on their accounts in ninety days. Quality and image standards have been upheld, and the required reduction in costs has been made.

More sophisticated retailers have the capability of mailing only to people who have purchased in a specific department, concentrating the mailing to established, and presumably satisfied, customers. This type of target mailing can eliminate considerable waste in direct mail operations.

THE IMPORTANCE OF TIMING

Timing is the key in most successful ventures. It has been said there is no stronger force than an idea whose time has come. To a retailer, the timing of an advertising program, even a single ad, is one of the most important factors in advertising success. Offering swimsuits for sale in October is bad; so is advertising snowshovels in August. Surfboards are never a best seller in Saskatchewan. The probability of selling air conditioners in Buffalo in the middle of winter is highly questionable, although the author accomplished it —once. Proper timing helps a lot.

More realistically, advertising swimsuits in March and April makes sense. In the Far West and Southwest, swimsuit advertising usually starts earlier in the year and lasts longer than in Eastern or Midwest cities. Back-to-school merchandise is advertised in August, when, throughout the land, families think about equipping their young ones for the classroom. At the same time, fashion stores start promoting fall fashions, fixing in the minds of shoppers that summer is over and it is time to buy warmer, darker-toned fashions for fall.

Timing of advertising is probably the easiest part of the sales promotion program to develop. The information is all there, documented in detail and easily available. The buying patterns of the American public are so consistent, varying so little from season to season, from year to year, that they are completely predictable.

The tables in Chapter 2 from the Newspaper Advertising Bureau Planbook give the percentages of the year's total sales done in each month (Table 2.1) and the percentages of the month's total sales done by each of the fashion stores' departments (Table 2.2). These are, of course, national averages and before they become the figures to live by, they must be evaluated alongside the regional and local sales patterns and the information from the store itself. The point, however, is that the sales pattern is a buying pattern. It then becomes very clear that the time when people traditionally buy swimsuits is the time to have swimsuits in stock, and when you have swimsuits in stock, that is the time to advertise to your customers to tell them!

A check of Table 2.1 indicates that the best months to sell women's and misses' coats are January, March, September, October, November, and December. Note that these figures are printed in bold type, indicating that more than 8.3 percent of annual sales occur in those months. If all months produced equal sales, each month would account for 8.3 percent of annual sales.

Table 2.4, which shows the percentages of the year's total newspaper advertising linage used each month by each category of merchandise, indicates some interesting facts. The linage figures for coats are listed separately—by untrimmed cloth, fur-trimmed cloth, and fur coats. January is not as good a month for the untrimmed coat category, so it is evident which types of coats should be advertised during that month. In March, however, untrimmed coats are the strongest of the three, with Easter and spring obvious factors in that statistic. All three groups do well from September through December, with fur coats, a holiday gift item, doing best.

This is an example of how the sales promotion planner can and should tailor the advertising plan to the sales plan. If the store's sales match up reasonably well with the national figures, it would be fairly safe to plan the budget the same way.

A Typical Calendar

Let us put together the first step of a sales promotion program to cover the basic needs of a typical fashion retail store (this calendar is adapted from the Newspaper Advertising Bureau Planbook, 1981).

January	Women's coats
	Intimate apparel
	Furs
February	Women's suits
March	Women's coats and suits
	Juniors' coats, suits and dresses
	Girls' wear
	Women's and misses' dresses
	Millinery
	Women's and children's hosiery
	Infants' wear
	Women's and children's shoes
April	Women's and misses' suits
	Juniors' coats, suits, dresses
	Women's and misses' dresses
	Housedresses and uniforms
	Millinery
	Intimate apparel and bras
	Women's and children's shoes
May	Juniors' coats, suits and dresses
	Women's and misses' dresses
	Blouses, skirts, sportswear
	Housedresses and uniforms
	Intimate apparel and bras
	Slips and lingerie
	Robes, lounging apparel
	Handbags and small leather goods

	Women's shoes
	Men's clothing
June	Women's and misses' dresses
	Blouses, skirts, sportswear
	Housedresses and uniforms
	Intimate apparel and bras
	Men's clothing
	Men's furnishings
July	None (no category sales 8.3% or better)
August	Juniors' coats, suits, dresses
	Girls' wear
	Furs
	Infants' wear
	Children's shoes
	Boys' wear
September	Women's coats
	Women's suits
	Juniors' coats, suits, dresses
	Girls' wear
	Women's and misses' dresses
	Blouses, skirts, sportswear
	Millinery
	Intimate apparel and bras
	Women's and children's hosiery
	Infants' wear
	Handbags and small leather goods
	Boys' wear
October	Women's coats and suits
	Juniors' coats, suits, dresses
	Girls' wear
	Women's wear
	Blouses, skirts, sportswear
	Furs
	Neckwear and scarves
	Millinery
	Women's and children's gloves
	Intimate apparel and bras
	Women's and children's hosiery
	Infants' wear
	Handbags and small leather goods
	Women's and children's shoes
	Boys' wear
November	Women's coats
	Juniors' coats, suits, dresses

Girls' wear
Blouses, skirts, sportswear
Furs
Neckwear and scarves
Handkerchiefs
Women's and children's gloves
Women's and children's hosiery
Underwear, slips, lingerie
Infants' wear
Handbags and small leather goods
Women's and children's shoes
Men's clothing
Men's furnishings
Boys' wear

December   ALL categories (all departments over 8.3%)

This calendar shows "probable" merchandising events. The fact that these are the best months for these merchandise categories does not necessarily mean they are the categories most likely to be advertised. An additional factor to be considered is how important that category is in relation to total store sales.

For example, examining Figure 2.7, we noted that although the sportswear division produces only 8.8 percent of its annual sales in May, sportswear represents 15.2 percent of the store's total sales for the month. On the other hand, although housedresses and uniforms ring up 12.3 percent of annual sales in May, the best month of the year because of Mother's Day buying, these account for only 5.6 percent of the store's total sales. This is where judgment and experience come into play—deciding where to place the promotional emphasis, and how much advertising money will be allocated to the various departments. Each department's need for advertising should be studied in relation to its importance each month—to annual sales, to monthly sales, to the store's merchandise mix, plus other factors. One of these factors is seasonality, or the traditional sales period for specific types of merchandise.

A Look at Traditional Sales

These traditional sales are an interesting phenomenon in the retail business. Their origins are as muddy as the chicken-and-egg which-came-first controversy. For some special reason, there is an intimate apparel and bra sale every January. Somewhere back in retail history, it was decreed that January and May (and sometimes August) was the time to run white sales. Swimsuits sales fill the newspapers and airwaves every July, with several weeks of good swimming weather still available in some parts of the country. Every Columbus Day is coat sale day. Explain that to customers still wearing bikinis and shorts in Southern California.

Some of these traditional sales do have rational explanations. The Columbus Day phenomenon probably happens because many of the fashion coat buyers and merchandise managers got their basic training in the New York area or in Eastern or Midwestern cities. There it made sense, from a weather and timing standpoint, to designate a holiday in the middle of the fall season as the logical time to launch a major coat promotion. As these merchants moved around the country from job to job, they took with them their experiences of successful coat promotions on Columbus Day. Why not follow the historical pattern? It worked once, why not again? Thus are retail traditions born.

Another interesting tradition is the annual swimsuit sale during the latter part of July, when practically every major store in every city in America simultaneously announces its annual sales of famous brand swimwear—$\frac{1}{3}$ to $\frac{1}{2}$ off. Originally established in the minds of retailers and manufacturers as the ideal time to unload swimwear stocks, to clear the stores of summer merchandise and prepare for the influx of fall goods, the swimsuit sale has become an annual event. Thinned-down stocks are augmented to round out selection, large ads are run, with radio and TV support, and customers respond in great numbers. It has almost become the official end of summer in many parts of the country and official notice that fall is just around the corner.

After checking the list of probable merchandising events based on "natural" buying patterns, the second step in organizing the sales promotion program is to list the holidays and special sales events that sometimes have the weight of real holidays:

January	New Year's Day
	End of retail fiscal year
	Home furnishings sale
	Clearances and sales
February	Valentine's Day
	Lincoln's Birthday
	Washington's Birthday
March	Easter (sometimes in April); St. Patrick's Day
April	After-Easter clearances
May	Mother's Day
	Memorial Day
June	Father's Day

	Graduation
	June brides
	Vacation time
	Pre-July Fourth clearances and sales
July	Independence Day
	End of fiscal half-year clearances and sales
August	Back-to-school
	August home furnishings sales
September	Labor Day
	Fall fashion introductions
October	Columbus Day
	Halloween
November	Thanksgiving Day
	Veterans' Day
	Election Day
December	Christmas

Add to these such "events" as Ground Hog Day, Home Sewing Week, Brand Names Month, and the like, and we have endless reasons for promotion.

Step three is checking the retail total sales promotion calendar (adapted from the NRMA Merchandising Planbook and Sales Promotion Calendar, 1981):

January. Cosmetics and drug sundries sales; intimate apparel and bra sales; lingerie sales; fur sales; fashion resortwear; white sales; infants needs sales; bridal promotion; art needlework; home furnishings sales—bedding, furniture, carpeting; fashion accessories; diamond sales; luggage sales; fashion fabrics sales; sewing notions, yarn sales; men's and women's apparel sales; women's and misses' coats and suits; year-end clearances

February. New spring fashions; Valentine's Day promotions; fashion fabric events; men's custom suit sales; men's wear sales; women's and misses' suits; spring home furnishing sales, bedding, furniture; Washington's Birthday sale; Lincoln's Birthday sale; President's Day sales; fur sales; art needlework; hosiery sales

March. Spring ready-to-wear; millinery promotions; pre-Easter sales; rainwear promotion; infants wear and furniture; spring fashion accessories, cosmetics, sunglasses; home improvement, garden supplies, china and glass; junior coats, suits, dresses; fashion fabrics event; women's shoes; children's wear; children's shoes

April. Easter and post-Easter sales; fashion clearances; spring millinery; misses' and women's fashions; children's shoes; sleepwear, lingerie promotion; summer fashions; juniors coats, suits, dresses; fashion fabrics; camp equipment, garden supplies, paint, wallpaper; women's shoes; intimate apparel and bras; pre-summer fabric sales; Mother's Day promotion; housedresses and uniforms; fashion accesssories; fur storage promotion

May. Mother's Day items; men's clothing; Baby Week sale; bridal promotion; summer sportswear; women's shoes; costume jewelry; fashion accessories; misses' and women's fashions, fine jewelry and watches; luggage sales; summer fabrics, trimmings; fashion clearances; Memorial Day sales; men's and boys' wear; intimate apparel, sleepwear; junior fashions; foundations and bras; white sales; home furnishings and housewares sales; diamond sales

June. Graduation promotions; fine jewelry and watches; camping clothes and supplies; sporting goods and cameras; vacation promotion; outdoor living promotion; silverware and clocks; luggage and typewriter sales; intimate apparel and lingerie sales; furniture, bedding, floor covering sales; Father's Day promotions; bridal promotions; fashion sportswear; men's wear sales; men's furnishings, clothing; men's shoes and slippers; summer wear for the family; women's and misses' dresses; summer furniture, accessories

July. Independence Day sales; summer fashion clearance; outdoor living supplies; sporting goods sales; August fur events; After-the-Fourth sales; annual swimsuit sales; August white sales; furniture and bedding sales; pre-inventory sales; Christmas in July events; Pre-fall fabric events

August. Final summer fashion clearances; August white sales; children's shoes; fall fashion accessories; August home furnishings sales; back-to-school fashions; fall fashion promotion; bridal promotion; boys' and girls' shoes

September. Labor Day weekend sales; men's and boys' fall wear; back-to-school fashions; home improvement events; fall fashion accessories; home furnishings, bedding, floor covering sales; fall fashions; children's shoes; sporting goods sales; fall fabrics, trimmings; millinery

October. Columbus Day sales; fall evening wear; men's wear; fall millinery; art needlework; ski season fashions; Halloween promotions; misses', women's coat sales; outerwear for the family; gloves for the family; woolen fabrics; fur sales; Baby Week sales; furniture, home furnishings events; Thanksgiving Day sales (often the biggest sale day of the year)

November. Early Christmas promotions; Election Day sales; pre-holiday sales; girls' and infants' wear; men's clothing, furnishings; Christmas toy opening; china and glassware events; Veterans' Day promotion; Christmas layaway promotions; furniture, bedding, and home furnishings sales; evening fashion wear; women's and misses' coats; fashion accessories; lingerie and robes sales; woolen fabrics; pre-Christmas sales; trim-the-home promotion; silverware and linens events; fur sales

December. Pre-Christmas sales; holiday fashion events; fashion accessories; bridal fashions; cruise wear; silverware, china, glassware; outdoor recreation events; misses' and women's apparel; post-Christmas sale events; Christmas gift events; fashion gift events; cosmetic gift events; men's and boys' wear; fine jewelry and watches; sporting goods and cameras; infants needs sale; luggage events; early January events

The sales promotion calendar includes many promotions and sales that may not be strictly in the "fashion" category, but they are listed for three reasons. The fashion sales promotion manager must be aware of the events going on in the marketplace because all stores are in competition for the same customer dollar. If they spend their money on bedding or furniture, they cannot spend it on fashions. If the fashion promotion is intriguing enough, the money will go there instead of for the new set of draperies.

The second reason for the inclusion of the full promotion calendar is to provide a checklist to prevent omissions from the store's own program. It is also possible to develop an offbeat idea for a fashion promotion by borrowing or adapting an event from another category of merchandise. For example, some fashion retailers run sales of winter-white fashions in January while the linen and domestics stores in town are advertising white goods. Some appliance stores offer their white goods (refrigerators, washers, dryers) to take advantage of all the white sale advertising and its impact on the public mind.

Another reason for the full promotion calendar stems from one of the premises of this book—that fashion is everywhere in our lives. Whether it is clothing, home furnishings, or the latest wrinkle in recreation, it is fashion. Its influence is apparent in the apparel we wear, the way we entertain, the food in our homes. The alert sales promotion manager has this awareness, and it shows up in the unique, unexpected, and memorable promotional events.

At this point, most of the elements for composing the store's promotion program are in the hands of the promotion manager— the calendars, the sales figures, the seasonal events. The input from the fashion director is also available to complete the picture.

PLANNING THE STORE PROGRAM

What happens next depends on the talents and experience of the sales promotion planners. Perhaps a brainstorming session, involving the entire staff, from writers and artists to secretaries and file clerks, is in order. This type of meeting is a freewheeling, mind-picking session aimed at getting ideas from the entire organization, to be screened and sifted at a later date for action. Perhaps a meeting of the section heads, the copy chief, the art director, the production chief, the fashion director, and the advertising manager takes place to develop the fashion themes and promotional ideas that will dramatize the store's fashion story to the public during the coming season. Or perhaps the sales promotion manager decides to do it alone, to go off and produce the series of fashion idea events that will capture the imagination and fashion dollars of the buying public. This one-person brainstorming technique is sometimes called "thinking." Full details of the brainstorming method of idea development and problems solving can be found in *Creative Imagination,* by Alex Osborn, of Batten, Barton, Durstine & Osborn fame.

The wealth of material available to the sales promotion planner may be more information than is wanted or needed. But a sound plan should have the proper backdrop against which to "paint in" the plan that is most effective for the store. The planner must select from the accumulated data those facts and figures that most closely apply to the store's particular needs and goals. You cannot be all things to all people. Our discussion about building a store image will cover some of the problems of spreading that image too thin, diffusing effort and inviting failure. If the market research has been accurate and relevant, the promotion planner has a good idea of what the market wants, needs, and expects from the store. The job is to present the correct mix of merchandise in an attractive, persuasive manner to convince as many as possible that your store is the best place for them to shop, the best place for them to receive satisfaction from their purchases. Studying the facts, and measuring the store's particular strengths and weaknesses against regional sales patterns, customer buying history, and growth and development over the years gives the planner the tools with which to fashion a workable sales promotion program.

In Chapter 2, we discussed the procedures followed by the merchandising division. Now that we have traced the path traveled by the sales promotion division during the same time period, it is time to put the two together. Again, we will use the larger retail unit to describe the procedure. The principles and the functions apply to retailers of all sizes.

Each merchandise division, building up from the departmental level, has put together its own six-month plan. Each sales-supporting division has worked out its plans for improving its operation during the coming season. The executive committee schedules a full-scale reporting meeting. Now is the time for divisional managers, both merchandising and sales supporting, to present their plans of action to the assembled management group.

The Six-Month Plan Reporting Meeting

A full day or two of meetings, outside the store and away from the daily pressures of business and telephone interruptions, is usually needed for this type of gathering. Key executives present their division's programs. Presentations range from 30 to 40 minutes in length, followed by a question-and-answer period at the conclusion of the formal report. By the conclusion of the reporting meeting, the participants will have received an overall picture of the store's plans. After the series of thorough discussions of all facets of the company's business plans, they will each have a good idea of what is expected of them for the coming season.

The merchandise divisions, of course, report on their fashion plans; the news in sportswear, apparel, and designer styles; trends in fabrics; trends in industry; information that affects the potential of the store's future fashion activities. The accounting people talk about how they plan to improve the efficiency of their operation; delivery and warehouse executives cover their departments and plans for progress; personnel discusses recruiting and training plans; and sales promotion presents the sales promotion program in some dramatic manner.

Sales promotion, the creative section of the store, is expected to provide the drama and romance of the total store picture to the management group at the meeting as a preview of what will be presented to the general public in the future. Its presentation is visually a welcome contrast to the statistical and detail reports that naturally constitute the bulk of the merchandising presentations. The promotion people use audiovisual devices, film, music, live models, and entertainment to dramatize the events that will make the new season exciting and successful. If the staid, conservative merchants and financial executives can be moved emotionally and imaginatively by the ideas presented, it provides reassurance for potential success later, when these ideas will be offered to the buying public. A truism in the retail business says the store must be sold on itself before it can sell itself to the public.

These planning or reporting meetings are sometimes held at vacation retreats, with wives and husbands of store executives sometimes invited at store expense. The activities for the meeting period are carefully planned, with work sessions scheduled from early morning through lunch. Afternoons and evenings are set aside for sports and social activities. Modern business practices encourage the periodic involvement of spouses under favorable conditions as beneficial to the long-range relationships of hard-working executives and their families.

The smaller retail store may not need, or be able to afford, the luxury of taking two days away from the business, and may not in fact have anyone to run the store while they are away planning for the next season. It is necessary, however, to back off from the day-to-day operation and pressure periodically, to look at the whole operation at "arm's length" in order to see things in perspective. Zero-base planning may sound a bit grandiose to the small retail chain operator or the individual entrepreneur, but its principles apply to businesses of all sizes. The idea of periodically reexamining every phase of the business makes good common sense no matter how good or bad economic conditions might be.

If necessary, the small retailer can hold these planning sessions on weekends. Sundays are great for relaxed, private thinking and talking exercises. Many companies schedule breakfast meetings, starting at 7 A.M. and digging into problems during the quiet hours before the phones start ringing. Planning time can be created with a series of these early morning meetings scheduled before it is time to open the store for the day's business. Leave it to the practical retailer to find time to plan, because good planning is part of running a sound fashion business.

Spring Plan

Table 3.3 shows a typical department store promotion program for a spring season. The predictability of a retail store's seasonal events is highly visible in this program. The variable factor each spring

3.3 SALES PROMOTION CALENDAR, SPRING SEASON

EEK	EVENT
lary 3	Valentine's Day gift promotions (through February 14)
February 10	
February 17	President's Day sales (Lincoln's Birthday through
February 24	Washington's Birthday)
March 3	Spring fashion promotions (starting date linked to Easter
March 10	date)
March 17	Spring homemaking time; St. Patrick's Day event
March 24	Easter fashion promotion
March 31	Girls' fashions, boys' Easter wear
April 7	Easter fashion promotions (continue to Easter Sunday)
April 14	
April 21	After-Easter sales and clearances
April 28	Mother's Day gift events
May 5	Lingerie and robe show
May 12	Summer fashion and sportswear show promotion
May 19	Memorial Day sale event; May white sale
May 26	Outdoor living promotions; June brides show
June 2	Graduation gift events
June 9	Father's Day gift events
June 16	Swimsuit and sportswear promotion
June 23	Vacation and travel promotions
June 30	Pre-July Fourth holiday events
July 7	Annual summer fashion sale
July 14	Semiannual storewide clearance
July 21	Early fall fashion events
July 28	Begin back-to-school promotions

season is the date of Easter Sunday. The date on which Easter falls has a marked effect on the amount of spring fashion business a retail store may do that year. It also affects the type of merchandise that can be promoted.

If Easter occurs in mid-April, there is a much longer selling period for spring and Easter fashions than if Easter Sunday is in March. Easter signals the height of the spring season, after which after-Easter sales and clearances take place and the promotion of summer goods begins. We discussed this in Chapter 2 as the Marpril planning procedure. If Easter falls earlier in the year, in March, it also means that more winter, or cold weather, merchandise will be in demand than the lighter, brighter spring fashions. Traditionally, the later Easter is more popular with the fashion merchant, since he or she has a longer period of time in which to advertise and sell spring items.

An interesting problem rises when Easter Sunday's date shifts from April one year to March the next. With the continuing goal of "beating last year" ever present in the minds of buyers, merchandising manager, and top management alike, an Easter date three weeks earlier this year than last raises havoc with sales figures. What were three weeks of healthy fashion buying due to Easter's date last year become three weeks during which special promotions must be planned this year to offset last year's sales figures.

Full-line stores like department stores move their annual spring home furnishings event or other special sales into the vacuum of "natural" traffic created by the shift of Easter. Specialty stores that carry only fashion merchandise have a more difficult problem. Their approach to meeting or beating last year's sales under these conditions might be to run, in addition the traditional after-Easter clearance and sales, special promotions of seasonal fashion items at reduced prices. By planning ahead of time, merchants can secure special items or extra concessions from key manufacturers for these occasions. The unwary buyer is caught short and "surprised" by the changes in the calendar for which the well-organized buyer has anticipated and planned.

A Six-Month Blueprint

The sales promotion calendar is distributed throughout the retail store organization to all key executives and department heads. The six-month sales promotion plan becomes the blueprint for the advertising and promotion activities for the season. Buying, merchandising, delivery, receiving and marking, distribution, and other functions of the store revolve around the dates and times contained in the program. For this is not just the program of the sales promotion department—it is the program for the entire store as it will be presented to customers.

The calendar shows that the seasonal buying patterns have been included—spring, summer, vacation, and early fall. The holidays, around which so much retail activity occurs, are there—Lincoln's and Washington's birthdays, Easter, Memorial Day, July Fourth. Merchandising events, real or contrived, are pinpointed—Mother's Day, Father's Day, June brides, Valentine's Day.

The degree to which any store takes advantage of these promotional opportunities depends on its merchandising policy, the size of the promotional budget, and the kinds of merchandise carried by the store. Obviously, the men's store ignores Mother's Day, and the women's fashion stores cannot promote Father's Day. Decisions whether to promote for extra business over the Memorial Day weekend or to do something special for President's Days is an individual matter. The full-line store tries to cover every base—the competition will probably do so, and the store cannot stand back and let them take any advantage.

Along with the sales promotion calendar, the sales and promo-

Table 3.4 SALES AND PROMOTION PLAN, SPRING SEASON

MONTH	PLANNED MONTHLY SALES	PERCENTAGE OF SALES BY MONTH
February	$ 154,000	11.0%
March	168,000	12.0
April	273,000	19.5
May	259,000	18.5
June	294,000	21.0
July	252,000	18.0
Total, spring	$1,400,000	100.0%

tion budget (Table 3.4), when approved by management, is distributed throughout the store on a "need to know" basis. The budget shows the planned sales for the six-month spring season on a month-by-month basis; the percentage of total sales of the season that each month represents; the promotion budget by month; the percentage of the total sales promotion budget allocated to each month; and the percentage of promotional dollars to sales by month. For example, total planned sales for March is $168,000. The six-month sales plan is $1,400,000, so the $168,000 represents 12 percent of the season's sales. The promotion budget for March is $7,900 or 14.9 percent of the total spring budget of $53,100. The promotion budget for March is 4.7 percent of sales. The seasonal percentage of promotion dollars to sales is 3.79, a figure arrived at by dividing $53,100, the total budget, into $1,400,000, total sales. Adding in a contingency reserve of $1,500, the percentage of advertising to sales becomes 3.86.

As the season progresses, and actual sales are recorded month by month along with actual promotional expenditures, the budgets for upcoming months are often adjusted to keep profit projections in line. If it happens that February and March sales fail to reach planned goals, management may decide to decrease or increase the advertising budgets for the remaining months. If the consensus indicates that promotional opportunities can be exploited, management may add dollars to the promotion budget. If the forecasts for business are conservative, management may decide to cut the budget for the balance of the season to minimize losses in profit. When this occurs, the advertising department must move quickly to make judicious budget cuts in the planned advertising program that save the required dollars but reduce the impact of the program as little as possible. Table 3.5 shows how advertising activity is planned to take changes into account.

PROMOTION BUDGET	PERCENTAGE OF PROMOTION BY MONTH	PERCENTAGE OF PROMOTION $ TO SALES
$ 6,800	12.8%	4.4%
7,900	14.9	4.7
11,300	21.3	4.1
9,200	17.3	3.6
9,400	17.7	3.2
8,500	16.0	3.4
$53,100	100.0%	3.79%
Reserve $ 1,500		
$54,600	with reserve,	3.86%

It is relatively easy to add special promotions to an advertising program. It requires more skill to trim ads, reduce frequency of broadcast spots, or limit the scope of mailing lists to save money without destroying merchandise commitments, buyer enthusiasm, or sales results.

In addition to the sales and promotion budget plan for the spring season, a sales promotion detail plan is published breaking the promotion budget into its media categories (Table 3.6). Each month, money is allocated to newspaper advertising, direct mail, radio advertising, and fashion promotion. The budget includes salaries plus a miscellaneous category. This enables each store executive to share knowledge of the store's total activities.

A Typical April Promotion Plan

Typically, the month of April, with its emphasis on spring fashions, is allocated a major portion of the total season's budget. The $11,300 is distributed, with heaviest emphasis on newspaper advertising ($6,400) and direct mail ($1,300). There is also money for radio ($600), fashion promotion ($1,000) and $1,000 in miscellaneous for this critical month.

Let us look at this month of April for our mythical store. The April sales promotion schedule for our store outlines the key promotions that will take place:

- Easter fashion promotions
- After-Easter clearance and sales
- Spring home sale
- Mother's Day campaign

The newspaper advertising space (in the *Times*, our major newspaper) is allocated to the merchandise divisions. Our contract

Table 3.5 ADVERTISING ACTIVITY PLAN

	MONTH					
	FEBRUARY	MARCH	APRIL	MAY	JUNE	JULY
Six-month plan for	July/ August	August/ September	September/ October	October/ November	November/ December	December/ January
Concepts for	June	July	August	September	October	November
"Talking out" for	May	June	July	August	September	October
Firm schedule for	April	May	June	July	August	September
Weekly meetings on ad merchandise for	March	April	May	June	July	August
Last chance for change/revision plus merchandise validation for	March (February 15)	April (March 15)	May (April 15)	June (May 15)	July (June 15)	August (July 15)

SOURCE: The May Company, Los Angeles. Used by permission.

Table 3.6 SALES PROMOTION BUDGET DETAIL PLAN

MONTH	NEWSPAPER ADVERTISING	DIRECT MAIL	RADIO ADVERTISING	FASHION PROMOTION	SALARIES	MISCELLANEOUS	TOTAL
February	$ 3,100	$1,100	$ 350	$ 400	$1,000	$ 850	$ 6,800
March	3,800	1,100	350	600	1,200	850	7,900
April	6,400	1,300	600	1,000	1,000	1,000	11,300
May	4,900	1,100	500	900	1,000	800	9,200
June	5,000	1,400	500	600	1,200	900	9,400
July	4,700	1,400	500	500	1,000	800	8,500
	$28,100	$7,000	$2,800	$4,000	$6,400	$5,200	$53,100

with the *Times* allows us to buy space at $10 per column inch, so the $6,400 in the budget will buy 640 inches for the month of April. To support the planned promotions—Easter, home sale, and Mother's Day, the newspaper space is divided as follows:

Smith division—fashion apparel—90 inches
Jones division—fashion sportswear—90 inches
Emerson division—children's fashions—120 inches
Morton division—fashion accessories and lingerie—120 inches
Jackson division—home store—100 inches
General store advertising—120 inches

Our basic advertising program calls for ad insertions in the Sunday paper for first-of-the-week business followed by a Thursday ad to carry us into the weekend (Table 3.7). To support the key promotions, we also purchase radio spot schedules, 35 spots spread over the final two weeks of Easter shopping; 20 spots to broaden the base of the after-Easter clearance and sale; 25 spots to build customer traffic for the spring home sale; and 20 spots to start talking about Mother's Day toward the end of the month. A key part of our Mother's Day promotion campaign is a direct mailer for which we have budgeted $1,300. We will discuss this item shortly.

There is a 40-inch ad schedule for the weekend before Easter to announce our traditional Easter Bunny Fashion Show, presenting Easter fashions for little boys and girls. This advertising is budgeted from general store funds. The advertising for the total store's after-Easter clearances and sales also comes from general store funds.

Each merchandising division takes its advertising allocation and assigns specific merchandise to fill the space, selecting items the buyer feels will produce the desired traffic and sales results.

Mrs. Jones has been assigned 90 inches of newspaper space for the fashion sportswear division—60 inches in the Sunday *Times* on April 2, equally divided, 20 inches each, among blouse, sweater, and skirt items; and 30 inches on April 9, to present a blouse and skirt item as a last-minute Easter fashion suggestion (Table 3.8). Mrs. Jones will also select 12 items for inclusion in the storewide after-Easter clearance ad which will run in Easter Sunday's newspaper. These are items that have been reduced in price to move them off the shelves and racks. The clearance ad is a catalog-type listing of these items from all departments in the store. This type of ad attracts the "bargain hunter" customer in great numbers.

Ms. Morton, who runs the fashion accessories and lingerie divisions of the store, is assigned 120 inches of newspaper advertising

Table 3.7 MONTHLY SALES PROMOTION SCHEDULE, TOTAL SALES, APRIL

SUNDAY	MONDAY	TUESDAY	WEDNESDAY	THURSDAY	FRIDAY	SATURDAY
LY$ TY$ (2) 60″—Smith 60″—Jones Easter fashions	LY$ TY$ Easter radio—20 radio ads	LY$ TY$	LY$ TY$	LY$ TY$ (6) 60″—Emerson, Children's Easter Fashions	LY$ TY$	LY$ TY$ (8) 40″—fashion show; Easter Bunny fashion show
LY$ TY$ (9) 60″—Emerson 30″—Smith 30″—Jones Easter fashions	LY$ TY$ Easter radio—15 radio ads	LY$ TY$	LY$ TY$	LY$ TY$ (13) 60″—Morton, Easter fashion accessories	LY$ TY$	LY$ TY$
LY$ TY$ (16) 80″—sales and clearances after Easter Closed—Easter	LY$ TY$ After-Easter sale—20 radio ads	LY$ TY$	LY$ TY$	LY$ TY$ (20) 40″—Jackson, spring home sale begins	LY$ TY$	LY$ TY$

LY$ TY$ (23) 60"—Jackson, spring home sale	LY$ TY$	LY$ TY$	LY$ TY$ (26) Mother's Day direct mailer	LY$ TY$ (27) 60"—Morton, Mother's Day fashion campaign	LY$ TY$	LY$ TY$	
	Spring home sale—25 radio ads		Mother's Day—20 radio ads				
LY$ TY$	LY$ TY$	LY$ TY$	LY$ TY$	LY$ TY$	LY$ TY$	LY$ TY$	

NOTE: General store—120 inches; Smith—fashion apparel, 90 inches; Jones—fashion sportswear, 90 inches; Emerson—children's fashion, 120 inches; Jackson—home store, 100 inches; Morton—fashion accessories and lingerie, 120 inches.

Table 3.8 MONTHLY SALES PROMOTION SCHEDULE, FASHION SPORTSWEAR, APRIL

SUNDAY	MONDAY	TUESDAY	WEDNESDAY	THURSDAY	FRIDAY	SATURDAY
LY$ TY$ (2) 60"—TIMES 20"—blouse 20"—sweater 20"—skirt	LY$ TY$	LY$ TY$	LY$ TY$	LY$ TY$	LY$ TY$	LY$ TY$
LY$ TY$ (9) 30"—TIMES 15"—blouse 15"—skirt	LY$ TY$	LY$ TY$	LY$ TY$	LY$ TY$	LY$ TY$	LY$ TY$
LY$ TY$ (16) 12-liners, after-Easter clearance	LY$ TY$	LY$ TY$	LY$ TY$			
LY$ TY$	LY$ TY$	LY$ TY$				
LY$ TY$	LY$ TY$					

Table 3.9 MONTHLY SALES PROMOTION SCHEDULE, FASHION ACCESSORIES AND LINGERIE, APRIL

SUNDAY	MONDAY	TUESDAY	WEDNESDAY	THURSDAY	FRIDAY	SATURDAY
LY$ TY$	LY$ TY$	LY$ TY$	LY$ TY$	LY$ TY$	LY$ TY$	LY$ TY$
LY$ TY$	LY$ TY$	LY$ TY$	LY$ TY$	LY$ TY$ (13) 60"—TIMES 20"—shoes 10"—scarves 20"—jewelry 10"—hats	LY$ TY$	LY$ TY$
LY$ TY$ (16) 10-liners; after-Easter clearance	LY$ TY$	LY$ TY$	LY$ TY$	LY$ TY$	LY$ TY$	LY$ TY$
LY$ TY$	LY$ TY$	LY$ TY$	LY$ TY$ (26) Mother's Day direct mailer	LY$ TY$ (27) 60"—TIMES 30"—robes 30"—slips	LY$ TY$	LY$ TY$
LY$ TY$	LY$ TY$	LY$ TY$	LY$ TY$	LY$ TY$	LY$ TY$	LY$ TY$

(Table 3.9). She participates in two major events during April— Easter and Mother's Day. Her fashion accessories department is important as the focus of last-minute purchases of jewelry, hats, shoes, and scarves to complete or augment Easter fashion outfits. For this, 60 inches of newspaper space is assigned. This division also provides 10 items for the after-Easter clearance ad.

Shortly after Easter has passed from the retail calendar, all attention zeros in on Mother's Day. This event, the second biggest sales period for gift merchandise for women (second only to Christmas) receives extra advertising support. In addition to the 60-inch ad, featuring robes and negligees as gift suggestions, a special Mother's Day mailer is produced—a booklet, usually in full color with fine-quality photography, highlighting brand-name merchandise suitable for gift-giving. A mail order form is enclosed, making it easy for the recipient of the mailer to select and purchase the illustrated merchandise without visiting the store. The merchandise is, of course, on display and available for purchase in the store.

The budget of $1,300 will allow the store to mail approximately 6500 booklets to its mailing list, estimating broadly the costs of printing, third-class carrier-routed postage, handling, design, and preparation of the book. A key to the success of a direct mail campaign is the list to which the mailing is sent. Preferred customers, charge account customers of the store, who shop and make purchases consistently, are the ideal target for this kind of advertising.

In some cases, where the store is trying to broaden its appeal and bring in new customers, the mailing may go to noncustomers. A store can buy a mailing list from a specialty mailing house and mail its advertising to potential customers. Lists are available in many demographic categories—by age, sex, income, occupation, education level. The store's advertising manager must be careful in buying this type of list because many people dislike unsolicited mail advertising, the demographic mix may be wrong, or the percentage of return may make this type of mailing unprofitable. Also, because of the predictably lower return from an unsolicited direct mail campaign, a cheaper mailing piece may have to be produced that does not accurately reflect the character of the store—and this compounds the problem and may lower results even further. Our discussion of advertising media will include more on this subject.

SOME BASIC PROMOTIONAL APPROACHES

The Mother's Day advertising will continue into the May schedule, building momentum right up to the Friday before the event. Although we will not show a typical May calendar here, we would like to point out certain basic approaches that should be considered in promotional events culminating on a specific day, like Mother's Day:

- Higher priced merchandise is advertised early in the campaign.
- Lower priced items are advertised as the "day" gets closer and closer, especially impulse and "idea" items.
- Larger retailers start their promotions earlier than smaller ones.
- Larger retailers often stop advertising several days before an event and "roll" on the momentum their earlier, heavier advertising has developed.
- Stores that are open on Sundays (where permitted by law) such as florists, drug and sundries stores, discount and promotional department stores, advertise right up to the last minute. Guess how many Mother's Day gifts are bought enroute to Mother's house for dinner.

The radio advertising campaign for April is not listed in the individual merchandise division's budget, since it is basically out of the general store budget and is written with the total store in mind, rather than a single merchandise division. The division will, of course, select the items to be included in those radio spots which feature specific merchandise.

The long, involved road we have traveled in outlining the sales promotion planning process may seem detailed to a point where its own weight would make it inoperable. Let us point out that every procedure is not followed every time by every store. Once the needs of the market have been explored, and the strengths and weaknesses of the store recognized, a pattern will emerge that will simplify and expedite the planning of effective sales promotion.

QUESTIONS FOR DISCUSSION AND CLASS ASSIGNMENTS

1. Collect newspaper retail ads reflecting the various stages of the acceptance curve. Discuss whether or not the stores present a balanced picture of their internal activities.
2. Compare the advertising presentations of four different kinds of local retail stores in your area. Do the ads truly reflect the character and image of the store? How might they improve?
3. Develop a sales and promotion plan (using the spring plan as a guide) with a sales plan of $2,000,000 and a 4 percent sales promotion budget for a medium-size department store.
4. Break down a sales promotion budget for the fall season of $80,000, in-

dicating allocations by month for newspaper, radio, TV, and direct mail advertising.

5. Plan the detailed day-by-day advertising plan for a men's store for the month of June using an ad budget of $9,400.

6. Collect examples of the advertising supporting a storewide event (anniversary sale, grand opening). Bring in samples and/or descriptions of direct mail, newspaper ads, radio and/or TV commercials, and so on. Comment on the consistency of advertising style from medium to medium.

7. With the lack of exclusivity in merchandise available to most retail stores, discuss how a store could develop a memorable image under these conditions.

8. Compare the national figures indicating the percentage of year's total sales done each month in the junior coat, suits, and dress departments with the figures of a local store's.

9. Prepare a sales promotion calendar of events for a specific department store in your city utilizing the listings in this chapter.

10. Prepare a detailed day-by-day advertising plan for the junior sportswear department for the month of August.

Chapter 4
Determining the Media Mix

Perhaps the most often asked question when an advertising professional addresses a group of students or newcomers to the business world is "What is the formula for determining what advertising medium or mix of media is best?" The answer approximates the reply to the question "How long is a string?"

Every advertiser would like to know how to get the most coverage, the greatest impact, and the maximum results for advertising money spent. An apocryphal story from the archives of advertising relates how one eager, enthusiastic neophyte sought out the resident advertising expert in the community in pursuit of this elusive formula. The wise man listened to the details of the project the young man had carved out for himself, hummed a bit under his breath, then replied: "I have in my files copies of readership studies of newspapers and magazines, so the advertiser can compare advertising efficiencies of the various publications." "That's all right," said the young man, "but I don't want to know which of the print media are best." "On the other hand, " continued the venerable expert, "the radio rating services are quite reliable in reporting

Figure 4.1 B.C. people, just like advertisers, puzzle over the proper choice of media for sales results. (SOURCE: By permission of Johnny Hart and Field Enterprises, Inc.)

information on listening habits of different radio audiences." Desperately, the interviewer blurted, "I'm not interested in comparing newspapers with newspapers or radio stations with radio stations. I want a formula that tells me which is best—radio, newspapers, direct mail, television, or whatever!" "Young man," said the elder statesman, in slow, deliberate tones, "if all that could be reduced to a formula, my job could be handled by kids like you!" (Figure 4.1)

The determination of which media to buy, and in what quantities, is a quest that has baffled several generations of advertising experts. But the search continues. Advertising professionals constantly study the audience patterns, the sales and advertising results, and the research information in pursuit of this desirable goal. All advertising media offer advertisers audiences to whom they can address advertising messages. Each medium gives the advertisers the opportunity of touching the minds, and perhaps the pocketbooks, of their audiences. Each works differently, and makes different kinds of impressions. Table 4.1 shows how much advertising was used in the United States in two recent years.

A newspaper ad with its illustrated product and written copy makes a different impression than a fleeting, sound-only radio ad. The newspaper ad can be read, saved and reread. The radio ad makes an auditory impression in a very short time, but if heard often enough, can be implanted into the consciousness of the listener. A direct mail piece can do a complete selling job, with its ability to show in great detail the workings of complicated products and complete the sales transaction with a handy order blank. This is quite different from the impact of a 30-second television commercial, which can be as transient as the radio spot. But no one can dispute the phenomenal impact of TV and its ability to motivate and influence people.

Each advertiser, retailer or national auto tycoon, must decide which combination of media will deliver the target market, deliver the story of the product or service best, and deliver the kind of message to be communicated. The type of store, the nature of the merchandise being offered for sale, and many other factors have an effect on the final media selection process.

FACTORS THAT AFFECT MEDIA SELECTION

Long before the layout artist begins to design the ad, or the copywriter rolls paper into the typewriter, the many facets of a store's personality have already determined many elements of the ad and how it will communicate its message to the public.

The decision where to advertise is influenced by the size and location of the store and any branch stores; by the characteristics of the market—where the customers are; by the life-styles of those customers—where and how they live; by the strengths and weaknesses of competitive stores; by the availability of advertising media in the market; and by the amount of money available to be spent on media, the size of the advertising budget. Not to be ignored are factors such as the type of store (high-fashion, semipromotional, or promotional); the desired clientele; the merchandise lines carried and the types of people to which the merchandise will appeal. Then fill in where they live, how they live, and what message the store will be sending them before a final decision is made on the medium, or media, to use.

Location and Size Makes a Difference

A large department store in a metropolitan area, open every day and requiring heavy daily customer traffic to sustain high overhead and operating expenses, must be a regular and constant advertiser. In order to reach the mass audience to whom they appeal, department stores rely on continuing programs of newspaper advertising as their main drive for business. A solid portion of the budget is spent on direct mail (10 percent or more), and a growing amount is allocated to radio and television advertising.

If the store is located in a healthy downtown location, with a thriving business community attracting shoppers on a daily basis, some budget savings might be realized. If, as is the case in many cities, population growth into the suburbs is cutting into downtown shopping, extra funds must be spent to keep the customers coming to the central shopping area. Advertising media that can best reach potential downtown shoppers are then added to the budget to extol the advantages of making the trip to the downtown area.

Table 4.1 ADVERTISING VOLUME IN THE UNITED STATES IN 1979 AND 1980

MEDIUM	1979 $ MILLIONS	PERCENTAGE OF TOTAL	1980 $ MILLIONS	PERCENTAGE OF TOTAL	PERCENT CHANGE
NEWSPAPERS					
Total	14,493	29.3	15,615	28.5	+ 7.7
National	2,085	4.2	2,335	4.3	+12.0
Local	12,408	25.1	13,280	24.2	+ 7.0
MAGAZINES					
Total	2,932	5.9	3,225	5.9	+10.0
Weeklies	1,327	2.7	1,440	2.6	+ 8.5
Women's	730	1.5	795	1.5	+ 9.0
Monthlies	875	1.7	990	1.8	+13.0
FARM PUBLICATIONS	120	0.3	135	0.3	+12.0
TELEVISION					
Total	10,154	20.5	11,330	20.7	+11.6
Network	4,599	9.3	5,105	9.3	+11.0
Spot	2,873	5.8	3,260	6.0	+13.5
Local	2,682	5.4	2,965	5.4	+10.5

RADIO					
Total	3,277	6.6	3,690	6.7	+12.6
Network	161	0.3	185	0.3	+15.0
Spot	659	1.3	750	1.4	+14.0
Local	2,457	5.0	2,755	5.0	+12.0
DIRECT MAIL	6,653	13.4	7,655	14.0	+15.0
BUSINESS PUBLICATIONS	1,575	3.2	1,695	3.1	+ 7.5
OUTDOOR					
Total	540	1.1	610	1.1	+12.8
National	355	0.7	400	0.7	+13.0
Local	185	0.4	210	0.4	+12.5
MISCELLANEOUS					
Total	9,776	19.7	10,795	19.7	+10.5
National	5,063	10.2	5,690	10.4	+12.4
Local	4,713	9.5	5,105	9.3	+ 8.3
Total					
National	27,075	54.7	30,435	55.6	+12.4
Local	22,445	45.3	24,315	44.4	+ 8.3
Grand Total	49,520	100.0	54,750	100.0	+10.6

SOURCE: Reprinted with permission from the January 5, 1981, issue of *Advertising Age*. Copyright 1981 by Crain Communications, Inc.

A medium-size store in a location off the main street has the problem of reaching out for customers who may not know where it is or what it has to sell. A high-traffic location does not require as much advertising as a store tucked away in a strip-type shopping center. Smaller stores cannot compete with the major retail organizations in advertising expenditures, and must spend their ad dollars carefully. The small store in the regional shopping center complex depends on the attractiveness and activities program of the total center to bring shoppers within reach of the store. A portion of the store's rental agreement includes contributions to the center's promotional program. The size of the "bite" varies, and it can be based on the store's square footage, a percentage of sales, or a fixed amount plus an override. Unfortunately, too much of most shopping center budgets is spent on attractions—art shows, petting zoos— and promotion managers are usually left with too little money to do a consistent, effective advertising job.

The traffic developed by the major stores in the centers, the retail giants, is the traffic off which the smaller tenants in the shopping center live. They may participate in the periodic promotions created by the center's promotion office with a small newspaper ad in the "shopper." On their own, private mailings to customer lists or a Yellow Pages listing could be the sum of their advertising efforts. The small store approach may seem parasitical, but it is all a smaller retailer can afford—after paying for leasing space, building and stocking the store, maintaining a sales staff, and so on. There is very little left to be spent on advertising—in any medium.

Where the Customers Are—the Market

Media selection closely follows that portion of the marketing research which locates the store's customers. Such research would also indicate where additional potential business might come from, the circulation of the various media in those geographic areas, and the related costs. Often, a new suburban area is not penetrated by the major daily newspaper in a market. So a neighborhood shopper publication containing ads from local merchants and delivered free on a weekly basis to the doorsteps or the driveways of the suburban homes might be a better place to advertise. Community newspapers, featuring local news and happenings to attract readership, provide a relatively inexpensive advertising vehicle for the small retailer trying to reach a limited portion of the market. Local, low-powered radio stations cover specific areas within their transmitter range and serve the local community with public service programming while offering the local retailer an audience for sales messages.

The large department store gravitates to the large metropolitan newspaper with its broad circulation, which covers the total market in an umbrellalike manner. Within that broad coverage there are bound to be holes, for whatever reason. Few newspapers reach more than 30 to 40 percent of the homes in their coverage area. Some additional medium or media must be added to the major store advertising mix. Determining where the customers are who might not be getting the message is the first problem for the ad manager; determining how to reach them comes next.

How the Customers Live—Life-Style

"We're dancing to the tune of the customer as never before," the sales promotion manager of a major retail organization said recently. He went on to describe the rapidly changing environment in which retail stores are operating compared to the much simpler days of a decade or two ago. He talked about the slowing rate of population growth, the growing singles market, and the changes in once-familiar family units. He noted the working woman phenomenon and its effect on the operations and advertising habits of the traditional department store.

No longer can the sales promotion manager blithely budget money into the daily newspaper and expect to reach the majority of the store's potential customers. As stores reposition themselves to accommodate changing customer attitudes and life-styles with new and different merchandise presentations, they must reexamine their promotional techniques to attract these new customers. Studies of what motivates people to buy, what factors determine where they want to shop, what importance is placed on decor, atmosphere, convenience, or service policies in making the ultimate buying decision are all reflected in advertising decisions.

The study of new customer habits will also reveal how to communicate with the elusive, mobile fashion customer. One continuing study by the National Retail Merchants Association indicated that retailers had increased their advertising budgets (1975 over 1974) by 55 percent for TV, by 50 percent for radio, but only 40 percent for newspapers. This shifting of advertising dollars among the media continues. Some stores, as they have expanded and grown in number of outlets, have adopted a policy of assigning any additional funds accruing from the additional sales volume of the new stores to broadcast while maintaining the dollars allocated to newspapers and print (See Table 3.2). The composition of the media mix is changing in retailing—more rapidly in the alert, volatile fashion retail world, and more slowly, but inevitably, in the slower-moving traditional department store fashion areas.

As life-styles change, and merchandising changes to fit new target audiences, media selection must follow the pattern. A typical breakdown of customer profiles revealed a major store chain had three types of customers: young juniors, who were highly fashion conscious; contemporaries, who spend more than any other segment on high-quality clothes; and conservatives, who are interested in comfort and value. The advertising media decision that followed shifted money into radio and TV advertising to reach the younger and contemporary segments of the market while continuing the print campaign for the older, conservative customers.

Strength of the Competition

Merchants probably enjoy stealing their competitors' customers almost as much as they enjoy beating last year's figures. With the leveling off of the population boom, the focus for most retailers is on increased market penetration—getting more business from their current customers or reaching out to lure other stores' customers into their fold. Future growth and profits lie in that direction.

The size and aggressiveness of any store's advertising budget is influenced by the promotional activities of the competition. If a market has stores that advertise regularly, offering consistently good value in their ads, a store is almost forced to compete in advertising impact to stay in the race. If competitors are content to float along, restricting their advertising to seasonal events and sales, a store could go along with that too. Or, one store could take advantage of the inertia and grab a sizable share of the potential market with a sharp, hard-hitting, well-balanced promotional and fashion advertising campaign that will make the town sit up and take notice.

Competitive advertising also offers the alert retailer the opportunity of learning by observation what to do and what not to do. The conservative approach, native to most retailers, suggests that the learning experience is better at someone else's expense. Most retailers watch competitors closely. They personally shop the stores, and notice what merchandise is in stock and what the customers are buying. Full-time comparison shoppers, professionals with retail and fashion knowledge, are hired to perform this duty to keep fashion buyers and merchandisers aware of trends and happenings in the marketplace. Equally close encounters (pun intended) of the advertising kind occur. Newspapers are checked daily and copies of competitive ads are clipped and pasted in loose-leaf books especially designed for that purpose. Radio and TV ads are monitored and reports written. Many stores take out charge accounts in competitive stores so their executives will receive copies of direct mail offerings by those stores.

Watching the competition is a favorite pastime in retailing. It is knowledge an alert operator must have. The danger lies in letting competitive activities dictate a plan of action. Copying the competition in advertising, no matter how successful the style being copied, results in a sameness in look and impression that reflects more often to the credit of the store being copied than the store doing the copying. Anyone imitating the distinctive style of New York's Lord and Taylor cannot help but make people think it is a Lord and Taylor ad. In every city there are ads that are unique and easily identifiable with the store running the ad. This is true in print, in radio, in television. That store has a special way of writing, printing, or delivering its messages. And then there are the great majority of ads that look alike. They are the great imitators; it takes a close look at the signature to find out which store is advertising.

You can conduct your own test. Remove the ads from your daily newspaper. Cover the store names or logos with strips of paper. Then ask students, parents, or friends to identify the stores by name, just by looking at the ads. It will surprise you how few can be named correctly. That is the ultimate penalty when retailers watch their competitors too closely. They copy each other so well they all look and sound alike. And since the customers cannot tell them apart, they react to the ads by going to the store where they usually shop. This means the advertising money has been wasted, for one of the purposes of advertising is to bring additional traffic to *your* store, not someone else's. Watch the competition, but don't let it lead you.

Availability of Advertising Media

The availability of various media in a market and its relation to costs is an interesting factor in the media selection process. In cities where there is only one newspaper, the monopolistic situation can result in unusually high prices for advertising space. This is understandable in a business sense, when "you're the only game in town" and the demand for ad space is constant, especially from local retailers. When there is competition, with two or more papers vying for advertisers' dollars, prices do not tend to rise as rapidly. Having a good paper in town, subscribed to by a good portion of the population, is the most comfortable situation for the average retailer.

The lack of a substantial daily publication creates problems. In Bakersfield, California, for example, there is a fairly good afternoon paper, but it reaches only a limited portion of the trading area. There is no morning paper. In order to reach the public and potential customers in the morning, and to reach the majority of the households who do not take the daily paper, retailers in that community turn to radio advertising. The residents of the Bakersfield area call radio their "morning paper," and the retail advertisers react accordingly. They are heavy and consistent radio advertisers.

Many communities find that their free-distribution publication, the weekly shopper, reaches homes with regularity. Retailers advertise in these papers at relatively low cost, and many find them adequate for their needs. The availability of a hand-delivery service in many areas has spawned a workable distribution system for circulars and shoppers for retailers seeking to avoid rising postal delivery costs.

The problem of covering the potential market when the local newspaper covers only a portion of the households has been partly solved by some enterprising publishers. By computerizing their home delivery subscribers lists, they are able to cross-check those addresses with complete city listings. Subscribers, who would be receiving the store's advertising in the paper (whether run-of-paper ads or special supplements), are dropped out of the city list, leaving a list of nonsubscribers to whom the advertiser can mail or hand deliver the advertising message. This combination of normal paper circulation plus door-to-door delivery comes close to perfect saturation coverage of the market at generally lower cost than direct mail alone. This system is utilized in major market areas for the dissemination of preprinted full-color special sections. Many stores, faced with rising postage and handling costs, have turned to inserting special sections into the newspaper's normal circulation. The material is delivered to those who happen to be subscribers to the paper, but in some cases this delivery is zoned, allowing the retailer some choice in the coverage.

Now that television is in most markets, many fashion retailers, with the assistance of co-op funds from vendors or manufacturer-produced commercials with local dealer tags, can make use of the advertising impact of the "tube." In larger markets, some department stores, fashion specialty stores, and chains have moved into TV on the nonnetwork independent stations, and many have the budgets to use the major network stations as well.

Radio is available in practically every market, with different stations attracting different audiences. Competition between radio stations is usually quite keen, resulting in sharp pricing practices and merchandising and promotion assistance to retailers, making radio a basic part of many small retailers' media buy.

But there are no easy answers. W. R. Simmons Research classifies consumers by their media usage patterns—how much time is spent with each medium. This type of research analysis points up the inadequacies of the various media in delivering substantial portions of the target population. Certain segments can be reached by newspapers, but others are better reached by radio or special-interest magazines. Light television viewers are usually heavy radio listeners. Older demographic groups tend to watch more TV and read more newspapers and magazines. Better-educated, more affluent segments are heavy newspaper readers. The various segments of the population also differ dramatically in terms of product consumption. It is in this area that the astute media selector must search to try to choose the best possible combination of media for the particular business or service being advertised.

NEWSPAPERS ARE FOREVER

Newspapers carry more advertising for more advertisers on more subjects than any other medium. Despite the existence and the growth of many different advertising media, retailers and other advertisers have determined through long experience that newspapers are their best selling force.

In terms of dollars spent in advertising nationally, even though television spending has increased astronomically in recent years, more money is spent in newspaper advertising than in any other medium. The publisher of a major metropolitan newspaper, in one of the country's largest markets, has been quoted as saying that the revenues from newspaper advertising in his paper exceed expenditures in all other media *combined* in that market.

Psychologically, this is easy to understand. When modern advertising began, somewhere around 1920, print was the only vehicle available to carry merchants' sales messages to the buying public. In the beginning, the ads were all words, all copy, with no illustrations. The skill of the writer was the only device the advertiser could use to convince people to buy products. But skillfully written, the sales message was able to attract, interest, intrigue, and motivate the reader.

History of the Retailer and Newspapers

Back in 1920, there were 437 morning newspapers and 1,605 evening papers in the United States. Their combined circulation was 27,791,000. There were also 522 Sunday newspapers with a circulation of 17,084,000. The only competition for the retail advertising dollar was among the various newspapers in an area. Mailings to customers of the stores was also a common practice, but advertising in the newspaper was the established retail pattern.

The story of John Wanamaker's remark that he knew he was wasting 50 percent of his advertising but didn't know which 50 percent it was has been told many times. He continued to advertise because his business was prospering and he did not want to tinker with success. It would have been a great boon to the modern retailer if Wanamaker, living before the age of broadcast, had been more of a marketer and had run tests and experiments to determine the true effectiveness of his advertising. To this day, the 50 percent waste factor is still bandied about, despite the acceleration of media costs and inflationary factors that eat up store profits. And the attitude of retailers toward newspaper advertising has not changed much over the years. As recently as 1950, it was reported that retailers were spending as much as 90 percent of their ad budgets in newspapers. In 1975, trade publications stated that the figure was still a very healthy 75 percent. Later figures place it as over 50 percent.

In the fifty years from 1920 to 1970, the number of newspapers in the United States dwindled from 437 to 334 morning papers and from 1605 to 1429 evening papers, but their combined circulations had grown to 62,108,000 from 27,791,000. The number of Sunday papers had increased over that period from 522 to 586, and the Sunday circulation was a whopping 49,217,000 in 1970.

At the end of 1978, there were 1,419 evening papers and 355 morning editions. (*Los Angeles Times*, Aug. 12, 1979). Newspaper circulation seemed to have reached its peak in 1973, when daily circulations nationally reached 63,147,000 and Sunday circulation hit 51,717,000. Since that time, the trend has been slightly down, with major newspapers in key cities closing for a variety of reasons. Papers such as the *Washington News, Newark News, Chicago Daily News, Chicago Today,* and *New York Morning Telegraph* stopped publishing in the 1970s. Attempts to start new newspapers have also failed, one notable case being the short-lived *New York Trib,* which published for less than three months in 1978 before folding. And the publisher, when announcing the closing down of the *Trib,* said that a major cause of the paper's failure to survive was "lack of support from local retailers." When the *Washington Star* ceased operations in 1981, a similar complaint was voiced by that publication.

Despite the competition from the electronic media, newspapers still corral the major portion of retail budgets and even on a national level continue to attract more advertising dollars than any other medium. Estimated expenditures for the year 1980 showed that of the $54.8 billion spent on advertising of all kinds, newspapers received over $15.6 billion or 28.5 percent of the total. This represented a 7.7 percent increase over 1979. Television, which has made tremendous strides, grossed $11.3 billion, an increase of 11.6 percent over the previous year and 20.7 percent of all advertising dollars. Radio grossed $3.7 billion in that same year and direct mail grossed over $7.7 billion (*Advertising Age,* January 5, 1981).

A close look at these figures, when local and national expenditures are broken out, show that the great strength of newspapers is at the local level. Over $13 billion of the $15.6 billion credited to newspapers was placed as local advertising. In television, 75 percent of the money was placed nationally. In radio, the local figures overwhelmed the national figures ($2.7 billion versus $935 million for national or spot radio), since in many ways radio, like newspaper, is primarily a local medium.

Advantages and Strengths of Newspaper Advertising

We do not want to leave an impression that retailers' decisions over the years to advertise in the newspaper are a result of whim or caprice on the part of storekeepers. Far from it: The successful retailer is an astute, hard-headed businessperson, aware of the many expense and operating factors contributing to success.

So let us direct our attention to some of the reasons why newspaper advertising has become the retailers' chief medium of communication with the buying public.

First of all, *newspaper readership is a habit.* We are all creatures of habit. We do many of the things we do the same way every time. We dress in a certain sequence each morning, do our regular chores in a regular routine. We receive our information and our news from specific sources. And we read newspapers, more or less, in an habitual manner. Many people still claim they get first reports of news events from newspapers, although radio and television devotees would challenge that statement.

The habit, once established, is hard to break. People who go to elementary schools where the daily newspaper (supplied to the classroom by civic-minded newspapers) is a part of the daily teaching routine grow up with the habit of reading the paper. The student learns to look in the paper for news events that will be discussed in the classroom. The clever ones, of course, read the newspaper at home so they are better informed than their classmates and make a better impression on the teacher. And the daily habit of reading the paper, instilled at an early age, sticks with the individual throughout life. A 1979–1980 report from Simmons Market Research indicates an average of 2.2 readers per Sunday paper, 2.1 per daily.

The pattern in which we read the paper may vary as we get older, the men looking for sports or business news, the women interested in fashions, home furnishings, and food information. In those cities where people ride to work on public transportation, the tedious hours riding to and from the job can be relieved by reading. The daily newspaper thrives in the big cities where workers who live in the suburbs and travel to their places of business in the urban areas spend an hour or more daily in a public conveyance. Newsstands still do big business in bus and train terminals, catering to the reading needs of travelers.

Homemakers read newspapers regularly to plan their shopping trips. Whether it is the weekly visit to the supermarket or the desire to keep up with current fashion and news happenings, surveys have shown that women tend to read newspapers more, and more thoroughly, than men. In studies that compare the parts of the newspapers read by men and women, after the main news, the fashion section or stories of interest to women rank high. Retailers realize this habit of readership exists, and place ads in the newspaper in the path of the readers they are trying to reach.

A strong business factor in the decision to advertise in the newspaper is its *low cost* per reader (Figure 4.2). In the advertising world, value is determined by what it costs to reach the target market. This is expressed in cost-per-thousand in newspapers and radio and in cost-per-household in television. This is one of the problems in comparing media, since each medium, as we will see, is different and has its own measure of effectiveness.

In newspapers, rates are published as cost-per-agate-line or cost-per-column-inch. Efforts are being made to standardize page sizes, but there are variations from market to market and within markets. Most papers are 8 columns wide and $21\frac{1}{2}$ inches deep. There are 14 agate lines to the column inch, with column depth of 300 lines. A full page would be 172 column inches, or 2400 lines. Regular advertisers sign annual space contracts with their newspapers and must run sufficient linage during the year to earn that rate. Smaller advertisers pay a higher rate. It is an accepted fact that newspapers generally reach readers at a lower cost per person than any other medium. Do not, however, confuse readership of newspapers with circulation. Circulation, especially paid circulation, indicates the number of papers sold, or the number of subscribers who "take" the paper. The readership of the paper is another subject, which we will discuss shortly.

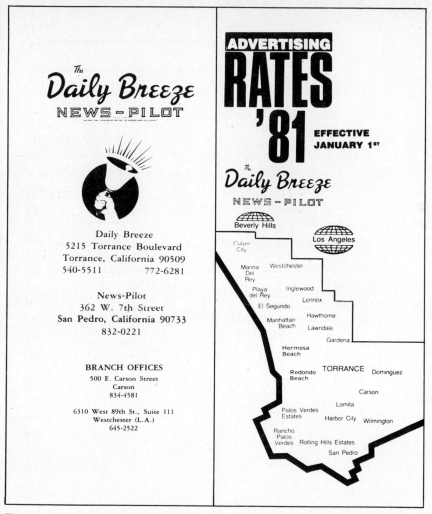

Figure 4.2   Standard newspaper rate card from *The Daily Breeze/News-Pilot,* Torrance/San Pedro, California, which gives complete information for advertisers. (SOURCE: By permission of *The Daily Breeze.*)

Another strong point in favor of newspapers as an advertising medium for retailers is its *market coverage.* Many newspapers reach a broad area and include large sections of the population. But the circulation of the paper is a factor over which the retailer has no control. Except for instances where special zone editions (Figure 4.3) allow the retailer to advertise to just part of the paper's circulation, the advertiser buys whatever audience the paper happens to have. From a retail viewpoint, the demographics of the typical newspaper subscriber may mean he or she is the exact person the

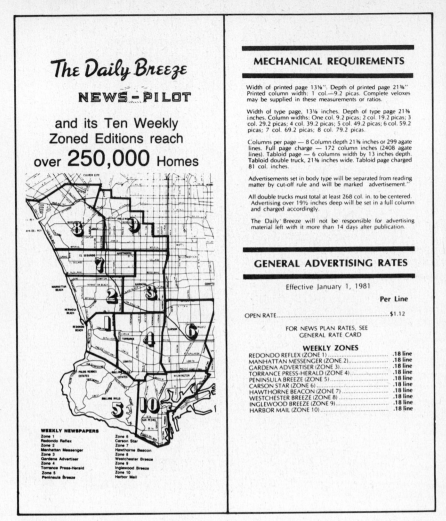

Figure 4.3   Weekly zone editions' circulation, mechanical requirements, and general advertising rates.

retailers are trying to reach—householder, upper income, family group, good level of discretionary spending power, better educated, and so on. The broad coverage of the paper delivers that type of audience in most cities.

Newspapers offer retailers *quick response* to their ads. Because of the daily publication of the paper, the short life of the news, there is a sense of urgency in newspaper advertising. It almost insists on quick reaction on the part of the reader, since the medium itself is replaced every day. Again, as part of the habit syndrome, people tend to respond to newspaper ads immediately. Items published in today's paper, are, to a great extent, on sale tomorrow. The customer can expect to see the merchandise in the store, on display in the department, and available in a selection of colors and sizes the day of or the day after the ad appears.

The retailer knows quickly whether the ad is successful or not. The "life" of an advertised fashion item may be three to five days, but within a day or two the retailer can gauge, by floor traffic or by actual items sold, whether the merchandise was wanted by the public. Along with the satisfaction of clocking the immediate response goes the headache when the response is not there and the item does not sell as well as expected. Other media strive for this quick action from their ads, but retailers expect every ad to work in the newspaper.

Quick response also means a *quick check on results*. This is highly important in the fast-moving fashion business. Information that a style or color is "hot" can mean quick reorders, fast shipments, repeat ads, and healthy added sales volume. With the here today, gone tomorrow pattern of newspapers, the information is rapidly available to the buyer, often within a short time after the store has opened on the day after an ad has run. Today's buyer gets next-day reports, computer printouts or hand-computed tallies (depending on the store's system), and can readily determine if the advertised item is a winner and worthy of further promotion.

A strong advantage of newspaper advertising is the *regular and periodic publication* of the newspaper. With retail stores open for business six or seven days a week, the daily publication of a newspaper offers the retailer an opportunity to advertise for customers every day (Figure 4.4). Even the weekly newspaper or shopper has this advantage of publication at regular intervals. This can create a reading and shopping habit toward which the retailer can target regular bids for business. The large retail establishment, needing daily traffic, needs the daily newspaper and its low cost per reader in its advertising arsenal.

The capability of responding with *speed and flexibility* to the ever-changing needs of the retailer helps the retailer-newspaper relationship. The constant problems of merchandise deliveries, manufacturing delays, and shipping delays require advertising flexibility. The high speed with which a daily newspaper is published can handle the retail advertisers' changes, modifications, or even cancellations of scheduled ads better than most other advertising media. Except for radio, with its live copy capability, other media cannot handle last-minute changes in prices, information, or items. Newspapers, aware of this need for quick reaction to merchandising crises, have developed and strengthened their relations with re-

RETAIL ADVERTISING RATES
MONTHLY CONTRACT RATES

The
Daily Breeze
NEWS - PILOT

These rates apply to all retail advertising appearing in the Daily Breeze/News-Pilot except the classifications of business otherwise specified on this card.

*To be used each month for 12 months
Effective January 1, 1981*

	SUNDAY EDITION	DAILY BREEZE	NEWS-PILOT	WEEKDAY COMBINATION
OPEN (PER COL. IN.)	$15.68	$13.51	$5.81	$15.68
10 IN. MO.	11.13	8.61	4.48	12.04
20 IN. MO.	10.71	8.40	4.41	11.69
43 IN. MO.	10.22	7.98	4.27	11.27
86 IN. MO.	10.08	7.84	4.20	10.99
172 IN. MO.	9.59	7.70	4.13	10.85
344 IN. MO.	9.31	7.28	4.06	10.15
688 IN. MO.	8.68	6.79	3.99	9.66
1032 IN. MO.	8.54	6.65	3.85	9.52
1548 IN. MO.	8.47	6.37	3.78	9.24
2064 IN. MO.	8.40	6.30	3.71	9.17
2580 IN. MO.	8.26	6.16	3.64	8.96
3544 IN. MO.	7.84	6.09	3.57	8.68
General Political (Comm.)	$15.68	$13.51	$5.81	$15.68
Transient Entertain. (Comm.)	15.68	13.51	5.81	15.68
Real Estate (Comm.)	15.68	13.51	5.81	15.68
Restaurant Page (Fri.)	12.25			12.25
Restaurants (Comm.)	14.70			14.70
Non-Profit:	9.59	7.70	4.13	10.85
Local Churches	8.40	6.30	3.71	9.17
Business Builder				
Min. 4 in. week, 13 weeks	9.59	7.70	4.13	10.85
Min 10 in. week, 6 weeks	9.59	7.70	4.13	10.85

	DAILY BREEZE	NEWS PILOT	COMBINATION
SPOT ADS 1 In. day, 30 days	$195	$ 115	$280
2 In. day, 30 days	370	215	525
3 In. day, 30 days	520	300	745
4 In. day, 30 days	655	380	940

Saturation Program: 5 ads daily for 6 days/6 ads daily for 5 days — Use Spot Ad 30 day rates.
Note: Spot Ad Program may also apply double space every other day for 15 insertions in 30-day period.

HALF DAILY AVAILABLE WEDNESDAY AND SUNDAY ONLY AT HALF EARNED RATES PLUS 30 COL IN SURCHARGE ALSO SEE QUAD RATES

DISPLAY COPY DEADLINE: 5 p.m. 2 Days Before Publication
SUNDAY DEADLINE: 5 p.m. Thursday
MONDAY DEADLINE: 3 p.m. Friday

SPECIAL PAGES: Wednesday...Food Thursday...Home and Garden Friday...Restaurants, The Entertainer Saturday...Churches Sunday...TV Week, Art, Real Estate, Travel Daily...Motion Pictures and Entertainment, Television page.

YEARLY BULK CONTRACT RATES

Effective January 1, 1981

	SUNDAY EDITION	DAILY BREEZE	NEWS-PILOT	WEEKDAY COMBINATION
OPEN, PER COL. IN.	$15.68	$13.51	$5.81	$15.68
172 IN. YR.	12.25	9.94	5.39	13.44
344 IN. YR.	12.04	9.45	5.32	13.37
688 IN. YR.	11.97	9.38	5.25	13.30
1032 IN. YR.	11.76	9.24	5.11	13.16
2084 IN. YR.	10.85	8.68	4.69	12.60
20,000 IN. YR.	9.10	6.79	4.27	10.64
35,000 IN. YR.	8.05	6.58	3.71	9.73
50,000 IN. YR.	7.84	6.37	3.43	9.45
60,000 IN. YR.	7.77	5.88	3.22	8.96
75,000 IN. YR.	7.63	5.74	3.15	8.61
100,000 IN. YR.	7.49	5.67	3.08	8.47

NON CONTRACT RATES

Effective January 1, 1981

	SUNDAY EDITION	DAILY BREEZE	NEWS-PILOT	WEEKDAY COMBINATION
OPEN	$15.68	$13.51	$5.81	$15.68
15 IN. MO.	12.46	10.08	5.74	13.58
43 IN. MO.	12.32	10.01	5.67	13.44
86 IN. MO.	12.11	9.73	5.60	13.16
172 IN. MO.	11.20	9.24	5.32	12.67
344 IN. MO.	10.85	9.17	5.25	12.46

WEEKLY ZONE PICK UP RATES
ALTERNATE DISTRIBUTION SYSTEM

Effective January 1, 1981

ANY 1 ZONE	$1.10 Each	$1.10 column inch
ANY 2 ZONES	1.05 Each	2.10 column inch
ANY 3 ZONES	1.00 Each	3.00 column inch
ANY 4 ZONES	.95 Each	3.80 column inch
ANY 5 ZONES	.90 Each	4.50 column inch
ANY 6 ZONES	.85 Each	5.10 column inch
ANY 7 ZONES	.80 Each	5.60 column inch
ANY 8 ZONES	.75 Each	6.00 column inch
ANY 9 ZONES	.70 Each	6.30 column inch
ANY 10 ZONES	.65 Each	6.50 column inch

Figure 4.4 Retail advertising rates are available at monthly or yearly bulk rates, depending upon advertisers' needs. There are noncontract rates for occasional advertisers, and weekly pickup rates for daily ads rerun in weekly zone editions.

tailers by working closely and cooperatively with them to handle these emergencies.

Newspaper advertising has practically *no size or quantity limitations*. Radio and TV are restricted to 10-, 30-, or 60-second limits. Magazine page sizes are standard and advance closing dates do not fit well with last-minute retail decisions. Newspapers, however, can accept ads of all sizes and shapes, with practically no limit to the number of pages the advertiser can buy within a few days of publication. The retailer can, within the 2400 lines of a full newspaper page, buy as much or as little of a page as suits the purpose of the ad. Major retail stores vary their newspaper impressions from part-page or single-page features on midweek days to 12- or 16-page sections for dramatic impact on Sundays. Since the newspaper can expand or contract the size of the daily paper at will, it can accommodate any advertising demand for space at any time within preset deadlines.

Most papers try to build the daily paper with a two-thirds advertising to one-third editorial content balance. This means that the editorial, or news and feature, content of the paper is determined by the amount of advertising that has been sold for that particular day. Notice that most daily papers are light on Mondays, Tuesdays, and Wednesdays, very heavy on Thursdays (traditionally retail and food shopping day), somewhat lighter on Fridays, very light on Saturdays (especially when stores are closed to Sunday shopping) and heaviest on Sundays. On each of these days, there is a direct connection between the number of pages and the number of lines of advertising in the paper that day.

Part of the theory governing the disproportionate use of the Sunday paper by most advertisers stems from the rationale that people have more time to read the newspaper on Sunday, the traditional day of rest and relaxation. This does not fit too well with the desire for immediate response to all retail advertising, because even though more advertising is scheduled for Sunday, a higher percentage of the week's business happens on Friday and Saturday. It is also felt that the Sunday paper, because of its size and feature material and special sections, remains in the household for a longer period than the weekday paper and therefore can be read during the early part of the week, not just on Sunday. Another point: Some people take the Sunday paper only, giving the ad wider coverage.

In recent years the Sunday paper, with its circulation higher than the weekday editions, has become the vehicle for special supplements, booklets, and other advertising material (Figure 4.5). Retailers find that these colorful advertising pieces, many diverted from direct mail because of rising costs and uncertain delivery, are profitable using the distribution systems of established metropolitan newspapers and gain wide awareness of their products and services. The problem here is lack of control of position in the paper, the presence of competition, and the contest for the reader's attention in the big Sunday paper.

High on the list of advantages of newspaper advertising is the *acceptance and believability* newspapers enjoy as part of the nation's way of life. If a story is printed in the paper, people tend to

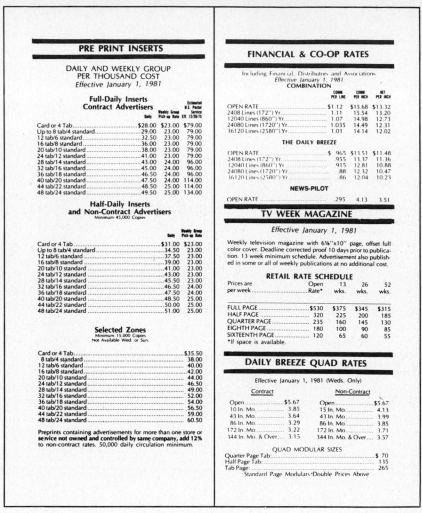

Figure 4.5   Preprinted supplements inserted in the paper's editions are priced according to size, number of pages, and distribution. Special rates are set for financial, co-op, the TV Magazine, and special editions. Many stores distribute preprinted sections through newspapers to cut down on postage costs.

believe it. Print has reliability. People learn by reading. If you can read it, it must be true. People get involved with their newspaper. They subscribe to it and have it delivered to their homes. The paper is accepted into the home, into the family. People write to their paper when bothered about public issues. They take the editor to task if they disagree with the editorial page viewpoint. They call or write indignant letters when a comic strip or favorite feature is discontinued. They care about their paper.

And the retailer, advertising in the paper, shares in this cherished and hard won acceptance. Retail ads, as part of the paper, inherit the believability and favorable reception into the home. They share the confidence the readers have in the paper. Since all good relationships are two-way streets, retailers contribute to the readership of the newspapers, because the advertising they run is part of the news content of the paper. They bring the reading public news of fashion, of home furnishings, of ideas to make their lives happier and more interesting. Many people buy the paper just to read the ads, to see what's new. It has been said that on many days, the only good news in the newspaper is in the advertising.

All these advantages of newspaper advertising have contributed to the stature of newspapers as the oldest established medium for retail advertisers. This close relationship will continue, because retailers who have asked their customers where they found out about new fashions, the new items in the store, or sales offerings were invariably told "the newspaper."

As newspapers have grown over the years, so have the retail stores. What were once individual, one-store operations have become large retail complexes, and with every change the newspapers have been there. Newspaper space salespeople have learned that it requires more than just accepting and placing ads from the local retailer to build a lasting, profitable customer for the paper. They have learned to service the retailer—to understand the problems, to write the ads, to design them if necessary, to deliver proofs and tearsheets, and to be on hand, in the store, on key sale days. The special relationship between retailer and newspaper is a precious, intangible asset that newspaper people must nurture and cherish if they wish to retain and improve their share of retailers' ad budgets as time goes on. Inroads by electronic media and special interest magazines can be offset, but only by newspaper people remembering what made them successful and reestablishing the close and continuing contact that used to separate the newspaper account executive from all other media salespeople.

Weaknesses of Newspaper Advertising

The best newspaper ads take advantage of the medium in which they are published. They are *timely*, as timely and topical as the daily newspaper. They are simple and direct, designed to be read quickly and easily. The ads have *immediacy*, and demand immediate action from the reader. The ads are *newsworthy*, or not worth placing in the daily paper. And the best retail ads are *local*, because that's the secret ingredient in inviting readership in newspapers.

But newspapers as an advertising medium do have weaknesses. Flip Wilson, the comedian, used to have a line that went, "What you see is what you get." In buying advertising space in a newspaper, the audience you get is the circulation the newspaper happens to have. This factor is of great importance to the retailer, who depends on the newspaper reaching his or her potential market area. The paper's circulation outside the store's shopping range is *waste circulation.* The existence of households where the paper is not delivered leaves gaps in the desired complete coverage. People who do not take or read the paper have no way of being reached if the only medium being used is newspapers.

Major metropolitan papers, whose broad coverage includes waste circulation for the smaller retailer, attempt to offset this weakness by publishing zone sections that reach specific smaller portions of the city, have their own editorial and advertising staffs, and print local news and features. The space rates are lower than the full circulation rates in these zones editions (usually published weekly), and more in line with the smaller retailers' budgets.

There are many more evening newspapers in United States than morning papers—more than four times as many, according to a recent survey. Remarkably, the *morning* papers are the giants of the industry in the largest cities in the country—the *Los Angeles Times,* the *New York Times,* the *New York Daily News,* the *Miami Herald,* the *Chicago Tribune,* for example. In some cities, however, the afternoon paper is still king; the *Atlanta Journal,* the *Houston Chronicle,* and the *Buffalo Evening News* dominate their markets. Most of the papers that have ceased publication in the past ten years were afternoon papers. Their deaths have been blamed on several factors: the flight of the middle class to the suburbs, the attraction of evening news television shows, and problems of late afternoon delivery of newspapers from downtown plants to the far-flung suburbs during commuter traffic hours.

Whatever the situation in your city, the dominance of either morning or afternoon paper can usually be traced to the vitality of the paper itself, the market it serves, and the paper's appeal to a segment or segments within the market. In either case, the retailer faces a disadvantage because of the limited hours of the newspaper's distribution. With a strong evening paper, retailers advertise for next day business. In other words, they place ads in the Wednesday afternoon paper, giving the shopper time to read the paper in the leisurely after-dinner hours and plan the visit to the store the next day. With a strong morning paper, the advertiser pitches for results that same day, with the expectation that there will be carryover results the next day and the day after. Sometimes, when there is doubt about same-day response (where there is limited commuter public transportation, a high percentage of women in the labor force, or curtailed newspaper reading time at the breakfast table), many advertisers will run ads in the morning paper for next day's business. In Los Angeles, the downtown department stores run their end-of-month clearance sales in the Friday morning paper, with the statement: "Sales Start Saturday." The dilemma here is, should the newspaper reader postpone a planned Friday shopping trip or wait until Saturday to take advantage of the advertised special? In a way, aren't you telling the customer not to shop on Friday, but to wait until Saturday? And don't we want to do business every day of the week? A continuing decision for the advertising manager and store management.

So, the limited hours of a paper's distribution give the advertiser a short span of time within which to deliver a message to potential customers. At best, the advertiser has only one opportunity for the attention of the reader, unless the paper is read more than once during a given day.

In the cities that are still fortunate enough to have two or more newspapers, additional problems arise. If there are morning and evening newspapers, there is always a percentage of duplication in the circulation, since many people who are habitual newspaper readers will take both papers. Commuters will often take the morning paper at home through monthly subscription and buy the evening paper from a newsstand to read on the way home. How great this duplication of coverage is varies by city, but the disadvantage to advertisers is deciding in which paper to advertise when they cannot affort to advertise in both. And even if they can afford to advertise in both papers, isn't there an inevitable duplication and waste of money? It can be justified, however, as making a second impression.

Another weakness is the *short life of the newspaper.* "There's nothing deader than yesterday's news" applies with equal truth to newspaper ads. When the day-old newspaper is used to line the canary's cage, the ads go to the same destination. The newspaper doesn't stay around very long.

Since newspaper reading is a deliberate process, where the reader sits down and "pages through" the newspaper, the advent of the mobile society has created competition for the public's time and attention. A high percentage of workers drive to work in many major cities, as many as 87 percent in Los Angeles, 66 percent in Chicago, 67 percent in Philadelphia, and 85 percent in Detroit. Where there is limited or no public transportation, these workers cannot read the paper going to and from work. They depend on the radio for news.

Within the pages of the newspaper itself, there is competition for the reader's attention. Starch newspaper readership studies indicate that the placement of an ad adjacent to, or on the same page as, a popular editorial feature does not ensure readership of the ad. Most readers go through the paper in some habitual pattern, and if your ad is not placed in the part of the paper that person usually reads, your ad may not be seen or read.

Sometimes, the ad from your chief competitor will appear on the same page as your ad, or on the page opposite. As much as the newspapers try to separate competitive ads, the complexities of page makeup prevent the paper from guaranteeing the advertiser a clear shot at a target. With every newspaper averaging 60 to 75 percent advertising, ads must be crowded, or stacked, to fit them in according to advertisers' requests. Fashion advertisers traditionally request positioning in the women's section of the paper and usually advertise on the same days of the week (Thursday, Friday, and Sunday). Confident advertisers do not worry about being in the company of competitors in the newspaper. Less confident advertisers want to be in the same section of the paper because they are afraid of being left out. Also, they gain in stature by being in the same "league" as the more successful retailers. But in the end, the competition for the reader's attention in the newspaper will follow the same path as the competition for the customer's loyalty. The better store, with the better merchandise and service, will win out. People tend to read the ads of the stores in which they regularly shop, so the two elements, ad readership and customer response, are always intertwined.

The *mechanical limitations* of newspapers have to be considered in any discussion of newspaper advertising limitations. The quality of newspaper reproduction is poor to begin with, since the paper is printed on the cheapest quality newsprint and at high speeds, with little time for quality control in the deadline-conscious pressroom. Ads that look great on the artist's drawing board in the ad office often lose detail, contrast, and clarity in the newspaper printing process. Papers that have converted to offset printing presses and modern ad preparation methods have made great strides toward defeating the problem of poor reproduction of retail ads. Unless your paper has offset presses, photographs and wash drawings will not reproduce as well as preproduction efforts warrant. Offset operations also use a better-quality newsprint, which helps the appearance of the advertisements.

The fashion retailer, buying newspaper space to display fashions as invitingly and in as complete detail as possible, is often frustrated by poor reproduction that fuzzes the contrast between the merchandise and the background and washes out the details of the garment, which may be its main selling points. Stores that use photography instead of artists' drawings to show merchandise constantly fight this problem of poor reproduction.

Many retailers would use color in their newspaper ads if color reproduction was available. Unfortunately, only offset newspapers and a limited number of major metropolitan papers are able to offer color reproduction with any frequency. Fashion retailers could present merchandise much more realistically and more invitingly if it could be shown in full color. This accounts for part of the attractiveness of catalogs and television to the fashion retailer, for styles, colors, and patterns can be shown to great advantage in these media. The increased use of color supplements, inserted in the newspaper for distribution but preprinted by the advertiser at another printing plant, can also be traced to the limited availability of color for advertising in many newspapers.

The most critical disadvantage of newspaper advertising is the historical fact that recent generations have grown up in what is called the electronic era and have never acquired the habit of reading newspapers. The traditional reliance of retailers on the newspaper as the sole method of reaching customers has been shaken by this problem. It is the major challenge facing newspapers today and in the future.

MERCHANDISING FASHION IN NEWSPAPERS

Readership surveys of newspaper advertising show that fashion advertising is the best-read part of the paper. Since women are the primary targets for most fashion advertising, and since it has been shown that women read newspapers more carefully and thoroughly than men, it follows that the fashion retailer should be advertising in the newspapers.

We made the point in our discussion on planning advertising that advertising should not be allocated to departments and categories in exact percentages merely to match their sales contributions to the store's totals. For example, recalling our five-year sales averages, we find that the dress department produces 10 percent of its annual sales volume in April. The dress department's contribution to the store's total is only 8.2 percent in that month. At this point, before a decision is made whether to allocate 10, 8 or another percentage to the dress department, other questions must be asked:

- Will advertising dresses importantly at this time sell dresses in such quantities that there will be immediate, direct sales results?
- Will advertising dresses importantly at this time sell the store

or the department as the best place to shop because of merchandise selection, price appeal, or fashion rightness?
- Will advertising dresses importantly at this time help test important fashion trends or items that can be developed into important large-volume promotions later?

Analysis of these questions will help determine how much space should be devoted to the dress department in April, and the same principles apply at any time of the year. Seasonality, trends in fashion acceptance of each category of merchandise in the store, the degree to which new items are catching on—all enter into the decision. The major portion of the store's fashion budget is going to find its way into the pages of the newspaper, for reasons we have already given. But the planning must still be done; the scheduling cannot be automatic. The newspaper must be merchandised, used to its fullest to gain the greatest results possible from advertising expenditures.

Most major daily newspapers are printed in sections to make the paper easy to read and to help the reader find the section of greatest interest to him or her. Most papers group subjects of interest to women into a section called "Women" or "Flair" or "Tempo" or some name to make that part of the paper easily identifiable as the area where news of fashion, home furnishings ideas, entertainment, and cultural and educational events can be found. These "women's" sections are read more consistently and thoroughly by women than any other part of the paper, sometimes even more than the main news section. Newspaper Advertising Bureau surveys indicate as many as 90 percent of women who read the paper read the women's pages. NAB statistics are reported as *page openings*, which means the page has been exposed to the reader.

It seems that most readers scan pages when going through a newspaper at a pace estimated at 4 seconds per page. That means a reader's attention must be grasped *within 4 seconds*, or the opportunity to talk to, and sell something to, that reader is lost. We must quickly note the same 4-second timing applies to all media. The point here is that the *subject matter* of the ad must stop the reader flipping through the paper. It is the merchandise in the ad that is going to grab the reader's interest. This is not to discount the importance of the design of the ad, the impact of the illustration, or the cleverness of the copy. Here we want to emphasize that the purpose of the ad, first and foremost, is to get attention. For without the reader's attention, no further communication is possible.

We have said that no store depends on the literal daily sales of its advertised merchandise for the major portion of its day-to-day business. The cost would be prohibitive if this were so. Each store has a fairly predictable daily sales pattern that has developed over a period of time. Increases in sales as a result of some form of advertising will show a measurable difference for a given period, but the basic pattern will not change until daily traffic increases.

The most effective kind of fashion advertising is the kind that talks to the reader about the merchandise of most interest to him or her. That sounds basic, even primitive. But a remarkably high percentage of advertising is placed for reasons other than customer interest. Because of the heavy involvement of cooperative advertising funds in most retail budgets, many items are included in a store's program that might not have been advertised if the store had to pay for the full cost of the ad. When the customer interest in a style or in a manufacturer's line is high, and there is co-op money available, fine. Because of the sharing of costs, the ad can be larger, more styles can be shown in greater detail, and a greater impression can be made on the buying public.

The sales history of the store will indicate what categories of merchandise are of most interest to most customers. The reader of a store's ads is usually a regular and loyal customer, looking for specific types of merchandise—the items from which he or she has received satisfaction through previous purchases. A store may be outstanding for swimsuits, or sweater selection, or the assortments of blouses may be special. Being superior in a category of fashion will ensure success. The store that is always there with the right items at the right time, with a full range of colors and styles from which to select, is the store with the steady, profitable flow of customer traffic.

The role of advertising is to give the public the store's message. Our five-year sales averages indicate that about 55 percent of fashion business comes from wearing apparel and 45 percent from fashion accessories. We can further divide these two groups of merchandise into items for which a buyer will make a special trip to the store and items purchased when in the store but rarely the object of a special visit. Ready-to-wear fashions, obviously, fit into the first group, as do shoes and millinery. These are the items that are of greatest interest to the shopper. A pair of shoes or a new hat can be the start of a costume that will result in several additional purchases being made at the store. A new dress or a suit immediately needs accessories to complete the ensemble. Wearing apparel motivates more customer traffic than any other item. The related, and also important, category of fashion accessories does not motivate as many special trips to the store. Fashion accessories sell in great quantities and are highly promoted by many stores. At times, a "hot" accessory item (remember the turquoise craze, when anything in turquoise was a necessary part of every outfit?) can be sufficiently in demand to require advertising to advise the public of the availability of the item.

As a basic rule, a retailer should divide advertising space usage based on the relative sales importance of the merchandise, but need not follow the percentages literally. For illustration purposes, let us list the merchandise categories and the percentages of the stores' total sales done by the departments in March:

Women's and misses' coats and suits	9.9%	Handbags	3.8%
Juniors' coats, suits, and dresses	6.9	Neckwear	2.4
Women's and misses' dresses	13.7	Gloves	1.8
Blouses, skirts, and sportswear	11.2	Handkerchiefs	.5
Millinery	3.7	Lingerie	6.3
Housedresses, uniforms	3.7	Hosiery	4.6
Women's and misses' dresses	8.6	Bras, corsets	5.7
Infants' wear	7.2	Children's shoes	2.0
Girls' wear	6.4	Furs	1.6

If we literally translated the percentage of sales into the budget for newspaper advertising, we could wind up with a series of ads that would present no coherent picture of the store as it should be presented to the public during the month of March, and we could dissipate valuable advertising dollars. The advertising pie would be cut up into so many pieces there could be no semblance of a fashion statement or impression through the advertising. The judgment of the advertising manager, in cooperation with the merchandising staff, would dictate an approach that would make important fashion impact in the newspaper in this manner: Assuming a total store budget of $30,000, with newspaper space selling at the rate of $1,500 for a full page, note how the plan on page 127 maximizes the advertising with 36 total impressions.

This budget will provide two full pages of newspaper advertising or more for the merchandise with the greatest customer interest. The highly important sportswear area has three full pages. The strong, traffic-pulling accessories, shoes and millinery, are well covered. Even though the allocation of 50 percent of the budget went to departments accounting for 41.7 percent of the month's business, it is basically a sound decision. The fashion accessories group, handbags, jewelry, and neckwear, are provided with three pages of advertising, and other departments, girls and infants' wear,

		Number of Advertisements
Coats and suits, women's and misses	$3,000	2
Junior coats, suits, dresses	3,500	4
Women's and misses' dresses	4,000	3
Blouses, skirts, sportswear	4,500	4
Wearing apparel	$15,000	
Millinery	1,500	4
Women's shoes	3,000	4
Major interest group	$19,500	
Fashion accessories group: (Handbags, jewelry, neckware)	4,500	6
Bras and corsets	1,500	2
Girls' and infants' department	3,000	4
Lingerie and underwear	1,500	3
Total budget, March	$30,000	36 advertising impressions

bras and girdles, and lingerie and underwear, get a fair share of newspaper exposure.

It is not essential that every department be advertised every month, although many buyers would disagree with that statement. Smaller sales figures can be achieved from regular store traffic. In fact, the responsibility of the advertising department includes bringing customer traffic to the store so that attractive impulse items can be sold in addition to the advertised items. Distribution of newspaper space to the departments with the most desirable merchandise from the customer's point of view is the most efficient method of budgeting.

In addition to allocating newspaper space efficiently, the ad manager must *schedule the space* in the newspaper for maximum effect and greatest sales results. As noted, most advertisers want to, and do, place a major portion of their advertising in the Sunday papers even though Saturday is traditionally the highest-volume day of the week. The desire on the part of the department manager to have the ad seen by the larger Sunday newspaper circulation audience sometimes overrides the better judgment of placing the ad in the Thursday or Friday paper, when Saturday shoppers might be looking for ideas of what stores to visit on the weekend. The ad manager must step in and make the decision for the store's best interests. In many markets, stores are open on Sunday, making it the second or third best sale day of the week. Where stores are closed on Sunday, the major portion of the week's business is done on

Table 4.2 AD DISTRIBUTION PATTERN

DAY	WEEK I	WEEK II	WEEK III	WEEK IV
Sunday	Coats and suits	Sportswear	Dresses	Accessories and shoes
Monday	Girls' wear	Bras and girdles	Infants' wear	Bras and girdles
Tuesday	Accessories and shoes	Women's shoes	Accessories and shoes	Millinery
Wednesday	Millinery	Lingerie and underwear	Coats and suits	Sportswear
Thursday	Sportswear	Juniors coats, suits, dresses	Sportswear	Juniors coats, suits, dresses
Friday	Juniors and accessories	Dresses and millinery	Juniors and accessories	Dresses and millinery
Saturday	Lingerie and underwear	Girls' and infants' wear	Lingerie and underwear	Infants' and girls' wear

Thursday, Friday, and Saturday. With Sunday openings, Saturdays have become slightly less important in total sales volume, while the Sunday business seems to be additional business. This gives the Sunday newspaper advertising more chances to be effective.

Table 4.2 shows how the 36 impressions the budget calls for could be distributed to give the public a continuing fashion impression. The size of the ads for the accessory departments would tend to be smaller than those for the major apparel categories, which account for more numerous appearances. Remember when advertising in a daily newspaper that readers should be getting a well-rounded picture of the entire store as time goes on. Assuming the continuity of the day-to-day reading habit, a reader would learn all about a store over a period of time. This is sometimes overlooked when a store runs advertising in more than one newspaper or in more than one medium. Even though there may be some duplication of audience, since people may take the two papers in a town, or hear the message on the radio as well as see it in the paper, the retailer cannot risk missing potential customers by eliminating items from the second or third medium. In fact, repeating the message serves to reinforce the story in the reader's mind.

Advertising experts generally agree that a message should be seen or heard at least three times before the sales story penetrates the consciousness of the individual. Newspaper readers receive these reinforcing messages as they read the paper day after day. Reinforcement is achieved in radio and television through repetition during the broadcast day.

The key to merchandising newspaper advertising space is to talk to the reader most often about the merchandise that interests him or her most. The purpose is to motivate frequent visits to the store, the more the merrier. Much too often, and this weakness seems to crop up mostly in department store promotion, advertising is wasted because ads are scheduled for the wrong reasons. Although advertising decisions are made by the advertising manager, or the executive responsible for advertising in a smaller retail operation, the critical decision—the selection of the item to be advertised—is made by the buyer or the department manager. The ad manager is subjected to pressure from the buying staff to allocate advertising for a variety of weak justifications:

1. The "I'm stuck with this merchandise and I need an ad to move it out of my stock" gambit. Some buyers feel that ads can work miracles, and that if the nondesirable styles were advertised they would somehow become more desirable to the customer. It does not work; all it does is throw good money after bad. If marking down the mistake, reducing the price on the floor, does not make it move, an ad will not move it either.

2. The "I had an ad last year this month, so I need an ad to make my figures" ploy. This is a plea based on past history. We appreciate the need for the buyer to meet last year's figures, but planning to offset those sales figures should have taken place earlier. Rushing an ad into the paper with an item that might not qualify from the standpoint of customer interest would be wasteful.

3. The "I bought this merchandise on my last trip to market, so I need an ad" story. This one might work, if the new item is "hot" and public demand is great. Here's where the ad manager dips into the reserve fund to get a fashion leadership item into the paper before the competition. But sometimes the item will move off the selling floor fast enough if prominently displayed; an ad is not always justified just because of the buyer's purchase.

The *Harvard Business Review* once ran an article on this subject which suggested that advertising people should ask four questions of every ad before releasing it for publication:

1. Why are we advertising this item?
2. How will the customer use it?
3. Why should the customer buy this item at our stores?
4. Have we advertised in an interesting and dramatic manner?

RECENT NEWSPAPER INNOVATIONS

Given the basic premise that the advertising content represents one of the most important and attractive factors in the life of a successful paper, newspaper publishers and other industry executives have

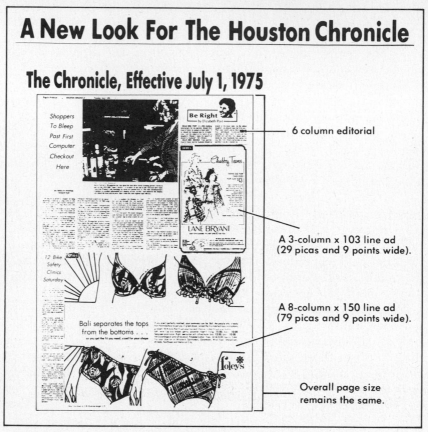

Figure 4.6   When the *Houston Chronicle* revised its format from the 8-column editorial/advertising pattern to the more modern 6-column editorial/9-column advertising format, it advertised the change in trade publications. (SOURCE: By permission of the *Houston Chronicle.*)

made strong moves to ensure and enhance that strength. After a period of changes in page sizes, column widths, number of columns per page, and other mechanical adjustments, newspapers generally have settled down into 6- or 9-column ad formats with which retailers are becoming familiar and comfortable. The Newspaper Advertising Bureau proclaimed a new age of newspaper growth in 1978, with the resurgence of the newspaper as a prime communications force in the United States.

Admittedly, the industry lost touch with the its communities in the post-World War II period with the move to the suburbs, the decline of center cities, and the competition from television and radio. The Vietnam war and the social upheavals of the 1960s were captured dramatically on TV. In addition, newspapers suffered from rapidly rising costs for paper and production, slow changes in management practices, and failure to adjust to the new ways in which leisure time was being spent. Eventually, they learned what they had to do, and many are now doing it.

Many newspapers have made dramatic changes in the product they are publishing in recent years. Some have changed the size of the page, many have changed the number of advertising and editorial columns per page, and quite a few have developed special formats to increase readership.

The change in the size of the newspaper page was partly induced by the newsprint shortage in the early 1970s. The availability of full-width newsprint (the paper on which most newspapers are printed) diminished, causing papers to buy narrower sheets. Judiciously making a positive out of a negative, these papers made other changes in page makeup and created an entirely new look for the paper.

Where papers had previously printed eight $1\frac{5}{8}$-inch narrow columns on a page for editorial matter, they now showed new formats with only six $3\frac{5}{16}$-inch wide columns. For advertising, however, they used a different format. The *Houston Chronicle,* for example, created a 9-column format for advertising where it previously had had an 8-column format (Figure 4.6). The *Minneapolis Star and Tribune* used the opportunity to "sell" the new format (Figure 4.7). The campaign included, among other themes, "We've replaced our 8 skinny columns with 6 fat ones" and used positive statements like ". . . much cleaner, more readable newspapers. We've gotten rid of a lot of those awkward eye-jumps and hyphens that can make newspapers difficult and tiring to read."

The more meaningful change in newspapers, one that relates directly to the content of the paper and the setting in which the advertiser's message is placed, is the development of target marketing of newspapers through the creation of special interest sections (Figure 4.8). The *Chicago Tribune,* for example, offers "Taste" and "Feminique" on Mondays—"Taste" being "a dramatic breakthrough in format and features . . . viewing food as part of Chicago life-style with emphasis on food as part of entertaining." "Feminique" contains "articles for every Chicago woman—features on home furnishings, and fashions for her job, her leisure, her social life." On Wednesdays, one special section is "Venture"—articles on tennis, camping, travel, fishing, and features that cut across all age boundaries. Wednesday's edition also offers the "Midweek Business Report"—"The Tribune's answer to a business magazine, with unparalleled coverage of the Chicago business scene." And

Figure 4.7 The *Minneapolis Star and Tribune* took a more humorous approach to advising clients of its page format change, using the familiar comic characters of Laurel and Hardy to illustrate the point. (SOURCE: Advertisement copyright 1975, Minneapolis Star and Tribune Company, 425 Portland Avenue, Minneapolis, Minnesota 55488. Reprinted with permission of the *Minneapolis Star and Tribune* and BBDO, Inc. Permission for the use of the Laurel and Hardy characters granted by Larry Harmon Pictures Corporation. Laurel and Hardy © Larry Harmon Pictures Corporation.)

Figure 4.8 The *Chicago Tribune* dramatized the development of special interest sections in the paper with ads to advertisers proclaiming "the sectional revolution" and pointing out the target marketing opportunities available through the new formats. (SOURCE: By permission of the *Chicago Tribune.*)

then there's Thursday's "Food Guide," Friday's "Sportsweek" and "Weekend." "Tempo" appears every day. This is an excellent example of a modern newspaper at work, bringing itself up to date and serving the retailer by developing better audiences and readership for the store's advertising messages.

Most major metropolitan newspapers have followed this lead and offer some variations on the themes. These special interest sections are usually focused on sports, fashion, leisure time/arts, home and at-home entertaining, and food. These sections offer the retailer the opportunity of reaching a specialized audience through the section's focused appeal.

The strong bond between retailers and newspapers has been forged over many years of service and attention to retailers' problems. The never-ending effort to reinforce the importance of newspapers as the prime advertising medium for retailing shows results every day of the week in every town and city in America. To the average retailer, advertising means *newspaper* advertising, and the wise newspaper publisher will see to it that that feeling never changes.

QUESTIONS FOR DISCUSSION AND CLASS ASSIGNMENTS

1. Compare the media patterns of the two leading department stores in your city. Discuss why they are similar or different.
2. Visit a major department store's advertising and sales promotion office. Determine (through questions and discussion) their agreement with and/or variations from traditional media patterns.
3. With more than 50 percent of the average retailer's advertising being spent in newspapers, what reasons can you give for this trend to continue despite the threatened inroads by electronic media?
4. What influence will the availability of more color in newspaper advertising have on retail store ads?
5. What advertising techniques, borrowed from other media, could be adapted to improve newspaper advertising readership?
6. Discuss the pros and cons of a newspaper advertising campaign that consistently features off-price merchandise.
7. A balanced advertising program presenting all departments in proportion to their importance month by month is considered the best approach. Trace a local store's advertising for an entire month and compare its advertising activity in relation to national sales averages.
8. Discuss why and how the newspaper has always been the primary advertising medium for retailers.
9. Discuss how the growing importance of women in the work force might affect the traditional role of newspaper advertising in retailing.
10. Discuss and show how your local newspaper has made changes to modernize and adapt to changing life-styles and buying habits in your community.
11. Design and write the copy for a full-page newspaper ad using the ad copy form (Appendix 9) as a source of merchandise and store information. Be creative. Develop an unusual way of selling this standard item.

Chapter 5
Talking Directly to
Customers: Direct Mail

No discussion of direct mail advertising can even begin without attention to the changes that have taken place in mail delivery in recent years. As a colleague facetiously suggested, the chapter could be dedicated to "those wonderful folks who gave us the Postal Service." Among the changes that have occurred, the one that has affected retailers most has been the uncertainty of delivery.

One of the most effective uses of direct mail by retailers was the "Courtesy Days" idea, which allowed charge account customers the special privilege of shopping for sale items a day or two before the store made a general announcement of the sale to the public (Figure 5.1). This device assured the successful launching of a major sale event, since the loyal, regular customer appreciated the opportunity of "beating the mob" and having first choice of the special bargains being offered. The Courtesy Day was often as big as or bigger than the official opening day of the sale event. The regular charge customer got special treatment, including an advance copy of the sale booklet and special shopping hours. To reinforce the "insider" aspects of the promotion, the date for the general public

Figure 5.1   Liberty House, Oakland, California, catalog mailed to the store's charge account customers announcing the "High Flying Sale" and the special preview day for regular customers.

was also included. For example:

Your Preview Day: Thursday, March 6
Special Hours: Shop Thursday 9 A.M. to 9 P.M.
Public Sale Starts: Friday, March 7

For our charge customers only
$5 off with coupon, March 6

$5   ONE DAY ONLY—MARCH 6 $5

$5 OFF
VOID

Charge Customer's Name:_____

Save $5 on the purchase price of any one item of $9.99 or more.
One day only, March 6, 1980. Coupon must be presented in
person with your Liberty House charge card.
Gift certificates, labor, installation charges and special orders are excluded.
Coupon is not redeemable for cash.

Marked price_____   Dept. No._____
Less coupon   5.00   Store No._____
$5   Sale price $5

Figure 5.2   Added inducement to attract customers to the special preview day—a $5 off coupon which could be redeemed only on that day.

An interesting innovation in the Courtesy Day idea was the inclusion of a "$5 Off" coupon, redeemable with the purchase of an
item over $9.99 and only on the Preview Day (Figure 5.2). This pro-
vided an added incentive for the customer to shop the sale on that
day.

In the past few years, however, especially since the govern-
ment-operated Post Office was turned into the private enterprise
Postal Service under federal control, promptness of delivery has
deteriorated. Quite often, customers receive notification of advance
selling dates days after the event is over. In one specific instance,
the jumbo postcard announcing a special "Private Sale" on the preceding Saturday arrived in the mail on Monday, carrying a post-
mark which indicated that it had been mailed seven days earlier as
first class mail. The intriguing part of the story is that the store was
located less than 20 miles from the home of the customer! Every
retailer in America can match this incident and add many similar
stories from bitter personal experience. This loss of the ability to
pinpoint delivery dates of mail has caused a change in sales promotion planning. Instead of stating on the envelope or self-mailer
"Sale Starts May 31," the retailer hedges by trumpeting "Sale on
Now!" so the customer can respond as soon as the mailing piece is
received. Retailers have had to find ways to work around the Postal
Service in order to continue to use this most effective and therefore
desirable advertising method.

FLEXIBILITY AND CONTROL:
THE ADVANTAGES OF DIRECT MAIL

Aside from being the retailers' second most favorite print medium, direct mail—or direct response—advertising is without question the most controllable medium. It is the one advertising process where every aspect affecting the cost of the campaign is in the hands of the advertiser. The retailer can determine how many pieces of direct advertising will be printed, how they will be distributed, what type of advertising will be produced, what kind of paper will be used, how many colors of ink will be used, and within certain limitations, even how much will be spent on postage. Part of the fascination with direct mail is this full control factor, for the very nature of retailing insists on as much control as possible of every phase of the operation.

The great flexibility of direct response advertising also makes it a medium that every retailer, large or small, can employ profitably. The basic plan for the small retailer includes two elements: a listing in the Yellow Pages of the telephone directory and a card filing system of regular customers to whom notices of special events can be sent. Each salesperson on the floor of the smallest fashion shop should keep an alphabetical card file of people they have served, with name, address, phone number, and a running account of what was purchased, in what sizes, and at what prices. This is the minimum advertising plan for the smallest retailer. It is easier to get a response from customers who have bought from you (and were presumably satisfied) than to spend limited advertising funds for any other advertising vehicle.

Listing your business in the Yellow Pages is standard. It is the perfect advertising medium for people who have made up their minds to buy something but do not know where to find it. The directory will give them the dealer nearest them who offers that product or service. It is a form of direct response advertising only in the sense that your phone will ring if you happen to be the most convenient source for a particular item or need.

Cost Control: Size and Distribution

Determining the size of the press run (number of pieces to print) of your direct mail campaign is the most important decision in controlling its cost. The type of store, its location, its size, the importance of the event—all are critical factors. Small retailers, with specialized clientele, limited-access locations, and standard, popular fashion merchandise probably cannot afford much beyond an occasional postcard mailing for semiannual or seasonal sales. Larger retailers, with a variety of merchandise to sell, plan direct mail campaigns on a year-round basis, matching seasonal trends and buying patterns as closely as possible. The size of any mailing is influenced by the budget, which is set up with seasonal, departmental, and storewide objectives in mind. The larger the store, the larger the event, the greater the number of pieces of mail distributed. Major department stores distribute as many as 80 or 90 "books" a year.

With the current availability of demographic data in stores that have and utilize computer-type registers or terminals, stores can pinpoint portions of their customer list for specialized mailings. This is an additional control on the size of the mailing, limiting distribution only to those customers most likely to buy the particular items. The advertiser can be most selective with the direct mail audience, thus eliminating costly waste distribution.

Unlimited Flexibility

A great advantage of direct mail advertising is its endless variety. The message can be packaged in as many ways as the creative minds of the advertising staff can concoct. The presentation can be tailored to fit the precise objective of the advertising. The range of possibilities is limitless. Actually, anything that can be sent via the Postal Service can be direct response advertising.

- A bag of walnuts with a tag proclaiming, "You'll go nuts over the sensational fall fashions now on sale at Blank's."
- A giant foldout piece that opens into a board game showing step by step how you proceed through the game to reach the goal of the new blouse excitement at Maury's.
- A booklet shaped exactly like a paperback best seller, listing page after page of values from every department in the store.
- A straight sales letter from the president of the store to the new homeowner presenting the family with an approved-in-advance charge account card.
- A catalog of preholiday savings delivered to charge account customers in advance of the normal newspaper ads announcing the event.
- Statement enclosures, single sheet announcements in full color with convenient mail order blanks, inserted and sent to charge account customers with their monthly statements.
- Handwritten notes on quality stationery, sent by experienced salespeople to special customers on their personal lists, advis-

ing them of the arrival of the newest spring styles in footwear or lingerie.
- The Christmas catalog, packed with gift-giving ideas for everyone on the family's list.
- A cutout in the shape of an elephant that unfolds into an elephant parade, to emphasize the enormity of the fashion warehouse sale now in progress.
- A newspaper-style tabloid jammed with current fashion items on sale mailed directly to the homes of customers, in addition to or instead of inclusion in the daily run of the paper.

Privacy and Ensured Delivery

Direct mail takes the advertiser's message directly into the home, along with other advertising, of course, but also along with letters, magazines, and other items welcomed into the household. The mail *is* delivered. Even if your message is easily recognized as advertising matter when the daily stack of mail reaches the kitchen table, it takes a very hardy soul *not* to open the envelope, especially if the cover and story are appealing. The piece may get a quick trip to the wastebasket once the contents have been evaluated, but it does get into the home, and it does get opened. Most advertising media cannot get that far. If the message hits the reader's interest button the message will get read, and at that stage the reader will probably read everything in the envelope and ask for more.

Direct mail is very private advertising. Your competitor has no idea what is being offered and cannot adjust to beat the offer. In the newspaper, the store is out in the open, a target for any retailer in the market. The customer likes to receive mail, especially if it is a limited clientele offer. There is an element of flattery, of being in the "in" group, that improves customer loyalty to a store.

Successful Advertising through Direct Mail

Direct mail advertising, designed to tell the complete story of the merchandise in full color and in great detail, is also designed to complete the sales transaction through the inclusion of a mail order form (Figure 5.3). The form must include all the necessary information—style number, size, color, and any other details needed to ensure that the customer is sent the right merchandise in the right color and correct size.

The popularity of direct mail as a retail advertising device has varied over the years. It has been estimated that 30 percent of all retail sales in the United States came through catalog shopping in

SHOP BY MAIL:

THE BROADWAY
P.O. Box 2072, Terminal Annex
Los Angeles, Calif. 90051

Your name _____

Address _____

City_____State_____Zip_____

Telephone(　) _____

☐ Check or Money Order enclosed
☐ Charge to my Broadway charge account

_ _ _ _ _ _ _ _ _ _ _
CHARGE ACCOUNT NUMBER AS ON YOUR CARD

SHOP BY PHONE:

**From anywhere in Southern California dial
toll-free 1-800-252-9174 Los Angeles 227-1177**

Our price comparisons, and what they mean:
Regular: The regular price of the item. This was The
Broadway's actual selling price before the sale. The item
will return to the higher price when the sale is over.
Original: The Broadway's original price before the sale.
After the sale, the price may either remain at the sale price
or go to the original price, depending on quantities.
Special purchase: Indicates merchandise from our
regular manufacturers which we've specially purchased at
low prices just for this sale.
Will be: Merchandise being introduced at The Broadway
for the first time. After the sale, the merchandise will be
priced at the "Will be" price indicated.

PAGE/KEY	ITEM	SIZE/STYLE	COLOR	QUANTITY	PRICE

Many items in this catalogue are covered by written manufacturer's warranties. Copies may be obtained by writing The Broadway at the address shown above.

We regret we cannot always avoid possible delays in merchandise arriving in our store. When these delays occur we will accept your order for the advertised merchandise and notify you as soon as it arrives.

Please add sales tax. Handling charge is additional beyond The Broadway's delivery area. Please add 1.50 service charge on orders under 15.00. 6/80. Sorry, no C.O.D. orders.

SUB.	
TAX/HAND.	
TOTAL	

51

Figure 5.3   Part of an efficient mail order catalog is the clear explanation of the store's pricing policy plus an easy-to-read and complete mail order blank.

1980. The Direct Mail/Marketing Association in New York stated that catalog shopping accounted for $33 billion in sales in 1974. About $13 billion was done by the "Big Three" catalog companies (Sears, Montgomery Ward, and JC Penney), with about 5,800 smaller companies accounting for the other $20 million.

The genius of the Sears, Roebuck catalog, which included showing customers how to measure themselves, proved for all time that practically anything can be sold through the mail. Ordering merchandise by mail is an American tradition that persists despite the inefficiencies of delivery and store system breakdowns. The business is huge and profitable. It is operated on a national scale by stores like Nieman-Marcus of Dallas, Saks Fifth Avenue, and mail order specialists like Spiegel's of Chicago, Horchow, L. L. Bean and others. Figure 5.4 shows some typical department store mailers.

Quick and Direct Results

Results of direct response advertising can be checked more accurately than most other advertising, since the customer must fill out the order blank, enclose a check or money order or charge account

Figure 5.4   (A) The Broadway, Los Angeles, California, humanizes its Father's Day mailer with a father-son photo. Photos of children and animals usually attract additional audiences to promotions. (B) The Broadway features a beach ball theme for its annual summer sale, with courtesy days included. (SOURCE: By permission of the Broadway.)
(C) Bullock's, Los Angeles, sticks to graphic design and bold colors to attract readers to its summer sale and clearance. (SOURCE: By permission of Bullock's.)

number, and mail it in. A simple tabulation of the mail received shows the retailer the direct results of the promotion. At the retail level, there is a second response—floor traffic. People come to the store as a result of receiving the mailing and buy the advertised items and other items as well. So much guesswork goes into the charting of most advertising results that it is comforting to be able to show a stack of mail order coupons indicating sales results in a most tangible form.

Cost Control: Production

Control of the direct mail campaign is important in the area that can be the costliest if it is not well supervised—the creative area. Creative people generally have poor business sense. Someone, usually a production person who understands printing processes and cost factors, should have veto power over the flights of fancy on which many art directors embark. We once discovered, at a point in the production of a mail order campaign when it was too late to stop, that the art director had ordered a change which blew the budget out the window. The campaign, with a "Life will be a bowl of cherries" theme, included an envelope with the imprint of two luscious maraschino cherries. The artist thought it would look better if we had cutouts of the cherries hand-affixed to the envelopes instead of merely printing them on it. Artistically it was a good decision; from a cost standpoint, no one had anticipated the extra cost of attaching 10,000 cherry cutouts by hand.

Production factors—the kind of paper; whether the right effect can be achieved with two colors of ink plus black, or four-color; saddle stitching or stapling—these and other technical considerations should be left to the experienced printer or artist, who will deliver the best job for the money. It is better to rely on the professionals, with the assurance that they will do more of your business if they handle the job properly, than to muddle through with limited knowledge and achieve mediocre results.

Many large retail operations, with skilled staffs, can produce professional mailings in-house, but few large department stores have the capability of producing full-color engravings right in their own facility. The smaller retailers must buy these services, but that does not mean they should settle for poorer quality because of limited budgets. The ability of talented printers to produce excellent work with less than generous budgets has always been a source of pleasant amazement.

The answer to most printing problems is *time*. Give the writer, the layout artist, the photographer time to use their skills. *Plan*

Table 5.1 A TYPICAL DIRECT MAIL PRODUCTION SCHEDULE

TARGET DELIVERY DATE: Week of March 15

1/10	Preplan meeting to determine content, number of pages and general theme of book (the concept)
1/17	Formats, including rough page layouts, based on merchandise plan—what goes in the book and where
1/23	Merchandise samples, copy and mail order information due
1/24	Paging due (page sequence for the book)
1/24	Lead sheets due (basic information about merchandise, headline, number of lines of copy)
1/24	Merchandise samples to art production department
1/24	Layouts due
1/24	Layouts approved
1/24	Production meeting

PHOTOGRAPHY DEPARTMENT

1/31	Photography complete, according to layout
2/3	Photography approved

COPY DEPARTMENT

1/25	Mail order blank copy due
1/25	Mail order blank copy approved
1/27	Catalog copy due; written to fit the layouts
1/31	Catalog copy approved and set into type for pasteup
1/31	Catalog copy in production

PRODUCTION DEPARTMENT

2/3	Photo sizing complete
2/8	Photo duping complete
2/9	Photostats on boards
2/13	Stripping complete
2/3	Catalog copy to typesetter to be set into type for pasteup
2/6	Checker proofs due
2/6	Checker proofs approved
2/8	Reproduction proofs due
2/13	Pasteup complete
2/14	Completed boards to clients
2/17	Completed boards approved

PRINT PRODUCTION DEPARTMENT

1/31	Mail order blank to printer
2/14	Film to color separator
2/21	Boards to separator
3/1	Film to printer; blueline (one-color copy of book) proofed and approved.
3/3	Catalog on press; printed, bound, labeled
3/8	Catalog due to mail house/post office
3/10	Mailing date

3/15 TO 3/21 DATE CATALOG IN HOMES

3/10	100 copies for in-house mailing
2/28	Post office check due
2/28	Post office labels due
2/28	Distribution list due
3/15	Store catalog samples due

Job No. _____

Printer _____

ahead, as we have said before. Color printing takes longer than newspaper printing. Each step in the printing process takes time. Find out from the printer how long it will take to produce the material. Better still, plan in reverse. Determine when the mailing should be received by the customer, and then work backward, allowing enough time for each step in the process to happen. You then have a time frame for each part of the operation, and a deadline for the buyers in the store to deliver copy and merchandise samples. Then keep to the schedule.

Table 5.1 shows a typical production flow schedule for a store catalog, based on a major department store's actual procedure. In practice, there may be more time allotted to each phase of production, but this listing covers all aspects of producing the mailer. Note that several operations happen simultaneously in different departments of the advertising office.

Very often the general theme, the cover page, and sample pages are created months in advance of the first planning meeting indicated at the top of this list. The plan of the book, along with estimated cost per page, circulation figures, and other pertinent data are prepared for the buyers to take to market. The plan becomes the vehicle for collecting commitments for co-op funds from the various vendors and manufacturers whose merchandise will appear in the book. The amount of money contributed determines how much space will be given to that vendor's merchandise. The results of the buyers' efforts are a major factor in the preplanning meeting that determines the merchandise content of the book, the number of pages, and the breadth of the distribution. The necessity for detailed production flow charts becomes apparent when the advertising department must produce from 12 to 36 direct mailings of various sizes and formats in a given year.

Postage

One additional point on cost control in direct mailing is postage. With continuing increases in postal rates, and with no end in sight, the decision on distribution method becomes a key factor. Should the piece go out first class or as third class bulk mail? Should it have a machine imprint or a regular stamp? Contrast the costs of first class and third class mail. Simple arithmetic may point the way to the appropriate decision. Note how postage costs have risen in recent years:

RECENT HISTORY OF POSTAGE RATES

YEAR	AIRMAIL LETTERS	FIRST CLASS LETTERS	THIRD CLASS BULK (MINIMUM PIECE RATE)
1955	6¢ per oz	3¢ per oz	1.5¢
1960	7¢ per oz	4¢ per oz	2.0¢
1965	8¢ per oz	5¢ per oz	2.8¢
1970	10¢ per oz	6¢ per oz	4.0¢
1975	13¢ per oz	10¢ per oz	6.3¢
1976	17¢ per oz	13¢ per oz	7.9¢
1978	—	15¢ per oz	8.4¢
1981	—	18¢ per oz	8.8¢

A recent development (1979)—the third-class carrier route presort—offers the advertiser a savings of 1.7 cents per piece off the normal rate if mail has been sorted and grouped by carrier route. The regulation offers postage savings for retailers with very large and frequently used lists or those with medium to smaller lists concentrated in a relatively small geographic area. Using the specific guidelines of the regulation, some major metropolitan stores have realized net savings of approximately 1 cent per catalog. In a heavy mailing, this adds up to a substantial amount of money.

Table 5.2 shows the estimated costs of various types of mailings, along with the rapid rise in prices, based on one million quantity runs. There was a myth that advertising mail (basically third class) was subsidized by the taxpayer. In August 1970, when the Postal Rate Commission went into operation, it was learned that third class mail paid 160.7 percent of its attributable costs. In other words, advertising mail was not only *not* a losing proposition for the

Table 5.2 TYPICAL COSTS OF DIRECT MAIL ADVERTISING

ITEM	1960 COST PER THOUSAND	1976 COST PER THOUSAND	PERCENTAGE OF INCREASE
Brochure—4 color	$19.14	$ 26.13	36%
Premium insert—4 color	8.60	10.30	19
Order card—4 color	3.81	7.36	93
Letter—2 color	4.17	6.64	59
Reply envelope—1 color	2.22	4.11	85
Outer envelope—2 color	4.83	6.69	38
Mailing list	15.00	30.00	100
Lettershop charge	6.50	7.57	19
Totals (1 thru 8)	$64.27	$ 98.98	54%
Third class postage	20.00	77.00	285%
Total cost per thousand	$84.27	$175.98	108%

SOURCE: Reprinted with permission from the March 28, 1977, issue of *Advertising Age.* Copyright 1977 by Crain Communications, Inc.

Postal Service, it was actually defraying some of the USPS fixed expenses as a *profit center!* Table 5.2 shows that costs for private business from 1960 to 1976 rose 54 percent, but costs for the government sector, third class postage, rose 285 percent during the same period! It's the kind of information that wrinkles the brows of retailers as they ponder the dilemma of how to absorb the continually rising costs of direct mail advertising.

THE VALUE OF CHARGE ACCOUNT MAILINGS

One of the most valuable possessions in the advertising arsenal of a retail store is its charge account customers. These are the loyal, regular customers, the frequent and consistent shoppers, who have programmed your store into their shopping habits. To have inspired and acquired the trust of families in the trading area as a good place to shop is an enviable position for a store to have. Taking out a charge account with a store is a mutual contract between the customer and the store, with the customer making a commitment to use that charge account card and the store making a commitment to assure the customer satisfaction with any purchases made in the store (Figures 5.5 and 5.6).

Ownership of a charge account with a store makes shopping easy and painless for the customer. Purchases can be made over the phone or by mail. With this attitude of "belonging" to a store goes an unspoken loyalty that is hard to measure, but certainly worth cultivating and nurturing on the part of the retailer. People think of themselves as "Magnin customers" or "Saks customers" and develop a possessive feeling about the stores in which they shop. They feel very comfortable calling directly to the store president if they see or experience something they do not like. It has been said that retail store presidents have more direct contacts with their clientele than the presidents of any other business. This feeling of being able to talk directly to the top is a two-edged sword—very nice to have that kind of open relationship, but also potentially a lot of trouble when customers call and call and call.

Charge account customers can receive an unlimited number of catalogs and direct mail pieces from each store with which they do business. They receive storewide mailers, divisional mailers, departmental and category mailers. Some possible mailings that could be sent out from a major department store during a year are listed in Table 5.3. In addition, there are individual mailings paid for by manufacturers of specific lines of merchandise, who preprint mini-catalogs in huge quantities, imprint the store's name, address and

Table 5.3 TYPICAL DEPARTMENT STORE DIRECT MAIL PROGRAM

Storewide Event	Divisional	Departmental	Category
Anniversary sale	Warehouse sale	Housewares carnival	Graduation
Summer sale	White sale	Father's Day	Bridal show
Year-end clearance	Fall fashion festival	Mother's Day	Cosmetic special
			Valentine's gifts
Christmas catalog	Life-style fashions	Summer sportswear	Shoe fashions
		Lingerie booklet	Tennis fashions
		Fashion clearance	

mail order information, and pay for the mailing of special booklets to the store's charge account list.

One of the minor, and least expensive, kinds of direct mail is the *statement enclosure*. These are the lightweight single-sheet pieces of advertising included in monthly billing statements to charge customers. There is no additional postage cost (hence the light weight) as long as the combined weight of the statement enclosures and the customer's billing information does not exceed one ounce. This keeps it within the first class postage limit. With the advent of computerized billing, the former limit of two or three of these messages no longer applies. The total cost of statement enclosures is borne by manufacturers of specific merchandise who have found this an effective medium. Among the regular users are manufacturers of perfumes and cosmetics, lingerie and bras, personalized stationery and Christmas cards, and magazines. The vendors supply the material in whatever quantity the store requires, with the store's logo and order-by-mail information imprinted at no cost.

Figure 5.5   (A) Manufacturer-supplied statement enclosures provide fine-quality, full-color photography to promote specific items. Intimate apparel is popular item in this medium. (B) Linens, household goods, stationery, and other standard items do well as statement enclosures. Note the store name imprinted by the vendor, plus specific mail instructions as required by the store. (SOURCE: By permission of Bullock's.)

The Broadway

HARRY SPITZER
15916 DICKENS ST
ENCINO,CA 91436

Account Number

0 863 794 409 7

Billing Date*

For prompt credit to your account please return
this portion with your payment.

If address is incorrect, line out and enter new. Please furnish zip code.

TYPE OF ACCOUNT	YOUR NEW BALANCE IS	MINIMUM PAYMENT NOW DUE	PLEASE ENTER AMOUNT PAID

The Broadway

P.O. Box   Terminal Annex
Los Angeles, California 90054

YES, I ACCEPT YOUR DEFERRED CHARGE OFFER.

SIGNATURE   DATE

DATE	REFERENCE NUMBER	DEPT.	ITEM DESCRIPTION ALSO SEE REVERSE SIDE	PURCHASES	PAYMENTS & CREDITS

FOR YOU----AS A SELECTED CHARGE ACCOUNT CUSTOMER, WE ARE
PLEASED TO MAKE YOU THIS SPECIAL HOLIDAY OFFER. CHARGE
PURCHASES MADE DURING OCTOBER THROUGH JANUARY, 1978 MAY BE
DEFERRED UNTIL FEBRUARY, 1978. MERCHANDISE PURCHASED WILL BE
ITEMIZED ON EACH MONTHLY STATEMENT. HOWEVER, THE AMOUNTS
WILL NOT BE ADDED TO YOUR STATEMENT BALANCE UNTIL FEBRUARY,
1978. IF YOUR FEBRUARY, 1978 BALANCE IS PAID IN FULL PRIOR
TO YOUR MARCH BILLING, THERE WILL BE NO FINANCE CHARGE. TO
ENROLL IN THIS PLAN, PLEASE SIGN AND RETURN THE TOP PORTION
OF THIS STATEMENT TODAY, IN THE ENCLOSED ENVELOPE. AS SOON
AS YOUR ACCEPTANCE IS RECEIVED, WE WILL BEGIN TO DEFER YOUR
PURCHASES. YOUR IMMEDIATE RESPONSE PROVIDES YOU THE USE OF
THIS PLAN TO TAKE ADVANTAGE OF THE VALUES IN OUR HOLIDAY SALE
WHICH STARTS WITH COURTESY DAYS WEDNESDAY, NOVEMBER 2ND.

BILLING CYCLE*
CLOSING DATE

ACCOUNT NUMBER

PAYMENT SHOULD
BE RECEIVED BY

TYPE OF ACCOUNT	TO YOUR PREVIOUS BALANCE	WE HAVE ADDED		AND DEDUCTED PAYMENTS & CREDITS	YOUR NEW BALANCE IS	MINIMUM PAYMENT NOW DUE
		FINANCE CHARGE	PURCHASES			

If we receive payment of the full amount of the NEW BALANCES before the next billing cycle closing date, shown above*, you will avoid a FINANCE CHARGE next month. The FINANCE CHARGE, if any, is figured on the PREVIOUS BALANCE before deducting payments and credits shown above. The periodic rates used are 1½% on the balance on amounts under $1000 and 1% on amounts in excess of $1000 (subject to a minimum charge of not more than 50c for balances under $33.50) which are ANNUAL PERCENTAGE RATES of 18% and 12% respectively.
NOTICE: See reverse side for important information - THE BROADWAY.

Figure 5.6 Many stores cater to their charge account customers to invite additional business. Using the billing form to announce a special credit arrangement is a novel approach and a welcome relief when the recipient realizes it is not another bill to be paid. (SOURCE: By permission of The Broadway.)

Long-range planning and precise scheduling is needed for an effective statement enclosure operation. Automatic stuffing machines in billing departments handle the physical stuffing of the advertising pieces, so they must conform to the size and weight specifications of the machinery. Many companies "buy" the outside portion of the store's billing reply envelope by paying for the printing of their advertising message on the outside flap and supplying the store with enough envelopes for the month's billing (Figure 5.7). The flap can be filled out and included with the payment being sent to the store, or torn off and discarded. In either case, the retailer is saved the cost of printing envelopes and has the opportunity of creating additional sales.

One of the added features of computer-controlled charge account bookkeeping, where the store has the capability of screening the activity of each account, is the ability to limit mailings to specific groups of customers. Where the sizes of fashion merchandise purchased can be recorded, the retailer can set up a computer run that will spill out only the names of customers who have bought junior size merchandise. This enables the junior fashion department to zero in on customers most likely to buy junior size clothes. When budget restrictions, or price increases, force a limitation of distribution of a store catalog, some stores can eliminate those customers who have not been active in the recent past or who may be delinquent in paying on past purchases. Again, this screening process allows the mailing to go only to current and potentially ready-to-buy customers.

The key to an ongoing direct mail program is the sifting out of the inactive charge customer in order to mail only to those who are currently buying. For example, if a store has a mailing list of 25,000 with 1,600 in the lingerie department, it can send the mailing to the 1,600 and test a random 500 for activity. Tests have shown that the savings in mailing costs more than made up the small amount of business not received due to the limited number of mailing pieces sent. When budgets require curtailment, total store mailings are limited to storewide sales—fall sale, anniversary sale, Christmas catalogs, and after-Christmas clearances and sales. If a store does multiple mailings during a season such as Christmas, some of the interim books may be sent to parts of the total store list.

Many retailers have access to demographic and psychographic information regarding customers and their buying habits. They can pull out very specialized groups for specific mailings, and many do. The cost in computer time becomes an expense factor, with the result that the decision might be made to spend the money on a broader, less precise, mailing rather than on computer time. The retail theory at work here states that the extra pieces mailed might bring in some business, but the computer time is just an outright non-sales-productive extra expense.

Many stores use their charge account lists to conduct surveys.

Figure 5.7   Example of a manufacturer (Elizabeth Arden) supplying a billing envelope to the store in exchange for an advertisement on the back of the envelope.

People enjoy being asked their opinions, especially from a store where they feel at home, and will give advice and suggestions freely. Research departments cull "focus groups" of customers from this same area when conducting in-depth interviews to dig into and solve current store problems.

Computerized letters, personally addressed and including the customer's name within the body of the letter to reinforce its "personal" approach, are a popular device for departmental special sales events (Figure 5.1). Inviting "Howard T. Jones" to a private 2-for-1 silver sale (see Figure 5.8) becomes a personal contact between the store buyer and the previously satisfied silver-purchasing customer. It is an effective, productive way of bringing the customer back into the store for the special event or to purchase other merchandise.

In cities where travel and parking are problems, mail order activity is high. The convenience of shopping at home from the store catalog is welcomed in areas where weather, security, traffic, or lack of in-store service are considerations. This is especially true of major downtown stores, when the people have moved into the suburbs and the stores have not moved with them. The telephone and the store mailings can keep contact with the customer alive and well, if the store arranges for and operates an efficient mail order and delivery service.

Since surveys have shown that many stores do 70 to 80 percent of their business from 20 percent of their customers, the care and feeding of the active charge account customer is a high-priority item on the agenda of most retailers. People happy with the store's fashion selections, service, and operating policies are more likely to spend more than the casual or occasional shopper. The aim of good sales promotion is to convert sale shoppers into customers—regular customers with active charge accounts.

UNSOLICITED MAILINGS

Competing media have constantly attacked that portion of direct mail advertising delivered without a person's name on the address label—so called junk mail. The target of the attacks—mail addressed to "occupant" or "resident" or "current occupant"—and delivered as third class mail by the Postal Service, either at bulk rate or regular, is not the only classification branded "junk mail." Have you ever wondered about the great amount of mail you didn't ask for that arrived in your mailbox *with* your name on it? Did you know that many of the companies with which you do business, and the magazines to which you subscribe, *sell* their customer lists to businesses looking for likely prospects to send advertising to?

LIBERTY HOUSE of California

1501 BROADWAY, OAKLAND, CALIFORNIA 94612 • 891-2121   EXECUTIVE OFFICES

July 14, 1980

Mr. Bob Smith
8059 Arroyo Drive #1
Pleasanton, California 94566

Dear Mr. Smith:

Our 10-day 2 for 1 silver sale is an exceptional investment
opportunity. As you know, silver prices have tripled in the last
year. Come in on your courtesy day, Thursday, January 24 and you'll
receive double your money's worth on magnificent sterling silver
flatware. Public sale starts January 25.

Choose from over 40 patterns from seven manufacturers: Gorham,
Wallace, Towle, Reed & Barton, Kirk, Oneida and International.

Here's how to receive your savings Bob Smith. Buy one 4-piece
place setting and receive two. Or, these silverplated bonus gifts
may be yours with a minimum purchase of two 4-piece place settings:

--Buy two 4-piece settings & receive 4, plus a $75 value covered
  bake and serve.

--Buy four 4-piece settings & receive 8, plus a $150 value
  Gorham candelabra and $35 value silver chest.

--Buy six 4-piece settings & receive 12, plus a $325 value Oneida
  tea service and $35 value silver chest.

Yours truly

J. Boyd
Silver Buyer

JB/sw

Use our Liberty House Silver Club Plan: There is no finance charge.
Minimum payment of $10 a month with minimum purchase of $100. Up to
36 months to pay. Cost of credit included in the price quoted for
goods and services.

AN amfac COMPANY

Figure 5.8 Personalized sales letters are popular with many stores for
certain kinds of merchandise. Departmental special promotions often
offer the charge customer presale opportunities to buy.

A retailer might want to advertise the arrival of new designer
fashions to prospects who might not know of the establishment. Notices have been sent to the people on the charge account list and an
ad has been scheduled in the women's section of the newspaper,

but how can the merchant find additional customers? Buy a mailing list! It is possible to solicit business from all the new Cadillac owners in town, or from all the homes located in the rich, suburban area beyond the city limits. Those names and addresses can be bought from one of the mailing houses that do a healthy business supplying that kind of information.

In many states, mail order houses acquire and sell names and addresses of licensed drivers, those who register autos, those who take out marriage licenses, home buyers, and many, many others. Subscribers to weekly newsmagazines might find themselves being asked to buy vacations in Hawaii, flight travel insurance, Book-of-the-Month Club memberships, and six other magazines. It seems that people who subscribe to weekly newsmagazines are in a demographic slot that says they are educated, professional, upper-income, literate and take foreign vacations. So companies selling those products and services advertise to this group, because statistically its members are good prospects.

Mailing lists purchased for specific purposes can be a valuable advertising tool when used properly. Suppose a men's specialty store adds an impressive fashion name to its merchandise selection. Of course it advertises in the newspaper in its usual position and sends an attractive mailing piece to its charge list. But wouldn't this be a great time to reach out for all those well-dressed doctors, lawyers and business executives who are not its customers to tell them the news? The investment of the advertising dollars to purchase a select list of upper-income professional men would certainly be in order.

But how to overcome the stigma of "junk mail"? Here is where the quality of the mailing piece comes in. Put it in an envelope—do not send a self-mailer. Hand-address the envelope, if possible, or get it typed—do not use address labels. Use a first class stamp—not metered mail. If the message is attractively packaged and looks first class it won't be treated as "junk" and it has a chance of being read. Unsolicited? Yes, but not tossed into the trash automatically.

Buying the right list is the key to most successful direct mail campaigns. It means the advertiser can talk directly to the most likely prospects instead of hoping that prospects will somehow get your message. The demographic approach is a sound one, based on historical experience and logic. If a family subscribes to quality magazines and owns expensive cars, there is a good chance its members are prospects for similar products and services. But there are no absolutes in advertising. We know of an instance where a family received, as a Christmas gift, a subscription to *Smithsonian Magazine*, an upper-level publication heavy in art, historical, and cultural information. When the first copy of the magazine was delivered, the computer addresser made a slight error, and the label read "The H. Sparks Famm" instead of "The H. Sparks Family." This did not prevent the family from receiving the magazine regularly, but it did highlight something else. Suddenly, there began to arrive all manner of expensive advertising pieces—from gold coin collectors, the Heritage Foundation, museums soliciting funds, around-the-world vacation tours, and at Christmas time, exquisite catalogs from the best stores and catalog houses in the country. And every one of them was addressed to "The H. Sparks Famm"! The constantly misaddressed address label proved that the Smithsonian subscriber list had been sold to other advertisers.

Why does this phase of advertising continue to grow? Because it works. People love to receive mail. Someone qualified "junk mail" as mail about things you are not interested in. If it's about scuba gear and you're a diver, you'll read every word. If it's about back-to-school clothes and you've been wondering what to buy and what the others will be wearing, you'll read it from cover to cover.

The Direct Mail/Marketing Association (DMMA), a national organization, has been running ads in magazines to help overcome the somewhat negative attitude with which the public perceives direct mail. Through a question-and-answer technique, DMMA points out that shopping by mail is not risky, because retailers depend on repeat business for their profits. More business is done by direct mail—over $60 billion in 1976—in both goods and services than ever before. DMMA explodes the myth that the Postal Service lost money because of advertising mail and shows that in actuality advertising mail is helping the Postal Service survive.

DMMA states that the sale, rental, or exchange of mailing lists does not constitute an invasion of privacy because most of these are one-time sales and do not include any other information about individuals. The major problem concerning unsolicited mail is answered in the following way: When something is bought by mail, the purchaser does not get on *every* mail order list, just some.

DMMA, in an ongoing campaign, offers readers the opportunity of having their names removed from the mailing lists of any or all of their nationwide membership companies. Or, they could fill out a mail order blank and have their names *added* to additional lists! Amazingly, according to DMMA, more people ask to have their names added to mailing lists than ask to have their names removed (Figure 5.9).

It would seem, therefore, that the "for" or "against" attitude toward direct mail is subjective, and not as widespread as some believe. If you are interested, you read. If not—into the circular file!

Want to get LESS advertising in the mail? MORE?
The DMMA gives you a choice!

Who's the DMMA? We're the 1,800 member companies comprising the Direct Mail/Marketing Association. Many of the manufacturers, retailers, publishers and service companies you've come to trust most over the years are among our members. ☐ And we think you deserve a choice, as to how much—and what kind—of advertising you receive in the mail. If you'd like to get less, mail in the coupon on the left. We can't stop all your mail,

but you'll see a reduction in the amount of mail you receive soon. ☐ If you'd like to receive more mail in your areas of interest—catalogs, free trial offers, merchandise and services not available anywhere else—mail the coupon on the right. Soon, you'll start to see more information and opportunities in the areas most important to you. Let's hear from you today!

LESS mail

I want to receive less advertising mail.

Mail to: DMMA Mail Preference Service
6 East 43rd Street
N.Y., NY 10017

Name (print)

Address

City   State   Zip

Please include me in the Name Removal File. I understand that you will make this file available to direct mail advertisers for the sole purpose of removing from their mailing lists the names and addresses contained therein.

Others at my address who also want less mail—or variations of my own name by which I receive mail—include:

MORE mail

I want to receive more advertising mail.

Mail to: DMMA Mail Preference Service
6 East 43rd Street
N.Y., NY 10017

Name (print)

Address

City   State   Zip

I would like to receive more information in the mail, especially on the subjects below (circle letter):

A All subjects
B Autos, Parts & Accessories
C Books & Magazines
D Charities
E Civic Organizations
F Clothing
G Foods & Cooking
H Gifts
I Grocery Bargains

J Health Foods & Vitamins
K HiFi & Electronics
L Home Furnishings
M Insurance
N Plants, Flowers & Garden Supplies
O Photography
P Real Estate
Q Records & Tapes

R Sewing, Needlework, Arts & Crafts
S Sports & Camping
T Stamps & Coins
U Stocks & Bonds
V Tools & Equipment
W Travel
X Office Furniture & Supplies

Figure 5.9   Ad published regularly by Direct Mail/Marketing Association offering readers the opportunity of action in relation to unsolicited mail. (SOURCE: By permission of the Direct Mail/Marketing Association.)

From the retailer's standpoint, it seems that the loyalty of customers, the consistency of a positive image, and the satisfaction delivered over the years have a direct effect on the degree to which direct mail will be read. They certainly affect the sales results produced by direct mail advertising.

BALANCING FLEXIBILITY AND CREATIVITY WITH COST

In the face of continually rising costs in producing effective direct mail programs, advertising managers are having to walk a fine line between the versatile capabilities of the medium and the volatile nature of the uncontrollable factors. While the variety of presentation is limited only by the talent of the art director, the costs of paper, printing, and production are creating limitations because of budget restrictions.

The fastest rising cost factor is postal rates. Most retailers would rather maintain the quality of their direct mail pieces and make the necessary cuts in distribution to maintain cost control.

Where stores have traditionally distributed their mailings to a 10- to 15-mile radius around each store, they reduce the circle to 8 miles to stay within budget. They also, of course, print fewer catalogs. Large retail operators use occupant-addressed mailing, depending on mass coverage to bring the desired sales results. In some cases, they take the money saved by the reduced postage costs, maintain the total number of catalogs printed, but distribute the balance of the press run by inserting the circulars into newspapers covering the outer areas. This is not an ideal coverage pattern. It is bound to include some duplication, since some of the newspaper distribution will fall within the 8-mile range of the store.

The practice of inserting mailing pieces, catalogs, supplements, and other items into the newspaper rather than using the mail is a growing trend. Advertisers are willing to accept the existing circulation of the newspaper for the distribution of their material, exchanging precise targeting for reduced costs. The use of these preprints inserted in newspapers increased 29 percent in 1979, totalling 27.1 billion circulation (Newspaper Advertising Bureau).

Under current rates, advertising mail, at its lowest cost (third class bulk mail), is mailed for $84 per thousand, (slightly less for routed mail), which means the total cost of distribution is $90 per thousand. Added to that, of course, is the cost of printing and preparation, which would apply in all cases. If the advertiser decides to insert the complete print job into the newspaper and distribute it to the newspaper's subscribers, distribution costs would range from around $20 per thousand and up, depending on how many pages the circular contained. If $20 per thousand was the cost for an 8-page tabloid-size insert, an 8-page standard-size insert would cost around $30 per thousand. Since there is no addressing cost, the total distribution cost is much below the cost of mailing through the Postal Service.

Another effort to reduce the cost of delivery of advertising is door-to-door delivery services. For relatively low prices, $26 to $36 per thousand, contracts can be made with one of these "walking man" operations, which will deliver circulars to a predetermined number of homes within range of the store. The only weakness in this type of delivery is the dependability of the delivery service. Such operations usually employ nonprofessionals, part-time workers, housewives, Boy Scouts, and other "irregular" troops. It is wise to spot-check when using this door-to-door delivery to be sure the store's area is covered as per contract. The Postal Service answers this challenge by pointing out the limited capability of the door-to-door service, the discrimination in income and geographical areas in the coverage, and the irregularity of service, since employees are not on hand full time. The Postal Service, of course, delivers wherever the mailer designates. Home delivery by private mailing systems may be a wave of the future. Mail experts are talking about private organizations taking over second and third class mail, leaving first class to the Postal Service.

One system, combining the best features of newspaper insertion with direct mail, has been used successfully in some areas. This concept seems to work best in areas where the daily paper is strong and covers 35 to 40 percent of the households in the market. This system, controlled by the newspaper, works as follows:

- The advertiser inserts the circular in the full circulation of the newspaper.
- The newspaper, which has its subscriber list on computer, interfaces the subscriber list against a household occupant list, bouncing out only those households that do *not* subscribe to the paper.
- The advertiser mails the circular to the nonsubscriber list.

This pattern gives the advertiser complete coverage of a market area with no duplication. Delivery costs are a combination of the low insertion rate of the newspaper plus postage costs only for the smallest number of pieces of mail delivered.

Other economies in the production of direct mail are constantly being sought to keep costs down and allow sufficient budget for the creativity in design necessary to make the mailing piece outstanding. Many retailers have installed their own typesetting or head-line-setting machines. The mechanical procedures, getting the material camera-ready for the printer, are often handled by the store's advertising department. Photography, original artwork, and pasteup, are created in-house so that the only outside service purchased is paper and printing.

The smaller retailer must rely on the capabilities of the full-service printing house, which can prepare, design, and produce the complete mailing campaign. The printer, acting as agent for the retailer, contracts for art, copy, photography, or any other service the job requires. The costs of these outside services are added to the retailer's invoice, plus a small commission or percentage to cover handling charges. If the printing job is large enough or profitable enough, or if the retailer is a regular customer, this add-on charge is sometimes waived.

The constant struggle to produce interesting, attention-getting, informative, and effective direct mail within the constrictions of rising uncontrollable fixed costs makes direct mail a never-ending challenge to the advertiser. Even the smallest retailer, whose entire advertising effort may be limited to sending postcard announcements to regular customers, must know that things have changed when the original penny postcard costs 15 cents in the post offices of 1982.

SOME DISADVANTAGES OF DIRECT MAIL

Many of the elements that should make the retail advertiser closely examine the use of direct mail have already been discussed, but some additional points should be made.

The American public is highly mobile. Nearly one out of every five people moves every year, according to the U.S. Census Bureau, although 63 percent of those who move stay within the same county. Some states are noted for having families move much more often than the national average—notably California and other western states. Keeping mailing lists current and accurate is a high priority in every mail order company, and it is difficult and expensive.

Retailers using third class mail for advertising have an additional problem in that third class mail is not forwarded and companies that compile and sell mailing lists to advertisers are often two to four months behind.

The much-sought-after young adult market is a big chunk of the mobile population. Thirty-four percent of the 18 to 24 age group moves every year, as do 27 percent of the 25 to 34 group. This important segment of the market, the target of the majority of fashion retailers, has rated "junk mail" very high on its list of nuisances in many surveys. Research (Target Group Index, 1979) has also shown that over two-thirds of the 18 to 34 age group never use mail "cents-off" and other coupons. Over 50 percent of the 18 to 24 group say they never buy by mail, and 39 percent of the 25 to 34 group also responded in the negative.

Another disadvantage of direct mail is its high cost per unit, which causes a continual narrowing of the number of pieces mailed unless budgets are being increased along with costs.

Repeat mailing to customer lists is sound business practice, since such high percentages of sales emanate from a small percentage of customers. However, this very selectivity can be an inhibiting factor in terms of growth. With a highly mobile population, mailing lists deteriorate and new names must be added. Customers who have moved away must be replaced. Other types of advertising must be used to build up charge accounts and customer lists. This means added expense.

But direct mail remains the most selective, most cost-controllable, most flexible, and most versatile of all advertising media. Looked-for or unsolicited, direct mail *does* get into the household.

Whether or not it is opened—and, if opened, read—is the problem of the creative department. The impersonal, inaccurate aspects, the uncertainty of delivery dates, the rising costs are negative factors to be considered by the advertiser. But the exciting possibilities of measured response by the precise people to whom the message is directed can tip the scales to direct mail advertising as a most effective tool for the retail advertiser.

QUESTIONS FOR DISCUSSION AND CLASS ASSIGNMENTS

1. Escalating costs of postage and mailing has created major financial problems for mail order and retail organizations. Discuss how these retailers can cope with rising costs and maintain profit levels.
2. Bring in to class all the unsolicited (occupant) mail received in your home for the past two weeks. Discuss the potential value to the advertiser of the mail sent to your family.
3. Prepare and sketch a direct mail advertising piece selling the merchandise listed in Appendix 9. Remember a direct mail piece must do the entire selling job, so be sure your piece is complete.
4. Select one direct mail item from your collection (question 2) and redesign it to make it more effective.
5. Discuss some reasons why direct mail will always be a primary method of advertising for small retail operations.
6. Discuss the pros and cons of developing your own direct mail campaigns versus hiring freelance direct mail specialists to do the work. Give reasons to defend your position.
7. Discuss the good and bad features of statement enclosures that solicit additional business from charge customers when they receive their monthly statements.
8. Discuss the phenomenon of people requesting that their names be added to mailing lists, according to the Direct Mail Marketing Association, when there seems to be popular resentment against unsolicited mail.
9. Discuss how direct response advertising, despite its high cost per unit, could be the most cost-efficient type of advertising.
10. There has been considerable growth of advertisers' use of newspaper insertions to distribute preprinted sections as a means of offsetting rising postage and distribution costs. What are the advantages and disadvantages of this type of distribution?

Chapter 6
Radio: The "New" Local Advertising Medium

At the end of 1980, there were 8933 radio stations operating in the United States, according to *Broadcasting Yearbook*, 1981 edition. Of these, 4575 were commercial AM stations and 3272 were commercial FM stations. In addition there were 1086 noncommercial FMs (educational, religious, and public service stations). It is estimated by the Radio Advertising Bureau, national sales arm of the radio industry, that there are 457.5 million working radios in the United States, 50 million purchased in 1980. A more graphic picture of the pervasiveness of radio appears when we note that there are 5.7 radio sets in the average American household. Ninety-nine percent of all homes have at least one working radio. (*Radio Facts*, Radio Advertising Bureau, 1981)

If we take into account that the estimated number of newspapers in the country is 1763 dailies and that newspapers have positioned themselves as the local advertising medium best able to serve retailers, it seems radio would fit that role as well, if not better. With almost 9000 stations serving the needs of many towns and cities that may not have a daily newspaper, the radio station is

Figure 6.1   B.C.'s comment on radio advertising, which points up the strong recall of an established product name. (SOURCE: By permission of Johnny Hart and Field Enterprises, Inc.)

the main source of news, information, and entertainment in many communities (Figure 6.1).

It seems strange, then, that it is only in recent years that the retail community has "discovered" radio as an advertising medium and has incorporated radio into advertising plans on a regular and consistent basis. Perhaps it was considered not necessary to use anything other than newspaper advertising, with a little direct mail thrown in to reach charge account customers. Perhaps it was the conviction that merchandise, especially fashion, must be illustrated, with art or photography, and that could only be done in print. And maybe it was because the radio industry was content doing business with advertising agencies and national manufacturers and did not need to seek out and convince retailers to advertise.

The positioning of radio as a local medium puts it into a perspective retail-advertisers can accept. Now we can talk about radio ads, instead of radio commercials. To the retailer, "ads" are devices for getting sales results and customer traffic. "Commercials" are the kind of advertising that only national advertisers can afford, and they are not designed to make people hurry to a store to buy merchandise.

The fact that radio stations operate, according to their licenses with the Federal Communication Commission, in the public interest, convenience, and necessity obliges them to become closely involved with the community in which they broadcast. Executives and employees of the station spend much of their time in the community, use their facilities to communicate with the people, help improve local conditions, and discuss civic, educational and economic problems. That's about as local a relationship as any business can have. This same description applies to retailers' relationships with their communities. The retailer ascertains the community's fashion needs, its requirements for all kinds of merchandise, and then purchases, displays, and advertises the merchandise to satisfy those needs. Wise retailers also involve themselves in general community problems and activities to establish themselves as good citizens and as "people with whom others like to do business." Chain stores often insist on local branch managers becoming involved in community activities, chambers of commerce, or merchants' associations. Retailers, media managers, newspaper editors, radio and TV station managers all get involved in the affairs of the market area they serve.

THE REDISCOVERY OF RADIO AS AN ADVERTISING MEDIUM

Prior to the early fifties and the arrival of network television, radio was, to a great extent, the all-purpose entertainment and information medium. Stations would program for the widest possible audiences. A typical day's output could include "wake-up" music to start the day, followed by farm news, the weather, and news reports; then the morning shows and soap operas to entertain the housewife and shut-ins; then the evening news, and the full spectrum of entertainment—drama, variety shows, game shows. The day closed with music and late news. When TV arrived on the scene, adding pictures to the sound that radio afforded, the demise of radio was predicted. But it didn't happen; radio adapted and grew.

In the "Golden Days of Radio," as stations changed programming as the day progressed, they discovered that they would gain or lose audience with each change. If the listeners did not like what was being offered at that time, they would switch to another station more to their liking. In a somewhat evolutionary manner, radio stations found that if they stayed with a particular type of programming for longer periods of time, they held their audiences for longer periods. From this evolved current programming techniques in radio, where stations program the same way every day, thereby attracting the same kind of listener all the time. These listeners, tuning in on a regular basis to their favorite stations, represent a segment of the market that can be reached by the advertiser who buys time on that station.

This demographic programming characteristic of radio was reported on by the *Los Angeles Times* in August 1976 under the headline, "You Are What You Listen To." The article said, in part:

"Your choice of radio station indicates more than your taste in music. The resting place of that needle on your radio dial, in fact, may be telling your friends as much about you as your Social Security number tells the government."

"By knowing what kind of station you listen to, they think they'll be able to guess your preferences in such items as salad dressings, toilet tissue, dog food, vacation spots and hair spray."

"The information comes from a 50-volume survey (Target Group Index) . . . of the buying habits of radio listeners, covering 13 formats ranging from classical music to golden oldies to farm reports."

"If you're a classical fan, you're one of the best targets for ads about European vacations (especially in Greece), wines, imported cars and banking and investment services."

"You're a good mark for a pitch about buying books or records by mail."

"You're one of the top consumers of Cinzano and Tribuno Vermouth, Heineken and Lowenbrau beer, gin and brandy."

"When it comes to advertising, radio has it way over television in pegging audience preferences."

Remember our previous discussion of targeting the advertising message to a specific audience? It is this ability to zero in on exact types of audiences that makes radio interesting to the retailer. Knowing the demographic breakdown of a medium's audience has become one of the strongest reasons for the growing use of radio as an advertising medium by retailers. Demographic information is available to retailers in many forms (Figure 6.2):

- Age. Most surveys report age by 12+; 12 to 17 (teenagers); 18+; 18 to 24; 25 to 34; 35 to 49; 50 to 64; and 65+.
- Sex. Knowing whether the audience is male or female is vital.
- Income. This is a strong determining factor in the price lines featured in the ad.
- Education. This is an indication for inclusion or addition of certain types of goods and services (for example, listeners with high school or less education would not be prime targets for sophisticated scientific or economics books).
- Occupation. White collar or blue collar might be a factor to be considered.

There are many more possible demographic breakdowns. Depending on research needs, they could include ethnic background, religion, and other data. Research departments for all media provide clients and sales staffs a wealth of information which is usually made available to advertisers on request (Figures 6.3 and 6.4).

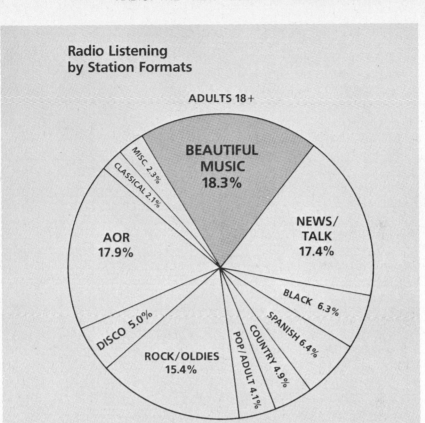

Radio Listening by Station Formats

ADULTS 18+

BEAUTIFUL MUSIC 18.3%

MISC. 2.3%

CLASSICAL 2.1%

AOR 17.9%

NEWS/ TALK 17.4%

BLACK 6.3%

SPANISH 6.4%

COUNTRY 4.9%

POP/ADULT 4.1%

DISCO 5.0%

ROCK/OLDIES 15.4%

ARBITRON Los Angeles Metro Share of Average ¼ Hour Estimates, Monday-Sunday, 6AM-Midnight, October/November 1979. Estimates subject to the qualifications in the original research.

Figure 6.2   Radio listening by station formats shows the percentage of listening to different programming. (SOURCE: By permission of Allen S. Klein & Associates.)

RADIO AUDIENCE RESEARCH SERVICES

The demographic story of radio is logical. It tells retailers that:

- Young audiences listen to contemporary or rock music (stations programming this kind of music carry ads for acne creams, blue jeans, records, and other youth-oriented items).
- Men listen to sports events (logical audiences for men's wear stores, home improvement merchandise).
- Women listen to stations programming mellow rock music (ideal for the fashion merchandiser).
- "Upscale" men and women listen to news broadcasts (logical for men's and women's fashions or family needs).

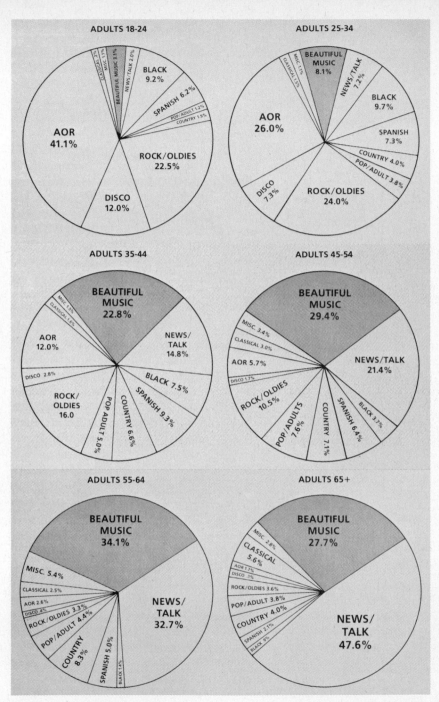

Figure 6.3   Listening patterns change by age groupings found in radio audience rating reports. (SOURCE: By permission of Allen S. Klein & Associates.)

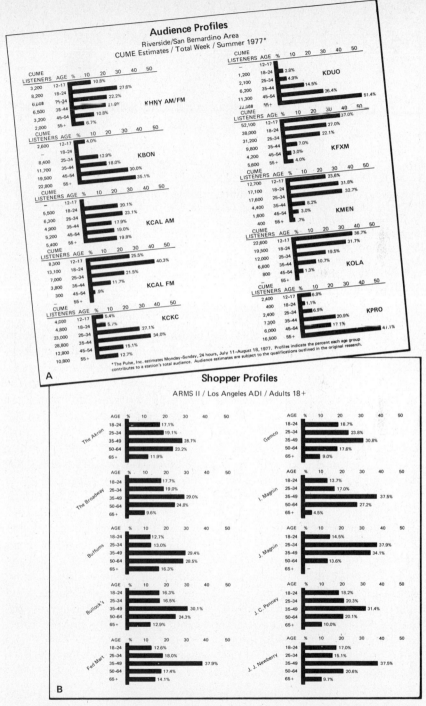

Figure 6.4 (A) Audience profiles: The percentages of each age group's contribution to the station's total audience. Age groups invariably match up with the traditional radio audience formats. (B) Shopper profiles: The age demographics of the stores' shoppers can be matched with the age demographics of the stations. (SOURCE: By permission of Allen S. Klein & Associates.)

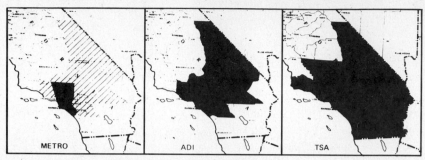

Figure 6.5   Map of Southern California depicting the areas covered by rating services. The metro survey area (MSA) generally corresponds to the Standard Metropolitan Statistical Area (SMSA). ADI, a television measurement, means area of dominant influence and reflects counties or area with the dominant share of viewing hours. TSA, total survey area, is a geographic area that includes the Metro Survey Area plus certain counties located outside the MSA. (SOURCE: The Arbitron Company, 1980. Used by permission.)

These demographic facts are gathered by audience research services, the most popular of which is Arbitron (originally known as ARB for American Research Bureau). In the past, audience research services such as Hooper, Trendex, and Pulse offered similar information, with varying methods of collecting data. They are no longer in business, however, and Arbitron is the widely accepted service measuring audiences for the radio industry. Other rating services, such as Media Statistics are in the radio ratings business, but they do not have the countrywide acceptance of Arbitron at this time. Arbitron also measures television audiences, as does Nielsen.

Since there is no way of measuring radio or television audiences exactly, as we can with newspaper readers (press runs and circulation can be counted), the broadcast industry depends on surveys to estimate audiences. It must be remembered that broadcast ratings and shares of audiences are *estimates* and not actual figures carved in concrete. However, in the absence of any other system, media buyers and advertisers rely on the rating numbers as "the only game in town." All rating services state that they give estimates, to cover themselves legally, but advertising people often tend to overlook that point.

The Arbitron method of collecting radio audience information should be understood by advertisers. Surveys cover market areas that are designated as (Figure 6.5):

Metro. Equivalent to the primary market area of newspaper audits

Total Survey Area (TSA). The full range of all radio signals in the district

Area of Dominant Influence (ADI). A TV measurement term applied to radio listening in major metropolitan areas

Households to be surveyed are chosen from telephone directories. In order to include nontelephone homes, such as in ethnic or low-income areas, households adjacent to telephone households are surveyed in those areas.

Four Arbitron reports are issued annually. Surveys are now taken over forty-four weeks during the year. The "books" are published seasonally. Advertisers concern themselves with "four book averages"—the average of a full year's reports of radio listening—as a more reliable measurement than any one report, which could rate a station accidentally high or low because of special circumstances in the survey.

After a household has been contacted by telephone, a letter is sent to the family enlisting its cooperation, and asking it to keep a diary of radio listening for seven consecutive days (Thursday through Wednesday), with each member of the family keeping a separate diary (Figure 6.6). The diary keeper must list the times of day spent listening to the radio and the call letters of the stations listened to. Special attention is given to diaries placed in ethnic households, with follow-up phone calls, diary retrieval by mail when personal calls are inconvenient, and so on. To assure the placement of sufficient diaries in the preselected sample area, as many as five phone calls will be made at various times of day and evening to solicit the cooperation of the selected households. Although great care is exercised in the distribution of the diaries to cover the designated sample area, there is no control over the number of usable (properly completed) diaries returned for tabulation or the sections of the survey area from where they originated. Imbalances can occur in the report when a disproportionate number of diaries come in from one section of the survey area. To offset this, diary return quotas are established for each sampling unit, with a probability factor included relating to the population in the survey area. As an example, in Arbitron, Summer, 1980 the average number of in-tab, or usable, diaries was 3801 in the Los Angeles/Orange County area, two counties with over 7.5 million people and 3.5 million homes. Each diary received and tabulated represented seven days of listening and nonlistening, so each day's listening was projected against the total sample.

Arbitron reports the average quarter-hour and cume listening estimates by *dayparts* (time of day) and by age and sex. *Average*

How To Fill In the Arbitron Diary

Please carry the Arbitron diary with you wherever you go during the seven days of the survey. *Then, each time you listen to radio*

❶ Please fill in the time you start listening and the time you stop. Be sure to use AM to indicate morning and PM to indicate afternoon and evening. For times that begin or end at 12 o'clock, please use Noon or Midnight ("Mid"). Whenever you change stations, please start on a new line.

❷ Check (√) either the AM or the FM column to indicate whether you are listening to the AM radio dial or FM radio dial.

❸ Fill in the call letters of the station you are listening to. If you don't know the call letters, fill in the name of the program, or the dial setting.

❹ Check (√) to show whether you are listening at home or away from home.

❺ If you don't listen to radio on a certain day, check (√) the circle at the bottom of the page for that day.

HERE'S WHAT A SAMPLE PAGE MIGHT LOOK LIKE

TIME		STATION			PLACE	
(Indicate AM or PM)		CHECK ONE (√)		FILL IN STATION "CALL LETTERS" (IF YOU DON'T KNOW THEM, FILL IN PROGRAM NAME OR DIAL SETTING)	CHECK ONE (√)	
FROM—	TO—	AM	FM		AT HOME	AWAY-FROM-HOME (INCLUDING IN A CAR)
6:40AM	7:30AM	❷ √		WWTM	❹ √	
10:10AM	NOON	√		PIERCE SHOW		√
4:45PM	5:20PM	√		WREF		√
6:30PM	8:30PM	√		WWAC	√	
10:50PM	MID		√	88.1 on the dial	√	

PLEASE CHECK HERE **❺** IF YOU DID NOT LISTEN TO RADIO TODAY.

IMPORTANT: Many stations broadcast on both AM and FM. For this Arbitron survey, it is important to correctly identify whether you are listening on AM or FM (even though the station may use the same call letters and broadcast the same thing over the air).

In order to have an accurate record of your radio listening, please fill in your own diary regardless of your age or handwriting ability. To keep your Arbitron diary from getting mixed up with any others in your home, please fill in your initials (or first name) here.

Figure 6.6 Instruction page from an Arbitron radio diary, telling the person keeping the diary how to fill it in correctly so that the information can be properly tabulated. (SOURCE: The Arbitron Company, *Quick Reference Guide to Arbitron Radio Market Report,* September 1977. By permission.)

quarter-hour means the average number of listeners tuned into a station during a daypart. *Cume* is the number of *different* people listening to a station over a given period of time. It is the net or unduplicated audience of the station. Retailers understand the difference between gross and net, and the two terms mean roughly the

KABC
TALKRADIO 790 abc

60 SECOND RATE

TIME	GRID I			GRID II			GRID III			GRID IV			PRE-EMPTIBLE GRID V		
	12x	18x	24x	12x	18x	24x	12x	18x	24x	12x	18x	24x	12x	18x	24x
AAA	$225	$220	$215	$195	$190	$185	$180	$175	$170	$160	$155	$150	$150	$145	$140
AA	150	145	140	125	120	115	100	95	90	85	80	75	75	70	65
A	85	80	75	75	70	65	70	65	60	65	60	55	60	55	50
B	45	—	—	40	—	—	35	—	—	25	—	—	25	—	—
TAP PLAN ⅓ AAA, ⅓ AA, ⅓ A	130	125	120	115	110	105	100	95	90	90	85	80	75	—	—

TIME CLASSIFICATIONS
AAA: Mon–Sat 5–10AM, 3–8PM
AA: Mon–Sat 10–3PM, Sun 8AM–8PM
A: Mon–Sun 8PM–Mid, Sun 6–8AM
B: Mon–Sun Mid–5AM

30-SECOND ANNOUNCEMENTS: 80% of applicable minute rate.
10-SECOND ANNOUNCEMENTS: 50% of applicable minute rate.

Figure 6.7   Rate card from a news/talk station with high audience ratings. Prices reflect the large number of listeners; rates vary by daypart at all times. The grid level varies in direct contrast to the pressure on the limited number of commercial minutes available for sale to advertisers. (SOURCE: By permission of KABC Radio, Los Angeles.)

same thing. *Dayparts* are the periods that make up the radio day:

6 A.M. to 10 A.M. is morning drive time
10 A.M. to 3 P.M. is mid-day (formerly housewife time)
3 P.M. to 7 P.M. is afternoon drive time
7 P.M. to midnight is night time
Midnight to 6 A.M. is late night time

Radio station rates are based on the size of the listening audience, with prices highest when the audience is at its peak. Generally rates are highest on AM stations during morning and afternoon drive times, while FM contemporary stations appealing to young audiences get their highest prices from 3 to 7 P.M., when youngsters are out of school (see Figures 6.7 and 6.8). The extent to which radio has grown as an advertising medium is best indicated by a continuing study of media audience trends and media costs conducted annually by McCann-Erickson, one of America's most successful advertising agencies. According to the 1980 RAB Fact Book, covering the period from 1967 to 1979, radio's costs-per-thousand have increased the least of all the measured media.

Cost-per-thousand, or CPM, is the arithmetic formula that

 **LOS ANGELES**
RATE CARD #16 EFFECTIVE NOVEMBER 1, 1980

GENERAL ADVERTISING RATES

	GRID I		GRID II		GRID III		GRID IV		GRID V	
	:60's	:30's	:60's	:30's	:60's	:30's	:60's	:30's	:60's	:30's
CLASS AAAA 5A-10A Mon-Sat. 3P-8P Mon-Fri. 10A-8P Sat/Sun.										
6X	$205	$175	$190	$162	$180	$153	$170	$145	$155	$132
12X	200	171	185	158	175	149	165	141	150	128
18X	195	167	180	154	170	145	160	137	145	124
24X	190	163	175	150	165	141	155	134	140	120
CLASS AAA 10A-3P Mon-Fri.										
6X	180	154	165	141	155	132	145	123	130	111
12X	175	150	160	137	150	128	140	119	125	107
18X	170	146	155	133	145	124	135	115	120	103
24X	165	142	150	129	140	120	130	111	115	99
CLASS AA 8P-1A Mon-Sun. 8A-10A Sunday										
6X	165	141	150	128	140	119	130	106	115	98
12X	160	137	145	124	135	115	125	102	110	94
18X	155	133	140	120	130	111	120	98	105	90
24X	150	129	135	116	125	107	115	94	100	86
CLASS A 1A-5A Mon-Sun.	32		27		22		17		12	

CONDITIONS

This rate card is for information purposes only and does not constitute an offer. Specific requests for selected days or hours within a classification available at a 20% premium. Frequency Announcements and Total Audience Plans are combinable for discount. Total Audience Plan preemptible by base-rate advertisers. Sixty second and thirty second announcements are combinable for discount. All Night Package rotates in each hour block over six days. This package does not combine for further discount. Commission of 15 per cent on net time only to recognized advertising agencies: no cash discount. All bills payable when rendered. No time sold in bulk for resale. Rates quoted are guaranteed for a period of 30 days from the effective date of any rate increase, providing that advertising is actually running at time of effective date of increase and continues without interruption. Advertising must conform to the standards of the station and the station reserves the right to refuse or discontinue any advertising for reasons satisfactory to itself. All advance material must be received at least 48 hours before first broadcast. 72 hours prior to a Monday start. Spots missed due to late copy will be billed.

Offices and Studios
3321 South La Cienega Boulevard
Los Angeles, California 90016
Phone: (213) 557-7000

Personnel
Vice President & General Manager. Bill Sommers
General Sales Manager. Lee Larsen
Sales Manager. Simon T.

National Representatives Katz Radio

News Service
AP Broadcast Wire, AP-A Wire, City News Service. UPI Broadcast Wire, UPI-A Wire, UPI Sports. UPI Regional, ABC Network News. American FM Radio Network.

Facilities
ERP 68,000 Watts horizontal and vertical polarization at 95.5 MHz, broadcasting 24 hours per day in full stereo, antenna is 2.970 feet above average terrain.

Figure 6.8 Rate card from KLOS, Los Angeles, a contemporary music station. Its rates reflect the heavier listening pattern of younger audiences during afternoons and early evenings and on weekends. For contrast, KABC's prices are highest during the morning commuter drive (Figure 6.7). (SOURCE: By permission of KLOS, Los Angeles.)

translates the cost of an advertisement and the audience it is expected to reach into a meaningful relationship. It answers the question: What will it cost to reach 1000 homes (or adult men, or women age 18 to 49, or whatever demographic group the advertiser is aiming for). CPM allows for comparisons within the same medium. The figure is the result of dividing estimates of the number of homes (or men, or women) into the cost of the time or space:

$$\frac{\$200}{100 \text{ M adult men}} = \$2 \text{ CPM}$$

It is difficult to compare media by CPM, because prime-time television could run quite high—$5 to $8 or more CPM—while radio and newspapers deliver lower CPMs—$1 to $2. Smart buyers avoid the danger of relying *solely* on the rating books in making media decisions by using ratings as *indicators* or *trends* and adding their own good judgment and expertise to the ultimate decision. The wide margin of error inherent in survey-type research requires the application of logic to final media-buying decisions.

The McCann-Erickson annual report on media quoted in the 1980 RAB Fact Book, showed that newspaper CPM increased 113 percent, in the 1967–1979 period; magazine increased 57 percent; outdoor, 105 percent, and television, 104 percent. During the same period radio CPM rose only 52 percent. This cost efficiency has been one of the motivating factors in the expanded use of radio as an advertising medium by retailers.

Another indicator of this trend is the percentage of radio business placed by advertisers on the local level compared to that placed on the national level by manufacturers and their advertising agencies. Although the figures for national versus local sales were 70 to 30 percent in favor of national as recently as 1970, reports from radio sources indicate that the numbers have reversed themselves; it is now closer to 70 percent local and 30 percent national sales at the average major radio station.

The burgeoning use of radio by retailers is a strong contributing factor to this swing to radio by local advertisers. A highly circulated report from the pages of *Women's Wear Daily* in January 1980, stated in part:

> No longer just a secondary medium used to promote traditional holiday businesses and sales, radio is steadily emerging as a year-round vehicle for selling regular-price merchandise—and even as a primary medium in some store's merchandising and positioning campaigns.
>
> Entering the Eighties, radio has several things going for it. It is the primary medium of the younger customer—a segment of the market

being hotly pursued by many of the nation's retailers—and a stronger medium with working women, a group which will grow in number and affluence in coming years.

The article dwelt on radio's ability to reach commuters driving to and from work and its programming focus on specific segments of the public.

An interesting quirk of fate also contributed to the growth of radio advertising at the local market level. When the Surgeon General of the United States declared that tobacco was injurious to health and cigarette advertising was banned from radio and television, radio stations turned to the local market, and to the retailers in their areas, to develop new business for their stations to replace the revenue cigarette advertising had given them in the past. This concentration of effort on retail sales, with research and sales development forces marshaled for the effort, has brought many more retailers into radio in recent years.

We discussed the population shift to the suburbs that took place after World War II, and how newspapers failed to move with the people. This factor opened doors for enterprising radio stations. Sales presentations were developed to show retailers the lessened coverage they were getting from their newspaper advertising, with suggestions and ideas showing how the addition of radio advertising could supplement and improve the efficiency of their advertising expenditures. The plan worked. Retailers learned again that radio advertising can bring sales results. The rest is current history.

For a business that was going into decline, as was predicted when television networks became a fact of life, radio is a very healthy "invalid." In 1976, total radio sales nationally topped the $2 billion mark for the first time in history. In 1980, sales reached the highest level ever—$3.7 billion nationally—with all indicators pointing to continued growth.

SIMILARITIES OF RADIO AND NEWSPAPER ADVERTISING

We have covered the local aspects of both radio and newspapers, especially their close connection with the community. There are other similarities. Both radio and newspapers are *personal* media. People read the papers alone. They listen to radio alone, for the most part. Many advertisers think the only time people listen to the radio is in their cars. However, whenever a survey has been taken asking where people listen to radio, at least 50 percent indicate that their radio listening occurs in the home. When you consider the statistics that the average home has 5.7 radios, including car radios, it seems reasonable.

Retailers who recognize the personal nature of radio write their radio copy for individuals—in effect, they *talk to one person at a time*. Anyone who has ever taken a course in sales or read an article on the basics of selling knows that the ideal situation for making a sale is face-to-face with a prospect. Both radio and newspaper afford the retail advertiser this kind of opportunity. Check your local newspaper or listen to radio commercials and notice how many retail ads fail to take this fact into consideration. They may consider it, or be aware of the personal nature of the medium, but the ads do not always reflect it.

Radio listening and newspaper reading are *habits*. You read the paper at a certain time of day, in a specific pattern. You have a favorite paper; you know the writers, the comics, the special features. The same is true of radio. People have favorite radio stations. They listen at specific times of day—on the way to work, while working in the yard, and so on. They know the announcers, the personalities, the kind of music the station plays. They consistently listen to one or two stations (nationally, according to a CBS survey, people have 2.5 favorite stations), and usually listen to their first choice 70 to 75 percent of the time. This loyalty does not extend to TV, where people switch channels to see favorite programs.

How does the retailer use this information? By placing advertising to coincide with the reading and listening habits of the store's customers. Men's wear ads go into the sports pages of the newspaper and on or adjacent to the sports news on radio. "Hard" news sections or radio newscasts attract consumers, both men and women, making them good locations for general merchandise ads. Young people generally listen to contemporary music stations and read the entertainment sections of the newspaper. Again, the placement of ads with a view to the reading and listening habits of the potential customer presents an ideal selling opportunity for the retail advertiser (see Figures 6.3 and 6.4).

The similarities of the two media support a technique many retailers employ—using radio to back up their newspaper ads. They use radio to talk about an upcoming event, to build anticipation, to call attention to the ad "running on page 22 in today's paper." They address the ad to the same kind of person to whom they are advertising in the paper. Since people have favorite stores where they do a majority of their shopping and tend to read the ads of the stores where they shop, retailers use radio to reach a broad segment of their markets—their own customers and people who might not be their customers.

Many newspapers advertise on the radio to build circulation for their papers, inviting subscribers to buy home delivery of the paper. They also use radio to increase the readership of the newspaper by talking about special features, major news stories, and newspaper promotions. Newspapers often invite radio listeners to look for the advertised values in the pages of the paper.

An outgrowth of the similar positions of radio and newspapers is intense rivalry and competition for the retailers' advertising budget. As noted, when radio stations were forced to look for new business prospects after they lost cigarette advertising, they turned to newspapers as the medium from which they could divert advertising dollars, using some of the reasons we have given to attract retail advertisers.

ADVANTAGES OF RADIO ADVERTISING

In addition to supporting newspaper advertising by reminding people to read the paper to get more information about special sales, retailers use radio to *call attention to special mailings and special events*. Since most direct mail is sent to limited numbers of charge customers or purchased mailings lists, some stores use radio to tell customers to watch for something special in the mail. They attain greater readership of the mailer, while telling the general public, or noncustomers, that something of interest is taking place.

One store used a heavy radio campaign during morning drive time at the beginning of a white sale event, inviting people who had not received a copy of the white sale catalog to come to the store to get one. Not only did they remind their charge customers about the sale, but they attracted great numbers of new customers who were not on the mailing list.

Adding radio to any advertising campaign seems to have the synergistic effect of making the impact of the advertising effort more than the sum of the media used. Greater awareness of an event occurs if newspaper *and* radio are used. There seems to be a combination of new people reached, plus a stronger motivation to action on the part of the people who are reached twice, by each medium, thus reinforcing the ad's strength.

High on the list of the advantages of radio advertising is its *cost efficiency*. Radio has always had the lowest cost-per-thousand ratio (next to newspapers) and reaches more of the target audience for less money than other media. This is because of the selectivity of radio, with the wide choice of program formats delivering specific segments of the population, keeping waste circulation down.

Radio is also efficient in production. The cost of producing television can be enormous, frequently 20 to 25 percent of the cost of the time. Print advertising production involves paper, printing, type, illustrations, engravings, and the like. Effective radio spots can be produced with just the cost of the air time, if you use the talents of the announcer or personalities of the station. Your station salespeople will help write the copy, arrange for the use of public domain music and sound effects (at your disposal at many stations), and the ad is on the air.

Of course, hiring professional commercial producers is recommended if the budget is large enough and if competition and the store image demands quality production. Even then, the cost of the most expensive radio commercial, including talent, musicians, writers, singer, and directors, is only a fraction of the cost of producing a television commercial of similar quality.

In radio, *your message stands alone*, with no other advertising competing for the listener's attention while yours is on. In a newspaper, unless the store buys most of the page, there is bound to be other advertising on the page, distracting the reader from your message. Sometimes, a direct competitor could wind up on the same page. On radio, nothing else can be on while your message is being delivered, and if the spot is attention-grabbing, interesting, and well written and produced, you will have the full audience of that station listening. Think of this: The smallest retailer is just as big, and can make as much impact with a 60-second radio spot, as General Motors, because 60 seconds is 60 seconds. A small retailer finds it hard to compete in print against multiple-page sections and full-color supplements, but radio is a great equalizer. However, it takes the right idea, presented in a unique, interesting way, to make the message memorable, and to motivate customers to action.

Radio has *more than 100 percent circulation!* How is that possible? Simple. We use newspaper circulation as a measure of market coverage. But it tells us only how many papers are sold to people and/or delivered to households. Since radios are in virtually every household in the United States, and in most cases there are five or six per household, by that standard radio has more than 100 percent coverage. Our point here is that circulation does not mean readership, any more than 5.7 radios means 5.7 people are listening.

In addition to great penetration of households, radios are in most automobiles. Radio Advertising Bureau surveys indicate that 98 percent of all cars are radio-equipped, and that over 70 percent have AM and FM capabilities (Figure 6.9). This makes radio the most *mobile* of all advertising media; it goes with people wherever they may choose to go. Radio is called the ubiquitous medium, of-

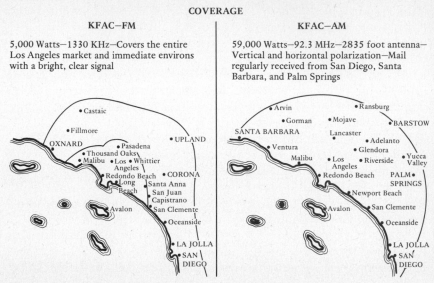

COVERAGE

KFAC—FM

5,000 Watts—1330 KHz—Covers the entire Los Angeles market and immediate environs with a bright, clear signal

KFAC—AM

59,000 Watts—92.3 MHz—2835 foot antenna— Vertical and horizontal polarization—Mail regularly received from San Diego, Santa Barbara, and Palm Springs

Figure 6.9   Radio station coverage map. Information piece distributed by a radio station company owning an AM and FM facility in the same market, showing the different coverage of the two stations. (SOURCE: By permission of KFAC, AM/FM, Los Angeles.)

fering advertisers the unique opportunity of reaching consumers virtually at the point of sale. The alert advertiser can talk to potential customers in their cars on heavy shopping days, while they're on their way, and perhaps convince them to visit X shopping center this Saturday instead of the usual Y.

Retailers love the *immediacy* of radio, with its ability to handle price changes and even item changes. This great flexibility has been limited somewhat by the arrival of automation in radio broadcasting. But if there is a schedule running, and programmed, it is possible to make copy changes faster in radio ads than in newspaper or television. This ability to keep messages current, to take advantage of sudden market changes, to beat competition to the punch, makes radio attractive to the aggressive fashion advertiser. It is not always possible to buy air time on short notice, but once on, quick changes can be made in your own copy most of the time.

Retailers always look for *quick response* to their ads. They want immediate reaction from the buying public in terms of store traffic and direct sales. Radio's *immediacy* and *timeliness* fit into this plan. Immediate increases in sales can be traced when radio is added to an advertising program that did not previously include radio. Retailers sometimes ask customers where they learned about the event that brought them to the store. Others report a general increase in store traffic and sales during and after an interesting, motivating radio campaign. Many small retailers spend all their advertising money in radio, finding it more effective than other media. In major markets, many retailers commit a sizable portion of their ad budgets to radio, building a balanced media mix based on the store's particular needs.

One weakness of newspaper advertising is the lack of thoroughness with which the ad is read. The reader might be stopped by the art work and layout, read the headline and the first few words of copy, but not all the rest. "Copy" is often viewed with disdain by the retail advertiser, and the ad manager is instructed to keep the copy to a minimum, thereby limiting the chance of the ad doing an adequate selling job.

In radio, however, each word of the copy is equally important. It is literally all headline. It means that every word of the message must be carefully selected, weighed, polished, and tested to be sure it says exactly what the advertiser wants it to say. There is no place to hide the disclaimers, no place for asterisks (with qualifications of the claim buried somewhere on the page). This is also one reason why some advertisers shy away from radio advertising.

Imagine if the warning in cigarette advertising required in print or on billboards was as large in type size as the headline. Do you think cigarette advertisers would devote 14 words out of a possible 150-word radio ad to say, in bold tones, "Warning: The Surgeon General Has Determined That Cigarette Smoking Is Dangerous To Your Health"? No chance. Even if it were permissible to advertise cigarettes on radio, manufacturers would shy away from the impact of that statement. It would, in fact, discourage sales, as the antismoking campaign did when cigarettes were advertised on broadcast media.

Federal Trade Commission rulings insist that all claims made in ads be fully substantiated in the ad. If there is a warranty or a guarantee, it must be clearly spelled out. In radio, there is no small print to hide the disclaimer. This could be construed as a weakness of radio as an advertising medium, but not necessarily. If the claim or benefit in the ad is straightforward, without strings attached, it can be advertised on radio. From the consumer's standpoint, it almost seems that only the completely honest advertiser can use radio, while the less openhanded operators resort to other means, and other media. This is not to say that these advertisers are less honest. Rather, they avoid the bother and potential problem by withholding certain items from the radio campaign.

No discussion of radio can omit one of its unique qualities—

the ability to create *pictures in the mind* of the listener. By use of the proper words or sound effects or music, any image can be created in the imagination of the listener (see Exhibits 6.1 and 6.2). Music can establish a favorable mood and setting for the advertiser's message. Want to talk about Parisian fashions? Start with a lilting French melody, with accordions, and the picture of Paris comes to mind. Want to sell Western-style jeans? A few bars of a typical Western song establish the scene. It works. Try it on your friends.

Remarkably, the words alone can do the trick. A well-written novel does the same thing, allowing readers to picture in their own minds the mists billowing across the moors in a Sherlock Holmes mystery; smell the fresh, invigorating sea breeze in a sailing boat; or visualize the filth and squalor of a Dickens slum. Each radio listener may not see the same two people comparing the whiteness or brightness of their laundry, but won't everyone see two people? And the human brain has an infinite capacity for remembering. The first few notes of an old song bring back the memory of a lost love, of fun at school, of a happy vacation. People can remember radio commercials they heard when they were small children. We can play a tape of pretelevision radio spots and find they are instantly remembered, even though they have not been broadcast commercially in over 20 years. In many cases, the jingle has outlived the product itself!

WEAKNESSES OF RADIO AS A FASHION ADVERTISING MEDIUM

Despite this easily demonstrated quality of radio—the ability to create pictures in the mind of the listener—fashion retailers have been slow to accept radio as a medium to advertise fashion. There have been too many years of print advertising, with the advertised fashion, drawn or photographed, illustrated on the page. The tangibility of the printed newspaper ad, the tearsheet taken from the published paper, and the unquestioned fact that the ad *did* appear in the paper are things in which the retailer believes.

Newspaper and direct mail advertising are concrete, solid. The advertiser can pick it up, re-read it, hang it on the wall, hold meetings about it. Hard to do with a radio spot, which is broadcast over the airwaves; who knows who is *really* listening?

Unless the advertising department or the radio station furnishes a copy of the commercial and a tape recorder on which to play it, it is difficult for a department manager to hold a meeting with the sales staff. With a newspaper ad, the manager can show the

EXHIBIT 6.1

RADIO SCRIPT, OHRBACH'S, NEW YORK (60 SECONDS)

Radio script from Radio Advertising Bureau, with the comedy team of Stiller and Meara. Slightly irreverent humor makes the selling point of fashion at popular prices.

ANNOUNCER: Stiller and Meara for Ohrbach's.

MEARA: Welcome to Last Chance, the sensitivity group for people who are flunking life. Now who wants to share their problems? Speak up, don't be afraid.

STILLER: I'll share.

MEARA: What's your name, Dummy?

STILLER: Sherman Doiley. Lately my life is empty and drab, I'd be better off dead. My mother's a trumpet player. When she sees me, she plays taps.

MEARA: Sherman, you're a victim! Look at you, you even dress like a loser. Nobody wears a noose for a necktie.

STILLER: It's my hang-up, I'm hopeless, I've tried everything . . . yoga, yogurt, tribal, primal. . . .

MEARA: Have you tried Ohrbach's?

STILLER: Ohrbach's the store?

MEARA: Yeah, Ohrbach's give you the security of being in style.

STILLER: My mother took me there.

MEARA: For once your mother was right. For years people have been shopping at Ohrbach's and getting top quality fashions.

STILLER: But can I afford it?

MEARA: You can't afford *not* to. Besides Ohrbach's expands your wardrobe without shrinking your wallet.

STILLER: Oh, you mean from now on I'll stop feeling the way I feel?

MEARA: No, Sherman, but at least you'll stop looking the way you look.

ANNOUNCER: When you're ready for the greatest fashion values in town, you're ready for Ohrbach's.

SOURCE: Radio Advertising Bureau, New York. Copyright RAB. Used by permission.

EXHIBIT 6.2

RADIO SCRIPT, DAYTON'S WAREHOUSE SALE (60 SECONDS)

Radio script for Dayton's, Minneapolis. Dick and Bert, popular radio commercial team, demonstrate the versatility of radio, making one of the dullest retail promotions—the warehouse sale—interesting and exciting. A most effective spot judging from sales results.

BOSS: And so, Shirley, welcome to the stenographic pool.

SHIRLEY (MALE VOICE): Thank you, sir.

BOSS: Any questions?

SHIRLEY: Uh, yes. May I be excused to attend Dayton's fabulous Warehouse Sale?

BOSS: Mr. Shirley, you've only been with the firm five minutes.

SHIRLEY: Well, I know. But Dayton's has this big sale.

BOSS: No.

SHIRLEY: Appliances.

BOSS: No.

SHIRLEY: Furniture.

BOSS: No. No. Just get to work, Shirley.

SHIRLEY: All right. (Sound effect—door closes, intercom buzzes)

BOSS: Yes, What?

SHIRLEY: Sir, I forgot. My moth . . . my sister is getting—let's see—married. So can I go to. . . .

BOSS: No. No. No. You're not going to Dayton's Warehouse Sale.

SHIRLEY: Oh, thank you, sir.

BOSS: Shirley, get to your shorthand.

SHIRLEY: Okay. (Sound effect—door opens) Sir.

BOSS: Yes.

SHIRLEY: I don't want to panic you or anything but I think an earthquake is due any second. So could I. . . .

BOSS: No. (Sound effect—door closes, then opens)

SHIRLEY: Ohhhh.

BOSS: What now?

SHIRLEY: Oh, I think my appendix is back.

BOSS: This is it, Shirley. The only way you're going to get out of here to go to Dayton's Fabulous Warehouse Sale is by being fired. Understand?

SHIRLEY: Yes, sir.

BOSS: Okay.

SHIRLEY: Fathead.

BOSS: You're fired.

SHIRLEY: Thank you. You won't regret this, sir.

SOURCE: Dick & Bert, a division of The DOCSI Corporation, Los Angeles. Copyright DOCSI Corporation. Courtesy of Grey Advertising, Minneapolis. Reprinted with permission.

tearsheet of the ad and talk about the special features of the advertised item. The ad can be posted for later reference by the sales staff. Records of sales made from the ad can be written directly on the ad for inclusion in the pasteup book for future reference.

A counterargument to the "we must see the picture" attitude is the ability of radio to create pictures in the minds of listeners. While an illustration of a fashion outfit can look very appealing in a newspaper ad, the merchandise is usually drawn or photographed on a tall, slender model to enhance the look and fit of the garment. The average retail fashion customer is not a tall, slender model and may look at that attractive fashion ad and think "nice, but would it look good on me?" When the listener hears the description of the dress or sports outfit on radio, he or she can picture in imagination how the garment might look on him or her. It might be intriguing enough to get the person to the shop for a closer look, and that's about all an ad can do, anyway. Once the customer is in the store, the ad has done its job and the rest is up to the merchandise and the sales staff.

Radio plays on the emotions, describing in vivid, image-producing words and music, the glamour, the beauty, the satisfaction the customer will derive from the fashions being talked about. It has been said that anything a person can visualize can be sold in a radio ad.

Radio also broadens the scope of fashion promotion. For example, even if a store could afford a full page of newspaper advertising, how many styles could be illustrated in that space? Six, perhaps even seven sketches, at most. But take the same budget, the cost of a newspaper page, buy radio time with it, and then say: "We have such an outstanding collection of styles, we could fill the main ballroom of the Waldorf-Astoria." Wouldn't that convey the idea of great selection and broad assortments to the listeners? Anyone can picture the ballroom filled with merchandise and think, "There's sure to be a style or two that's right for me in such a big selection."

One weakness of radio advertising for the fashion retailer is its transitory nature. The message is perishable; once the words are spoken, they are gone. There is no way the listener can turn back the clock to hear again the information that was missed. People do not listen attentively to every word of copy unless their attention is grabbed by the first few words. Sometimes they pick up the commercial in the middle, when a key word breaks through to their consciousness. Newspapers and direct mail can be picked up and read again. The interested radio listener must be alert to catch the commercial from the beginning the next time it is aired.

This is one reason why radio ads are run with great frequency.

The rule of thumb is that every radio ad must be heard at least three times before the information registers. It's like a new song—the first time you hear it, you hear part of it. If you like it, you hear more of it the second time. By the third time, you've heard enough to decide if you really like it. Repetition is the key to success in advertising in all cases, but mandatory in radio. An ad must be heard often enough to be remembered, and an interesting radio spot will be remembered faster, and longer.

Radio cannot show a product or service in use. A new kitchen utensil cannot be demonstrated. A word picture cannot show how a skirt drapes, how a blouse hugs the shoulders. Most people want to see before they buy, so as long as fashion remains a business of items and styles, print will be the primary medium for most retailers. Radio has a place, but it probably will never replace print.

Although radio stations have loyal listeners and strong followings for their particular type of programming or music, patterns change. When rock and roll music became popular, it pushed middle-of-the road music out of the top spot. As kids grow into adults, their tastes change from heavy rock sounds to those of more mellow groups. Listening patterns change over the year, and listeners move from station to station looking for programming more in tune with their current life-styles.

This movement of audience makes some kind of audience measurement necessary, hence the rating services. The advertiser must keep up with these changing trends to be sure the stations on the schedule are currently delivering the same demographic audiences in the same quantities as before. This constant attention to changing information is sometimes too much trouble for retail advertisers. They sometimes employ a media buying expert or consultant to analyze the radio situation, make recommendations, and then buy radio time on the "right" stations. It is often necessary to hire media consultants in the larger markets around the country. The many radio stations (over 40 in New York, Los Angeles, and Chicago), with their various formats, that cover the metropolitan areas also fragment the audiences of those areas. The analysis of who, and how many, are listening to what stations becomes an important factor in the media buying decision. Larger stores have their own media planning person, whose job requires a thorough knowledge of all the media in the market, their strengths and weaknesses, prices, availabilities of air time, and so on. In many cases, the very need to have this additional staff member may keep the fashion retailer out of broadcast advertising.

RADIO AS CATALYST

The dictionary describes a *catalyst* as a substance that accelerates a reaction but itself remains virtually unchanged. That is a chemical definition, of course, but to a great extent it describes a unique capability of radio as an advertising medium.

Radio adds a dimension to any advertising campaign. It increases the reach and frequency of advertising budgets by getting the message to more people more often without any increase in cost. ARMS II (All Radio Marketing Study, Fall 1974), the prestigious study of advertising impressions conducted for the Radio Advertising Bureau, showed many examples of increased effectiveness through the addition of radio (Figures 6.10 and 6.11).

Taking an all-newspaper campaign that statistically reached 36.4 percent of its target audience—middle- and upper-income men 25 to 49—1.1 times during the campaign and made 713,000 impressions, the study showed that splitting the budget so that half the money was spent in newspapers and the other half in radio produced better results. The half newspaper/half radio budget increased the audience reach to 42.7 percent with 1.8 average frequency while making 1,387,000 impressions. An all-radio campaign would have yielded a 45.1 percent reach, 2.3 average frequency, and 1,852,000 impressions.

Another section of the ARMS II study took an all-television campaign aimed at upper-income adults and divided it two-thirds TV and one-third radio, then one-third TV and two-thirds radio, and finally all radio with the following results:

	Reach (%)	Frequency	Impressions
All TV	52.3	1.8	3,890,000
2/3 TV 1/3 radio	67.2	2.2	5,997,000
1/3 TV 2/3 radio	71.6	2.8	8,071,000
All radio	66.1	3.5	9,535,000

This study shows the potential for greater effectiveness in spending advertising dollars through use of more than one medium. The advertiser must experiment and try different combinations to determine what works best for each individual campaign.

Adding radio to an existing budget requires very little additional money, because air time is generally the least expensive of all advertising media. When the advertiser is unwilling to increase

A CROSS-TAB ANALYSIS FROM

ARMS II
ALL-RADIO MARKETING STUDY

COMPARISON OF 3 MEDIA STRATEGIES TO REACH...

MEN 18 +
(NEW YORK ADI)

HOW 3 MEDIA STRATEGIES COMPARE IN TOTAL IMPRESSIONS DELIVERED AS WELL AS REACH AND FREQUENCY

STRATEGY 1	STRATEGY 2	STRATEGY 3
ALL TV	1/2 TV - 1/2 RADIO	ALL RADIO

Target audience measured: Men 18+—New York ADI
Equal weekly budget for all strategies.

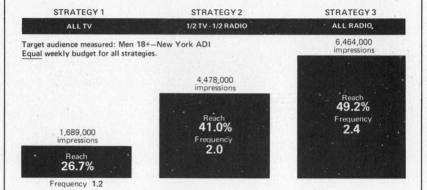

1,689,000 impressions
Reach
26.7%
Frequency 1.2

4,478,000 impressions
Reach
41.0%
Frequency
2.0

6,464,000 impressions
Reach
49.2%
Frequency
2.4

HOW 3 MEDIA STRATEGIES COMPARE IN PERCENT OF AUDIENCE REACHED AT VARYING FREQUENCY LEVELS (FREQUENCY DISTRIBUTION)

Men 18+ reached	STRATEGY 1 ALL TV	STRATEGY 2 1/2 TV - 1/2 RADIO	STRATEGY 3 ALL RADIO
1 or more times	26.7%	41.0%	49.2%
2 or more times	3.6	20.1	30.7
3 or more times	.5	10.2	17.8
4 or more times	0.0	5.3	9.9
5 or more times	0.0	2.8	5.4

Figures above show how the Media Strategies differ in "frequency distribution." Strategy 1 (All Tv) reaches only small percentages of consumers more than 2 times weekly. All Radio does far better.

DETAILS OF 3 MEDIA STRATEGIES

A $10,000 weekly budget was used in New York ADI. Strategy 1 is Tv in early and late fringe and prime. In Strategy 2, $5,000 of original budget remains in Tv. $5,000 goes into morning and afternoon drive and evening Radio. In Strategy 3, Radio gets total $10,000 budget. Tv strategies based on 30' announcements, Radio based on 60's. Further details available from Radio Advertising Bureau Research Department.

RESEARCH DEPARTMENT • RADIO ADVERTISING BUREAU, INC. • 555 MADISON AVENUE • NEW YORK, N.Y. 10022

Figure 6.10   The ARMS II Study, sponsored by the Radio Advertising Bureau, produced a series of media strategies that revealed increases in reach and frequency when radio is added to the media mix. This is a TV-radio mix. (SOURCE: By permission of the Radio Advertising Bureau. Copyright RAB.)

A CROSS-TAB ANALYSIS FROM

ARMS II
ALL-RADIO MARKETING STUDY

COMPARISON OF 3 MEDIA STRATEGIES TO REACH...

PRESTIGE STORE SHOPPERS

HOW 3 MEDIA STRATEGIES COMPARE IN TOTAL IMPRESSIONS DELIVERED AS WELL AS REACH AND FREQUENCY

STRATEGY 1	STRATEGY 2	STRATEGY 3
ALL NEWSPAPER	1/2 NEWSPAPER-1/2 RADIO	ALL RADIO

Target audience measured: Prestige Store Shoppers
Equal weekly budget for all strategies

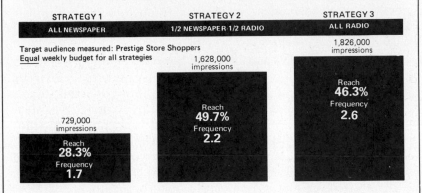

729,000 impressions
Reach **28.3%** Frequency **1.7**

1,628,000 impressions
Reach **49.7%** Frequency **2.2**

1,826,000 impressions
Reach **46.3%** Frequency **2.6**

HOW 3 MEDIA STRATEGIES COMPARE IN PERCENT OF AUDIENCE REACHED AT VARYING FREQUENCY LEVELS (FREQUENCY DISTRIBUTION)

Prestige Store Shoppers reached	STRATEGY 1 ALL NEWSPAPER	STRATEGY 2 1/2 NEWSPAPER - 1/2 RADIO	STRATEGY 3 ALL RADIO
1 or more times	28.3%	49.7%	46.3%
2 or more times	20.5	24.7	30.3
3 or more times	—	15.6	19.5
4 or more times	—	9.5	12.2
5 or more times	—	5.4	7.3

Figures above show how the Media Strategies differ in "frequency distribution." Strategy 1 (All news- paper) reaches no customers more than 2 times weekly. All Radio does far better.

DETAILS OF 3 MEDIA STRATEGIES

An $8,300 weekly budget was used in New York ADI. Strategy 1 is 2 insertions in the main news section of the New York Times. In Strategy 2, $4,150 of original budget remains in newspaper, $4,150 goes into morning and afternoon drive and housewife Radio. In Strategy 3, Radio gets total $8,300 budget. Radio strategies based on 60′ announcements. Further details available from Radio Advertising Bureau Research Department.

RESEARCH DEPARTMENT • RADIO ADVERTISING BUREAU, INC. • 555 MADISON AVENUE • NEW YORK, N.Y. 10022

Figure 6.11   Another example from ARMS II, showing the total impressions possible from the combination of radio and newspaper advertising. (SOURCE: By permission of the Radio Advertising Bureau. Copyright RAB.)

the dollar outlay for advertising, dividing the budget among two or more media might be the better idea.

Many advertisers are looking for alternative advertising media to offset the increasing costs of direct mail, newspapers, and television advertising. Including radio can help lower the average cost to reach customers. Including radio in the advertising mix also allows the advertiser to maintain daily contact with customers, to advise them of impending sales, to remind them to read the direct mail piece when it arrives, or to look for ads in the newspapers. Radio, with its emotional impact, can motivate customers to action—to read, to visit, to remember your store, to think of your store first when deciding to make a shopping trip.

As a catalyst, radio makes things happen. People get their first news of a breaking story on radio, then go to newspapers for details and to weekly newsmagazines for background information. As a catalyst, radio functions and produces results by itself. For many advertisers throughout the country, radio is the primary medium. They buy radio first, then back up the radio schedule with advertising in other media. Certain categories of merchandise, with specific appeal for selective audiences, find radio is the only medium they need for success. For example, the waterbed industry admits it could never have grown as rapidly as it has without the use of radio to reach the young, modern, innovative audiences it was seeking. As much as 90 percent of the advertising in this industry goes to radio. Other producers and sellers of merchandise designed for specific types of people find the unique qualities of radio perfect for their needs. Not only can advertisers determine the stations to which potential customers are listening, but the times of day the most people tune in.

The versatility of radio, newly rediscovered by retail advertisers, has opened up new vistas for imaginative, creative advertising by even the smallest retail advertiser. There is no patent on ideas. Anyone can develop the idea, the combination of words and phrases that perfectly describes a store and what it stands for. Often the unimaginative, conservative buyer or store owner can supply the key word that tells the story best. Retailers know why they are successful, why customers keep coming back, but they may not be able to articulate it. It is the job of the advertising person to ferret out what it is that makes the store different and translate that revelation into an exciting, informative, memorable message to the public.

The conversational quality of radio allows the advertiser to *talk* to the customer, to establish the one-on-one relationship all advertisers seek. A major ad agency creative director once stated that radio is the only full-participation medium, for if people listen, the brain reacts and something happens. This, he claimed, did not always occur with other media.

In summary, radio seems to work well alone, or with other media. To some extent, it has the selectivity of direct mail, the visual qualities of television, the timeliness of newspapers, and a sound all its own.

QUESTIONS FOR DISCUSSION AND CLASS ASSIGNMENTS

1. As a class project, have all students record their radio listening (stations listened to) for a three-day period, using the Arbitron diary sample instructions as a guide. Tabulate the class' total listening. Determine the average number of stations listened to per student and compare the amount of in-home versus out-of-home listening. Compare with national averages and discuss.
2. Survey 10 homes in your area and report the number of radios and television sets per household and where they are located in the home. Also record the number of AM versus AM/FM radios. Discuss findings.
3. Discuss the theory of radio as a "local" advertising medium similar in its retail applications to newspaper advertising.
4. Monitor the five most popular stations in your market and compare the demographics of their audiences versus the population percentages in your market area.
5. Write a 60-second radio commercial (150–175 words) using the information in the advertising request form (Appendix 6). Set the scene with music and/or sound effects and develop an interesting, memorable radio ad for this item.
6. What reasons would you give to overcome the objections of a fashion retailer refusing to advertise on radio because of the belief that a picture must be shown to sell fashion merchandise.
7. It has been said that "Anything a person can visualize can be advertised on radio." Discuss whether or not you agree with this statement.
8. Monitor your favorite radio station all week and report on the "best" radio ads you've heard. Compare your selections with those of the rest of the class. Discuss what makes the radio commercial memorable.
9. Discuss the special advantages of radio as an advertising medium. What are its weaknesses? How do these apply to a specific local retailer?
10. Name six ways in which radio helps the retailer's advertising program achieve better results.
11. To demonstrate the "magic" of the word, see if you can picture in your mind where you were, who you were with, and perhaps, especially for the women, what you were wearing when you heard:

• that John Kennedy had been shot?
• that three astronauts had died on the launch pad at Cape Canaveral?
• that your favorite dog got loose and failed to return?

These are all tragic events, to be sure, but the dramatics of the examples do not negate the fact that the mere statement of the event, if you have lived through it, would bring it back to mind in a flash. Try to think of similar events in your lifetime that would fit into this exercise.

Chapter 7
Here Comes Retail
Television

At the end of 1980, there were over 1000 television stations in the
United States, 1020 to be exact. Of these, 519 were commercial
VHF (very high frequency) and 233 were commercial UHF (ultra
high frequency) stations. There were 106 noncommercial VHFs and
162 noncommercial UHFs (*Broadcasting Yearbook,* 1981). VHF
stations operate on channels 2 through 13; UHF stations, channels
14 to 82.

Most commercial TV stations are *network-affiliated.* This
means the stations contract with one of the three major networks,
ABC (American Broadcasting Company), NBC (National Broadcasting Company), or CBS (Columbia Broadcasting System) for a majority of their programming. Approximately 150 stations operate as in-
dependents, with no network affiliation. Many of these TV stations
are in major markets, like New York, Chicago, San Francisco, and
Los Angeles. They offer local advertisers the opportunity to advertise on television at much lower rates than network affiliates.

Under Federal Communications Commission rules, no single
entity may own more than seven television stations, and no more

than five of them may be VHFs. Future FCC rules may alter these guidelines. No owner may have two stations in the same community, and if a company owns three VHF-TV stations in the top 50 markets in the United States, it cannot purchase additional stations without convincing the FCC there is a compelling public interest that the new ownership can serve. There are also regulations prohibiting newspaper owners from buying television stations in the same market; nor may radio station owners acquire TV stations there, nor TV owners radio outlets. The purpose of these regulations is to prevent limitation of communication and editorial viewpoints in the public interest. The existence of multimedia ownership in many cities has been "grandfathered" by the federal government, which allows existing newspaper-radio-TV combined ownerships to continue, but bans the creation of any new potentially monopolistic arrangements.

Commercial broadcasting—radio and television—had total revenues of $10.6 billion in 1979, according to Federal Communications Commission reports, with $1.9 billion in profits. Television accounted for 74.5 percent of the revenues ($7.9 billion) and 89.5 percent of the profits ($1.7 billion). Radio registered 25.5 percent of broadcast revenues ($2.7 billion), with 10.5 percent of profits ($241 million). Public broadcasting income was only $603.5 million, with 27 percent coming from the federal government (*Broadcasting Yearbook*, 1981).

Television is practically everywhere; it is in 98 percent of homes in the United States. There are 76 million homes with television sets, and 50 percent have more than one set. Over 83 percent are color sets. With the advent of all-channel television, requiring that all TV sets be manufactured with UHF capabilities, 94 percent of homes can now receive UHF signals. New on the scene and growing rapidly is cable television, with wired systems that will change the country's viewing habits in the future. About 21 percent of American homes are linked with cable systems—and the number is growing (*TV Digest*, January 1980). According to Nielsen, the widely accepted TV rating service, the average American family spends 6 hours and 36 minutes a day with TV. The Roper research organization reports that 64 percent of the American public says it turns to TV for most of its news, and 51 percent rank TV as the most believable news source (Table 7.1).

Small wonder that television has become the most powerful communications force in our lives today. Political candidates are elected not only for their stands on issues, but because of how they look, talk, and project on television. Office seekers hire public relations experts to "package" them for presentation on television to

Figure 7.1   B.C. rarely omits any phase of a selected target. His commentary on TV might apply to retail advertising in the cosmetics/drugs area. (SOURCE: By permission of Johnny Hart and Field Enterprises, Inc.)

the voters. The combination of sight, sound, motion, and color makes television the biggest thing in many peoples' lives and offers advertisers vast audiences for their messages.

TELEVISION COMES TO THE RETAIL WORLD

National retail advertisers (Sears, Ward's, JC Penney, Kmart) can afford to and do use television to advertise their merchandise. Larger department stores and chain store operators find that their budgets can accommodate television costs. In many instances, individual retailers have also found ways to use television. The ability of television advertising to produce direct sales results, build store traffic, and improve store image have moved more and more retailers into TV in recent years. Successful retail TV advertisers report that the higher costs are offset by greater results. Many have utilized the services of advertising agencies, TV production companies, and media buying services to handle their television efforts. Others, in true retail tradition, try to develop in-house capabilities so they can do it themselves, thereby controlling costs, creativity, and other aspects.

When television appeared on the scene at the conclusion of World War II, many enterprising and far-sighted retailers welcomed the newcomer. Retailers, in fact, were one of the largest TV advertisers during the first few years of TV's existence. In Atlanta, Georgia, Rich's, the South's largest and most prestigious department store, experimented for a year, broadcasting from the store during an extended bus and trolley strike. It was called "Rich's in Your Home," and literally brought the merchandise to the city, since the residents could not come to the store because of the public transportation strike. The plan did not work too well at that time because of the limited number of television sets then in homes and the small audience that could be reached.

Table 7.1 SOME TV STATISTICS FROM THE TELEVISION BUREAU OF ADVERTISING

TV HOMES CLIMB TO 77.8 MILLION

Number of TV Homes .... 77.8 Million
Number of Color TV Homes ..... 66.3 Million (85% of TV Homes)
Number of Multi-Set Homes .... 39.8 Million (51% of TV Homes)
Time spent with TV per home per day 6 Hrs. 36 Mins.
Total time spent with TV per day ... 504 Million Hours

Source A.C. Nielsen: TV Homes, Jan 1981; time spent, 1980 annual average

TV SET OWNERSHIP AT 98%...
AND VIEWING IS HEAVY

	Avg. Viewing Time per TV Home per day		Avg. Viewing Time per TV Home per day
TOTAL U.S.	7:02	LADY OF HOUSE	
TERRITORY		18-34 Yrs.	7:19
Northeast	7:13	35-54 Yrs.	8:01
East Central	7:01	55 Yrs. & Over	6:36
West Central	6:50	HOUSEHOLD INCOME	
South	7:14	Under $10,000	6:15
Pacific	6:39	$10,000-$14,999	7:13
COUNTY SIZE		$15,000-$19,999	7:31
A	6:56	$20,000 and Over	7:20
B	6:58	$30,000 and Over	6:54
C & D	7:12	EDUCATION OF	
HOUSEHOLD SIZE		HEAD OF HOUSE	
1	4:37	Under 4 Yrs H.S.	7:28
2	6:20	4 Yrs. H.S.	7:22
3+	8:38	1+ Yrs. College	6:21
4+	9:08	4+ Yrs. College	6:08

Source: A.C. Nielsen, Nov. '80

GROWTH OF COMMERCIAL TELEVISION STATIONS

TV Stations	1955	1960	1965	1970	1975	1980	1981
Total	411	515	569	677	706	734	757
VHF	297	440	481	501	514	516	519
UHF	114	75	88	176	192	218	238

Source: Television Digest, Jan of each year

TV VIEWING NOW 6 HOURS 36 MINUTES PER DAY

Daily TV Viewing Per TV Home

1950	4 hours 35 minutes
1955	4 hours 51 minutes
1960	5 hours 6 minutes
1965	5 hours 29 minutes
1970	5 hours 56 minutes
1975	6 hours 7 minutes
1980	6 hours 36 minutes

Source: A.C. Nielsen, annual averages

SUMMER VIEWING INCREASES...
AND VIEWING LEVELS ARE HIGH

Daily TV Viewing per TV Home		% Homes Using TV During Avg. Minute—1980	
		Summer June-Aug.	9 "other" months
1955	3 hrs. 58 mins.		
1960	4 hrs. 10 mins.	Daytime M-F	
1965	4 hrs. 36 mins.	10 am-4:30 pm	26%	27%
1970	5 hrs. 5 mins.		
1975	5 hrs. 20 mins.	Late Night M-S	
1980	5 hrs. 54 mins.	11 pm-1 am	32%	33%

Source: A.C. Nielsen

TV ATTRACTS THOUSANDS OF ADVERTISERS AND BRANDS

	Network TV	Spot TV
Advertisers	558	2,598
Brands	2,522	10,612

Source: BAR, 1980

TELEVISION REACHES PEOPLE

In an Average Day	In an Average Week		Daily Hours of Viewing
88%	95%	of all TV households	7:02
73%	89%	of all men	4:06
78%	91%	of all women	4:47
68%	90%	of all teens 12-17	3:17
83%	95%	of all children 2-11	3:52

Source: A.C. Nielsen, Reach—Feb. '77, Viewing—Nov. '80

DISTRIBUTION OF TOTAL TIME SPENT DAILY WITH MEDIA BY ADULTS

	All Adults	In $20,000 + Income Homes	Better Educated
Television	53%	49%	45%
Radio	32%	34%	36%
Newspapers	9%	11%	11%
Magazines	6%	6%	8%

Source: TvB/R.H. Bruskin, Jan 1980

ADVERTISING AGENCIES THE TOP 10 TV USERS IN 1980

		Millions of Dollars		TV's Share of Total Billings
	TV Network	TV Spot	Total TV	
1. Young & Rubicam	$491.0	$208.0	$699.0	56%
2. J. Walter Thompson	440.2	211.9	652.1	71%
3. Dancer Fitzgerald Sample	215.6	168.3	383.9	76%
4. BBDO	253.4	119.5	372.9	55%
5. Leo Burnett	294.0	78.0	372.0	51%
6. Ogilvy & Mather	176.1	113.4	289.5	52%
7. Grey	199.2	85.2	284.4	55%
8. Doyle Dane Bernbach	163.0	94.0	257.0	54%
9. D'Arcy-MacManus & Masius	142.5	110.2	252.7	57%
10. McCann-Erickson	171.5	80.5	252.0	53%

Source: Broadcasting Magazine

LEADING LOCAL TV CATEGORIES

	Add (000)		%
	1979	1980	Change
1. Restaurants & Drive-Ins	$263,290.4	$287,873.1	+ 9
2. Food Stores & Supermarkets	133,802.4	148,708.6	+11
3. Banks, Savings & Loans	139,760.5	140,948.2	+ 1
4. Department Stores	118,002.8	131,241.1	+11
5. Furniture Stores	103,519.8	111,420.0	+ 8
6. Movies	94,203.3	102,401.4	+ 9
7. Auto Dealers*	122,229.3	99,106.1	−19
8. Discount Department Stores	68,458.4	73,505.4	+ 7
9. Radio Stations & Cable TV	53,364.3	69,264.2	+30
10. Amusements & Entertainment	57,532.7	68,024.5	+18

Source: BAR   *Dealer Associations Not Included

CABLE TV OPERATING SYSTEMS AND SUBSCRIBERS

	1960	1965	1970	1975	1980	1981 (pre.)
Operating Systems	640	1,325	2,490	3,366	4,048	4,300
Subscribers (millions)	0.7	1.3	4.5	9.8	15.5	17.0
% of TV Homes	1.4%	2.4%	7.6%	14.3%	20.5%	22.0%

Source: Television Digest, Jan. 1 of each year

The arrival of the coaxial cable, linking the East and West coasts and major cities in between, established network television by allowing for simultaneous broadcasting nationwide. This occurred during the early 1950s. During the next two decades, retailers gradually began to turn to television. It was not until 1970, however, when the rising costs of newspapers and direct mail, the mainstays of retail advertising, began pricing themselves almost out of reach that retailers made a determined effort to find alternative media. Declining newspaper circulation and failure to cover the movement to the suburbs led retailers to experiment with TV and radio and gradually to build broadcasts into their regular advertising programs.

Table 7.1 (cont.)

CABLE HOUSEHOLDS CONTINUE TO VIEW
OVER-THE-AIR STATIONS...ONLY MORE SO.

	Viewing By Type of TV Household (avg. hours per week)		
Viewing:	Non-Cable Homes	Basic Cable Homes	Pay Cable Homes
Over-the-Air	48.2	50.0	53.2
Cable Originated	—	1.7	2.5
Pay Cable	—	—	6.2

Source: A.C. Nielsen, Nov. 1980

TOTAL ADVERTISING VOLUME REACHES $54.8 BILLION:
MAJOR MEDIA: $36.2 BILLION

	Millions of Dollars			
	1979	1980	% Change	% of Total
Total Advertising	$49,520	$54,750	+10.6	100.0
TELEVISION	10,154	11,330	+11.6	20.7
Newspapers	14,493	15,615	+ 7.7	28.5
Magazines	2,932	3,225	+10.0	5.9
Radio	3,277	3,690	+12.6	6.7
Outdoor	540	610	+13.0	1.1
Business Papers	1,575	1,695	+ 7.6	3.1
All Others	16,549	18,585	+12.3	34.0

Source: McCann-Erickson 1/81

NATIONAL ADVERTISING INVESTMENTS
IN MAJOR MEDIA $17.0 BILLION

	Millions of Dollars			
	1979	1980	% Change	% of Total
TELEVISION	$ 7,472	$ 8,365	+12.0	49.3
Network	4,599	5,105	+11.0	30.1
Spot	2,873	3,260	+13.5	19.2
Newspapers	2,085	2,335	+12.0	13.8
Magazines	2,932	3,225	+10.0	19.0
Radio (Network & Spot)	820	935	+14.0	5.5
Outdoor	355	400	+12.7	2.4
Business Papers	1,575	1,695	+ 7.6	10.0
Total Major Media	$15,239	$16,955	+11.3	100.0

Source: McCann-Erickson 1/81

LOCAL ADVERTISING INVESTMENTS
IN MAJOR MEDIA REACH $19.2 BILLION

	Millions of Dollars			
	1979	1980	% Change	% of Total
TELEVISION	$ 2,682	$ 2,965	+10.5	15.4
Newspapers	12,408	13,280	+ 7.0	69.1
Retail	7,801	8,600	+10.2	44.8
Classified	4,607	4,680	+ 1.6	24.3
Radio	2,457	2,755	+12.0	14.4
Outdoor	185	210	+12.5	1.1
Total Major Media	$17,732	$19,210	+ 8.3	100.0

Source: McCann-Erickson 1/81

COLOR TV PENETRATION TOPS 85%...
66.3 MILLION TV HOMES HAVE COLOR

	Color Households	Penetration of TV Households
1960	340,000	0.7%
1965	2,810,000	4.9
1970	23,400,000	39.2
1975	48,500,000	70.8
1980	63,350,000	83.0
1981	66,250,000	85.2

Source: NBC, 1960-75; A.C. Nielsen, 1980-81

TELEVISION SET SALES TOP 17.5 MILLION IN 1980

	Total	Color	Monochrome
1975	10,637,000	6,219,000	4,418,000
1976	14,131,000	8,194,000	5,937,000
1977	15,431,000	9,341,000	6,090,000
1978	17,406,000	10,674,000	6,732,000
1979	16,619,000	10,043,000	6,576,000
1980	17,508,000	10,779,000	6,729,000

Source: EIA, Domestic & Imports

TV VOTED MOST AUTHORITATIVE

Which medium/advertising is the most authoritative:	% of Adults 18 Yrs. +	
	The Medium	The Advertising
Television	50%	50%
Newspapers	29	26
Magazines	8	9
Radio	7	5

Source: TvB/R.H. Bruskin, June 1975

TV VOTED MOST BELIEVABLE

	% of Adults Responding						
	1959	1964	1968	1972	1976	1978	1980
Television	29%	41%	44%	48%	51%	47%	51%
Newspapers	32	23	21	21	22	23	22
Radio	12	8	8	8	7	9	8
Magazines	10	10	11	10	9	9	9
Don't know	17	18	16	13	11	12	10

Source: TIO/Roper

TV VOTED SOURCE OF MOST NEWS

	% of Adults Responding						
	1959	1964	1968	1972	1976	1978	1980
Television	51%	58%	59%	64%	64%	67%	64%
Newspapers	57	56	49	50	49	49	44
Radio	34	26	25	21	19	20	18
Magazines	8	8	7	6	7	5	5

Source: TIO/Roper

LENGTH OF ANNOUNCEMENTS—
THE 30 SECOND DOMINATES

	Non-Network			
Announcement Length	1965	1970	1975	1980
10 seconds	15%	11%	8%	8%
20 seconds	13	3	—	—
30 seconds	1	54	83	87
60's piggybacked	7	9	1	—
60 sec. or more	64	23	8	5
	100%	100%	100%	100%

	Network			
Announcement Length	1965	1970	1975	1980
10 seconds	—%	—%	—%	1%
20 seconds	—	—	—	—
30 seconds	—	32	83	87
60's piggybacked	25	45	12	10
60 sec. or more	75	23	5	2
	100%	100%	100%	100%

Source: BAR, Nov. of each year

By 1975, department and discount stores were spending over $145 million on television, a 40 percent increase over 1974, and the trend has continued. The impact of TV advertising is being felt most by the retailers who consistently plan and schedule the medium. The only measure of success for the retailer is sales results, and good results come from good planning. Long-range investments of advertising dollars will bear fruit. The one-time or once-in-a-while advertiser will have the same sporadic results from television as from any other medium.

The Television Bureau of Advertising, the sales arm of the TV industry, provides the retail advertiser with excellent materials to help develop successful and effective television advertising campaigns (Table 7.1). The National Retail Merchants Association has published a book with a compilation of information from professionals in retail sales promotion on many of the technical aspects of planning and producing retail television advertising. A glaring omission from both sources is specific data on fashion TV advertising. The growing emphasis on retail television advertising is evident, but applications to the field of fashion have yet to emerge with much consistency. Retailers are acquiring greater confidence in using television. They have seen remarkable results when advertising items or sale merchandise. About 50 percent of retail TV advertising is spent on sale and off-price promotions. Most of the remaining dollars are spent on special promotions and manufacturer-involved programs, with a small percentage devoted to image or personality advertising. Many retailers feel their "image"—the way in which the customers perceive the store—is a reflection of all the things they are, and the total impression made on the public is merely a sum of all the parts.

The NRMA reported that 66 percent of its member stores were using TV, an increase from 1973, when 58 percent did. It is interesting to note that the increases in expenditures on TV in certain categories of retailers from the Television Bureau of Advertising's annual statistics (figures in millions):

	1976	1979	PERCENT CHANGE
Department stores	129.4	140.4	+8.5
Discount stores	57.4	81.4	+41.8
Furniture stores	61.7	122.5	+82.5
Clothing stores	28.1	47.3	+68.3
Shoe stores	8.5	22.7	+167.0

The department store figures would be higher except for a statistical change in 1979 by TvB assigning product commercials with single-store tags into the spot TV categories. These were in effect national ads listing local stores, one at a time, as a place to buy that product. Previous statistics had listed these ads as local. It is assumed that a percentage of the money spent by department stores includes the fashion departments, and that the discount stores promote their low-priced fashions heavily on TV. The percentage increase in shoe stores is relatively high, although the dollars involved are not as great as in other categories.

Clothing stores, both men's and women's, are increasing their use of television, selling items, image, and special promotions. Stores committed to broadcast advertising have developed skills and techniques to present their particular kinds of merchandise. They have learned how to present the character of their stores, using the capabilities of television, by consistently displaying the stores' best features over a period of time. When planning to develop a program for TV advertising, the retailer takes into consideration the same factors all other advertising planning includes:

- The audience they're trying to reach
- The best time periods to reach them
- The number of messages to schedule
- The content of the message
- What the video (visual) portion of the commercial should show
- What the audio (sound) should say

Men and women seem to have different viewing patterns. And the patterns vary by age as well as sex. Since everybody watches some television, the advertiser needs information on when each target audience is likely to be watching.

The television day is divided into dayparts, as in radio, but the dayparts are different. These are the TV dayparts:

Morning	7 to 10 A.M.
	10 A.M. to 1 P.M.
Afternoon	1 P.M. to 4:30 P.M.
Early evening (early fringe)	4:30 to 7:30 P.M.
Prime access	7:30 to 8 P.M.
Night (prime time)	8 to 11 P.M.
Late fringe	11 to 11:30 P.M.
Late night	11:30 P.M. to 1 A.M.
Late late night	1 to 7 A.M.

The charts from the Television Bureau of Advertising graphically indicate the general TV viewing patterns of men and women, giving the advertiser estimates upon which to make judgments (Figures 7.2 and 7.3). If the target audience is working women, a growing factor in today's life-style marketing, the charts show their general viewing levels are lower than those of women aged 25 to 54, but basically the same as women 18 to 49, with the exception of afternoon and morning viewing. The men's charts show fairly consistent levels, with night and late night viewing increasing as the audience grows older. Men also seem to watch less television than women at all demographic levels. Young audiences watch during prime time and late fringe. Older audiences are heavy viewers of early news shows and early fringe time. The programming being offered during the dayparts is an important factor. If it is sports or news, you can be sure of your male audience. If you are selling

Here's the percent of women of different ages and family incomes reached by television in a day vs. the other major media:

Daily reach of	TV	Newspapers	Radio	Magazines
Women, Total	85%	69%	63%	32%
18–34	86	62	67	35
35–49	84	72	62	32
50 and over	86	75	58	29
Family income:				
$10–14,999	87	73	64	36
$15,000+	82	80	67	40

Source: TvB/R. H. Bruskin, 1975

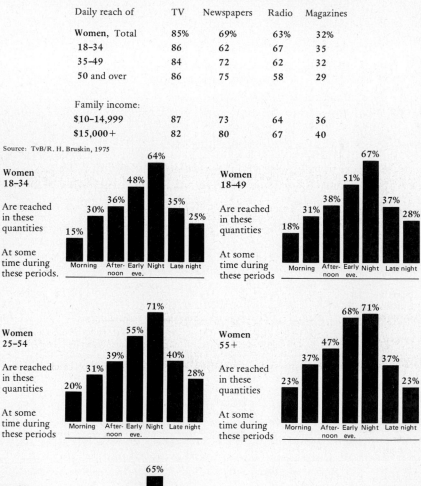

Women 18–34
Are reached in these quantities
At some time during these periods.
Morning 15% After-noon 30% Early eve. 36% Night 64% Late night 35% 48% 25%

Women 18–49
Are reached in these quantities
At some time during these periods
Morning 18% After-noon 31% Early eve. 38% Night 67% Late night 37% 51% 28%

Women 25–54
Are reached in these quantities
At some time during these periods
Morning 20% After-noon 31% Early eve. 39% Night 71% Late night 40% 55% 28%

Women 55+
Are reached in these quantities
At some time during these periods
Morning 23% After-noon 37% Early eve. 47% Night 71% Late night 37% 68% 23%

Working Women
Are reached in these quantities
At some time during these periods
Morning 15% After-noon 17% Early eve. 23% Night 65% Late night 34% 50% 26%

Dayparts
Morning	7–10 am
	10 am–1 pm
Afternoon	1–4:30 pm
Early evening	4:30–7:30 pm
Night	8–11 pm
Late night	11–11:30 pm
	11:30 pm–1 am

Source: A. C. Nielsen, Feb. 1977.
Avg. daily cumes, M–F, except night, M–S.

Figure 7.2   Television viewing patterns, women. Women watch TV at different times, depending on age, life-style, and family income. Note the statistics on working women. (SOURCE: By permission of Television Bureau of Advertising.)

Here's how television compares with the other major media in reaching men:

Daily reach of	TV	Newspapers	Radio	Magazines
Men, Total	84%	77%	73%	34%
18–34	80	69	83	37
35–49	86	84	70	34
50 and over	87	80	65	31

Source: TvB/R. H. Bruskin, 1975

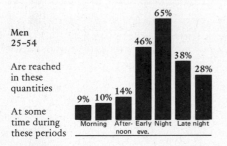

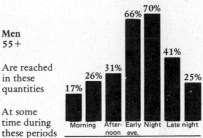

Dayparts

Morning	7–10 am
	10 am–1 pm
Afternoon	1–4:30 pm
Early evening	4:30–7:30 pm
Night	8–11 pm
Late night	11–11:30 pm
	11:30 pm–1 am

Source: A. C. Nielsen, Feb. 1977
Avg. daily cumes. M–F, except night, M–S.

Figure 7.3   Television viewing patterns, men. Men watch TV at different times, based on their availability. According to these figures, men can be reached in all dayparts regardless of age. (SOURCE: By permission of Television Bureau of Advertising.)

fashion, be sure there is a program that appeals to women scheduled at that time.

With the number of commercial, or nonprogram, minutes limited by license agreement, the availability of air time becomes a key factor in the pricing of television spots. The more popular the program, the more advertisers want to buy time on the show. This limited inventory of air time has made television time buying a supply-and-demand business. Obviously, with advertisers clamoring to buy time on the popular news show, the costs for those spots will escalate. On network stations, national advertisers must commit for the major portion of the available spots, occupying five-sixths of the air time. Local advertisers, including retailers, compete for the limited number of commercial minutes the local affiliate can sell during prime time. The stations sell these spots for the highest price possible.

When an estimated 104 million people were watching the 1981 Super Bowl telecast, national advertisers were paying $550,000 per 60 seconds of air time. Local stations were probably asking and getting as much as $5,000 to $15,000 for station breaks and thirty-second commercial announcements (*Broadcasting Yearbook,* 1981). That sounds like a lot of money, but when figured on a cost-per-thousand basis, it is not too unreasonable. For "Super Bowl" type programs, local stations get as much as double their normal rate because of the potentially larger audience and the number of advertisers wanting to advertise on those shows (Table 7.2).

Television uses certain terms (as does radio) to report the sizes of audiences, how often they are reached, how the audience grows over the period of a schedule, and what it is costing to reach that audience.

- A *rating* is the percentage of the people or homes in an area reached by an advertiser's commercial. If a spot reaches 10 percent of the homes or people in a given area, it is said to have a rating of 10.
- *Gross rating points* (or GRPS) are the number of rating points for a specific schedule of spots. If two spots each had a rating of 10, the two spots together have a GRP of 20, by simply adding the rating of each spot on the schedule.
- *Reach* is the percentage of *different* homes or people reached by a specific spot schedule. Since a schedule, over a period of time, accumulates homes and people, this is also referred to as *cume,* or cumulative audience. If two 10-rated spots in a schedule are run so that half the homes are reached twice, the reach of the two spots would be 15 (5 homes reached by one spot, 5 by the other, plus 5 that were reached by both spots).
- *Frequency* means how often the average home or person is reached. If a TV schedule reaches the average home or person twice during a certain period of time, it is said to have an average frequency of 2. Radio, newspapers, and television all talk about frequency, the number of times they reach their audiences.

The ideal situation in budgeting advertising is to reach 100 percent of the store's trading area. Of course, this rarely happens, because no one medium can reach every person every time. Media planners strive to reach as many potential customers as possible within the financial limits of the budget. In setting up TV schedules, a choice must be made between the amount of money that should be spent and the amount of money the store can afford to spend. If advertisers buy higher-rated spots, they pay more but reach larger audiences. If they buy lower-rated spots, they must buy more frequency to reach enough audience to make the advertising effective. If a schedule estimating 100 gross rating points was purchased, the schedule would presumably reach 100 percent of that store's trading area. In a metropolitan area, the cost of 100 GRPs would be beyond the budget of most stores. In smaller markets, if the rating services are available, the cost would be more affordable. Arbitron and Nielsen, the two television audience research services, sweep the country three times a year in all markets (February, March, and November), and their results become the basis for air time costs for the ensuing period.

For example, a store with a $5 million six-month sales volume and a 3 percent advertising budget would have $150,000 to spend on promoting the store. If we allocate 10 percent of the budget to TV, we would have $15,000 to spend. Using our previous budgeting methods, planning advertising expenditures somewhat in line with sales volume, we could develop a reasonable television schedule for this fashion retailer. The key months for fashion in the spring season are March, April, and May, with June added if the men's division is included. Assuming a small market situation, with TV spots averaging $50 per 30-second commercial (96 percent of all network spots are 30 seconds long, as are 87 percent of non-network spots. 8 percent of non-networks spots are 10 seconds). The $15,000 budget will buy 300 spots during the season. Keeping sales trends and seasonal needs in mind, note the schedule on page 206.

Many stores have discovered that they can apply co-op advertising dollars to TV advertising. At first there was reluctance on the part of manufacturers to include television (or radio) in cooperative advertising contracts. There was as much habit as prejudice against broadcast media on the part of the vendors as on the part of retailers. Used to the tangibility of the newspaper tearsheet, many vendors felt uncertain about proof that the radio or TV schedule really ran. The newspaper ad could be held, hung on the wall, shown to salespeople, and saved for future reference. The proof of performance from a broadcast schedule consists of a copy of the script, an excerpt from the station's log indicating the times and dates the

Table 7.2 TV ADVERTISING EXPENDITURES AT THE LOCAL LEVEL

	RANK	TV $ IN MILLIONS	PERCENT CHANGE OVER 1979	BY DAYPART				BY LENGTH			PERCENTAGE OF COMMERCIALS — BY MONTH											
				DAY	EARLY EVENING	NIGHT	LATE NIGHT	10	30	60	JAN.	FEB.	MAR.	APR.	MAY	JUNE	JULY	AUG.	SEPT.	OCT.	NOV.	DEC.
Amusements and entertainment	10	68.0	+18	36	23	9	21	18	79	2	8.8	**10.9**	9.3	8.6	7.1	8.5	10.0	8.6	8.4	8.1	6.7	5.0
Appliance stores	13	37.9	0	35	20	9	27	9	89	2	7.0	7.9	7.6	7.1	8.0	7.3	8.1	8.4	8.3	7.8	9.9	**12.6**
Auto dealers	7	99.1	−19	20	25	11	34	12	83	4	8.3	9.9	**10.4**	8.9	7.6	7.9	8.0	8.6	8.4	7.7	8.5	5.8
Auto repair and service stations	15	28.0	+ 9	12	30	14	31	18	82	—	6.8	8.7	9.0	9.0	7.9	**11.0**	9.0	9.3	9.4	7.6	6.9	5.2
Auto supply stores	33	12.3	− 5	15	26	12	34	10	90	—	5.3	7.1	7.8	9.1	9.7	7.4	9.3	8.6	7.7	9.2	10.8	8.0
Banks, savings and loan assns	3	140.9	+ 1	20	31	21	22	9	83	3	**9.3**	9.3	9.2	8.4	7.8	8.2	7.4	5.6	8.0	8.8	9.3	8.7
Builders and real estate agents	18	25.9	−44	33	23	10	25	14	80	5	8.1	10.5	**10.6**	8.3	8.6	9.2	8.6	9.5	9.3	7.3	6.3	3.7
Carpet and floor covering stores	19	24.2	0	47	16	6	24	9	85	6	7.5	9.2	**10.0**	8.6	8.6	7.4	8.1	6.7	8.4	9.3	9.8	6.4
Clothing stores	11	46.0	+16	36	23	9	25	18	81	1	6.3	5.3	7.5	6.4	6.6	6.9	5.2	10.4	7.6	8.7	10.3	**18.8**
Dairy stores	39	6.3	−10	37	22	6	21	22	78	—	6.6	10.8	9.7	8.0	8.3	10.5	7.7	7.7	8.5	5.0	6.0	11.2
Department stores	4	131.2	+11	40	28	10	19	15	85	—	6.1	6.0	8.7	6.5	7.3	7.7	4.7	9.0	7.5	7.2	10.9	**18.4**
Discount department stores	8	73.5	+ 7	42	29	10	15	5	94	1	4.3	4.2	6.5	6.4	10.8	7.3	5.6	13.9	5.1	7.0	10.6	**18.3**
Drug stores	17	26.3	+17	41	26	9	19	3	95	2	6.5	8.8	7.2	6.9	7.3	6.2	5.8	6.7	6.1	7.5	9.5	**21.5**
Exterminators	40	5.2	−10	30	28	15	24	14	86	—	1.0	3.1	10.6	16.2	**17.0**	12.2	13.3	8.5	10.3	5.4	1.7	0.7
Food stores and supermarkets	2	148.7	+11	40	28	15	15	11	87	2	7.4	7.3	8.0	8.3	8.6	8.7	7.9	7.9	8.8	8.6	9.0	9.5
Furniture stores	5	111.4	+ 8	42	20	8	23	14	85	1	8.7	9.2	8.6	8.1	8.1	7.8	8.1	**9.5**	8.1	8.1	8.3	7.4
Gas, electric and water companies	26	15.7	+ 6	21	31	19	24	4	82	14	5.4	7.3	7.1	6.0	8.4	8.7	10.3	10.9	**13.1**	7.3	10.2	5.3
Hardware stores	22	19.0	+43	23	34	10	26	2	97	1	5.3	5.4	5.8	11.2	12.0	8.2	5.0	7.0	8.5	9.4	9.5	**12.7**
Health clubs and reducing salons	21	20.5	+ 8	73	13	3	8	10	76	14	8.4	9.5	9.4	9.3	**10.6**	8.5	7.4	6.7	9.1	8.2	7.5	5.4
Home improvement contractors	14	35.0	+21	39	22	8	23	10	86	4	6.0	7.2	9.4	9.9	**11.2**	9.5	8.5	7.2	9.0	9.0	7.9	5.2

Category																						
Hotels and resorts	24	18.0	+10	33	22	11	25	7	84	8	6.1	7.3	6.5	7.5	9.7	**16.2**	14.1	8.3	6.6	5.2	7.0	5.5
Investment brokers	37	6.9	+60	36	21	13	23	3	82	10	8.4	10.2	9.4	7.8	7.4	6.0	5.8	6.0	10.0	11.0	**11.7**	6.3
Jewelry stores	23	18.6	+ 9	35	22	10	27	18	81	1	3.1	4.4	5.2	5.5	9.1	6.1	4.1	5.0	6.1	7.1	15.1	**29.2**
Leisure time activities and services	12	42.2	+14	31	26	11	21	17	81	2	4.4	5.8	6.7	7.3	10.4	16.8	19.7	14.6	5.5	4.1	2.5	2.2
Loan and mortgage companies	34	11.6	− 3	37	16	10	29	4	95	1	9.1	10.9	7.5	4.5	6.9	5.1	7.3	8.2	**11.2**	**11.2**	11.1	7.0
Mail order catalogs and showrooms	32	12.5	+ 6	40	24	9	21	9	83	3	3.7	2.2	2.0	2.4	6.9	3.7	3.8	3.1	10.3	8.0	19.8	**34.1**
Medical and dental services	30	13.4	+24	77	7	4	8	4	87	9	6.9	7.7	8.0	7.5	7.7	8.5	9.2	9.4	**9.7**	9.3	8.8	7.3
Mobile home and camper dealers	36	6.9	−17	31	22	9	25	3	93	4	9.4	9.6	9.2	8.9	**10.2**	9.7	7.3	7.9	9.2	6.2	7.7	4.7
Movies	6	102.4	+ 9	15	28	13	37	5	94	1	7.0	9.4	8.7	7.2	8.4	7.9	11.3	**11.9**	7.1	7.8	7.8	5.5
Music stores	38	6.7	−11	33	19	8	30	15	81	3	6.7	6.6	6.5	5.8	5.2	4.9	4.3	7.3	8.3	9.4	11.6	**23.4**
Newspapers	28	15.4	+18	26	30	17	21	13	80	7	9.7	8.2	11.7	7.4	6.8	4.1	6.4	5.0	10.8	**12.8**	10.4	6.7
Optical services and suppliers	29	14.0	+46	47	23	7	19	10	89	1	7.2	8.9	**11.5**	9.9	10.5	10.2	8.4	9.7	8.1	5.8	5.9	3.9
Radio stations	9	69.3	+30	31	26	13	22	21	77	2	6.7	5.7	7.1	**19.6**	8.9	3.5	4.6	3.7	5.5	14.5	15.2	5.0
Rental services	27	15.5	+45	61	14	3	12	2	97	1	7.0	8.0	8.1	8.0	8.3	8.8	8.4	8.5	8.7	8.6	8.6	**9.0**
Restaurants and drive-ins	1	287.9	+ 9	21	33	16	20	7	92	1	5.6	6.7	8.6	8.6	8.5	**9.6**	9.2	9.6	8.5	8.3	8.5	8.3
Schools and colleges	25	17.3	+11	66	12	3	13	11	82	6	8.3	8.1	8.1	7.1	7.5	8.1	8.3	**11.2**	10.5	7.6	8.0	7.2
Shoe stores	16	27.3	+41	35	29	9	21	17	83	—	1.9	2.6	16.0	9.7	9.2	3.5	3.2	**18.7**	6.9	8.1	10.5	10.0
Shopping centers and assns	31	12.5	+ 9	52	21	7	15	33	66	1	4.2	7.2	6.3	4.3	4.2	4.2	6.8	9.3	7.9	6.7	9.3	**29.6**
Sport, hobby and toy stores	20	23.3	+11	33	24	9	23	15	83	2	5.3	4.9	5.4	4.4	6.0	5.7	5.9	6.6	5.9	6.4	16.7	**26.8**
Variety stores	35	7.0	+21	51	27	10	11	1	99	—	5.3	4.8	9.1	7.0	8.3	7.7	4.7	9.5	8.8	9.8	11.9	**13.1**

SOURCE: Television Advertising Bureau, New York. Used by permission.

NOTE: A number in **boldface** shows this month is the category's highest TV month.

NOTE: A change by BAR in assigning product commercials with single store tags has resulted in dollars shifting from local TV to spot TV in 1979. The Department Store category appears to be most affected by the change.

	BUDGET	NUMBER OF SPOTS	EVENT
February	$1000	20	Valentine's Day, President's sale
March	$2500	50	Spring and Easter fashion events
April	$3000	60	Spring sale, After-Easter sale
May	$3500	70	Mother's Day event, Memorial Day sale
June	$3000	60	Father's Day event, brides, graduation, summer fashions
July	$2000	40	July Fourth sales, summer clearances
Total	$15,000	300	

spots were broadcast, and a notarized affidavit signed by the station manager certifying that the information is correct. Sometimes tapes or air-checks are provided to support proof of performance, but unless the vendor monitors and hears every spot, there can always be doubt.

There is an interesting angle to this problem of seeming lack of credibility of broadcast. Retailers accept without question the circulation figures issued by newspapers as the Publisher's Statement, and certified by the Audit Bureau of Circulations. The figures are not questioned, and there is no higher court, in case there is a question. The publisher cannot lose a license to publish because of a misstatement, because there is no license involved. All radio and television stations *are* licensed by the Federal Communications Commission. Any falsified statement, document, station log, or any other record could result in the station losing its license, which is valued in the tens of millions of dollars. Therefore, the signature of the station manager on an affidavit of performance is equally creditable and believable as a publisher's statement.

The reluctance to offer co-op advertising on equal terms to radio and television advertising for retail use stems more probably from lack of knowledge about broadcast on the part of the manufacturers. This, too, is passing. More and more vendors are developing their own commercials for stores to use, giving the retailer the benefit of nationally produced TV spots of higher quality than could be produced by the retailer alone. Many categories of merchandise now offer packaged spots to retailers, with time at the end of the spot to drop in store identification or provision for superimposing the store's logo in the final seconds of the spot. More innovative retailers are taking the manufacturers' spots and, using a store spokes-person, re-recording the sound track, the audio portion of the commercial, to make it sound more like a store-produced spot. By writing their own copy, stores can also be sure the store's name is mentioned more than once, as in the case of the quick tag at the end of the spot.

ADVANTAGES OF TELEVISION

Television contains the best elements of other media. There are the words and pictures of print; the sound of radio; the motion of the movies; and the color of motion pictures, direct mail, and magazines. There is standardization of size, in that most television ads are 30 seconds in length, although ads on local and independent stations are interspersed with 10-second and some 60-second spots. The limitations of time can be turned to advantage by creative advertising people, who can distill the story to be told to its barest, simplest minimum. This makes for better selling, for in 30 seconds one idea, well presented, can do the job. In addition to the item or product being shown, the camera is also picking up the background story. This could be the store itself, the setting in which the fashions should be worn, or a landscape vista that establishes a comfortable atmosphere in which to tell the store's story (Figure 7.4).

Television, with its broad reach, sends the retailer's message out beyond the scope of the newspaper into the suburbs that most newspapers fail to cover. Television is intrusive. While watching a show, unless the viewer takes some action to avoid receiving the message, the message will be delivered. One of the strongest advantages of television advertising, and important to retail fashion advertisers urging the viewer to shop in their store, is the depth of impression made by television commercials. The powerful combination of sight, sound, motion, and color creates emotion and involvement by the viewer. The medium can generate moods that enhance the merchandise being shown. The realism of television gives the viewer the feeling of actually being there. When budgets allow, the basic advertising attributes of continuity and repetition can be added to increase television's effectiveness.

The opportunity to talk one-to-one to the viewer is an advantage salespeople always look for. Even though many people may be watching a show or hearing and seeing a commercial, the advertiser is talking and demonstrating product or service to just one person at a time—you. The very personal nature of TV has kept many questionable products off the air. Broadcast executives, through their broadcast standards departments, are constantly on the lookout for

Figure 7.4 Television storyboard. The creator of a television commercial must visualize the synchronization of sound and picture. The storyboard lays out the plan for the commercial in advance so all concerned —director, producer, actor, and technicians—know what the objective

material that might offend the sensitive or have a negative effect on the viewing public. The advertiser is thus assured that the spots will be shown in compatible surroundings which will not disturb the viewer.

The retail advertiser should plan the placement of the store's spots in and around the programs that attract the kind of audience the message is designed to reach and influence. People will not turn off the set just because they are not customers. Seeing the spot might make them decide to visit your place of business. Therein lies the opportunity to grab the attention of uninterested people and, by the quality of your commercial, convert them into new customers.

The fashion advertiser seeking to enhance the store's image can move in that direction with TV advertising. Your store's mere presence on television gives a favorable, up-to-date, modern impression. Just using the latest, most prestigious advertising medium could change the attitude of some people toward your business. People like to feel they are "with it" (or whatever the current phrase is for being current and aware of what's going on). Customer surveys sometimes show that people indicate they heard or learned about the store event on TV even when the store had not advertised on TV! Since people feel that television advertising is

WONDERFUL LIVE-IN COLORS
FROM HERALD HOUSE..........

NOW........AT ROBINSON'S!!!!

is. It also spells out the "look" of the commercial for the store buyer or merchant prior to production so he or she can give approval to proceed. (SOURCE: By permission of Robinson's, Los Angeles.)

exciting, modern, and influential, it follows they will think more highly of a store if they see its ads on TV.

The power of television to communicate with viewers can be important to the advertiser endeavoring to change customer attitudes about the store—that the prices are too high, that the sales people give poor service, that the return policy is too strict. These can all be transmitted as secondary messages or tag lines at the end of the commercial. Constant repetition of slogans about the store eventually find their way into the consciousness of the public—like "Nobody Undersells Gimbels" or Alexander's "How Lucky Can You Get."

As in radio, every word of spoken copy in a television commercial is headline copy—there is no small type (except, perhaps, for disclaimers). The retailer can describe the fashion while it's being shown, almost like a mini fashion show. All the color, the motion, the fit, or the graceful lines of the outfit can be shown, in as real and lifelike a setting as possible. Being able to show products in use, demonstrated in an ideal environment, is a great TV advantage. Sophisticated camera work can show multiple images in fractions of seconds, pouring forth a kaleidoscope of fashion impressions sure to motivate any viewer to a positive feeling about the store.

Television advertising is delivered, for the most part, to people in their homes, while they are relaxed and receptive, in a comfortable atmosphere. What better opportunity for delivering a selling message? Advertisers can simultaneously reinforce the acceptance of regular customers, convert the fence-straddlers, and start the campaign for future shoppers. Among young women aged 18 to 34, the store advertising on TV is often considered to be the leading fashion store when compared with their attitude toward stores advertising in newspapers. This is the market most fashion stores are trying to reach. If this survey is right, more fashion advertising will be done on television than ever before.

OPPORTUNITIES FOR THE FUTURE

According to TvB, each succeeding generation of shoppers is more influenced by television. The influences come from all aspects of the medium. Life-styles presented on situation comedies or serials find their counterparts in real life. The hairdos of Farrah Fawcett changed the way women throughout America wore their hair. Fashions worn by popular television personalities, both men and women, find their way onto the racks and shelves of every fashion store.

Television, in some ways, is larger than life, even though its former 25-inch size has jumped to 84 inches. As it grows, as audiences continue to spend more than six hours a day per household watching the "tube," the influence on fashion and other merchandising will be felt. The personalities themselves become the advertisers, the products. Johnny Carson suits, Jack Nicklaus' sport clothes (although a sports great, without TV Nicklaus would not be the recognizable personality he is), many products by Arnold Palmer, Farrah Fawcett's line of cosmetics, and many more were born and nurtured on television. The implications for fashion retailing are obvious. It becomes mandatory that the fashion retailer develop an attitude of alertness to the changing pictures on the tube, for television is and has become one of the strongest influences on fashion today. This is not to downgrade or negate the fashion designers of Paris, London, New York, or wherever; their influence too will continue.

A recent trend—the saturation use of television to create consumer demand for fashion items—is changing the standard pattern of some fashion promotion. A highly intensified campaign on television launched Jordache jeans, Gloria Vanderbilt jeans, and Sasson. Customers coming to stores to buy these items were often disappointed because the items were not in stock. The promotion had preceded the distribution of the merchandise, and shipping had not kept pace with demand. It caught up quickly, however; these items now sell to millions of customers all over the country. The traditional pattern of the store's buyers going to market; selecting merchandise from manufacturers' lines; waiting for shipment to the stores; and *then* planning and running ads timed for the arrival of the merchandise was broken by this TV blitz technique. It will be interesting to see if this high-powered, expensive approach to selling fashion merchandise is copied by others.

Consider what happened to tennis and tennis clothing in the 1970s. Until it became a television sport and spectacle, thanks to Billy Jean King and Bobby Riggs, tennis was a minor sport. It was an activity for the rich or well-to-do, existing basically in an amateur world of its own. Tennis departments in fashion stores were nonexistent; there were probably a few tennis outfits hanging in a corner of the sporting goods area. Tennis shops outside of tennis clubs were rare. There were other influences, of course, but thanks to the impact of TV, more prize money and the emergence of new personalities, tennis wear is now a major fashion industry. In 1975, American women spent $50 million on tennis clothing, and the growth continued. Many women wear their tennis clothes to the supermarket and never go near a court. But it's "in" to be in tennis clothes. TV tells us so. Opportunities for the fashion retailer? Why not? The store that's first in town with a new fashion idea on television can establish itself as a fashion leader in that area.

A future potential use of television for the retailer is the two-way cable TV system called *Qube*, which began operating on an experimental basis in Columbus, Ohio, in 1977. This system of "interactive" cable TV offers the subscriber the choice of 30 channels, with every possible variety of programming available. The revolutionary aspect of the system is that subscribers can talk back to the TV station. Response buttons on the minicomputer console in the home allow viewers to respond to questions flashed on the screen. Retail opportunity? Couldn't this be the beginning of a true Catalog of the Air? Merchants could show their wares to the family assembled in the comfort of the home. By pushing a button, the viewer could order the advertised product, which would be automatically charged to his or her account. Pickup and delivery could be arranged.

Think of the potential for fashion testing of new merchandise. The retailer could put on a fashion show of the latest styles and items, and viewers could vote whether or not they liked them or would buy them, or what colors would be most popular. With this information, the retailer could estimate the full potential of each particular style and order enough pieces to cover customer needs while eliminating overstocking. Buying in the correct quantities could mean many more profit dollars, for markdowns mean money lost. How far this experiment will go and how successful it will be remains to be seen. We point this out as one of the ways in which television of the future could involve the fashion retailer.

Another exciting advance in television technology opens up new vistas for fashion retailers—the hand-held portable television camera called the minicamera. The minicamera makes possible in-store, outdoor, on-the-spot commercial production. The commercial can be shot right in the store, in the department of choice, giving the viewer an impression of the entire store, not just the fashions being shown. This technique opens the doors to creativity previously possible only on film, which is more costly and time consuming than videotape. If necessary, videotaped television commercials can be produced as quickly as print ads, often more quickly. This improvement in the time factor is welcomed by retailers who have to fight late deliveries and unavailable samples in the production of TV spots. The added flexibility of being able to go right to the store, to do live demonstrations, to re-create actual selling situations, holds great promise for more imaginative, more creative commercials (Figures 7.5 and 7.6).

The development of the videocassette recorders for home and office use will bring great changes in TV viewing habits. By plugging the devices into the TV sets, viewers can automatically record programs for later viewing. Being able to play back the program at another time also gives the commercial added life, unless the spots are eliminated by some new gadget. The advertiser then gets added coverage on top of the audience watching the show at its normal time.

An interesting aspect of the electronic revolution taking place is the growth of cable and subscription television with the absence of commercials as a key attraction for subscribers. We must distinguish between cable systems established to give homes better television reception in certain areas and pay-TV subscription television that provides special programming with no commercial interruptions. The rapidly developing innovations in the entire field of telecommunications—satellite transmission, low-powered TV broadcasts, increases in the number of broadcast facilities—all will have an effect on the future use of television by retail advertisers. The television industry, primarily the three networks, will, in all probability, combat these threats by utilizing its own vast technological inventiveness and resources. It also seems that when cable TV grows to a point where it achieves 30 percent penetration of American homes (forecast for 1985), it will be big enough to move from

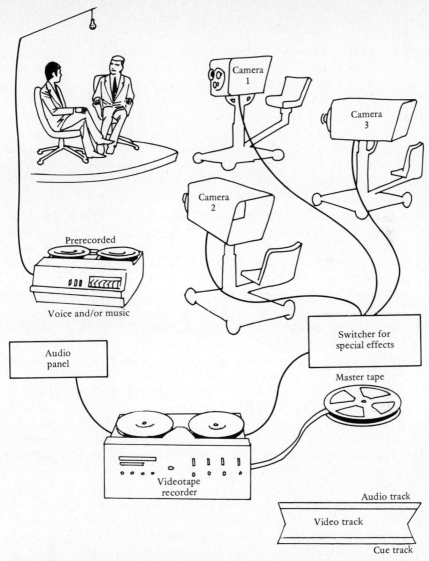

Figure 7.5 Production procedure for television, videotape. Step-by-step diagram of the elements involved in the production of TV spots with videotape.

"an electronic communications medium to become a broadbased advertising medium" (*Newsweek*, July 3, 1978). Then cable will take commercials to reduce its subscription price, and the race will start all over again. This is another development for the retail advertiser to watch, for what it all points to is fragmentation of audi-

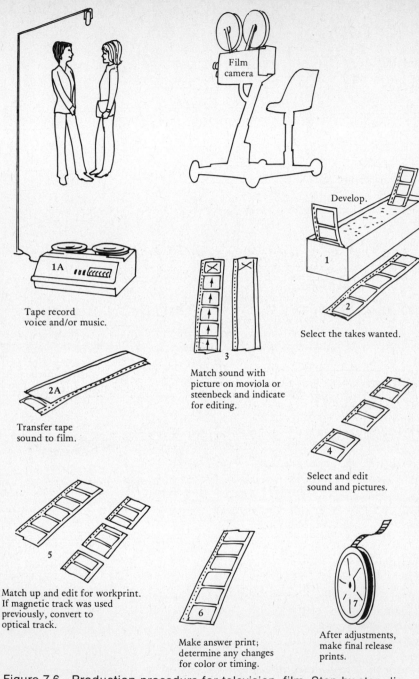

Tape record
voice and/or music.

Transfer tape
sound to film.

Match sound with
picture on moviola or
steenbeck and indicate
for editing.

Match up and edit for workprint.
If magnetic track was used
previously, convert to
optical track.

Develop.

Select the takes wanted.

Select and edit
sound and pictures.

Make answer print;
determine any changes
for color or timing.

After adjustments,
make final release
prints.

Figure 7.6   Production procedure for television, film. Step-by-step diagram for producing a TV spot on film. Production of TV spots should be handled by professionals, but retailers need to understand the scope and limitations of the process.

Table 7.3 DEPARTMENT STORE'S QUARTERLY PERCENTAGES OF BUDGETS AND SALES

DEPARTMENT STORE TELEVISION SCHEDULES			
	1ST QUARTER	2ND QUARTER	3RD QUARTER	4TH QUARTER
2-year average	(Feb., Mar., Apr.)	(May, June, July)	(Aug., Sept., Oct.)	(Nov., Dec., Jan.)
(1973–1974)	15%	24%	21%	40%
DEPARTMENT STORE SALES			
5-year average	20%	23%	22%	35%

SOURCE: Television Bureau of Advertising, New York, BAR, 1975.

ence, similar to radio, and the opportunity to advertise specific types of merchandise to specific groups of people.

DRAWBACKS OF CONSISTENT TV ADVERTISING

Because of high costs, television advertising continues to be an inconsistent outlet for retail fashion advertising. So many retailers are locked in to long-standing advertising habits, mainly newspaper and direct mail, that they find it hard to make the break to broadcast with any regularity. At the point when television expenditures (and radio, too) more closely match seasonal sales patterns, TV will have arrived as an integral part of retailers' advertising.

Contrast the quarterly percentages of sales in department stores with the percentages of their television budgets, also by quarters (Table 7.3). Note that the second and third quarters match up quite well, with dollars spent on TV very close to sales percentages. In the first quarter, and again in the fourth quarter (the Christmas shopping period), there is a 5 percent variance. The probable cause for the imbalance is the availability of co-op funds during the holiday shopping time. Since the November–December period represents 20 to 40 percent of the year's sales for most categories of merchandise, manufacturers make co-op dollars available during that time to be sure their products are advertised when customers are in the best buying mood. Since co-op dollars are not available as readily for fashion merchandise as they are for many other merchandise categories, many fashion TV ads are paid for completely by the stores, without vendor participation. This would account for less fashion advertising on TV, shorter schedules when on the air, and less money spent on production of the spots. These factors tend to make the fashion efforts less effective, reflecting unfavorably on the medium in the minds of the retailer.

Table 7.4 LOCAL COMMERCIAL ACTIVITY BY DAYPART

	DAYTIME	EARLY FRINGE	NIGHT	LATE FRINGE
Clothing store	40%	19%	16%	25%
Department store	47	21	15	17
Discount store	46	22	14	18
Jewelry store	38	18	16	28
Shoe store	54	19	12	15
Furniture store	44	19	15	22

SOURCE: Television Bureau of Advertising, New York, BAR, 1975.

Another set of statistics which indicates that retailers have not entirely embraced television as a full-time advertising medium is shown in Table 7.4. Remembering how the audiences vary in the different dayparts, note the distribution pattern. National averages indicate that 47 percent of department store TV commercials run in daytime; 21 percent in early fringe time; 15 percent in nighttime, and 17 percent in late fringe.

It is obvious that the best times, with the largest audiences and the most selective shows, are utilized only by the national advertisers. Sears, JC Penney, Montgomery Ward, Kmart, and other national retail chains can afford network spots. The local retailer is usually limited by budget to less than the best dayparts, or he or she can buy "prime time" on independent stations if they exist in that market. Some major retailers do buy prime time for important events.

In addition to high cost in air time, television production costs drive many advertisers away. It is recommended that 15 percent of the TV budget be set aside for production to create quality commercials that can stand up against the national advertiser commercials that might be competing with them for attention. National spots, which run for extended periods of time in many markets, can carry a heavy production cost, since the initial cost is spread over the spot cost of the entire schedule. Retail spots, which run for short periods of time, and on much smaller schedules, cannot afford the luxury of top-quality production. Many techniques are not available to the local advertiser because of cost, but retailers have found ways to produce commercials that look more expensive than they are.

Fashion stores endeavor to create the illusion of quality, to reflect the grace and elegance implied in the word "fashion." Some do it by featuring the look of the fashion store itself, others by staging the department's highlights, and others by shooting on location in attractive settings. Presenting the merchandise in a charming environment establishes a mood to which the viewer can respond.

Overcoming the costs of live talent is a problem for retailers in markets with strong AFTRA and SAG union offices. Some cooperative unions, to which broadcast performers belong, have special retail performer rates, taking into consideration the short-term use of the commercial by the retailer. Special rates are also created for voiceovers, where only the performer's voice is used. Every AFTRA local in the country negotiates its own local rates representing everything from actors, singers, and dancers to TV news reporters and sportscasters. Music rates and regulations are the province of the American Federation of Musicians (AFM). Contracts and rates are established in each market depending on the importance of TV production there, economic conditions, and the supply and demand for talent in each market. Studio time is expensive. It involves the hiring of many technical people, such as cameramen, lighting people, floor supervisors, and prop handlers. When shooting on location, some studio costs can be avoided, but trucking and transportation costs are added.

Every step in the production of television commercials must be watched in order to keep costs under control. Each expense item must be estimated as accurately as possible. Establish a simple form listing studio facilities, talent costs, music, graphics, props, trucking costs, and so on. Allow for technical items such as tapes or film dubs. The better the planning, the less chance there is of going over budget. (See Exhibits 7.1 and 7.2)

Other drawbacks to the consistent use of television by fashion retailers include the lack of viewer loyalty to programs and the ease with which viewers can turn off your message. The TV message is as transitory and as perishable as the radio spot, and unless there is sufficient frequency, the message won't stick.

Much has been said and written about the clustering of several commercials at breaks in the programs, with the resultant competition for the viewer's attention and memory. The resultant "cluster" (also called "clutter") can sometimes cancel out one or the other of a three-spot series. The challenge to the advertiser is to make the store's spot so attention-grabbing and interesting that *it* will be the spot that is remembered. The size of the challenge is magnified when the retailer's spot is sandwiched between a dynamic General Motors spot and a tempting Kraft cheese commercial. And the production budget is just a fraction of theirs.

Retailers have learned that the technical help available at the TV production studios can work wonders when given the chance. Unless the store's staff has the experience to the job right, it is wiser to allow the professionals to take over. With proper preplanning and an approved storyboard that spells out every phase of the com-

EXHIBIT 7.1

HOW TO PRODUCE A TV COMMERCIAL FOR UNDER $1000

Most retailers have limited budgets for production of advertising and would therefore do better to produce their commercials in the television studio. Most TV stations are equipped and willing to assist the smaller operator in creating effective commercials on low budgets. Their talents are available to you. A sure way to cut costs is to shoot more than one commercial at a time. Here are two examples:

PRODUCING THREE COMMERCIALS ON TAPE

Studio time at station (including full crew, availability of Chroma Key, props, all facilities)—six hours	$1200
Talent Fees (5 to 6 actors)	600
Editing time (3 hours total)	300
Cost for three commercials	$2100
Average cost per commercial	$700

PRODUCING TWO COMMERCIALS IN THE STORE—TAPE

Remote truck with videotape machine (including director, crew of 3, lights, mikes, camera)—approximately 4 hours on location	$1100
Talent fees (4 actors)	400
Editing time (4 hours)	400
Cost for two commercials	$1900
Average cost per commercial	$950

mercial, rehearsals with the performers before going to the studio, and completed graphics, supers, and props, the studio crew, with a competent director who knows what is expected from the commercial, can produce a satisfactory commercial with a minimum of difficulty.

Making the most of studio time by planning to shoot several commercials in the same day is a recommended way to save time and money. As stores become more involved in broadcast media they will discover that their expertise will improve, their timetables will lengthen, and before long they will be producing spots and achieving many of the same economies of operation they used to think only newspapers could give them. Retail TV commercials need not have that "local" look. TV spots don't have to be expensively produced to be effective. Having a talented in-house staff helps as does having enough budget to hire the right talent. Either can produce quality TV commercials that sell.

EXHIBIT 7.2

HOW TO PRODUCE A TV COMMERCIAL FOR UNDER $35,000

Producing high budget commercials? Few retailers can afford to spend large amounts for TV spots when their life expectancy (as in most retail promotions) is so limited. For the occasions when the money is available, plan to spend wisely. Here are typical costs for producing a television commercial on 35 mm color film, on location, in a major city, with four on-camera actors. Shooting time: 12 hours.

Production company (including talent)	$20,000
Postproduction (editing, blending, etc.)	3,000
Voiceover announcer (fee and recording)	600
Music (composition, arranging, recording)	3,000
Color-corrected packages	800
10 percent production reserve (remakes, etc.)	2,000
Agency commission (15 percent)	4,410
Total cost	$33,810

WEIGHING THE GLAMOUR AGAINST THE RESULTS

As more and more retailers discover that, when used effectively, broadcast advertising can pack tremendous impact and bring in results, certain decisions must be made and certain factors taken into account.

The *ego factor* must be discounted. The novice in television, enthralled by the excitement of seeing himself or herself on the tube, must resist the temptation of being the spokesperson for the store. This avoids paying some talent costs, but the average retailer is not an entertainer or even a qualified public speaker. It is best to leave the job to the professionals and to let them show the merchandise; that's why the advertiser is buying TV in the first place. It is true that some store owners have become celebrities because of their roles on TV commercials, but aired side by side with national TV spots, the local retail message often looks like amateur night versus a Broadway production.

When *buying air time* the retailer must exercise judgment to be sure the TV package has the best chance of reaching the target audience with the proper merchandise. Ask a media planner for a choice of broadcast packages to determine which is best suited to achieve the goal. Many stores employ advertising agencies or media buying services to handle their broadcast needs. These outside services take many of the problems of producing broadcast advertising out of the hands of the store's advertising staff and can assist with many phases of the job which the store's ad people might not be capable of managing.

Look for loopholes in the schedule. Be sure the spots are positioned according to product appeal and target audience. If scheduled spots are preemptible and can be moved because someone will pay a higher rate for that spot, it could be wasteful if the commercial for teenie-bopper blue jeans eventually ran in the late news segment. Because of the negotiable nature of television buying, it is often worth paying more in order to be sure the spot runs in the right location.

The mere presence of the retail fashion store on television does not guarantee results. The campaign must develop increased awareness of the store name, its merchandise values, and all the reasons why people should shop there. Simply increasing the number of spots will not do it, for unless the commercials attract attention, develop interest, demonstrate the product, and motivate the viewer to action, very little will happen. The spot must be memorable. The idea must be presented clearly and distinctly. The schedule, especially when limited, should concentrate the spots on a limited number of stations for the greatest impact. The tendency to try to be on as many stations as possible, so "everyone can see my commercials," spreads the schedule too thin and reduces the chances of making the number of impressions an ad must make to be effective.

Many retail advertisers require postanalyses from their buying services or advertising agencies. These consist of a certified log of when the spots actually ran compared to the plan indicating when they were *going* to run. If some spots are "bumped" from their planned positions, the store is entitled to have the spots run at another comparable time, on a comparable program, with a comparable audience (called "make goods").

With the short-term runs of many retail schedules, the event may be over by the time the error is noticed. In that case the store is credited with the time, and it is "banked" for use at a later date. This procedure is no different than the usual retail habit of counting the pieces of merchandise in a shipment to be sure everything tallies with the original order and the shipping invoice. Making sure you get what you pay for is just a sound business practice.

After the retailer agrees to accept a cooperative arrangement with a national advertiser to participate in a television campaign, processing the paperwork that goes with such an arrangement can offset the increased sales results. Systems have been developed (see Appendix 7 and Chapter 2) to smooth the flow of the inevitable paperwork. The stations on the schedule must be notified that certified proof of performance will be required, and should know that this information will be needed before the schedule starts. All parties must be aware of deadlines, including the dates during which the spots can be aired, and the date by which the claim for reimbursement must be submitted to the manufacturer. If run too late, or claimed too late, the retailer could wind up paying the entire cost of the TV campaign, with no rebate coming from the vendor.

This kind of problem arises in co-op advertising in every medium and requires constant vigilance on the part of the retailer. Lost rebates mean lost profits. Failure to collect co-op claims inflates the advertising costs of the store and causes other problems. If a campaign was planned at $10,000, with the manufacturer paying 50 percent of the costs, and through some slipup the store fails to live up to the co-op agreement, the manufacturer's $5,000 does not materialize and the advertising department is $5,000 over budget. That means curtailment or elimination of some future promotion and loss of an opportunity to promote for additional sales volume.

Despite the problems of integrating the new medium of television into the basically print-oriented advertising departments of retail stores, the results can make the effort worthwhile. Retailers throughout America report good and improving results from their television advertising. And, as in many things, retailers learned to do it their own way.

Since retail copywriters were originally print writers, filling space in newspapers and direct mail, the challenge of writing for television forced them to write for the eyes and ears of their customers. No longer could they just write copy for a stand-up spokesperson to read in front of a camera. They now had to do more than just gather the facts about the merchandise. They had to visualize how to present it, and think through step-by-step, frame-by-frame coordination of words, pictures, and music. Copy, music, and visual elements had to exist in harmony to present a pleasing result for the viewer. The copywriter, from whom flow the ideas that make effective commercials, had to keep in mind the functions of the music and the visuals while securing enough attention from the viewer to ensure close attention and eventually participation.

The basic premise of a productive commercial involves getting attention by trying to stand out as different and worth listening to. Remember the line "What do you say after you say Hello?" If you've got attention, you've said "Hello." Now get on with the selling. Show and tell how the fashions being presented make the viewer look good, feel good, attract glances, or bring whatever benefit the commercial can promise—and deliver. The ad promises, the merchandise delivers. If the spot offers enough reasons to buy to motivate the customer to visit the store, its job is done. If the merchandise in the store fails to live up to the promise of the ad, the ad has done more harm than good. Not only has the store failed to make a sale, but the failure has probably cost the store a customer. Television, as we have said, is a powerful medium. It realistically plays back what the camera sees. The viewers must want what they see, and the store is responsible for satisfying the desire or need the commercial stimulated.

The impact of broadcast advertising cannot be denied. It has been pointed out that public and legal notices, required by law, must be published in newspapers. They usually wind up in the back pages, hidden among the classified ads and obituaries. Could it be the rule was promulgated so that they would not be seen? Think about the ruling that took cigarette advertising off radio and TV. The selling force of the media was so influential that the advertising had to be prohibited by law.

As the television industry grows, with technical advances that promise many more channels and methods of receiving televised information, TV may become more fragmented, with more diversified, but smaller, audiences. Networks as we know them today will probably change. But however it happens, TV's future development will have a continuing and growing influence on our daily lives. Within this brilliant world of things to come, the retail fashion advertiser of tomorrow will learn how to use this medium to advantage, as retailers through the years have learned to use print. Techniques to deliver messages, tailor-made to attract the precise target audiences, will be developed. Retailers usually move slowly into new territories, but when they move, when they have seen it work, they move with determination. Somehow, sometime, the sight, sound, motion, and music of television will find its way into the daily operation of fashion stores, for the nature of the medium lends itself to fashion presentation as no other kind of advertising does.

QUESTIONS FOR DISCUSSION AND CLASS ASSIGNMENTS

1. As a class project, have all students record their TV viewing (programs and stations watched) for a three-day period, using the Arbitron diary instructions as a guide. Tabulate total viewing by program and determine the average per-person viewing patterns. Compare with national Nielsen ratings in your area. Discuss.

2. Survey 10 homes in your neighborhood and determine the number of TV sets per household. Ask the amount of daily viewing per home. Discuss the number of sets versus the number of people per home.
3. Monitor both network and independent stations in your market area. Record the number and variety of retail commercials over a one-week period. Discuss results in relation to the store's newspaper advertising activities.
4. Name four special advantages television advertising offers retail advertisers. Note four disadvantages. Discuss the potential increased use of television by retail stores.
5. The launching of Jordache jeans via saturation television was a retail phenomenon. Discuss the possibility of this technique being applied to other retail advertising categories.
6. Cable television and subscription TV are growing in importance but have yet to penetrate retail advertising budgets. Discuss the potential of this intriguing new medium.
7. Production costs have discouraged some retailers from producing quality TV commercials. Comment on some techniques retailers might employ to improve the quality of their TV spots without adding excessive costs.
8. Discuss the problem of TV "clutter"—the grouping of several commercials during programs. What would be the best position for an advertiser to have in a four-spot cluster? Why?
9. What are some of the problems retailers face in scheduling television ads, in adapting retail procedures and timing to television production needs.
10. Discuss cable television in the home as a replacement for department store catalogs. Is cable feasible as a future communications vehicle for retailers?

Chapter 8
Other Advertising Media

We have confined our discussion so far to external advertising media—newspapers, direct mail, radio, television. There are others we will talk about, but first let's consider the internal advertising media.

INTERNAL ADVERTISING

If a store advertised to the limits of its financial capabilities it would, at most, display about 15 percent of its total merchandise through advertising. This figure holds up under examination, for if a store traces more than 15 percent of its sales volume to advertised items, that store will have trouble showing a profit. Most stores derive a smaller percentage of their business through promotion, and many small retailers promote very little. A profitable fashion operation must sell the customers who are in the store *more* than what they planned to buy when they arrived. The opportunity is there, because the shopper is certainly in a buying mood if he or she is in the store at all. (See the section on internal advertising in Chapter

2.) An alert merchant makes use of internal advertising media to make it easy for the customer to find the advertised merchandise and also see everything else possible while in a receptive frame of mind.

Internal advertising possibilities are limitless. Initially, copies of the newspaper or magazine ads—*tearsheets*—can be mounted and displayed at entrances, elevators, main aisles, and in the department. Actual pages from the paper, or enlargements (blowups) are used. They serve to remind those who saw the ad, reinforce the ad at point of sale, and gain new readers who may not have seen the ad. As an aid to the sales staff, the tearsheet is essential. It reminds *them* of the event, whether they read the paper or not, and provides a ready reference for customer questions.

Manufacturers often provide professionally produced *counter signs,* reproductions of slick magazine ads and fashion magazine hang tags to enhance the quality image of the store and the manufacturer.

Many stores still print daily or weekly *handbills*, which are distributed at entrances, at the wrapstands, and at other key points. They list unadvertised specials, give fashion news, and tell about items not planned for advertising.

Manufacturers tags contain instructions for care of the garments and details of the fabric and construction to help the customer decide to buy. Labels in garments carry washing instruction and fabric content, information the customer may want to know before buying.

Merchandise that is packaged attractively tends to be displayed by the stores in traffic aisles. The package itself is a sales aid. Even the backs of sales and restaurant checks carry advertising messages.

Store signs of all kinds are the silent salespeople of any store (see Appendixes 17–20). Signs should list any information about the merchandise not easily apparent to the casual shopper (Figure 8.1). The more the sign can include, besides item and price, the easier it becomes for the customer to make a buying decision. Well-written, informative signs can convert people who are "just looking" into customers. Signs should be written by advertising copywriters, especially for advertised items. Too often the writing chore is given to an unqualified person in the department or the person running the sign machine.

Store windows, posters, banners, even the restaurant or snack bar menus can carry advertising about store events. If there are elevators, a neat sign at eye level or above will surely be read by the occupants. Most people don't know where to look when riding in an elevator, so why not take advantage of the circumstance?

This Is the Upright Type of Sign

- Order only as many signs as you need.
- A sign is a silent but influential salesperson—always on the job.
- Make each sign do a thorough selling job.
- Eliminate signs that merely repeat or give no information.

Good signs tell a complete story. The customer wants to know:

- Why should I buy it?
- What is it?
- What are its special points of value?
- What is its price?

Each selling sign must answer these four questions forcefully, quickly, clearly.

Write a selling sign as follows:

- Headline. Describe the merchandise or service briefly, clearly, and with scrupulous accuracy; include a powerful selling phrase.
- Outstanding Selling Points. List briefly, in the order of importance, three or four sound reasons why *you* would buy the article.
- Price. Most of all, *the customer wants to know the price of the article*—tell her!

Figure 8.1 Budd Gore's suggested sign procedure. Emphasis on good signs varies from store to store. This basic plan tells how to write effective signs. (SOURCE: By permission of Budd Gore, Inc.)

A recent addition to the arsenal of internal advertising media is the *videotape recorder* and its adaptations. Many stores run their television commercials on strategically situated TV monitors. They run tapes of spots from manufacturers, some of which may never get on the air, selling products available in the store. Extended versions of the 30-second spot can be shown in the store to reinforce the message just as a posted tearsheet does, or to attract the attention of a new prospect. National advertisers' training films describing in detail, for salespeople's education, the care and selling points of merchandise often make interesting and productive viewing for shoppers.

Some stores employ *public address systems* to tell shoppers about in-store specials, fashion shows, and demonstrations. The technique is frowned upon by quality image stores, but others find the public address system an effective device for getting more sales volume out of existing store traffic.

WHY NOT BILLBOARDS?

While it is true that few retailers use billboards and other outdoor advertising, many other advertisers find it effective. Despite pressures from civic organizations and environmentalists, the outdoor advertising industry continues to grow.

There is great variety in the medium—poster billboards (12 by 25 feet), painted bulletins (14 by 48 feet), smaller painted and posted signs (Kennedy boards), transit ads, bus benches, and the super-sized three-dimensional spectaculars. New variations are constantly being developed. The advertiser is offered large audience circulation at a low cost per reader. There is wide choice of location, with availability of dramatic color and graphics to deliver quick, direct messages.

Outdoor advertising has many of the same advantages as an advertising medium as radio, for its audience is the same mobile, outdoor-living, auto driver listening to the car radio and looking around while rolling along the streets and highways. Outdoor advertising develops great awareness for products and advertisers. According to the Institute of Outdoor Advertising, billboards were used by Richway, the discount division of Rich's, Atlanta, to advertise the opening of new stores in and around the Atlanta area. There were no Richway stores in this market previously. Using billboards exclusively, the chain increased awareness of the Richway name 187 percent.

Outdoor has great flexibility in that the message can be placed where the advertiser wants it. Choice locations—high traffic intersections—are in great demand, and costs rise accordingly. Most contracts are for 30-day showings, with the boards rotated within an agreed-upon area. Outdoor signs work all day long, every day of the week. Lighted signs have great visibility at night and less competition from unlighted signs.

Outdoor reaches all kinds of people—young, old, affluent, not-so-affluent, professional, managerial—anyone who travels. It is a strong supportive medium, reinforcing and reminding viewers of products, store names, and events. Major department store chains, like Gimbels and Stone & Thomas, use billboards for added exposure of specific products and special sales (Figure 8.2). Unquestion-

Figure 8.2 Examples of major billboard campaigns by department stores. Special events provide reasons for reaching out to customers. (SOURCE: By permission of Pacific Outdoor Advertising.)

ably, outdoor advertising has potent impact as an institutional medium. But the value of institutional advertising has always been a question in the minds of most retailers. This accounts for its limited use despite individual successes around the country.

In San Francisco, Hastings Men's Stores developed an effective billboard campaign using copy lines that created a mild public sensation (Figure 8.3). The word-of-mouth, both positive and negative, indicated that the billboards certainly were noticed. JC Penney uses painted bulletins to keep the corporate name continually be-

A

B

C

fore the public while generating support for advertising efforts in other media. Automotive products advertising has been effective in reaching the prospect behind the wheel, in touch with the car's operation and keenly aware of the car's performance (Figure 8.3).

Supermarkets have found ways to give price and item flexibility to their painted bulletins. The technique consists of painting half the bulletin while using the other half of the space for a cut-out area that changes periodically with weekly specials. This combines company identification with price/item adaptability.

There are several drawbacks for the retailer in outdoor advertising. The medium requires short messages of very few words. Unless the store has an easily recognizable slogan or signature, there is a problem of recognition. There is lack of audience selectivity, but then most Americans travel. The 30-day rotation of billboards, with limited opportunity for change, may be too slow for the fast-moving retailer, but reaching the same audience every day (people usually drive to and from work the same way daily) with a good fashion message has value. The location of the boards and the speed with which traffic passes those locations places a limitation on the message content. Readership and recall of the advertising message vary widely because of these factors. From a cost standpoint, most retailers spend little of their own money on outdoor advertising. They accept tie-ins with national campaigns for products they sell, but limit their own use to store openings and major sale events.

Whether it is the high cost of production, the inability to pinpoint results, or the image the outdoor industry has acquired through bad publicity from environmental groups, outdoor advertising is low on the list of the retail advertiser's preferences.

WHERE MAGAZINES FIT IN

So little magazine advertising has been produced by retailers that it is usually included in the "all other" section of the advertising budget. But the magazine business is changing. The era of specializa-

---

Figure 8.3   (A) Hastings Men's Store in San Francisco ran a highly effective campaign that developed great awareness through dramatic design and strong, clever copy. (B) Sears' outdoor campaign includes price specials neatly fitted into the 30-day change schedule of most billboard operations. (C) JC Penney, a national retail organization, uses billboards to promote its private brand merchandise and to compete with other national brands. (SOURCE: By permission of Pacific Outdoor Advertising.)

tion and the growth of the high-level "city" magazines are creating new interest in a print category that has been largely ignored by the fashion retailer.

Up to now, the widest use of magazine advertising by fashion stores consisted of listings run (and paid for) by fashion manufacturers in *Vogue, Harper's Bazaar, Glamour*, and similar publications. The manufacturer would take a full page in the magazine and list (with permission of the stores who bought that particular item) the stores where the merchandise could be purchased. Stores like Bonwit's, Saks Fifth Avenue, Neiman-Marcus or Rich's would have their names listed at the bottom of the page. Sometimes only one store would be involved, and in that case the store's logo might be used.

The prestige value of these ads worked both ways. It identified the manufacturer as one of nationwide importance, and it served as a bonus for the store, which also gained prestige points by being mentioned in a quality publication. The ad also included an implied endorsement for both parties. While not as heavily sought after as in the past, these fashion credits give stores an aura of authority they will usually accept.

To make their publications more accessible and useful as an advertising medium for major department stores and regional fashion specialty stores, many magazines have begun to "zone" their circulations. An advertiser can buy just the distribution of the magazine in the area where that store does business. Zones vary by the type of magazine, but choices range from whole sections of the country (Northwest, Southeast) to life-style area (Sunbelt, Far West) to zipcode distributions (*Time, Newsweek*). Today you can notice in most national magazines ads for local businesses, which benefit from the acceptance and influence of the publication while buying a small portion of the magazine's circulation (Figure 8.4).

High-fashion stores use this approach to reach the more affluent people in their area who may not be reachable by other means. The prestige of the magazine might be strong enough to interest these people in a store and its merchandise. Costs for ads in these regional editions average 40 percent higher in cost-per-thousand than the national rate, an expensive buy for the fashion retailer.

On the positive side of the magazine picture, caused in part by the amazing growth of special interest magazines, are some interesting statistics from the Magazine Publishers Association:

- Magazine circulation is at an all-time high.
- People buy more copies of magazines and pay more for them than ever before.

Figure 8.4   This *New Yorker* cartoon, part of an ad to promote the select market available in the readership of the magazine, shows the variety of specialized subject matter offered in magazines today. (SOURCE:
Drawing by Whitney Darrow, Jr., © 1976 The New Yorker Magazine, Inc.)

- Nine out of ten adults read magazines during the average
  month. They each read an average of seven different copies
  per month.
- The average magazine reader is young (34.9), married, and
  living in a single-family home in the suburbs, which he or she
  owns; is better-educated, employed, and has a 24 percent
  above average household income.
- There is no seasonal dropoff in magazine readership.

This sounds like the perfect target consumer for the fashion retailer
and specialty store. Can these targets be reached by magazines regularly, consistently, economically? The trend is there. Major retail
organizations like Sears, Kmart, Saks Fifth Avenue, JC Penney, and

Federated Department Stores spend hundreds of thousands of dollars in magazines. Sears, always the leader in advertising expenditures, spent over $18 million in magazines in 1976, *nine times* more than its nearest competitor, Kmart, which spent $1.7 million. In 1979, Sears' total advertising expenditures were $709,312,000; Kmart spent $287,095,000, and JC Penney spent $278,000,000. (*Advertising Age,* November 3, 1980). The average fashion retailer cannot play in that league, but if the leaders in the industry are using magazines, smaller retailers will find a way to use the publications available in their areas.

The first indication of this trend at the major city level is the curiosity retailers are showing in the new, special interest "city" magazines. Monthly publications like *Chicago, New York,* and *Los Angeles,* featuring the entertainment, life-style, and personalities of the major cities of the nation, offer the fashion retailer an audience with better income, better education, more discretionary dollars to spend, diversified interests, and the desire to be up-to-date in all things, from gossip to fashion. Specialty shops and designer name sections of department stores are putting ad dollars into this medium as part of the growing campaign to upgrade the stores' fashion image and improve their market share of better-quality customers.

Entire departments, featuring exclusive merchandise from Calvin Klein, Gloria Vanderbilt, Yves Saint Laurent, Bill Blass, and others have been established in many major department stores. They appeal to a special segment of the consumer public and operate with separate open-to-buy, management, and promotional funds.

A trip to your neighborhood newsstand will fill you in on the great variety of special interest magazines now on sale, competing for the consumers' attention. Here are some:

For men	Automotive Science Fishing and hunting	Mechanics and service Sports
For women	Fashion Baby care Brides Romance Self Improvement	Home decorating Dressmaking, needlework
For men and women	Arts and antiques Boating, yachting	Aviation Business, finance

Camping	Recreation
Crafts, hobbies	Dogs, cats,
Fraternal, clubs	pets
Photography	Horses
Religious	Music
	Sports

And under sports, there is everything from tennis to skiing to mo-
torcycles to hot rods to boxing, baseball, hockey, and football. The
practical result of this overload of information is new fashion needs
and life-style requirements for enthusiasts who want to pursue
their special interests.

The life-style marketing that many fashion retailers are geared
up for lends itself to the specialization trends taking place in most
media. It remains for the media planner to seek out the specific audience for the specific merchandise and position the two for maximum efficiency.

CONSISTENT ADVERTISING IN ALL MEDIA

When great advertising campaigns are studied, they usually reveal
a common trait—consistency. Along with consistency is continuity.
And with consistency and continuity comes recognition—and with
recognition, memorability. Positioning the name, the product, the
store in the mind of the public as the one people recall when it's
time to buy—that's advertising success. Successful campaigns
show that throughout the ad schedule—in whatever medium—
there is a consistency of theme, a thread of continuity, an easily remembered main idea.

This concept is most noticeable in national advertising. Ad
agencies understand the need for multimedia campaigns and plan
variations of the basic theme for each medium being used. Consistent, regular impressions, made over a period of time in newspapers,
on radio, on television, and in other media instantly bring to mind
ads from McDonald's, from Crest, from Datsun. Repetition is the
"secret" of advertising—if there is a secret formula—but the same
theme must be repeated, or variations of that theme, to achieve
maximum results.

Unfortunately, this is not always true in retail advertising and
sales promotion. Sometimes it seems the left hand does not know
what the right hand is doing. The style of advertising in newspapers often differs from the store's look in direct mail catalogs. The
look of the television commercial makes the radio spot sound like
it's coming from another store. The home furnishings ads look one
way, the fashion ads have another style. Even with a prominent

logo or signature, tests have shown that readers have trouble deciding who is doing the advertising.

With the exception of the Christmas campaign or anniversary
sales, few stores have a consistency of appearance, of copy style, of
technique that immediately says to the casual reader or viewer,
"Aha! That's a Jones Brothers ad coming up!" A Lord and Taylor ad
is easily recognized. Macy's is Macy's. Bloomingdale's has its
unique style. But for many retailers this is not true.

The missing link is planning—long-range planning; constant
and consistent planning. Formats, type styles, copy approaches
should be consistent to be recognizable, to be remembered. The
voices, or the copy style, or the musical intro of the radio and TV
spots should immediately identify the advertiser. The time interval for grabbing the attention of the uninterested, preoccupied listener, reader, or viewer is five seconds or less, so there must be instant recognition.

One of the enemies of consistent advertising by retailers is
boredom. Many advertisers tend to get bored with their work long
before the customers have begun to recognize the style. National
advertisers have said that it takes two years to sell a slogan or a tag
line to the public. The trouble is that the creative people, who
worked on the project months before it saw the light of day, are sick
of it just about the time the general public is catching on.

The synergistic effect we described when discussing how
radio increases the impact of advertising when added to the mix applies to all media. Imagine the combined impact if the catalog, the
newspaper campaign, the radio and television spots, store signs,
window treatments, bus cards, truck banners, and bumper stickers
all heralded the same story, the same design, the same message!
There would no longer be an identity crisis, for everyone who received the message, from whatever medium, would get the same
message. And each additional time the message was seen or heard
its effectiveness would expand geometrically.

This concept is not new. Most knowledgeable advertising
people know it. Too often things get lost in the day-to-day struggle
to meet deadlines, to settle buyer hassles, to get the ads out no matter what. The daily problems tend to obscure the big picture.

Somehow, despite the pressure of the daily grind that is standard operating procedure in most retail advertising offices, there
should be a pause to look at things from a broader viewpoint. Unless there is a planned break in the action, a time to look at everything in perspective, errors will occur, mistakes will slip through.
In addition to checking proofs and reading the ads for typographic
errors, there should be an additional checkpoint to determine if

every ad contributes to the basic advertising theme, the sales promotion goals of the season, and the long-range objectives of the company.

QUESTIONS FOR DISCUSSION AND CLASS ASSIGNMENTS

1. What reasons do retailers give for their limited involvement in outdoor advertising? Do you think their reasons are valid?
2. Discuss the importance of internal advertising as a natural conclusion of the marketing/advertising cycle.
3. To what degree should a retail store allow manufacturers' signs to be displayed in the store to promote the sale of merchandise?
4. Should special signwriters, department assistants, or advertising copyriters write the copy for the store's merchandise signs? Discuss the pros and cons of each situation.
5. Name four reasons outdoor billboards offer advertisers advantages similar to radio advertising.
6. National fashion magazines and popular "city" magazines have attracted retailers in many sections of the country. Discuss how advertising of this type could be beneficial to the retailer.
7. One of the weaknesses of retail sales promotion is the absence of continuity of advertising from medium to medium. How can this lack of consistency be prevented?

Chapter 9
Developing a Fashion
Advertising Image

One of the most overworked words in the business world is "image." It falls into the language category called cliché, a trite phrase or hackneyed expression. Someone once said a word or phrase becomes a cliché because so many people find it is the best way to express what they mean to say, so they use it over and over again. As in most clichés, however, the original, or true, meaning of the word is often lost. One dictionary definition of *image* says: "A mental representation of anything not actually present to the senses; an imitation or likeness, a copy or symbol," and, of course, "a reflection."

The latter is the closest definition in its application to the "image" of a retail store. *Image* is the word retailers use to talk about their stores. The idea they are trying to convey would more accurately be expressed as the store's personality or character. Most often, store principals feel their image is what *they* think it is. In most cases, however, the personality of the store is the opinion *people* have of the store—the way in which the store is perceived by its public. The true reflection of the store is the sum of how all the things it is impinges on the minds and opinions of the buying public.

Advertising is a mirror. It can only reflect what is in the store and of the store and by the store. But as a mirror, advertising can quickly convey to the public the true character and personality of the retail store.

Some store managements are more interested in customers' attitudes towards the store than in finding out customers' personal and demographic characteristics, their shopping habits, their lifestyles, and their media usage. Using the mirror analogy, this is a looking inward attitude instead of the broader marketing attitude of looking outward. To establish the store's position in the marketplace, to nail down its identity, the attitude of the retailer must swing away from inward, merchandise-oriented factors to those that involve the customers and the market the store serves.

This is the role of the marketing executive in the retail organization and in the larger department stores. It is a distinct change from the routine retail patterns of the past, when store buyers scanned the racks of their manufacturer resources, selecting items and styles for their stores from whatever was available in the market. More recently, retailers have regarded themselves as purchasing agents for their customers. To implement this attitude, merchandise managers and fashion directors confer with individual department buyers before the buying trip to the market and again during the trip to make sure all buyers are buying to the "looks" and themes that conform to the store's plan and that are most likely to succeed with the store's customers. This development in retailing reflects modern marketing strategy. The marketing vice-president is a major executive in some department store organizations, and the responsibility for the store's image is assigned to that executive. If not assigned to a specific person, the marketing function becomes part of the sales promotion manager's responsibility.

ALL THE THINGS YOU ARE IS YOUR IMAGE

If you query a retailer and ask who the store sells to—who would be the target audience—the answer could possibly be "Everyone!" Large retailers imagine that they cater to the entire population, but the use of modern marketing tools would report a more accurate analysis of the store's audience. The smaller retailer, much closer to the day-to-day operation of the store, has a much more accurate evaluation of the customers being served.

Knowing your store and what it stands for in the eyes of the public is valuable information sought by all alert retailers. Budd

Gore, in his excellent, experience-based *Retail Marketing Newsletter*, quoted the findings of a study conducted by a trio of professors who asked customers of small retail stores what was important to them in deciding in which retail stores they would shop. The results appeared under three headings indicating the degree of importance of the various factors:

Very Important to the Customer

1. Quality of goods and services
2. Quantity of goods and services
3. Neatness of establishment
4. Cleanliness of establishment
5. Spaciousness of establishment
6. Uniformity of appearance of establishment
7. Management's knowledge of product or service
8. Speed of service
9. Prestige of business
10. Satisfaction of customer complaints
11. Quality of advertising
12. Dependability of business
13. Employees' knowledge of product or service
14. Helpful attitude of employees
15. Friendly attitude of employees

Important to the Customer

1. Convenience of location
2. Variety of choice of goods or services
3. Hours open each day
4. Days open per week
5. Availability of latest fashion or style
6. Adequacy of merchandise display
7. Adequacy of liberal credit policy
8. Adequacy of delivery service
9. Adequacy of product guaranty
10. Adequacy of after-guaranty repairs
11. Adequacy of product return policy
12. Adequacy of purchase bonuses
13. Availability of parking facilities

No Significant Importance to the Customer

1. Adequacy of layaway service
2. Employees' appearance

3. Price of goods or services
4. Sales pressure
5. Traffic congestion in street
6. Traffic congestion on sidewalk
7. Traffic congestion in store
8. Air conditioning

We don't agree with all the findings, of course, and most retailers seeing the list would say "They're not talking about *my* store!" But some of the answers are surprising in regard to the image of the store—the way in which customers perceive it and what *they* think is important. Note the importance on neatness, cleanliness, and spaciousness. It should not be necessary to point out that a store should always be neat and clean, with judicious placing of mirrors and good lighting that give an illusion of spaciousness at modest cost. Management's knowledge of products and service ranks higher than employees' knowledge, because if management does not bring in the right merchandise, the employees will not have the right merchandise to sell, no matter how knowledgeable they might be.

We do not know what types of stores were included in the survey, but "availability of latest fashion or style" would undoubtedly rank much higher in importance if the store were a fashion store. Substitute the basic retail line of "the right merchandise at the right time at the right price," and the score would certainly be higher. Note the importance to the customer of displaying the merchandise well. Attractive displays of merchandise, in realistic settings, in neat, clean areas with a feeling of spaciousness, help the customer buy more. The lack of interest in traffic congestion is the "go to where the action is" idea, because crowds attract more shoppers than empty stores.

The low ranking of air conditioning is a strange item. Customer comfort in many areas of the country is a high-priority consideration. Since most brand name merchandise is available in many stores in every city, the store that offers the comfort of controlled temperatures and pleasant surroundings is sure to rank high in the minds of the public.

The findings of this survey are, of course, not conclusive, but they do give some insight into the elements of store merchandising and operation that some customers look for. The individual components of the questionnaire apply to all stores, large or small. It would be interesting to conduct such a survey in the stores in your town, as a marketing project. This is information the retailer must have to respond to customers' needs. With this kind of input, the retailer can have an idea of how the store is perceived by the public, provided the information is used to initiate a study of the store itself, and an examination of its merchandising and service policies.

A store's image is the sum of all its parts. It is a composite of many factors. It is what comes to mind when the store's name is mentioned. Blank's store may be known for service. Jones' is a great place to meet friends, to have lunch in the restaurant. Smith's is the place to find the latest trendy fashions. Or: "Don't ever go to the BonTon, they never have what they advertise."

The impression a store makes is a combination of its stated policies and the execution of its policies. A store can't call itself "The friendliest store in town" if the salespeople are grumpy or discourteous. A store president once illustrated the principle of a friendly, courteous attitude to his employees with a commentary on the reputed ability of whisky to offset the effects of snakebite. The whisky, he said, didn't work as an antidote to the snake venom unless the whisky was *in* the person at the time the person was bitten. In the same way, he said, courtesy and politeness is not something to be put on when the employee comes to work in the morning and discarded when he or she goes home. It has to be part of their personalities, all the time, or it doesn't work. A good point; a "friendly" store should be sure to hire friendly people.

Topping the list of items of importance to customers is "quality and quantity of goods and services." No surprise here. Merchandise policies are the heart and soul of the fashion business. Paraphrasing the saying, you are what you sell. Fashion stores establish their positions in the market by the brand-name merchandise they offer for sale. The specialty shop corrals the designer names that spell "high fashion." The popular priced shop sells the fashions that are the peak of their appeal and most in demand by their clientele. Often the brand names carry with them an additional identification of a type of merchandise category the shopper readily understands. For example, "Levis" used to mean the pants manufactured by Levi-Strauss. Now it has become the generic term for the entire jeans division. A "Judys" or "Contempo Casuals" immediately brings to mind a certain type of fashion and the assurance that selections of contemporary styles, with the necessary accessories, will be available in those stores. Merchandise policies also dictate the price lines of merchandise to be carried and the depth of selection by brand, style, and price to be stocked in each store. From these policy decisions, and others, an overall merchandise image develops that the promotion department must project to the public (see Figure 9.1 on pages 244 and 246).

Sales promotion policies—the look of the ads, the sound of the

A

B

C

D

244

commercials, the selection of typefaces—contribute to the image the store reflects. Many people get their first impression from advertising. When a store tries to change its image, advertising is used to tell people about it. And, of course, the advertising must reflect merchandising and service policies.

The second impression people get, after the advertising, is from salespeople. Part of the store image is established by the decision whether or not to give service, and if so, how much. Think of the quick influence a self-service store projects in contrast to a store that has eager, friendly salespeople standing by, ready to help with the customer's selection.

Other policies that affect a store's personality include standards of delivery, the availability of parking space, exchange and return procedures, and phone and mail order service. Less tangible, but also important, is the design and layout of the store. Wide aisles, lush carpeting, comfortable, colorful surroundings, suitable lighting are all conducive to a pleasant shopping experience.

THE IMPRESSION FASHION MERCHANDISE MAKES

Fashion is everywhere in today's life-style—not just in clothes, but in every phase of modern living, as we have previously noted. It is part of our mode of living, the decor of our homes, the cars we drive. Everything we do is, in some way, in style or in fashion. It is reflected most often in the clothes we wear, for the clothes are suitable to the lives we lead.

We have noted the growth of active sportswear fashions—warm-up suits and tennis apparel—worn even by people who do not jog or play tennis, but like the look of the clothes. The outdoorsy, mobile society of southern California fostered a fashion trend in sportswear that has indicated fashion directions for years. The bundled-up, indoor life of northern, colder climates created the need for warm, lightweight clothes with a minimum of bulk. Within each broad market there are minimarkets, each with its own

Figure 9.1   (A) Establishing the personality of Liberty House in a new community. Store openings provide great opportunities for stores to present their story to a new group of potential customers. Sonoma County had a good idea of what Liberty House was all about by the time the store opened. These are layouts of pre-opening ads. First, the outdoor look in fashion. (B) Liberty House promises the evening look in fashion. (C) Ad designed to show Liberty House will stock the merchandise to furnish the homes of Sonoma County. (D) Liberty House will have men's furnishings to fit the life-style of the community. (Figure 9.1 continues on page 246.)

E

F

G

characteristics and fashion needs. Knowledge of these social, economic, and cultural differences must be ascertained by the retailer.

Knowing the needs of the community leads to sound buying decisions in merchandise. The job of the store's advertising is to let people know the store is equipped to satisfy their fashion requirements. In each community, large or small, there are the trendsetters, what the trade publication, *Women's Wear Daily,* has dubbed the "Beautiful People" or BPs. They are the fashion leaders, the people who set the styles for a fashion-conscious public. Their counterparts are found on the high school and college campuses, setting fashion trends for their classmates. Pictures appear in the women's or fashion sections of the newspapers, the people-oriented mass magazines, and other public places where the elite gather or are seen. Styles they adopt soon appear in the stores for the general public's acceptance. Many fashions to which trendsetters give their stamp of approval are merely fads; they have a short life in the public eye, then fade from view and wind up on the markdown racks in the stores. Others take hold, are received with acclaim, and soon are worn by the masses. When a fashion becomes popular, it is a signal for the fashion leaders to start looking for something different.

It is easy to see why retailers place great emphasis on offering the latest in fashion to their customers, often advertising in advance of the season as "Forecast Fashions" or "The Look Is . . ." in order to make an impression on readers and viewers that they are the stores in which to shop for up-to-the-minute fashion. Not all customers are looking for the newest and latest, however. Many retailers have segmented their fashion shoppers into life-styles and viewpoints that dictate their fashion preferences:

The Establishment Customer. Conservative, mature and generally older; traditional in life-style.

The Updated Customer. Under 40, but possibly in his or her fifties or older; primarily interested in newness in fashion.

The Contemporary Customer. The advanced, fashion-conscious person totally interested in the most advanced fashions.

Figure 9.1 (*continued*)   (E) Closer to opening day, the ads talk total store, with each merchandise ad carrying a specific idea that follows the total plan. (F) The quality inherent in recognized fashion brand names is part of the total message of the merchandise ads. (G) Here it is! Opening day! The time and date are part of the message. The pre-opening ads have whetted the curiosity and interest of the people of Sonoma County, and they are now invited to an Open House.

This awareness of consumer differences in life-style and interests is reflected in the development of free-standing specialized shops within department stores and in specialty shops. Entire retail chains have been established to cater to the needs of special groups. Lane Bryant provides fashions for large-size women, tall women, and chubby girls. The Gap sells sportswear to active young men and women. Liberty House is known for its gourmet food shop, Gump's for its fabulous jade collection, Loehmann's for quality fashions at low prices. Mode O'Day brings popular fashions at moderate prices to women all over the country. Discount stores serve the woman seeking current fashion but not conventional store prices. Certain stores concentrate on apparel for tall women, petite sizes, short women, or big men. And there is still the special customer for Neiman-Marcus, Saks Fifth Avenue, and other fine stores.

The impression the store's fashion merchandise makes carries over into all phases of the operation. Bloomingdale's, New York, has the justified reputation of having the best selection of the newest trends in women's clothing. It started by being the best in home furnishings. The store has created a position for itself that has become the envy of every fashion retailer in America. A visit to Bloomingdale's is a "must" on every visitor's list in New York. Even the Queen of England had to tour the store when she came to the United States. On Saturday afternoons, Bloomingdale's is the place to be in New York. The store has captured the imagination of the city and most closely matches in merchandise presentations the upwardly mobile and affluent population of its market. People have said: "I go there to buy most everything"; "The prices are not 'reasonable' but the service is terrific"; "I love Bloomingdale's. They have everything one would want—and more of it than anyone else"; "Whatever's newest just seems to end up here first"; "I love their clothes . . . I can get everything here from housewares to children's wear—they carry the latest trends." What more could a retailer ask? When customers state publicly their favorable reaction to merchandise, selections, prices, and service, the store has made the right impression on its market.

In every city there are stores that enjoy the acceptance and loyalty of their customers. They cater to their clientele's needs and have built a long-lasting business and a valued reputation over the years. Names like Rich's in Atlanta, Ivey's in Charlotte, North Carolina, and Diamond's in Phoenix quickly come to mind. These quality-image stores exist in most cities, large or small, metropolitan or suburban.

SALES AND SERVICE POLICIES
MAKE THE DIFFERENCE

When the time comes to chart a course of action, to nail down the details of merchandising and service policies the store is to follow, hard decisions must be made. The executives who chart this course, who describe in writing their instructions to the merchandisers and buyers, to the operations and sales promotion people, set the stage for all phases of the store's existence. They must weigh the costs against the benefits to the store, both short and long term.

- Should the price lines be high, medium, or low?
- Will the store sell designer or brand-name merchandise?
- Will there be dress standards for employees?
- What about the return policy?
- Should there be free delivery and pickup service?
- How about selection and training of salespeople?

Here are two sets of answers that add up to two different images:

Pricing	High	Moderate to low
Brand names	The finest	Where necessary
Dress standards	Yes	None
Return policy	Liberal	Five days, with salescheck (Anytime, if charge account)
Delivery/service	Free	None
Salespeople	The best	Very limited
Interior	First class	Clean but simple

Add to the lists the stores with twice-a-year sales versus those constantly promoting; the rare clearance versus the monthly end-of-month clearance event. What a marked difference these elements make in determining the character of the store!

If you are operating a fashion leadership type of store, you establish a percentage of relationship between total stock and the trend-setting merchandise. The true fashion leader starts with a commitment with the initial order, planning not to reorder. If a store starts with a higher markup, the markdowns come quickly if the styles show up in cheaper copies or if the merchandise doesn't sell. A higher markdown percentage is planned for this type of store or department. The medium-priced store stresses assortments and selection of the most popular fashions. This type of store "checks out" new items, testing for customer reaction before reordering for store display and advertising.

Sales promotion policy reflects merchandising and other policies. The fashion leader advertises forecast fashions, with ads that emphasize fashion ideas and designer names and minimize prices. The medium-price store avoids talking about the "latest," and more cautiously advertises "This is what's new . . ." or this is "right" this season. Promotional stores and smaller retailers make price a dominant element in their ads, and stress availability and selection.

ATTITUDE BEGETS PERSONALITY— NOTHING FILTERS UP

As in chemistry, attitudes toward customers start at the top. Nothing filters up. If the feeling toward the public is genuinely one of concern and desire to serve, it will filter down to the sales floor and to the customers. If management is only giving lip service to the idea of satisfying the needs of shoppers, it will penetrate the organization, and the customers will feel it.

If store management is interested in its employees, a spirit of teamwork and total store involvement shows on the selling floor. It's the difference between having salespeople who are warm, friendly, alert, interested, knowledgeable, and helpful, or brusque, nasty, short-tempered, uninterested, curt, and unpleasant. The first assures success, the second practically guarantees failure. And no amount of advertising or publicity proclaiming "the friendly neighborhood store" can help.

The sales promotion manager may not be able to affect changes or improvements in this area, but he or she must be aware of their effect on advertising results. In practical terms, lower-level executives must conform to front-office directives and policies and adjust their activities and expectations accordingly. The advertising manager should exert as much influence as possible in this area, reminding top management of the importance of developing positive attitudes throughout the organization.

Achieving this feeling of oneness, of being part of the team, is a difficult task for any organization. After the rebellious years of the 1960s and the "me" attitude of the 1970s, any attempt to develop an esprit de corps in a retail store may seem almost certain to fail. Yet there are examples all around of people proud of the organization for which they work. There are stores in every town where people are eager to tell where they earn their living. And others where they show up on the job just to collect the paycheck.

Whichever is the case, the attitude of the employees can usually be traced to the attitude of store management. We remember storewide meetings in major department stores where everyone who worked there was invited to attend. Whether it was the kickoff of an anniversary sale, the announcement of a major policy change, or the date of a new store opening, each person in that store felt he or she was a part of the store family, not just a number on an employee payroll sheet. That feeling, we can report, carried over to the selling floor. These were the stores that gave their people time off to vote, to help them be good citizens. They had personal improvement courses paid for by the store. The store's top executives were known to all employees; they were not just mysterious names that delivered edicts and thunderbolts from the executive suite. Top management made it a point to drop in on departmental and divisional meetings, just to keep in touch. The mood of those stores was friendly, happy, and, of course, successful and profitable.

Stores that "give a damn" about their people find that their people "give a damn" about the store and do their best in dealing with customers. A store image that is reflected in the attitudes and actions of its employees, from executives to salespeople, to delivery people and cashiers, is an honest image, and one to be cherished and nurtured.

CHANGING THE ESTABLISHED STORE IMAGE

Some retailers are never satisfied. If sales volume is good, they complain about profits. If profits are good, they worry about markup. If store traffic is healthy, they are concerned about the size of the store's average sale. When everything else is going well, they start to worry about their image.

It would be interesting to ask a typical retailer to describe or define the store's image. It would be of minor concern to the individual storekeeper, but could be a major consideration to a major department store board of directors. The customers might say: "We love you for records, appliances, hard goods and cameras, but we don't know you for fashion." "We buy our children's clothes at Blank's, but for shoes we go to Clark's." "You're great for sportswear, but your coat department is nowhere." Customer surveys tell store owners and operators what customers like or don't like about their stores. Marketing studies with "focus groups"—average shoppers representing the public—give store managements ideas of what the public thinks of products, services, advertising concepts. When stores are troubled, concerned about current activities and future growth potential, they often look for ways to change the status quo, to change the trends of their stores.

Making the Decision to Change

Before the store makes the critical decision to change its image, it would be well to conduct a scientific customer survey to collect the vital information on which the decision to make a change would be based. There are many specialists in this field of marketing analysis, and we would recommend hiring a professional firm to assure an objective, thorough job.

Retailers often tend to rely on one-person surveys. "My wife thinks . . .", "My brother-in-law, the lawyer, says . . .", "I saw an article in *The Wall Street Journal.* . . ." Quoting a third party is an old retail ploy, designed to give a privately held opinion added credibility. It reinforces the retailer's opinions, which are not necessarily based on the facts.

We recall an instance when the store president casually mentioned to the new sales promotion manager that he'd been to a party recently (he couldn't remember when), at which a woman (whose name he couldn't remember) thought that the store's radio commercials needed updating. After the meeting, one of the other store executives explained to the newcomer that the store president had not lost his memory. It was just his way of conveying an apocryphal third-party suggestion to lend weight to something he wanted done without giving a direct command. In fact, the dinner had taken place at this friendly executive's home the previous weekend and the woman whose name the president couldn't remember was his wife!

A sounder approach to the problem of deciding whether to start a campaign to change an image would involve getting answers to a lot of questions. The following list, courtesy of Ralph Heineman Inc., Advertising, is in three sections:

1. What do you KNOW about your customer?
   Who is she? Or he?
   What is her age? Or his?
   Single or married? Or sharing?
   Does she work? Or he? Or both?
   How many in the family?
   What ages are the children?
   What is the family income?
   Where do they live? House? Apartment? Farm? Town?
   Who does most of the family buying?
   What is her favorite store? Or his?
   If they had more money to spend, would they continue to
      shop at your store?
   What is the favorite shopping day?

What are the favorite shopping hours?
What life-style do they have?
How about hobbies? Tennis? Swimming? Skiing?

2. WHEN does your customer shop at your store?
   Regularly? How many times a week? A month?
   Occasionally? When last shopped?
   Only on impulse?
   After their favorite store doesn't have what they want?
   Only for advertised items?
   Only for sale items?
   Only for items for the family?
   Do they shop your store for gifts? Why? Why not?
   Only for very special purchases?
   Only for clothes? Men's wear? Children's wear?

3. What does your customer THINK about you?
   Is your store attractive?
   Is it neat and clean?
   Are the salespeople helpful?
   Do they think they get good value in your store?
   Do they think your values are reliable?
   Do you have what they want, when they want it?
   Do they think you are out of stock too often?
   Do they wish you had more assortments to offer?
   Do they enjoy their shopping experiences in the store?
   Do they like to shop your store even when they have no specific need?

If a sufficiently large number of answers to these questions are received and analyzed, you would emerge with a fairly reliable profile of your customer. Note that the first series of questions was about the customer, not about your store. This is the outward-looking approach of current marketing practice. This type of information lets you know what the customer will want to buy, based on life-style, socioeconomic level, and cultural interests. It leads to research that tells you where and when, in what form and at what price customers will buy. If the answers to the questions are not satisfactory to the management of the store, then it might be time to consider a change.

Before that decision is made, one should research all phases of advertising and sales promotion to see if they are synchronized with the customers' attitudes. Are the newspaper ads talking to the shoppers about things in which they are interested? Do the ads convey the feeling or the image the store wishes to impart to the public? Do the radio ads talk a different theme from the television spots, and do they both seem different from the mail order catalog? When deciding to change, be sure to make the right change.

Planning and Implementing the New Image from Within

At all costs, the retailer should avoid making cosmetic changes in the advertising and sales promotion presentations of the store. Merely changing the look of the ads, or presenting a well-known personality as spokesperson for the store on television and radio, without making comparable changes within the store, is a waste of valuable time and money.

Snappy catch phrases like "the store with more," "your friendly neighborhood store," or "the store that understands your fashion needs" are not believed by the shopping public. They know better. They know if you have changed your merchandise policies and sufficiently back up advertised items. They know if you have shaped up your sales force with people who know and understand fashion. They know if you have just put a coat of paint on that tacky sportswear department and not added any of the better lines of merchandise to round out your stocks. Today's customer is smarter, more sophisticated than ever before. So many stores have similar, sometimes even identical, merchandise that it becomes increasingly difficult to keep their loyalty. The worst thing to do to your customers is to fool them, or try to.

There are many instances where stores have closed their doors "for complete renovation and remodeling—to reopen with a brand new approach to fashion for you." Mail is sent to current customers and former customers. Ads are run announcing the "new" fashion shop. Comes the big day; the customers arrive. They see the limited renovation, the slightly different assortment of the same merchandise lines, the same tired and bored salespeople. Many of the customers have given you a second chance, but you've struck out— for good.

If the decision to change image is made, it must be made all the way, from top to bottom, from ceiling to floor. Stores that have successfully made a change in fashion personality start at the beginning—with the merchandise. The manufacturer lines that are recognized by the public as the "right" fashions are the lines to be added to your stocks. The lines that are not right, even those represented by the boss' brother-in-law, should go. The department should be refurbished, redesigned with an open, flowing floor plan that invites the shopper, surrounding him or her with a pleasant atmosphere that matches the tempo and mood of the merchandise and the life-style it represents. Freshen up the sales staff. If the clothes are younger, more tuned to the contemporary customer, staff the department with young, well-dressed salespeople who wear and look good in the clothes they are selling. Transfer the older, experienced salespeople to departments with merchandise more suited to their selling style and ability.

Suppose the decision is to improve the service image of a store that specializes in women's apparel. The first step would be a close examination of the sales staff. Are they knowledgeable about fashion? Are they aware of company goals and policies? Are they naturally courteous and helpful? Are they good salespeople? Do they know how to close a sale or are they just order takers? Are they aggressive without being pushy? How do their sales records compare? Are they trainable? Which ones should be replaced?

One retailer instituted a three-month training program, bringing in sales experts to lecture to and train the staff. Selected employees were sent to a finishing school to teach them poise. Others learned the fine points of multiple-unit selling. At the conclusion of the training sessions, a new, higher-percentage commission system was installed. Sales quotas were increased. The added incentives and added skills helped the salespeople reach their goals, and both retailer and sales staff were happy.

Using the approach of installing new and different customer services could result in giving a store a competitive edge in the minds of the public. The service aspect of a store probably registers faster with the buying public than other factors that might bring people to the store. Using service to attract people to the store for various reasons and exposing them to the merchandise is a technique that will always be popular with merchants. Services have a way of giving a store a certain character and differentiating it from its competitors.

Here are some examples of what stores have done to give themselves a different image by offering something extra:

- A custom shirt department for men and women
- Serving free coffee to shoppers waiting for the store to open
- Maintaining an efficient lost and found department
- A kitchen demonstration area
- A designer eyewear shop
- A career woman's shopping service or shop
- A gourmet cooking school
- Free self-defense classes for women

- Money management courses
- Courses on how to reenter the job market

Many of these special shops or services can be classified as special events, depending on their duration. The lasting effect they have on the image of the store will be contingent on the continuity of the program and the cumulative impact of the various elements.

Generally speaking, lack of space is the main reason specialty shops and one-outlet businesses are not as interested as department stores in building up services. There's very little room to spare for concrete programs and conveniences. These stores turn to what they do best—servicing customers by stressing the fundamentals of retailing to make it easier for the shopper to understand the new fashion looks and by offering the right merchandise at the right time in sufficient depth to satisfy customers' needs.

A major change in a store's personality can be achieved by the changeover of the traditional department store tearoom into an interesting, appealing theme restaurant. Smaller specialty stores install health food bars and yogurt counters to attract a certain kind of customer. Bloomingdale's, with its famous 40 Carrots, was the first to open a restaurant with special appeal for specific shoppers. It followed with another called the Greenhouse. Many department stores have copied this idea, and have spent large sums to build theme restaurants, complete in design and ambiance, to attract the contemporary customer and to offer one more reason to shop.

Research has shown that when people go to retail stores to eat lunch (and many stores depend on working women shopping while on their lunch hours), more than half of them make an additional purchase while in the store. Just as a good cup of coffee can help make a restaurant successful, a good restaurant can add to the store traffic and sales volume of a retail store.

QUESTIONS FOR DISCUSSION AND CLASS ASSIGNMENTS

1. Conduct a survey of a major department store in your area using the list in this chapter. Score the results on a scale of 1 for unimportant to 5 for very important. Discuss whether the advertising presentations of the stores match the survey results.
2. Select a store in your area that has changed its image in recent years. Investigate and report on the strategy employed internally and how it was reflected in the store's sales promotion.
3. List 10 retail stores in your area and give a one- or two-word commentary describing the store. Compare your evaluations with those of other members of the class.
4. Many retail stores are successful because of great acceptance of certain

departments or categories of merchandise in which they excel. Name six stores in your town and the merchandise for which they are noted.

5. Using the Ralph Heineman survey list in this chapter, conduct a study of a major store in your community. Interview store principals and give them your results. Discuss whether the store's sales promotion is a reflection of the survey's results.

Chapter 10
How Advertising and
Promotion Sell the
Store Image

Many books and articles have been written on advertising, filled with formulas and lists and patterns, describing the step-by-step method of producing effective advertisements. These methods, techniques, and devices are good and useful, but in the practical daily world of writing and producing retail ads to run in the various advertising media, there are no ironclad, sure-fire rules.

No one sits down and says, "I'm going to use the Blank method of advertising in this ad, with a 'reason-why' headline and four motivating selling points." It does not work that way. When a good ad is written, however, the writer can use many of these "how-to" lists to check to see how many of the elements of the "method" appear in the ad (Figure 10.1). If it is a well-constructed, informative ad, chances are most of the elements of the copywriting system will be there.

One of the oldest and simplest "formulas" for ad writing is the favorite of opera lovers—AIDA—which lists the four steps to a

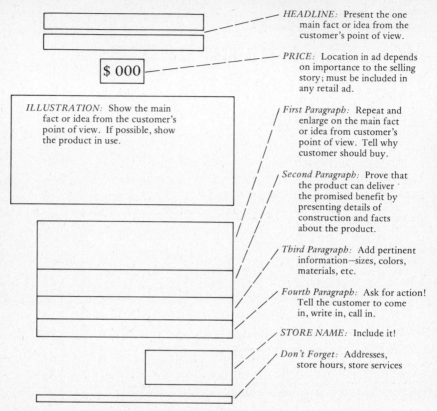

Figure 10.1   Diagram of a basic retail newspaper ad. The elements of a complete ad, adapted from Clyde Bedell's material, include all those listed here.

good ad as:

A—Get the prospect's *attention.*

I—Get the prospect *interested* in your product or service, promising benefits.

D—*Demonstrate* the facts showing how and why the product or service will deliver the promised benefits.

A—*Ask* for action, for the order, for the sale.

Check to see how many ads in your daily paper follow this general rule. You may be surprised how many do or do not do a proper selling job. Be sure to note how few ask for the order or suggest the prospect do something, like "Come in tomorrow," "Order today, call 784–5204," "Come in and see our fall selection," or "Visit our store nearest you, there's one at Fifth and Main."

Many of the soundest principles of good writing have been set down by Clyde Bedell, probably the finest retail copywriter of all time, whose book *How to Write Advertising Copy That Sells* has been virtually the Bible for generations of copywriters. One of Bedell's techniques is as follows:

- *Get attention* with your headline, mentioning the prospect and his or her interest and promising benefits.
- *Arouse interest and create desire* by enlarging on the promise of the headline, telling how the product or service can deliver the promise, giving facts to support the promises.
- *Distinguish your offering* by making it look and sound "special" and different from others; remember, you want people to come to *your* store.
- *Create conviction* by emphasizing the main idea of the ad, adding proofs and assurances of the product's or service's reputation or acceptance.
- *Try for action* by giving the prospect good reasons and excuses to buy now, and where, when, and how the purchase can be made.

To add one more way of saying it again, which should convey the idea that advertising is selling and the job of any ad is to sell, here's a more visual description of the advertising process: Think about going fishing. The headline, the opening of your radio or television commercial, is your bait or lure. That's how you *attract* the reader, viewer, or listener. You must get them to stop. Once you have their attention, the first sentence of your copy, the first five seconds of your commercial, is the hook. That's where you impale the prospect on the major *benefit* so hard and so well he or she is forced to find out what it's all about. Then you give the line—all about the "thing" that will give the benefits the person is seeking. As in fishing, it is important not to let the prospect off the line. Each sentence, each statement, should carry the prospect to the next, right to the very end, easily and smoothly. Then you hit the person with the sinker, the statement, the *urge to action* that tells him or her what to do, makes him or her want to do it, and do it now.

SELLING THE IMAGE IN NEWSPAPERS

The basic elements of a print ad are these:

- The headline—the heading or caption of the ad
- The body copy—the text or descriptive copy
- The illustration—the artwork or photo showing the merchandise

LIBERTY HOUSE

Wide wale
corduroy
from England

Figure 10.2   Layout of high-fashion ad from Liberty House. Strong impression of quality imported men's wear adds to the store's fashion image.

- The logo or signature—the name of the store, usually an identifiable design or artwork

The *layout* is the design or plan of the ad, the arrangement of the elements in a pleasing, easy-to-read sequence. The layout indicates where the headline, illustration, body copy, and logo are to be

Figure 10.3 Layout of trend-setting shoe ad. Fashion stores predict coming fashion directions for their clientele.

placed in the ad. The layout design, including the selection of type styles, gives the store's advertising a "look" that makes it easily identifiable to the public (Figures 10.2 and 10.3).

Stores that have used the same layout style over the years attain a strong degree of recognition. In New York, the look of the Lord and Taylor and Macy's ads are so constant that readers know, without even looking for the logo or signature on the page, whose advertising it is. The same would apply to Marshall Field's in Chicago, Eaton's in Toronto, and many other stores in many other cities. With consistency, the visual impact of the ad design becomes familiar to the public. Stores that get bored with the look of their ads and periodically change the layout style run the risk of losing recognition during the transition period. It takes the public a relatively long time to associate the new look with the advertiser. Consistency pays off in all advertising.

There is one good test to determine if the stores in your town have strong recognition value in their ads. Check to see if they are instantly identifiable by appearance without the name of the store.

In addition to competing with other retail ads, your newspaper ads compete with national and local ads of every description for the attention of the reader. The purpose of an ad is to sell the merchandise in that ad, and to sell it for your store. With the widespread distribution of identical fashion merchandise to many retail outlets in every city, the job of advertising is to make the customer buy that merchandise in your store, and not somewhere else. Remember that the purpose of cooperative advertising from the manufacturers' viewpoint is to sell their merchandise; they don't care in which store the purchases are made. The retailers' objective is to make customers buy the merchandise in their stores. This is difficult if a store's advertising is so similar to that of competitors' that the customer cannot be sure who advertised. An ad that engages the attention of the reader must establish the identity of the advertiser without question. National ads develop customer awareness of new products and services that are sold in the marketplace. The retailer, in sharing the cost of the cooperative ad, must be sure the identity of the store is not lost in the process of keeping ad costs down.

ELEMENTS OF PRINT ADS

Let us examine the various elements of print ads to see how they can carry the story of the store's fashion image to potential customers.

The Basic Idea

Over the years the question of which comes first—copy or layout—has been debated without resolution. There are as many reasons for starting the ad from the copy standpoint—writing the headline and the body copy, then turning the information over to the art department for layout and finished art—as there are for the reverse method. In the latter case, the visual design and art concept the art group creates allows space for the headline and text copy which the writer obligingly fills.

The *copy-to-layout* method is the oldest, since in the beginning ads consisted solely of words. When artwork and photos were added through technological advances, the ability to show the actual merchandise gave the advertisement added impact. Most retail stores use the *layout-to-copy* technique because they can see in advance what the ad will look like. The danger in this method, although it accomplishes the visual recognition we have been talking about, is that the selling story is often cramped or diminished by the amount of space allocated to it by the layout artist.

The best method, if time and system within the ad department permit, is the *team method,* where artist and writer get together with the store buyer and the team works out the *idea* of the ad. Once the questions (1) What is the main selling point of the merchandise? (2) How much space is needed for the selling story, the copy? (3) How large should the headline be and what will it say? and (4) How can we show the item best? are settled, the team agrees on the basic idea of the ad. Then they do their separate jobs. The copywriter writes the headline and text copy, the artist arranges for the layout to be designed and the illustration made, and the buyer provides the sample of the merchandise for the artist or the photographer.

The Headline

The headline, to most advertisers, is the most important part of the ad. Some ads, using the same amount of space, the same type of illustration, and the same newspaper, will outpull other ads as much as 2 to 1. The difference usually is the appeal of the headline, the attention-grabber that hooks the reader. The strength of the story stems from the merchandise, of course, but the words used to express that story are the key.

The most effective headlines are those that appeal to the reader's self-interest. There is no greater appeal. People are most interested in themselves. If you doubt that, think what you do the day the new phone book arrives—you look for your name! Headlines that offer the reader benefits, something the reader wants, work best.

Good headlines are also news headlines. Remember that most of your ads run in newspapers, and people are interested in "what's new," whether it is a fashion item or a civic crisis. The news, however, must be to the point. "New" and "now" are probably the most overworked words in advertising, so be sure the story is really news or the customer will be misled. If you use a false or misleading headline to "hook" a reader and don't deliver the promise, the reader will feel cheated and may not respond to your next lure. Use curiosity in your headlines, but again, be sure it is pertinent and connects to your selling story quickly and smoothly. Combine the curiosity factor with the news or self-interest angle, and you have a strong headline. Key words and phrases that attract attention and strengthen headlines include these: "Announcing . . . ," "New" and "Now," "Beginning tomorrow . . . ," "For 3 days only. . . ." If the price is the story, feature the price or the savings in the headline. If newness is the feature, tell about it. If it is selection, include that. The headline must reflect what is being advertised, or the point the writer is trying to put across. If possible, mention the product, and how it will benefit the purchaser.

A Starch readership study, produced by Starch/INRA/Hooper, one of the nation's leading advertising readership and research firms, estimated that readers give an average ad *half a second* before they decide to read any more (The *Toronto Star,* "Retail Street," July 1978). That's the real job of the headline—and the headline writer—to stop the readers at the ad. If not stopped within this time limit, chances are they will turn the page. Other research has indicated a *four-second* interval during which the reader's attention can be grabbed. This applies, however, to the total ad, with the attractiveness of the layout and art adding to the chances for success.

When the retailer has limited space within which to advertise, chances are the ad will use a label headline. The most a label headline can do is identify the merchandise being offered. Unless it is an unusual one-word headline, the mere statement "Dresses," "Blouses," "Slacks," "Shoes," often has limited appeal. It will attract those readers already interested in buying, but does not do much to intrigue or interest the casual reader flipping through the paper. Sometimes, however, a single word can be meaningful and selective of a specific audience from among the paper's readers: "Lawyers," "Reduce," "Disco," "Beautiful," "Style." Two-word headlines can do even more: "Large Women," "New Shoes," "Vacation Spot," "Itchy Scalp," "Bed Wetter." The readers could feel that the ad is addressed to them if the words fit into their sphere of interest or concern.

Techniques for writing headlines are many and varied. Often writers do the headline *after* they have written the full copy story of the merchandise. Sometimes the first few words of the body copy contain a much better headline idea than the headline that was used. This happens when the writer writes the headline to "get it out of the way so the layout person can get started," then gets to work writing the selling story.

The Copy

The copy, the text of the ad, should enhance and enlarge on the promise of the headline. It is frustrating and irritating to the reader to find there is no connection between the provocative headline and the facts presented in the ad. Good copy is believable, persuasive, and offered in an interesting, clear, simple style. It should answer the question uppermost in the minds of the reader: "What's in it for me?" This attitude of self-interest is not just the phenomenon of the "me" generation of the 1970s. People have always been dominated by their own needs, wants, and desires. They are more interested in how a product or service will benefit them than they are in how the designer and manufacturer collaborated to create the great new fashion. Customers are interested in their own problems, not those of the retailer. Is it better to say "We're overstocked with dresses, so we've reduced prices," or to say "You will save because we've reduced prices on these dresses"? The "you" in the story gets the reader involved.

Many advertisers advance the need for short, limited copy because of the short attention span of the reader. Lack of readership of ads should be more correctly directed to *how* the copy story is presented rather than its length. If the copy is well written, with facts and information moving the reader through the story, the reader will probably read it all. Consider this: You may never have read a word of copy about fur coats in your life, but if it happens that family finances indicate a fur coat might be purchased for Christmas, you can bet the recipient of that fine gift will read everything possible about furs before the purchase is made.

The depth to which an ad is read is determined by a combination of merchandise factors and advertising presentation ideas. David Ogilvy's famous ad "At 60 miles an hour the loudest noise in this new Rolls Royce comes from the electric clock" is probably one of the best read ads of all time. His Hathaway shirt ad created readership and memorability, establishing the shirt as the quality product in its field. Studies have shown that strong, well-written ads can achieve four to five times the readership of weak ones. It is a good practice for a store to repeat successful ad techniques while discarding less productive ones. Effective techniques can be applied to many categories of merchandise. Repetition of specific types of ads helps connect the technique with the store, improving the store's ad identity. Constant checking on results of ads and product testing can help determine what works best for the store.

Imitating what has worked well for another store does not always ensure success. We can remember running historically successful promotions in one city that failed to produce results comparable to those the same kind of ad had achieved in another city. Many aspects of the ad—the believability of the claims, the acceptance of the store, the unfamiliar appearance of the imitated ad— were different and did not reflect the image of the store in the minds of the public. Result: disappointing store traffic in response to the ad.

The essential elements of good copywriting, true of all good writing, include these:

Simplicity. Advertising copy should be easy to read and understand. The writer should use the language of the day, but not be faddish, so the reader understands what is being said. Sentences should be short, direct, and uncomplicated. Avoid vague, general statements. Be specific. Copy, for retail customers as well as others, must be so clear that anyone can understand it.

Naturalness. Select words that are familiar, natural, and informal. Avoid "copywriters' copy"—esoteric and high-sounding phrases that only the elite may comprehend. Communicate with the reader. Test the naturalness of the copy by reading it aloud to yourself or a friend. If it sounds stilted or stiff, rewrite it. Remember, the customer is a real person.

Information. People are looking for information when they read an ad. They are not looking for a clever turn of phrase that might be more suitable in a poem or essay. Copywriting is selling, offering benefits to the potential customer, with facts about the merchandise that will convince the reader the product will deliver the benefits. Anticipate the questions the reader may have and answer them.

Enthusiasm. The first attribute of a successful salesperson is enthusiasm. If you can't be enthusiastic about the merchandise or service you are writing about, that lack will show in your writing. Some have said that *nothing* can be achieved without enthusiasm. That may or may not be true, but it is certainly necessary for successful selling. Writers who must persuade people to spend their money must believe in the products. This may be a lot to ask in these days of cynicism, but some less enthusiastic types find a compromise by visualizing the enjoyment the customer will get from the merchandise, and get satisfactory results by this transference of the enthusiasm.

Interest. These elements of copywriting are not in order of importance, or this item would be higher on the list. Copy must be interesting to readers. Show them benefits they will gain, unpleasantness they will avoid. Relate the merchandise to their life-styles, show them and how and why to use the product. The more reasons you give the prospect, the greater the chance the sale will be made. All copywriters should be told that buying advertising space or time does not give them the right to bore the customer. Unfortunately, many ads bore people into inaction. Interesting copy finds its way into the minds of the readers and motivates them to action.

The Illustration

The illustration is a critical point in the success of the ad. For all the advertising experts who say the headline is the stopper—the thing that makes the reader pause and read the ad—as many insist that the illustration is the basis on which most readers decide whether or not to read the ad. The half a second, more or less, within which the decision to read or turn the page is made can turn on the quality of the artwork or photo as well as on the impact of the headline. A carryover from the days when all ads were composed entirely of type lingers to this day in the minds and pocketbooks of some retailers, who resist paying for anything they consider unnecessary to the operation of the business.

Production costs—photo and engraving costs, copywriters and artists' salaries, and equipment costs—are questioned constantly. The tendency to "save" on these expenses in an advertising department can affect the quality of the finished ad and drastically affect sales results. Merchandise should be presented in the best possible light, enhanced, beautified, even exaggerated, to look as appealing as possible to the reader.

The current trend toward realism in advertising has led many advertisers to present merchandise photographically. This is a highly skilled technique, requiring expert photographers, top-quality fashion models, studios, lighting, makeup, retouching, and other items, all of which add to production costs. Those stores using the skills of high-fashion artists to sketch their merchandise pay the price for the artwork, but have no additional production costs to worry about.

With most retail advertising appearing in newspapers, the type of printing presses used by the paper can help determine whether a store should use art or photographs for fashion ads. The spiraling costs of photography and photographic film, which doubled during 1979–1980 due to inflation and rising silver prices, could also have a decisive effect on decisions to use photos or art work in ads.

Printing Processes

Printing is the process of transferring an image from one surface to another through the medium of ink. The two principal types of printing of concern to retailers and their newspaper advertising are *letterpress* (or relief) printing and *offset-lithographic* printing. In letterpress printing, the oldest process, all the image areas are raised in relief about the non-image areas. Only these raised areas receive the ink, and the image is transferred to the paper as it rolls across the letterpress plate. In this process, metal type, engravings, forms combining both, or duplicate forms to carry the image are used. Letterpress impressions are sharp and clear, but vary with the smoothness and texture of the paper. Newsprint, the paper used by newspapers, is the poorest quality of paper, and consequently prints unevenly. It does not always reproduce photographic art well, requiring the artist to highlight areas of the photo for greater contrast, to compensate for some of the loss of detail.

In offset-lithography printing, both image and non-image plates are carried on the same plane or level. Ink receptivity and transfer is controlled by the natural principle of oil and water not mixing. Image areas are chemically sensitized to accept ink and repel water. Non-image areas accept water and repel ink. In printing, the plate first contacts rollers of water or dampening solution, then the inked rollers. The inked image is then transferred or "offset" from the plate onto a rubber blanket cylinder, then onto paper. The resilience of the rubber blanket permits offset-lithography on a wide range of surface textures. This flexibility of offset presses provides advertisers with good, clear reproduction of photographs. This is especially helpful to smaller retailers, whose limited facilities and budgets depend on the use of manufacturers' photos in their ads. Fashion vendors are anxious to provide stores with photos of merchandise. The retailer gets quality illustration at minimum cost and manufacturers are assured that their merchandise is properly presented.

Another printing method, usually restricted to large-quantity printing runs, is *gravure* or *intaglio.* This process is the opposite of relief printing, with the etched image areas recessed into a metal plate to form reservoirs or wells for ink. The total image is screened, with the depth of the well controlling the amount of ink transferred and the density of tone on paper. Gravure provides quality reproduction on both smooth and textured surfaces.

Both offset-lithography and gravure are excellent for color reproduction. Retailers in cities where papers are printed offset find the color reproduction of fashions greatly increases the effectiveness of their ads. The greatest use of gravure is in Sunday magazine sections, very popular in many metropolitan areas. For more technical explanations and descriptions of printing processes and the preparation of materials for reproduction, we recommend Dean Phillip Lem's *Graphic Master,* a workbook and guide of inestimable value to any advertiser (see Appendix 16).

Elements involved in deciding whether to use artwork or photography to show fashion merchandise include these:

The availability of printing facilities.

The merchandise to be presented. For example:
- Fashion shoes look best when sketched, allowing for angles that elongate and flatter the look. Photos tend to add thickness and weight to objects, as does the television picture.
- Television sets or major appliances may look better shown in a real-life situation.

The availability of talent to produce the desired illustration.

Good artists, like good photographers, are expensive. The retailer may not want to pay the costs, and may settle for inferior or amateur work or depend on mat service artwork or photos provided by the local newspaper.

One of the truly great creative art directors and advertising managers in the history of retail advertising, M. L. "Rosey" Rosenblum, laid down some specific guidelines for artwork in retail ads:

- Art should be used only when necessary: for merchandise information, to create emotion or drama, or as an innovation. Sometimes words can describe the merchandise better than artwork. The words "silky smooth" can hardly be illustrated, yet a photo of a very fat man tells the story of clothes for big men faster than "sizes 44 to 56."
- Don't use art for the sake of having a picture in the ad, although any picture has some attention value. Use it to show

special features of the merchandise that reinforces the copy story. Everyone knows what a pair of pantyhose look like, yet many ads use large areas of costly white space to show a pair of women's legs. Unless there is a design or workmanship feature to be highlighted, the ad might gain impact with a neatly designed type-only approach.

- Good artwork reflects the store, fills a necessary function in the ad, and communicates quickly and clearly to the reader. Good artwork sells, by creating the desire to buy. Artwork contributes to the success of an ad by helping attract the reader's attention, by illustrating the main idea of the ad and supporting the headline and copy story.
- Good artwork can give ads an impression of flair and sophistication. It can create a mood for the reader by showing the merchandise in a situation or setting. Photo art can give the reader the illusion of being there—"there" being the scene in which the merchandise is being shown.

The important decision between artwork or photography as the ideal illustration for the merchandise must be based on a complete understanding of the strengths and weaknesses of each technique, the printing process to be used, and the purpose of the ad and the impression you want it to make.

Typography

The typography of the ad plays an important part in the impression the ad makes. Many artists and layout artists are not as aware as they should be of the impact type makes in the overall mood and feeling of an ad. The choice of typeface as an integral graphic element is often as important as the choice of an art style (Figure 10.4).

The function of type is to be easily read and understood. The mood it can convey through its design is a secondary asset. When the style of the type attracts more attention than the message itself, the result is bad advertising. This view of what is important applies to artwork, overly clever copy, humor, and any other element in an ad that distracts from its main purpose—to sell merchandise.

Light typefaces whisper. Bold typefaces shout. Some faces are modern, others classic, still others futuristic. Some types are elegant, graceful, flowing. Others are stiff, circusy, or casual. There are typefaces to fit any mood the ad means to convey. Skillfully handled, type can add a great deal to the total impression. Most typefaces have a "family" of type variations that are adaptable to changing needs. We suggest that when a store decides on an advertising style as one of the continuing elements of the store's advertising

**Cacharel French jeans & tops:
the accent's on your curves**

It's the European Plan with lots of leg and a sensational fit.
Top with the French Tee sporting classic bateau neck,
3/4 sleeve and signature on shoulder.
5-pocket western jeans: indigo blue cotton denim, 4-14 **$38**
Stripe top: cotton/polyester, color choice, S,M,L **$18**
See the entire collection in Designer Jeans (389)
all stores

LIBERTY HOUSE AN dmfac COMPANY

CALL TOLL-FREE 24-HOURS: IN NO. CALIF. 800-772-3103. IN NEVADA 800-227-1830.
SHOP DAILY 10 A.M. TO 9 P.M, SATURDAY 10 A.M. TO 6 P.M, SUNDAY NOON TO 5 P.M.*except Oakland Tues., Wed. 'til 6. Sunday closed;
San Francisco Mon., Thurs., Fri. 9:30-9, Tues., Wed., Sat. 9:30-6; Southland Mon.-Fri. 9:30-9, Sat. 9:30-5:30; Concord Mon.-Fri. 9:30-9, Sat. 9:30-6; Dublin Mon.-Fri. 'til 9:30.

Figure 10.4 Liberty House fashion ad, ready to be printed. Note the consistency of typeface throughout—different sizes, same type family.

personality, it chooses a type family that contains enough variety to portray the many moods its merchandise assortments require (see Figures 10.5 through 10.9). Rosenblum's book, *How to Design Effective Retail Advertising,* is recommended to any serious student of retail store advertising design.

Figure 10.5 Fashion manufacturers use retail advertising techniques in presenting merchandise to prospective store buyers in trade publications. This series from Pendleton Woolen Mills illustrates the effective use of type to portray mood. Each type selection is in keeping with the kind of woman for whom the clothes are designed. Layout of the matching pages is the same throughout, but photos, merchandise, and typefaces change. (SOURCE: By permission of Pendleton Woolen Mills, Portland, Oregon.)

Figure 10.6   Country clothes in the new gentle mood.

Figure 10.7   Knockabouts in the liveliest mood.

Figure 10.8   Young Pendleton in the new gentle mood.

Figure 10.9   Pendleton women's sizes in the new gentle mood.

SELLING THE IMAGE THROUGH DIRECT MAIL

All the principles discussed in the preceding section on newspaper advertising apply equally to direct mail or any other kind of print advertising. The great plus in advertising by direct mail is the almost limitless variety at the advertiser's disposal. From full-run catalogs to billing statement enclosures, the shape, size, color, and distribution of direct mail messages are restricted only by imagination, talent, capabilities, and, of course, budget. No matter what message is to be delivered, a printed piece can be developed to do the job. Most stores have customer mailing lists, whether compiled from saleschecks or charge account computers. These lists represent people who have shopped in the store and should be the first group to be notified of any change in the store's personality. They will also be the easiest to convince, since the store is not a stranger to them. The information might almost be considered a message from a friend, as in the following examples:

- An invitation to a showing of a nationally known brand of women's sportswear could be designed as a formal engraved invitation, or printed on a cutout of a tennis racket, or attached to a booklet showing a sampling of the merchandise in full color.
- The announcement of your semi-annual clearance event could be on a tag attached to a miniature broom, or printed on a jumbo price tag, listing some of the highlights, or the front page of a booklet announcing a courtesy day of early shopping for charge customers.

There are probably as many variations of direct mail catalogs, package stuffers, statement inserts, direct mailers, and remittance envelopes as there are opinions about their effectiveness. Decisions on what to use are usually based on past experience. Manufacturers involved in supporting direct mail campaigns and mailings with co-op money reflect the same kind of mixed feelings about the medium. Some like statement enclosures (enclosed in monthly billings to charge customers) but hate catalogs. Some stores have no trouble getting vendor support for their Christmas catalogs, but find it tough collecting for other seasonal events. Many manufacturers will participate in a store's catalog only if similar categories of merchandise will be featured. In other words, cosmetic or fragrance vendors will want to be included in a store's Christmas fragrance gift guide, but will not cooperate in a store wide presentation in a general merchandise book. As a general rule, many stores depend on manufacturers' support to help underwrite direct mail activities. Catalog costs doubled from 1967 to 1977, causing many stores and vendors to reevaluate their advertising strategies. Postage increases, for both first and third class mail, have forced many retailers into considering newspaper inserts as an alternate distribution system (see Chapter 5).

All things considered, direct mail to customers and to selected mailing lists of prospective new customers can be an effective method of telling the story of a new store image and a new fashion personality. As part of a multimedia campaign, direct mail, used astutely to reach specific sections of the population, can be a powerful advertising tool.

Direct mail, personally addressed to the individual, received in the home under the best possible circumstances and conceived to tell the complete story of the new store image fully and clearly, offers the advertiser unique opportunities. The ability to control every aspect of the design, production, distribution, and cost of the advertising message exists with no other medium.

Once the customer has had a satisfactory transaction by mail order, the tendency to order more often from mailings and catalogs will grow. As the number of women in the work force increases, more women will think about shopping by mail as a time-saving device. The catalog houses and catalog stores that have sprung up around the country attest to the increased acceptance of mail order shopping. Once just a Christmas-time phenomenon, mail order catalogs now appear in the mail boxes of middle- and upper-income households throughout the year. They sell every conceivable product from foods to musical instruments, clothing to kites. As this trend continues, these businesses become another competitor for the retailer to consider. Everyone is competing for the same customer dollar, and the individual storekeeper must keep up or expect to be shut out. If the customers are reacting favorably to catalogs (public favor ebbs and flows), the retailer must decide whether to join in or stick to what has been successful and ride out the advertising storm.

The most successful direct mail campaigns have two basic elements—consistency and regularity. The story must be told at regular intervals—weekly, monthly, twice a month—systematically. The story must be consistent. It may take many shapes and colors and treatments, but there must be a continuity of theme, the main idea that carries through everything.

It is rare that people hear a new song in its entirety the first time it is played. The second time, more of the words come through and the melody is more familiar. By the third or fourth hearing, the listener has heard it all and knows whether or not he or she likes it.

It takes at least three impressions for an advertising message to break into the consciousness of the average person; and some take even longer.

SELLING THE IMAGE BY RADIO

The special qualities of radio as an advertising medium lend themselves to the job of selling the new personality of a store. After the store has been remerchandised, redecorated, reorganized, and redesigned, the story of the changes must be told. Your regular customers can be told through direct mail or by messages enclosed in the store's billings. Visits to the store will reveal the changes to regular shoppers. The sought-after new customer (probably the reason the image change took place) must be reached by the intrusive media—radio and television.

The story must be told repeatedly, over and over again, to convince noncustomers to come to the store. Radio, with its low cost-per-spot, can deliver the message with great frequency. Because of its specialized programming, which attracts specific types of listeners, radio advertising can reach more of the store's potential customers. The key words "reach" and "frequency" crop up often in discussions of advertising media. Radio offers both.

As an integral part of the total promotional program to introduce the "new" store image:

- Radio reaches potential customers who do not take or read a newspaper regularly.
- Radio reaches potential customers beyond the newspaper's circulation.
- Radio grabs the attention of regular customers who may not be aware that things are happening.
- Radio reminds listeners, customers or not, to look in the newspaper or in their mail for news of the store.

The intrusiveness of radio lets you "slip up" on uninterested, preoccupied listeners before they are aware you are selling to them. This points up the importance of the first few words or the first few seconds of the radio commercial. This also parallels the importance of the headline for a newspaper ad—if the attention is not grabbed in the first few seconds, the page is turned and the opportunity to communicate with a customer is gone.

Nothing grabs the attention of an individual faster than a good idea. And that's what it takes to create an effective radio ad—a concept or an idea. Once you have the idea, you can start to paint the picture you want the listener to see. Radio *is* visual. Some say it is the most visual of all advertising media. You can create characters, situations, and whole scenes, many of which would be impossible to duplicate in print or on TV from a cost or a technical standpoint.

A few words bring in a background of the Taj Mahal. A strain of accordion music establishes Paris as the scene. A squeaky door sets the stage for mystery. The history of radio is full of the stories and scenes created in the imaginations of generations of listeners. This same visual capability, when used in creating radio commercials, can create pictures and settings within which you can sell fashion, home furnishings, or anything else the listener can visualize.

The Basic Elements

There are *four basic elements* to the radio ad, once the concept has been established: the copy, the sound effects, the music, and the voice (or voices). There are always copy and voice. The degree to which music and sound effects are employed is determined by how well they fit or enhance the effectiveness of the commercial, and by whether or not the budget contains money for production.

Without words, of course, there is no commercial. It is the foundation on which the message is built. But a lot of words strung together will not do the job of one cogent thought or phrase. With the outside limit of 150 words in a 60-second commercial, every word must count. Write simply and clearly. Short sentences are better than long sentences. Involved clauses and roundabout phrases are hard to understand. Some words sound better than others. When writing to catch listeners' attention, the words must be carefully chosen.

Use unexpected words, unusual combinations of words. Use verbs, especially active verbs. Avoid superlatives, clichés, hackneyed expressions. Be specific rather than general. Make it sound as though you know what you are talking about.

A favorite radio commercial technique is the "slice of life"— setting a scene with characters in a dialog who talk about the product or service. In writing dialog, think about the characters. Are they real? Believable? Is this how they would talk? Do they relate to each other? Is the message consistent with their character? The answers should be "yes," but we have all seen and heard commercials that do not meet these challenges. There are many reasons why "bad" or poorly written commercials get on the air, but there is no excuse for not trying to do it better.

Many dialog commercials sound as though the characters are actors reading their lines without talking to each other. Too often the listener is set up by the dialog with a humorous sketch, and then suddenly one of the characters delivers the sales pitch from out of nowhere. Try to make the message part of the flow of the dialog. A good test for any piece of radio copy is to read it out loud. Read it to a friend or associate. It may look right on paper, but not sound well. Some words do not read well together. Some phrases may sound awkward. Some sentences written by copywriters, trained to write copy for print ads, do not sound natural or conversational. Remember to write for the ear, not for the eye. Does the message come through? Is it clear? Is the product mentioned at least twice? The store name at least three times? If not, rework the copy. Try to write so the last words in the commercial include the store's name. It has been said that good copy is not written—it's rewritten. When it has been rewritten to a point where it is good copy, then decide how to present the message.

The Role of Music

Consider *music*. Music can set a tone or a mood that carries the listener into a situation. It can be quiet or reflective for a cosmetic product, contemporary for men's trousers, bouncy for active sportswear, or nostalgic and comfortable for home furnishings. Music can create a geographical or historical atmosphere. Music can induce shades of emotion, can lighten or darken moods, define character and refine personality. Music can generate momentum or create tension and add warmth or coolness to the picture being painted with the words (Exhibit 10.1).

Musical themes can be very effective in reflecting the personality of the store and quickly identifying the advertiser. The lively sound of "Get it at Bullock's," played repeatedly every time that southern California store is on the air, builds recognition in the minds of listeners every time a spot is played. The special flavor of "Fall in to the Gap" identifies the mood and feeling of that sportswear chain clearly and distinctly. Lilting strains of violins and semiclassical music easily establish a store offering elegant fashions. The military beat of a marching song brings to mind the heavy-hitting campaign of the discount store. The variety of ways music can "tune in" to a store's personality is endless.

These nuances of music's capability are best handled by professionals. We recommend that retailers allow the creative people they hire to perform and create by establishing the atmosphere of confidence and trust within which most artists work best. The natural tendency to refer to one's own musical tastes is difficult to resist. Many retailers concern themselves too closely with details of broadcast production in which they have limited expertise. This

EXHIBIT 10.1

RADIO SCRIPT, ROOS/ATKINS, SAN FRANCISCO, CALIFORNIA (60-SECOND RADIO SPOT)

This clever, two-character vignette quickly establishes the situation and setting, and in a humorous, easy style works in the selling story of After-Six Formal Wear. Good example of visual radio. Good use of co-op advertising with After-Six and Roos/Atkins.

WOMAN: The mud flats are beautiful tonight.
MAN: Yeah, Prom Night is kind of special. Stop it, Eunice, I'm driving.
WOMAN: It marks a change, doesn't it? Suddenly we're grown up.
MAN: It's probably my After-Six Formal Wear from Roos/Atkins that's got you fooled. I'm still just plain old Freddie Spencer.
Sound Effect: Giggles
WOMAN: You're so handsome tonight, Freddie, so "Ten."
MAN: It's After-Six from Roos/Atkins, Eunice. They lead the way in style. Stop it!
WOMAN: Freddie, we're not children any longer.
MAN: Don't be taken in by the bow tie. Roos/Atkins has After-Six Formal Wear at 15 percent off. And top hats, canes and capes that make me look mature and elegant. Oh, look, Eunice, it's already 8:30 and I promised Dad I wouldn't be out late.
WOMAN: Freddie, let's throw caution to the wind. Let's make memories!
MAN: Oh, geez. We're out of gas!
WOMAN: Oh, Freddie, you're so sly.
MAN: I don't believe this. Look, Eunice, I'll be right back.
WOMAN: Don't leave me, Freddie!
MAN: I was going to walk to that gas station a few miles back.
WOMAN: Freddie! Freddie!
MAN: I shouldn't be gone more than a couple of hours.
WOMAN: Freddie!
MAN: Play the radio. No, don't play the radio. You'll run down the battery.
Music: Roos/Atkins musical theme up and out.

SOURCE: Radio Advertising Bureau, New York. Copyright RAB. Used by permission.

stems from retailers' desire to have complete control of all aspects of their businesses. In dealing with temperamental artistic and creative types, it is usually better to let them have their way. Remember that the client always has the privilege of accepting or rejecting the finished commercial. Difficulties in this area can be avoided if the concept and basic outline of the commercial are discussed and approved in advance by all parties.

A favorite cliché in the trade says: "There's never time to do it right, but there's always time to do it over." When doing it over involves musicians, studio rental, equipment, engineers, and actors, as in radio and television commercials, it can be expensive. Better planning in advance is always more satisfying than emergency remakes and patching. It will also result in better commercials.

A third basic in the production of radio commercials is *sound effects*. Radio buffs know how sound effects set the scene for all the dramatic shows, how the right sound effects could create the mood or setting the story required. The devices that established those moods and settings still exist in the recording studios of today. The sound of waves crashing on the shore sets the scene for a swimsuit commercial. The sound of a car's squealing brakes leads into an ad for radial tires. The famous line "Piston engine goes boing, boing, boing, but Mazda goes hummmmmm" launched the Mazda auto in the early 1970s. The roar of the crowd, coupled with the tense voice of the announcer, puts the listener in the grandstand at a ball game. It is these combinations of sound effects, music, and voices that create the pictures in the minds of radio listeners and establish the receptive atmosphere for the sales message.

Add the Right Voice

The fourth element of the radio commercial—*the announcer*, or *the voice*—can make or break the commercial. The manner in which the message is delivered is often more important than the message itself. A flat, routine delivery can kill any potential interest in the story it might generate. We've all heard "live" announcers or disc jockeys "excuse" themselves from the news or music portion of the program to "take care of" a few commercial messages. The negative tone of the announcement alone can convince the listener to switch stations for a few minutes to avoid listening to the spots. On the other hand, many station announcers, personalities, and disc jockeys read their commercials with conviction and enthusiasm. The reading of a retail spot by a popular radio personality can improve the results of the commercial because it includes the implied endorsement of that personality. Many radio people with strong public followings make it a point to visit the stores and try the products of their advertisers to ensure the believability of the commercials they read.

When creating a radio commercial, you know how you want the message to sound. It pays to audition voices to be sure the ad sounds right. Sometimes a woman's voice works better than a man's. Some insist on the same voice for all their commercials, believing that the continuity of a single spokesperson adds to the recognition factor in their advertising. This is essentially true, but if the spokesperson is that good, chances are he or she will be in demand by other advertisers. If you have a good spokesperson, it is advisable to make arrangements to have that person's services available on an exclusive basis. If you cannot afford that luxury, you may be able to keep the announcer from working for any competing store in the market area.

Not all announcers at all stations read copy well. Since many retailers rely on station personnel to handle their "live" copy because retailers love the flexibility of radio and take advantage of the opportunity for last-minute copy changes, there is a risk that the messages will not produce similar results on all stations. Unless you take the time and trouble to acquaint each individual announcer with your point of view, your attitude toward your customers, and the personality of your store and your merchandise, you may be disappointed with your radio advertising results. One approach to the problem is to find a suitable spokesperson at one of the stations. Then prerecord the commercials using that voice, making "dubs" or extra copies of the taped commercial for the other stations on your schedule. That will give you continuity of sound wherever the spot runs, and the cost is minimal. Usually the station does not charge the advertiser for the use of an announcer on that station. There is a charge—a talent charge to the announcer—if the spot is played on any but the home station. This technique has been effective for retailers who want to avoid the costs of outside production studios and who write and produce their own radio spots.

Now that you have written good copy, selected good music and sound effects, and have an announcer with good presence and a convincing voice, you have to put the radio commercial together. Be sure the music is appropriate to the sound effects, that they blend, rather than fight each other. Be careful when mixing the elements to be sure the message comes through. The mixing after the recording session, tested on the small speakers to re-create the conditions under which the commercial will be heard, is critical. We have all heard commercials in which the music or background noise drowns out the message.

One additional point: We are convinced that radio, being a local medium, works well in combination with newspaper advertising and on its own for the same reasons. To support this contention, Appendix 5 contains procedures for effective newspaper advertising as suggested by the Newspaper Advertising Bureau, the sales arm of the newspaper industry. An adaptation of the NAB rules works for effective radio ads. We also prefer the terminology "radio ads" rather than "radio commercials" when discussing retail advertising. To the retailer unfamiliar with broadcast, the word "commercial" implies the kind of national advertising produced for manufacturers and big advertisers, not for the local merchant. There is an implied impression that commercials are institutional in nature, and not designed to get a direct response from the public. A newspaper ad, on the other hand, translates into a device for getting customers into the stores right now or no later than tomorrow. Radio, as we have indicated, is an immediate-response medium. Handled properly, it can develop as much "next day" business as print media.

The 60-second radio commercial can be structured in many ways. Here are two examples:

15 sec	*Opening*
	musical
	sound effect
40 sec	*Middle*
	"live" copy
	announcer-read
5 sec	*Close*
	musical tag
	store hours
	"sound" logo

This pattern relies on the opening and close to carry the responsibility of store identification. When a store has an established musical theme, the breakout might look like this:

25 sec	Opening
30 sec	Middle
5 sec	Close

The middle live-copy section may be used to sell items, special sale events, department features, new fashion trends, or new store services. By recording the opening and close, stores ensure store identification. The middle section is used for the fast-moving changes of copy that radio can accommodate. The way in which the store uses the 60 seconds depends on the objectives of the advertising. Since

60-second radio commercials usually cost only 20 percent more than 30-second spots, we recommend taking the full minute of time to tell your fashion image story.

SELLING THE IMAGE BY TELEVISION

Television is the nation's mass medium, with the capability of reaching great numbers of people simultaneously. It offers the retailer one of the fastest methods of announcing a new fashion image. So many people have television sets and viewing numbers are so high that it is hard to imagine any medium getting the word out more quickly. No one questions the broad base of the television audience. It is well known that people plan their time, especially in the evening, around what is on television. Family life revolves around favorite programs. Meals are eaten in front of the tube. Silence reigns in the household while a certain program is on. The Television Bureau of Advertising (TvB) reports that the average amount of time per TV home spent with television during 1979 was 6 hours and 28 minutes.

The audience is there. Retailers, with their limited advertising budgets, have the problem of reaching that audience without overspending their advertising resources. It is not just a matter of buying air time. The cost of producing television commercials is an added factor. Many newspaper production costs are built into the line rate. Radio spots can be produced for very little money. It takes planning, preparation, and knowledge to produce quality TV commercials—and money.

Stores are always looking for ways of producing low-cost television commercials that reflect class, that promote an image of elegant and current fashion. Good planning is the first step in the process of keeping control of production costs. The best way to control costs is to create estimates as accurately as possible on each item of each planned commercial (the lists that follow are courtesy of KNXT, Channel 2, Los Angeles).

Studio Facilities. Rental of production facilities includes lighting, camera crew, floor manager, directors, and technicians. Some major department stores have built their own studios, making the investment in the facilities and hiring full-time personnel in an effort to control expenses.

Cost of Talent. This will vary depending on the kind of commercial being produced. If the commercial is to run beyond the standard 13- or 26-week period, talent is paid residuals or additional fees, usually under AFTRA or SAG contracts.

Music. Fees for music are also standardized under union contract. Recorded or background music is inexpensive. When live musicians are used, residuals again come into the picture, with additional payments when commercials run for long stretches. It is possible, under certain conditions, in cities where unions are not a factor, to buy the talent and music costs for a fixed fee.

Graphics. All artwork, scenic backgrounds, logos, prices, and other printed materials must be included in cost estimates.

Props. All the property elements—chairs, rugs, walls, anything involved in set design and setting the atmosphere for the commercial—must be calculated.

Other Costs. If shooting "on location" (in an actual setting) there are no studio rental costs, but the costs of transporting camera and crew and props and talent to the site have to be figured. Proper lighting becomes a major problem. If additional tapes or film dubs (copies) of the commercial have to be made for distribution to several stations, these costs should be included.

The real savings in producing television commercials come in the preproduction stages. If everything possible is prepared and completed *before* you start paying for expensive studio and talent time, you are much better off. Rewriting the script on the set sounds dramatic and creative, but it is also wasteful and costly. By the time you head for the studio, many things should be nailed down, agreed to by all concerned, and ready to shoot:

Budgeting and Scheduling. All budget elements should be discussed and approved in advance. Everyone involved should have a printed schedule listing the order in which the commercials will be produced. Each person should know who is due on the set and when and for what purpose. Scripts should be sent out for bids by qualified production houses.

Script. The first step in the process is the writing of the script. The copywriter writes both the audio and the video portions of the script, visualizing everything audiences will see and hear when the commercial appears on their television sets. In a sense, the writer is also the director, the cameraman, the set designer, the musicians, and the actors—all at the same time. The writer creates a shooting script indicating, side by side on the typewritten page, the video (picture) on the air while the audio (sound) is being heard. This is a job for professionals, and some retailers should avoid the temptation to do it in-house.

Storyboards. The storyboard was invented because of television's need to show clients what the commercial would look like in order to get approval to go ahead and produce it. Very simply, a storyboard is a series of sketches indicating what action is taking place on the screen, with the words being said at that time printed under each sketch (Figure 10.10). It is comparable to the layout in print advertising, and gives a fairly comprehensive presentation of the idea of the commercial. Rarely does the commercial come out exactly as indicated by the storyboard; rather, it is the working model for the finished product. The writer works with the art director and the television producer in preparing the storyboard so that the ideas presented to the client represent the combined thinking of the creative team.

Props, Graphics, and Supers. Much of this material can be prepared in the store in advance, or by the ad agency or production house before you get to the studio. The *supers* (the words that run across the bottom of the TV screen to reinforce the selling story or some other point) have to be ready so they can be set up in the control room for insertion at the proper time.

Film or Videotape. The creative or production requirements of the commercial indicate whether film or videotape should be used. This is a decision to be made early in the production process. Constant improvements are being developed in both media, suggesting again that the decision be left to the professionals, unless members of your staff are qualified enough to make a judgment. Portability, the cost of making duplicate copies, and the creative limitations of the media enter into the decision.

In making the decision to use television to convey the fashion image of the store, many retailers believe in the philosophy that the store that advertises on television is considered to be the fashion leader. A TvB report pointed out this belief was especially true with young women 18 to 34 years of age, the customers most fashion stores are trying to reach. Developing a fashion campaign on TV, and buying air time where and when this desirable segment of the market will be exposed to it, is the problem.

Retailers, being resourceful and ingenious in finding ways to achieve their goals with limited budgets, have been creative. Some stores have prevailed upon local union officials to create special low retail rates for talent and musicians more compatible with the limited, short-run pattern of retail TV ads. Others have achieved economies by organizing to shoot several commercials the same day. Poor planning increases production costs tremendously. These retailers build one set with several products in mind, shoot on tape, and edit on computer. Time is saved by prerecording the audio portion and voiceovers, then shooting the commercial to match the sound track. Fashion retailers preplan the selection, fitting and rehearsals of the models to be used in their television presentations by running through the entire procedure in the store before going to the studio. In many fashion TV ads the models just move around, showing off the apparel items being advertised, with the message delivered by on off-camera performer. Good rehearsals avoid expensive retakes in the studio or on location.

Many stores take the agency-produced commercials furnished by manufacturers as part of their co-op advertising program and redo the audio portion to give the store more identity. If a store has a regular spokesperson, that familiar voice ties the national commercial to the local store much more convincingly than the usual 5- or 7-second tag and logo allotted by the vendor.

Another inexpensive technique developed to offset filming or videotaping costs is the multislide approach. For a limited cost, the store can create a number of 35 mm slides which can be shown on screen in coordination with the sound track to create an acceptable television spot. The slides can be made from photos, artwork, or manufacturer materials, or be store studio-produced, using models, still life, or interior displays. Movement, one of the key ingredients in TV, is achieved by the rapid flashing of the slides, while allowing 2 to 5 seconds per item or fashion pose to freeze the viewer's eye on the screen while the sales message is delivered.

Considering that a local retailer's commercial could conceivably be sandwiched between expensively produced national spots, some consideration must be given to offsetting that probability. Commercials should have a logical starting and stopping point, an opening and a close. Since most TV spots are 30 seconds (87 percent of all nonnetwork spots in 1979), the advertiser is sometimes reluctant to "waste" time with an opening and a close. Think how often you go from one commercial to the next without being aware one has ended and the other has begun. Think of this idea as similar to the "white space" in a newspaper ad that is designed to make your ad more visible on the page, no matter what other ad may surround it. A quick identification of the advertiser, with a definite close (urge to action, logo) can ease this problem.

Does your commercial create a memorable visual image, a picture that stays with the viewer? It is tough in a clutter situation, but there should be a focal point in every TV spot that keys in on the

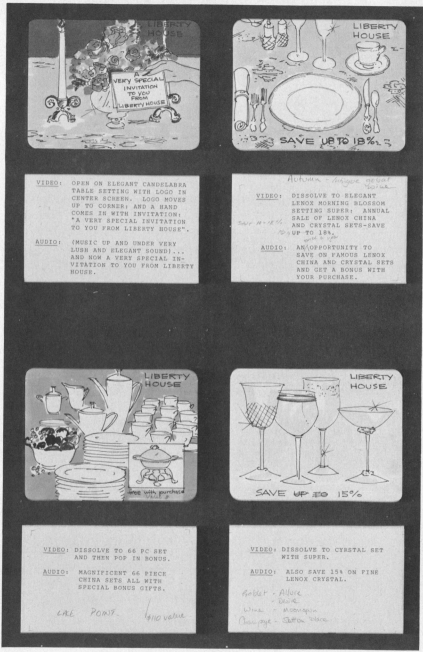

Figure 10.10 Television storyboard from Liberty House. The commercial delivers a strong impression of home furnishings quality while presenting a sale of Lenox china.

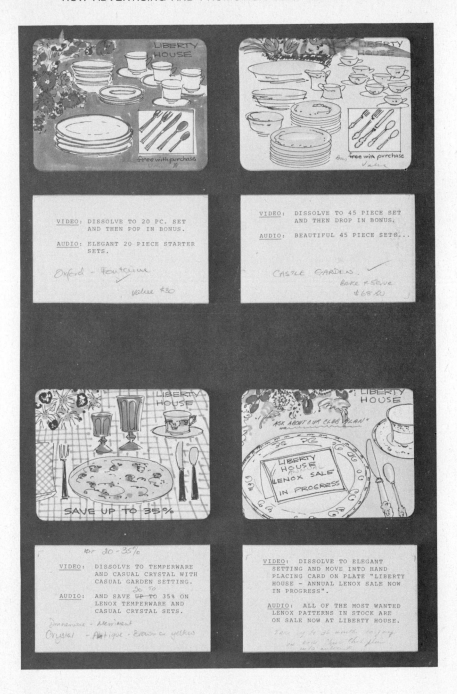

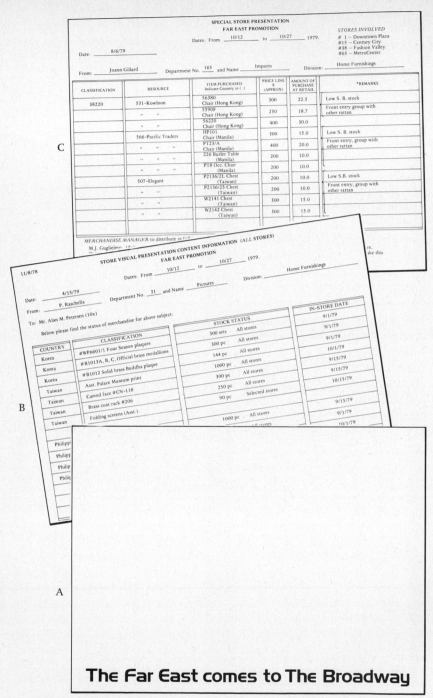

Figure 10.11   Case History of a Sales Promotion Event, The Broadway, Los Angeles, California. Theme: ''The Far East Comes to The Broadway.'' (A) A bright, Chinese red folder was used throughout the cam-

image you want the viewer to retain. Is the message clear, simple, and direct? Most viewers will not take the time to figure out what you are up to if you get too cute.

Will the spot be repeated often enough to reach a sufficient percentage of the potential market to make the effort worthwhile? That answer lies in the budgeting, of course, but it is a consideration in deciding how much to spend on the production of the spot.

One of the most effective television techniques is the demonstration—*showing the merchandise in use.* It is the main reason why television should be used by retailers, to show the viewer how to use the product, where to wear the apparel, or the setting in which the merchandise is most suitable. It is TV at its best. Many spots show the merchandise, either on display or in use, with a *voice off-camera* talking about it. This is a popular technique, used heavily by some advertisers because it costs less if the performer is only heard and not seen. The *on-camera spokesperson* can be a strong image builder, if the personality has relevance to the product—Douglas Fairbanks, Jr., selling Lincoln Continentals; John Wayne and other Western movie stars selling for Great Western Savings & Loan; sports figures selling athletic equipment. Hiring and paying for a "big name" to add prestige to your store may be great for the ego of the store president, but might be out of order in relation to other factors in the advertising budget. In many markets, a well-known local personality can be convinced to appear as spokesperson for a prestigious fashion organization. Not every market has television or motion picture people from which to draw for impression-building commercials. But most markets have radio personalities, city officials, respected businessmen and women. This is a television device largely neglected by retailers.

There are other television techniques that rarely make it into retail commercials:

- The slice of life (a scene from "real life")
- Humor (very difficult to do real humor)
- Animation (creates great illusions and is very costly, but computerized animation may make it more feasible)

---

paign to carry the elements of the promotion. It is a distinctive, attractive, professional package. (B) Sample of information for the visual merchandising department highlighting those items available in sufficient quantities to be included in press releases, ads, displays, exhibits, and special events. (C) Example of report to advertising and sales promotion office from merchandise manager indicating the merchandise purchases for the event, with other pertinent information. (SOURCE: All Far East promotion materials by permission of The Broadway.)

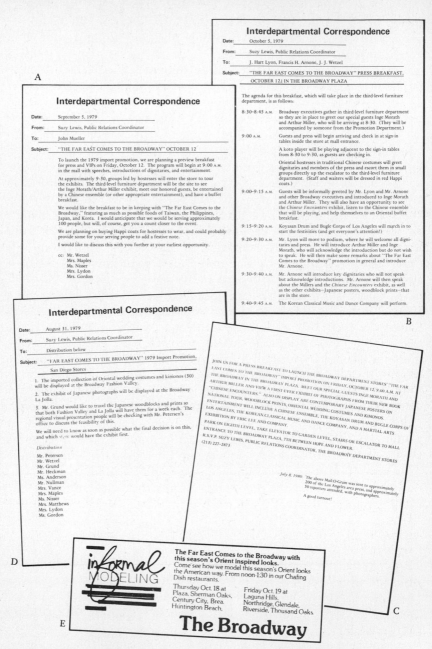

Figure 10.12   (A) Public relations bulletin notifying key personnel of planned preview breakfast for press and VIPs. (B) Detailed outline of agenda for press breakfast sent to store executives from public relations office. (C) Copy of text of Mailgram sent to Los Angeles press inviting its members to the press breakfast. Over 50 attended, with

Television is one of the lively arts. Too many retail TV commercials are not only not lively, they are hardly artistic. In a medium where the retail commercial will be seen and must be judged cheek-by-jowl with $50,000 nationally-produced spots, retailers of the future will have to make commitments to television that will include funds and talent to produce ads that will compete favorably and effectively.

BLENDING THE ELEMENTS TO CREATE THE TOTAL STORE IMAGE

Once a store's management comes to the conclusion that it cannot re-create the magic of Bloomingdale's in that city and decides to serve its public according to the public's needs, wants, and desires, the formula for communicating the news must be devised. What combination of media is best suited to the problem of reaching as many potential customers as possible? What will be the message? What theme best conveys this message? What vehicles of communication will carry the dramatized message best? Figures 10.11 to 10.16 show one major theme sales promotion by The Broadway.

When Lord and Taylor keyed in on the European look of the wide-shoulder dress, it launched a strong promotion under the title "Shoulder to Shoulder." It put together a collection of shoulder-emphasizing dresses, especially aimed at late day and evening, in many sizes and colors. The merchandise was set up in a special shop in the Fifth Avenue store, with dramatic window displays and traffic aisle emphasis inside the store. A double-truck (two-page) ad was run in the Sunday *New York Times* showing a dozen of the trend-setting styles. Customer response was good.

When Gimbels, New York, conducted a two-week fashion promotion presenting the natural soft look of spring—the Natural Look—it used newspaper, television, and radio ads. After six months of planning and working with manufacturers, the campaign was staged to make a dominant, concentrated impression of Gimbels as headquarters for moderate-price fashion. The total promotion included 18 newspaper ads, a 30-second television spot that was shown over 100 times during the two weeks, plus heavy radio support. Special events within the store included fashion shows, physical fitness and dance programs, and appearances by health

---

photographers. (D) As part of the storewide scope of the promotion, some elements of the program are scheduled for branch stores in suburban areas and in other cities. (E) Announcement ad for the Orient-inspired fashion show, listing dates of showings at branch stores.

A

Ad date	Wednesday, October 24								Schedule Control					
Ad #	Newspaper, dept. (s) and merchandise	Ad size	Lead sheet	Layout	Type room	Art Assign	Finish Art			Shipped	Killed	Moved	H.F.O	
	Holiday Sale Book in customers' homes													
# 3133	Times — P. 8 — Far East Comes to The Broadway 70 Brass and wood	132"												
# 3134	Times — P. 9 95 GE Festival, 5 days only	132"												
# 3135	Times — P. 11 33 York Gold series luggage													

Ad date	Friday, October 12							Schedule Control						
Ad #	Newspaper, dept. (s) and merchandise	Ad size	Lead sheet	Type room	Art Assign	Finish Art			Shipped	Killed	Moved	H.F.O.		
	Far East Promotion begins (thru 27th)													
# 3045	Times — Fashion '79 (60% gen. funds) The Far East Comes to The Broadway 215 Splendid silk shirts of the Orient	132"												
		40"												
# 3046	Times — P. 5 73 Plaza item													
# 3047	Times — P.8 — The Far East Comes to The Broadway Levinson pyramid omnibus page	132"												

B

ACTION-EVENT
Promotion Department:

October 8, 1979

From: SPECIAL EVENTS OFFICE

Subject: "THE FAR EAST COMES TO THE BROADWAY"

To: ALL CALIFORNIA STORES Store Manager; Operations Manager; Service Manager; Security; Executive Secretary; PBX

There will be a martial arts demonstration in all Broadway stores in California on:

Saturday, October 20 — 1:00–2:00 P.M.

Advertising October 11 132" ad in Los Angeles Times
October 12 18" ad in Santa Ana Register
October 11 Inclusion in 100" ad in San Diego Union Tribune

The groups in each store are as follows:

PLAZA	Kung Fu Association
HOLLYWOOD	Julio & Company Martial Arts Demonstration, Mr. Julio Hernandez
PASADENA	Ed Parker, Kempo Karate, Mr. Frank Tryo
CRENSHAW	Black Karate Federation, Chinese Kempo, Mr. Steve Sander
WESTCHESTER	Ralph Alegria Karate School, Mr. Ralph Alegria
PANORAMA CITY	Chong Lee Tae Kwon Do, Mr. Chong Lee
ANAHEIM	Samurai Academy, Mr. Burt Raush
LONG BEACH	Champion Studio, Mr. Young Lee
DEL AMO	Yamashita Karate, Mr. Richard Rabayo
WILSHIRE	William William 3 System Kung Fu, Mr. William William
WHITTIER	Fighting Grandpa Demonstration Team, Mr. Dick Hatch
WEST COVINA	Kim's Hapkido, Mr. Sae Kim

Figure 10.13 The Far East comes to The Broadway. (See caption on page 298.)

C

D

E

and media personalities. The storewide package delivered extra business and excellent customer response.

When Saks Fifth Avenue sought to increase store traffic in certain suburban stores, it devised a unique newsletter containing fashion and beauty stories plus merchandise designed for mail order, which was sent to charge customers in those areas. A special feature, tailored to each store, was a single-page insert describing special events at that store only. These events included designer personal appearances, social affairs, and fashion events.

Smaller stores and specialty store chains, with less money to spend than Gimbels and Lord and Taylor, can, and do, accomplish the same goal of total store sales promotion within the limit of their budgets. Every element of sales promotion cannot be used for every event, but shrewd planning and knowledge will give the store more exposure and better results. Sometimes the combination of a direct mail campaign with newspaper and radio will do the job. Often newspaper ads, backed up by good fashion publicity and invitations to a fashion show, make the event a success. In San Francisco, Hastings Men's Stores used billboards as the added ingredient in its sales promotion campaign. It seems that some combination of media, or media mix, is needed for effective advertising. A single-medium campaign, whether newspaper, radio, or mail order, may not be enough for today's complicated retail marketing problems.

All over the country, successful stores adapt to new fashion trends. They do not throw out the successful pattern upon which their business has been built; they create a variation within the pattern that lets the public know who they are and what the news in fashion is all about. The stores take a position, support it with merchandise and promotion, and know their customers will respond.

As customers become more sophisticated, they become more fickle. The fashion retailer knows today's customers are not as loyal

---

Figure 10.13   (A) Portion of The Broadway's newspaper advertising schedule indicating dates, size of ad, ad position, and other data. (B) The Broadway's multistore operation requires efficient communication at all levels. This schedule of martial arts demonstrations, involving every store in the southern California division, indicates the professional (and successful) approach to sales promotion by this retail operation. (C) Press photo of Inge Morath and Arthur Miller supplied by The Broadway. Many papers will reprint photos when furnished if the editor feels the event has enough reader interest. (D) Press release listing full schedule of special events for the duration of the Far East promotion. (E) Sample of press release announcing "The Far East comes to The Broadway."

Figure 10.14   Opening day newspaper ad of "The Far East Comes to The Broadway" outlining details of the promotion and dates and locations of the special attractions.

as previous generations of shoppers may have been. There is the constant need for reestablishing customer communications. Stores that stay flexible and competitive and never forget their basic identity survive customer change and fickleness. Stores that stay fashion- and quality-conscious will retain their share of shoppers as time goes on, although they must constantly work to bring in new

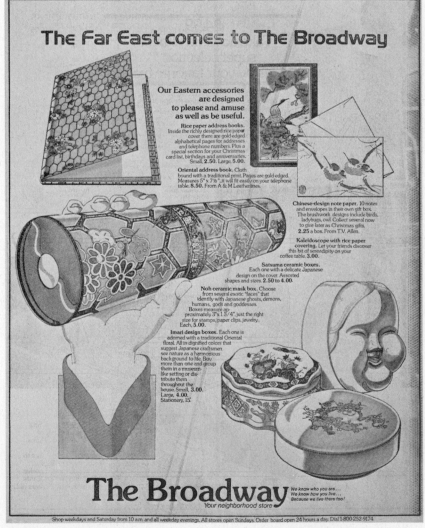

Figure 10.15 Follow-up newspaper ad offering exotic merchandise from the Far East and including a reminder of the Oriental art exhibits available for public viewing.

Figure 10.16 Specific merchandise ad featuring Japanese *kimono* from The Broadway's junior fashion department.

customers to replace those lost through attrition. New customers enlarge the base on which a store can grow.

The economic climate will dictate a future for advertising and promotion that will inform, educate, and help customers to buy. Stores will have to find new ways, using media they never used before, techniques that are strange, consultants they never needed before, to reach customers. As new living patterns, new attitudes, new thinking, and new needs arise and must be serviced, the stores that

Figure 10.17 California fashions from Robinson's, Los Angeles. This dramatic presentation combines the dual impact of the two-page newspaper ad with the power of the multi-image pose to make an important

keep up with and anticipate customer needs will be most successful.

Innovative sales promotion is not an end in itself. It must incorporate all elements in the store to make it work, especially if the promotion is aimed at changing the image of the store. The merchandise must reflect the new personality. The salespeople must be aware and enthusiastic about the change. Each buyer and merchandise person must be involved early in the planning stages. The direction, the driving force, must come from management, for as we

fashion statement. Robinson's uses this effective design principle to establish and maintain its fashion image in southern California. (SOURCE: By permission of Robinson's.)

have noted, nothing filters up. Although the building of a new image starts at ground level, where both the customer and the salespeople are, the inspiration for the change comes from the executive level. From the shipping clerk to the cashier, from the delivery truck driver to the stock help, the entire store family must exude the confidence that makes customers believe what the store is saying in its advertising (Figure 10.17).

The themes must be the same in newspaper ads, in direct mail, in radio, and in television. The cumulative effect of all elements inside and outside the store, funneled in one continuing direction, can make a town, a city, a state, even a country, sit up and take notice. It doesn't happen overnight. Bloomingdale's—the Bloomie's that is every retailer's dream—didn't become the retail phenomenon it is in a day. At one time Bloomingdale's was a very promotional, poorly directed store without much personality or charm. Through in-depth research and enlightened management leadership, the store became aware of the migration of a special class of people in the East Side of Manhattan during the 1950s and 1960s. It mapped out a merchandising and promotional strategy to take advantage of the situation, and the result was "overnight success." It was years in the doing, but the focus, the direction was there for a long time before it "suddenly" became a retail showplace. Like the movie star who achieves instant success, the public is not aware of the years of training, practice, heartache, and suffering preceding the sudden arrival in the public consciousness and the crowning of another "overnight sensation."

Retailing changes, yet retailing is the same. With changing times and changing fashions comes a changing public. The function of sales promotion is to keep up with the store's customers, to reach them with the stories the store has to tell, to motivate them to continue to shop at the store (Figure 10.17). The sales promotion person will always be the chemist, mixing the media, the appeal of the merchandise, and the desires of the customers into a smooth-running, interesting blend of communications. Sales promotion is the catalyst that makes the retail juices flow.

QUESTIONS FOR DISCUSSION AND CLASS ASSIGNMENTS

1. Select a dozen ads from the Sunday newspaper. Cover the store logos or names. See how many stores the class can identify from the "look" alone. Discuss the consistency of the advertising of those most identifiable.
2. Pick six ads at random from your daily newspaper. Check them against the AIDA formula of advertising. Discuss good and bad elements of the ads.
3. Bring into class examples of ads (newspaper, direct mail, radio, and television) that do and do *not* offer benefits to the consumer as reasons to buy.
4. Bring into class six examples of newspaper ads where the headline is unrelated to the text or body copy of the ad.
5. Select six ads using news and other key words indicating immediacy or urgency in the headline.
6. Discuss the advantages and disadvantages of using photographs instead of artists's sketches as illustrations in newspaper ads.

7. Bring in to class examples of retail ads using varieties of typefaces to indicate the mood the ad seeks to convey.
8. Collect all the direct mail received in your home for a month from a major department store where your family has a charge account. Compare your collection with those of others in the class. Discuss your findings in relation to the type of store involved.
9. Bring in the most unusual examples of direct mail you can find. Discuss the versatility of direct mail advertising.
10. Describe radio commercials you have heard recently that use (a) emotion, (b) humor, (c) unusual music to get the attention of the listener.
11. Report on three store-produced retail television commercials that reflect the quality image of the stores they advertise.
12. Discuss why changing life-styles, the increased number of women in the work force, and economic conditions foster the need for multimedia exposure for better sales promotion results.

Chapter 11
Fashion Promotion
in Action

Earlier we stated that effective advertising is advertising that talks to its public most often about the merchandise that interests *them* most often. This will result in maximum readership of newspaper and direct mail ads, and greater awareness of television and radio ads. The best promotions, therefore, are those that will inspire the most visits to the store at the most frequent intervals.

Yet studies and surveys have shown that as much as 65 percent of many stores' advertising budget is eaten up by 15 to 20 big sale events annually, leaving a mere 35 percent to promote the rest of the year's programs. In addition, the obligation to allocate large portions of that 35 percent to participate in vendors' co-op programs takes a bigger chunk out of the total budget than many retailers would care to admit. Therein lies the problem many stores face when planning advertising and promotion programs that will enhance or change their fashion personalities. It requires the inclusion in the management team of a person whose sole responsibility is the building and maintaining of the store's fashion reputation, the fashion director.

THE FASHION DIRECTOR

The position of fashion director has traditionally been held by a woman. In past years the position was, in most major department stores, limited to the function of fashion coordinator. These women, easily identified by their big hats and long white gloves, regardless of season and weather conditions, were regarded with suspicion by the more conservative buying and merchandising people in the store. Fashion coordinators were considered frivolous, unreliable people operating in a tiny circle all their own, with little regard for or effect on store sales or merchandising. Their sole function was to provide commentary for fashion shows and schedule informal modeling when necessary. They were considered a necessary evil if a store was to project a fashion image, but not very important in the total store picture.

Things have changed remarkably in recent years: Stores depend on fashion promotion to build and maintain their fashion reputations. In a major department store, with its fragmented departmental organization and split buying responsibilities, it is more vital than ever that fashion promotion be an integral part of the total promotion program.

The fashion director's importance and influence is apparent by the title and position in the chain of command accorded that person. The degree of influence can be measured by noticing to which store executive the fashion director reports. If she (or he) reports to the store president, you can be sure the fashion image of the store is of primary interest to the company. If the fashion promotion responsibility is under the divisional merchandise manager's banner, there can be strong influence and guidance in merchandise purchases. If the fashion director is reporting to the sales promotion manager, the influence is felt directly in advertising and display presentations.

The role of fashion sales promotion, regardless of store size or organization, is the presentation of the store's fashion personality in a consistent, effective manner no matter which medium of advertising or promotion is being used. The fashion director advises and counsels the sales promotion manager and advertising manager in their fashion advertising planning. The fashion director analyzes and studies market trends, fills in the background on the merchandise for the advertising department, and helps plan the presentation of the merchandise stories for advertising. Store management depends on fashion promotion for the continuity of the store's image in all media.

In recent years the stature of the fashion director has been enhanced by the elevation of fashion directors to vice-presidencies in many major department stores. Several of these have risen through the ranks from buyer to merchandise manager to fashion vice-president. These people gain enormous respect when they make buying trips to the showrooms of New York manufacturers. Instead of playing a mere advisory role, they have the clout to direct and cause merchandise to be bought with fashion promotion in mind. Manufacturers have great respect for this kind of authority and respond accordingly. The new stature of the fashion director in the large stores cannot help but have a corresponding effect on the stature of fashion promotion people in medium and small fashion operations. The increased competitiveness for fashion business has enhanced the position of the fashion director.

In many stores the fashion director works with the training department to teach the sales staff about the new season's fashions. Informing the salespeople of the reasons behind purchases is a vital responsibility. Uninformed salespeople can cause a store to lose sales—and customers. Well-informed salespeople can make a mediocre store a winner. Merchandise information cannot be limited to garment labeling or store signs. Knowledge of fashion trends, what to wear with what, the latest fashion news—are all part of the sales staff's selling arsenal, and it must be provided to them by the fashion promotion person.

The training of salespeople can take the form of employee fashion shows, after-hours rap sessions, show-and-tell meetings before store opening, or routine information reports. Each store determines its own best method of sales training, but no successful store operates without good training methods.

Qualifications of the Fashion Director

With the growing importance of the fashion director's role in the planning and buying of merchandise, it almost follows that anyone interested in a career in fashion should begin at the ground level—in a store. To get to the top in any job, it is usually necessary to start at the bottom. How long you stay on that bottom rung depends on you. The climb to the top may be slow and tedious, with much competition for the limited number of fashion director positions existing throughout the country.

A fashion director must be dedicated. A wealth of knowledge about the fashion business is mandatory; a fashion director must be fashion-wise. The presentation of a store's fashion image often requires a flair for the theatrical. The staging of fashion shows has blossomed from the simple parade of models on a runway to most of the elements of a Broadway production. A fashion director must have the talent to present fashion merchandise stories in a dramatic, exciting, and creative way.

The fashion director is the spokesperson for the store in all fashion-related matters. Contacts with the trade and consumer press are necessary for the proper presentation of fashion stories about the store. The fashion office is the area of the store that generates most of the news the papers find fit to print. The fashion director must have an appreciation of the value of fashion publicity and the ability to create fashion news to build and maintain the image of the store.

To be effective, the fashion director must have the confidence and cooperation of the buyers and merchandise executives of the store. Advice, direction, and suggestions from the fashion office should reflect the authority and acceptance of the fashion director. Unless the store buys and carries the merchandise the fashion director suggests, the image the store projects will be confused, fuzzy, and ineffective. The fashion director must have clout.

Fashion directors have climbed the ladder to fashion leadership by various routes. The qualifications for this position are different from store to store. The attributes we have cited cover most of the requirements a successful fashion director should have, plus the other characteristics of most successful business people—intelligence, enthusiasm, stamina, good health, the ability to work under pressure while maintaining a positive mental attitude toward the job, the store, and the fashion industry. This, of course, is not an all-inclusive list, but a person with these characteristics has a good chance for success in retailing and in fashion.

Coordination with Sales Promotion

The fashion director is the middle position in the marketing pattern between merchandising and sales promotion. Awareness of the goals and problems of both segments of the store operation must be maintained at all times. The sales promotion or advertising manager depends on the fashion office for the reasons why certain merchandise is planned for advertising. Buyers and merchandisers know why certain buying decisions were made, but do not always articulate those reasons to the advertising staff. Sometimes the interpretation of the merchandising information can be presented to the advertising group in a more understandable form. It is the responsibility of the advertising people to describe and present the merchandise story from the customer's point of view. Without the complete story of why each particular fashion item was purchased in the market and selected to be advertised, the store could get weak, generalized ads that do not generate business.

Since many fashion directors make market trips with the buyers and merchandise managers of the store—some even travel abroad to Paris, London, Rome, and the Orient—they can assist the promotion department with firsthand insight into the styles and colors and fabrics that make the fashion news. With this kind of arrangement, the enthusiasm the fashion director brings to the advertising/merchandising meetings easily translates into more excitement and interest the advertising people can develop in their presentations to the public.

As the fashion authority in the store, the fashion director's office could also have the responsibility for checking all accessorizing of models appearing in the ads and of all mannequins on display throughout the store. This will ensure that all fashions are presented with proper accessories—the right shoes, hats, handbags—to show that the store is fashion-right in all departments. Some large retail advertising departments and most display departments have their own fashion coordinators or stylists. When there is more than one fashion authority in a store, confusion may result unless there is a clearly defined store position on fashion to which all promotion departments conform.

Stores that are filming television spots always employ the talents of a fashion person to be sure the models are "put together" correctly. Stores that use photography in fashion ads must have full-time fashion people on staff to dress the models. Every time the public is shown a fashion item in an ad or on display, it must be correct in every detail. One wrong item—a belt or scarf improperly included as part of an ensemble—can negate the fashion impression the store is trying to make. In some cases, the fashion director may have veto power over a television commercial or newspaper or magazine ad if the presentation does not conform to the store's image. When the sales promotion manager and the fashion director do not agree, the conflict can be resolved in the office of the merchandise manager, or if need be, the office of the president.

Proper planning and communication well in advance of the TV shooting date or the photo session for the print ads can prevent unnecessary problems and expensive remakes. Remember the old saying in the advertising business: "There's never enough time to do it right, but there's always time to do it over." But it costs money. Since the fashion director's sole role in relation to sales promotion is usually advisory, the relationship between the two departments should be cordial and pleasant.

One solution to the fashion image presentation problem in ad-

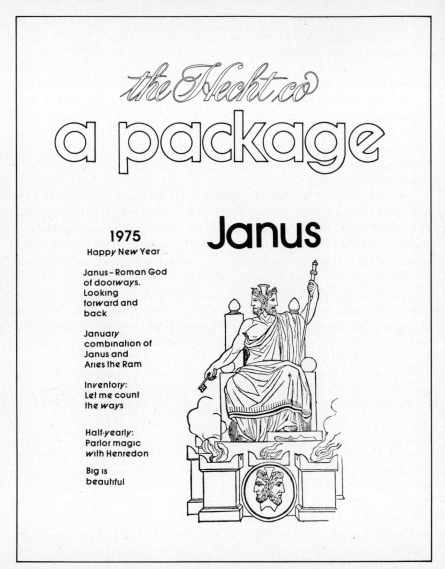

Figure 11.1   Case History of a Sales Promotion Package. The Hecht Company, Washington and Baltimore. Cover folder of a typical sales promotion package distributed from the headquarters sales promotion office to branch stores. Similar procedures exist in multistore chains. This illustration covers stores in Washington, D.C., and Baltimore, Md. Detailed information and instructions are issued to ensure continuity in the sales promotion impression delivered to the public. (SOURCE: By permission of David Dunay, Merchandise Communications.)

vertising was developed by a major Eastern department store. The weekly, full-page ad in the Sunday paper in which the store made its regular fashion statement was placed under the control of the fashion director. This person had free rein to select the fashion item to be advertised, the manner in which it was to be sketched (no photos here), which artist was assigned to the drawing, and even the person to write the copy! The ad department staff, bogged down with the heavy load of the regular ad schedule, was unhappy about this special arrangement. But the result of the campaign was a consistency of presentation week after week that made a strong fashion impact on the public.

Once a store has taken a fashion position and has spelled out its fashion philosophy to all departments and executives in the store, the job of coordinating fashion elements from various parts of the store becomes simple. Either the fashion items fit or they do not. The merchandise assortments are reflected on the shelves, racks, and counters, in the advertising, in displays, and in all stories released by the publicity department (Figure 11.1).

PLANNING THE FASHION PRESENTATION

Fashion promotion starts when the fashion director announces the look or looks the store "believes in" for the coming season. This belief is a composite of the materials, colors, silhouettes, and textures that will be found in the store in the months ahead. Fashion promotion follows the seasons in much the same way as the store's total sales promotion calendar.

There is an interesting pattern in the sequence of fashion buying and delivery and store promotion and advertising. The fashion calendar tallies with the sales promotion calendar, with certain types of merchandise requiring longer lead time for store delivery, as Table 11.1 shows.

Markets where seasonal factors result in expanded or contracted selling periods will deviate from this kind of scheduling, but the basic pattern exists in most parts of the country.

To make the most of the traditional seasonal fashion events most stores promote, the stores look to fashion promotion department for ideas and themes that can make an impact on the buying public and enhance the store's fashion personality. The three most important "seasons" are fall, spring, and summer, with the other periods providing bridges to the longer, more profitable seasons.

The program the fashion director publishes includes the names, dates, and themes of the major fashion events of the season (Figure 11.2). Key fashion shows are listed, and whether they will

Table 11.1 THE CONNECTION BETWEEN BUYING AND PROMOTING

EVENT	BUYING PERIOD	DELIVERY	ADVERTISING/ PROMOTION
Back-to-school	May	July/August	August/ September
Fall fashions	April/May	July/August	August/ September
Holiday fashions	September	October/ November	November/ December
Resort/cruise wear	September/ October	December/ January	January
Spring fashion	October/ November	December/ January	January
Summer fashion	January/ February	April/May	May/June
Transitional	May	July	July/August

take place inside or outside the store. They could be tied in with community organizations and become, in fact, charity or benefit shows for local church or hospital groups. These can become important social functions, and reflect great credit to the store in the eyes of the public.

Also in the fashion schedule are planned visits of fashion designers and key manufacturers. These visits are important from at least two standpoints: the impression made on the public by the appearance of these fashion leaders in the store, plus the establishment of good customer/client relationships between the designers and manufacturers and the store. These visits also provide the store with opportunities for good publicity stories in the local press and interviews on local radio and television talk shows. Many designers bring with them samples of creations not yet available to the general public and take special orders from store customers. These so-called trunk showings also serve to indicate to the store and the designer which styles have the most appeal to the clientele of the store.

With the spread of branch stores into the suburbs, a designer or manufacturer may spend several days in a city, visiting many of the stores on a tight, frantic schedule, bringing the fashion news to the store's customers wherever they are. Some manufacturers prepare packaged fashion shows, complete with fashion commentator and models, which travel from market to market showing their latest looks to as broad an audience as possible. These touring fashion shows, when scheduled into the total store program, provide the fashion promotion department with some relief from the job of creating and producing individual shows for key fashion lines on sale

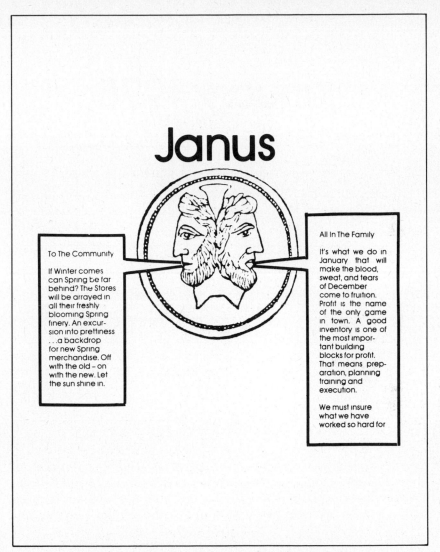

Figure 11.2   Theme of the month is described and explained.

in the store. Final approval of the show, however, rests with the fashion director and the merchandise manager, to ensure that the show content fits in with the store image. It must be scheduled so that all aspects of good promotion can be included—announcements to the public and to store personnel, staging, advertising, publicity. Touring shows can become important fashion events in smaller markets where people are not exposed to promotional events as often as their big-city counterparts (Figure 11.3).

january 1975

	SUNDAY	MONDAY	TUESDAY	WEDNESDAY	THURSDAY	FRIDAY	SATURDAY
WASH.	Half-Yearly 5 Book ---- Budget White Sale Insert Post	6	7	8	9	10 (-----------------PRE-INVENTORY SALE	11 -----------------)
BALT.	Budget White Sale Insert N.A.				(-----------------PRE-INVENTORY SALE	-----------------)	
WASH.	12	13	Inventory 14 F Street	Inventory 15 Branches	16	LOM/TC/MH 17 Private Sale	18
BALT.			Inventory Howard Street	Inventory Branches	White Sale Mailer		RFIS/ED/NO Private Sale Last Year in Dec.
WASH.	White Sale 19 Insert - Post	20	21	LA Carpet Event 22 MM Men's Event	F Street 23 Private Sale & Men's Clothing Event	24	Golden Opportunity 25 Day
BALT.							Golden Opportunity Day
WASH.	26	27	28	29	30	31	1 REMNANT DAY
BALT.		HO Street Private Sale					REMNANT DAY

Figure 11.3 Detailed sales promotion and advertising calendar.

Fashion shows must be informative as well as entertaining. Showing the customers of the store what to wear with what, talking about fashion trends and how the fashions being shown fit with the season's looks, all help convert shoppers into regular customers.

Informal Modeling

On busy traffic days, many stores will provide informal modeling, with models wandering throughout the store in a casual manner, visiting the restaurant, the beauty salon, and other traffic areas, calling attention to new merchandise. Again, this kind of activity does not just happen. It must be planned and scheduled, so that details can be attended to and the proper impression is made on the buying public.

The following is a typical planning procedure for informal modeling in an independent or branch store. The guidelines are similar to those followed by most stores, and provide the fashion person or the department manager with a practical checklist from which to proceed.

1. Determine the date for the modeling and advise store personnel of the date and the merchandise involved. Be sure to include this information in the monthly in-store bulletin, with dates, hours, and locations.

2. Promoting the event: "Coat News for Fall"
   Timing: Two to four weeks prior to the informal modeling
   a. Advertising: Run ads in local media announcing "fashion presentation" with specific time and place. Include mentions in any ads scheduled to run during this period.
   b. Direct mail: Mail invitations and/or call special customers who might be interested in the merchandise. Tell them about the modeling, the reason for the event, the time and place, refreshments and any personalities involved.
   c. Merchandise: Arrange for the buyer or department manager to be on hand during modeling to answer questions and help close sales.
   d. Other: Arrange for refreshments, with personnel to serve refreshments and clean up.

3. Selecting the fashions
   Timing: Two to four weeks prior to the informal modeling
   a. Coat fashions highlighted in the store's merchandise bulletin on the fall coat collection should be featured. A representative sampling of the fabrics, colors, and styling you have in depth in the store should be shown.
   b. Accessorize the coats with boots, hose and shoes, hats, scarves and gloves.
   c. Select more fashion outfits than you intend to use. Some will not fit the models. Make notes on each outfit with details concerning fabric, care, color, price, and styling. This information is for the model so she can answer questions as she goes through the store.
   d. Plan to have the merchandise being modeled highlighted on forward fixtures in the department to make it easy for customers (and models) to find them.

4. Selecting the models
   Timing: During the two weeks prior to the modeling
   a. Hire professional models (if the budget allows) or establish contacts at modeling or charm schools, offering practical experience for their best students as an inducement. Take only the best students.

    b. If you plan to use customers as models, offering gift certificates or other considerations in lieu of payment, check for the following qualities:
- Women with current, attractive makeup
- Women with up-to-date hair styles
- Pleasant-looking customers who walk with poise, grace, and self-assurance
- Customers with friendly, outgoing personalities who can answer questions and give information just like professional models
- Customers who look well in your fashions

5. Meeting with the sales staff

Timing: During the week prior to the modeling

    a. Hold a briefing session about the informal modeling with the store staff, in small groups or at a regular weekly get-together.

    b. If you are using customers as models, have them appear at the meeting. Using customer models is a risky business, but it can work if handled carefully.

    c. Discuss the timing of the informal modeling, the fashions being featured, the location of backup stock, a review of the promotional activities, and each person's responsibilities on that day.

    d. Encourage the sales staff to promote the event in conversations with customers, reminding them of the day and date and inviting them to attend.

    e. Check to be sure store signs at the entrances are posted to remind shoppers of the coming event.

6. Matching the models with the fashions

Timing: About a week before the modeling

    a. If selecting customers or nonprofessionals as models, begin to visualize which outfits are best suited to which person. Mature styles look better on mature models, and so on.

    b. Have each model try on each outfit to be sure the lengths of the garments are appropriate.

    c. Accessorize each outfit carefully and just enough to get the message across. Give each model a cue card—notes about the fashion details, price, fabric use and care, and location of the merchandise in the store (department name, which floor).

    d. Make sure the models know what time to be at the store and how to get in, and remind them to have their cue cards.

7. The fashion presentation
   a. Checklist time!
      • Everything ready in the store?
      • Refreshments on hand, with people to handle?
      • Dressing room all set, with helpers ready?
      • Outfits arranged in sequence? On hangers?
      • Models on hand on time? Do they have cue cards?
      • Department manager or buyer on hand?
   b. Watch the action. If there is good attendance and interest in certain fashions, you may want to rearrange the sequence of the models, allowing some to stay on the floor longer.
   c. Watch for sales response. Pass the information along to the merchandise people; this is valuable material. Be sure the nonprofessionals handle the merchandise carefully to avoid damage and markdowns. Send the nonpros thank you notes with their gifts. Thank the store staff for its cooperation.

Promoting and Executing Fashion Shows

This guide to informal modeling contains much of what the average retailer needs to know about handling a fashion show in the average fashion store. It gets a bit more complicated when it comes to staging a full-scale fashion show. Guidelines for organizing a fashion show would include some of the following:

1. Planning the event
   Timing: Six to eight weeks prior to the show
   a. Determine the theme (The Wonderful World of Coats)
   b. Decide on the date, the time, and what location in the store will be used for the show. An open area near the ready-to-wear section works well to absorb the crowd at the end of the show. Stores that have auditoriums can stage more elaborate presentations, but creative planning can make a fashion show on the selling floor quite effective.
   c. Plan and schedule the advertising media to promote the show.
      • Newspaper. Include in fashion calendar listing; prepare special fashion show ad; include mentions of show in regular ads (copy, with show information, should be in the ad department's hands several weeks prior to show).

- Invitations. Mail to charge account customers, especially those who have been coat customers in past few years; design an attractive mailing piece to get customers' attention.
- Radio. Buy a radio schedule on stations whose listeners are women age 18 to 49; commit to the buy early, to ensure getting spots on the air at the best times.
- Store posters. Keep them simple but attractive; place at all traffic locations—entrances, restaurant, lounges.

d. Arrange a meeting with the visual merchandising people to plan the physical setup for the show. Points to cover include overall decor of stage and show area; runway location; microphones; lighting; music (piped or live); seating arrangements; refreshments for audience. Don't forget to check and double check all electrical equipment in advance and on show day. Have extra lightbulbs and extension cords on hand.

2. Selecting the models
   Timing: Two to four weeks prior to the fashion show
   a. Hire a minimum of five models to allow for costume changes.
   b. Establish high standards for the models:
      - Current makeup for the right look
      - Attractive, current hair styles
      - Pleasant, attractive facial features
      - Ability to walk with poise, grace, and self-assurance
      - If music is important, models with dancing ability
   c. Prepare file cards on each model, including photo, listing name, address, telephone; dress and shoe sizes; hair color; height and weight; age. Keep card file current, with running comments on each model's performance, attitude.

3. Selecting the merchandise
   Timing: Two to four weeks prior to the fashion show
   a. For a 30-minute fashion show, you need 25 to 30 outfits. Preselect at least 40 suitable outfits to allow for fit problems.
   b. Select the fashions that best demonstrate the new colors, styles, and fabrics for fall. Be sure there is sufficient stock on hand or en route of the merchandise you select.
   c. The fashion office stylist should assist in the selection of accessories for the show, with a fitter on hand to dress the models and cope with emergencies.

4. Sequencing the show
   Timing: Two weeks before the show
   a. After the models have been fitted and accessories chosen, prepare the commentary to flow logically from outfit to outfit. Often the theme of the show will suggest natural groupings of merchandise.
   b. Sequence the garments to fit the commentary and allow the models to appear sequentially, with time between calls to make outfit changes.
   c. Number the garments in order of appearance.
   d. Hang the outfits in order of appearance and tag each outfit with the model's name and the number of its appearance.
   e. Hang the accessories with the outfit or tag them with the same number and model's name as the outfit. Sometimes models will bring their own accessories with them, especially when there is a problem finding shoes that fit comfortably. Indicate on the outfit that the model is using her own accessories.
5. Final preparations
   Timing: One week before the fashion show
   a. Release all ads to advertising media—newspapers, direct mail, radio. Place all sign posters at store entrances and in concerned departments.
   b. Be sure store's weekly bulletin includes fashion show announcement.
   c. Hold meeting with fashion sales staff, inform them of show details, encourage them to tell shoppers about the show and to call special regular customers.
   d. Assign one person to assist each model to help dress the model and assist in outfit changes. Each assistant should be briefed in advance concerning the model's outfits.
   e. In addition to the commentary, the fashion director should prepare a cue card with a full description of each outfit, including the model's name, the description of the garments, the price, the fabric story (including use and care), and the department name and location in the store.
   f. Prepare a list of the outfit sequence by number and model name and post inside and outside the dressing room for easy reference.
   g. One fashion assistant should be charged with the responsibility of backing up the fashion director. They should review the commentary together, checking the lineup of

models and garments and fully understanding the procedure. Rehearse with the models if necessary.

h. This person becomes the "starter" on show day, responsible for sending out the models in the proper order, and on cue.

i. A final check should be made of all electrical and lighting equipment, refreshment arrangements, and all other mechanical details.

6. The day of the show

   a. Be sure everyone has the proper assignment and arrives on time, ready to go to work.

   b. On with the show! Good luck!

   c. When the show is over, clear the department as quickly as possible to allow the attendees to shop.

   d. File the cue cards for future reference; customers may ask for an outfit that was modeled.

   e. Thank the people who helped with the show.

FASHION PROMOTION IN DEPARTMENT STORES

Much of our attention has been directed to the fashion sales promotion problems and opportunities in large department stores. This emphasis has been deliberate. The segmentation of the department store operation was used to spell out the fact that all functions in the sales promotion procedure take place in all stores regardless of the size of the store. The only real difference is the number of people available to carry out the job.

In the department store organization, with the fashion director as vice-president, there is a staff of assistants, clerks, fitters, seamstresses, secretaries, and the like. In a large store, the fashion position is a big job. To cover the production of shows, the training of salespeople, the coordination of television commercials and interior displays, the working with consumer groups, and the public relations activities requires divisional coordinators, assistants to handle specific functions. The fashion director attends social and civic affairs, takes market trips, contacts the trade and local press, and travels to fashion openings in foreign cities. These activities necessitate the existence of backup organizations that can handle the regular responsibilities of the department.

The fashion sales training function is usually a staff function. An assistant is assigned to work with the training director to train the salespeople. This can be done through lectures, slide demonstrations, employee fashion shows, and training films. After the main (downtown) store has gone through the training for the new season, the fashion assistant moves on to the suburban or branch stores with the same information. It is important that the same fashion image is projected by each store in each community. This can only be accomplished through constant training and communication.

When the branches are far-flung, at great distances from headquarters, frequent personal visits are impractical. At this point, there is greater reliance on bulletins, booklets, memos, and other materials that managers and salespeople can read and study. The use of videotape for this type of training is growing, with many of the presentations made publicly to inform and educate the buying public (Figure 11.4).

The fashion director, in the final analysis, despite multiple responsibilities—to management, to the buying and merchandising staff, to sales promotion, to sales training, and to the public—has one basic responsibility: to convert consumers into customers.

FASHION PROMOTION IN SPECIALTY STORES

The specialty store, dealing in fashion only, avoids the problems of the large department store, where management's attention is fragmented among many departments and activities. Concentration on fashion, and only fashion, results in the unique ability of the specialty store to create, operate, and prosper in the face of department store and chain store competition.

When it comes to offering the public narrower, deeper assortments of the most popular fashions at moderate-to-better prices, the specialty store cannot be surpassed. They tend to avoid the vacillation of department store fashion departments, which flit from manufacturer to manufacturer from season to season. Specialty stores also tend to capitalize on this vendor loyalty factor by "scooping" the competition in satisfying customer demand.

They have the ability, through mobility and singleness of purpose, to pick up and capitalize on the newest, hottest trends. When a style is at its peak of popularity, the fashion shopper heads for the specialty store that carries the line of the season in sufficient depth of assortment to ensure her finding her size and color. These stores do not predict or dictate fashion looks and trends. Their role is to package fashions for customers. They must be able to feel the fashion change, anticipate it, present it, capitalize on it, and then get ready for the next change. Under these conditions, the fashion direction comes from a less specialized person than in the big department store. The person filling the role of fashion director could be a former big store buyer or assistant fashion director or coordinator.

Figure 11.4 Trends in fashion that will be reflected in the store's merchandise, displays, and fashion presentation are regularly communicated to branch stores.

She or he works with a small staff or an assistant or two, but in many cases may have to do it all alone.

With limited access to the New York and California markets, the fashion director in a medium-size operation tends to operate by contacts. Close contact is maintained with the store's buyers. Great reliance is placed on the store's resident buying office, which takes on the responsibility of feeding fashion trends, hot item information, and promotional possibilities back to the company's executives. Market reports, manufacturers' bulletins, books and trade publications offer information that would not otherwise be available to the nontraveling fashion promotion person.

In specialty stores and some smaller fashion chains, the same buyer could be responsible for several categories. This results in somewhat natural coordination, for the buyer is aware of what goes with what and selects merchandise with that in mind. No need for a special person to coordinate activities if the multidepartment buyer is the fashion expert that kind of position demands. If coordination is necessary it is a simpler process, for with fewer buyers offering fewer opinions there is bound to be less friction. Also, the fashion coordinator's job is easier because there are fewer people to work with and to train, and probably less physical area to cover. Smaller operations also benefit from the closeness of smaller staffs because there are more frequent intra-store contacts and better communications.

When the independent fashion store delves into the area of fashion coordination, the role of the fashion director is usually just one facet of that person's total job. In many cases, the responsibility for fashion direction may be delegated to the boss's wife, the boss, or the family's youngest son. Often, the store's buyer doubles as the fashion authority, coordinating the elements of several categories or classifications. Salespeople are trained to sell across departmental lines, to be knowledgeable in all merchandise categories. With less regimentation, sales can be made in various departments by the same salesperson. This type of selling is profitable, allowing the salesperson to stay with the customer while he or she is in a buying mood and developing larger total sales per shopper. The technique maximizes the effectiveness of the store's advertising and promotion program by getting the most out of the store traffic the advertising generated.

When the merchandise manager in a specialty store or small department store handles the fashion director function, it is usually because that person loves doing it and enjoys the challenge of promoting fashion. It also allows that individual the rare opportunity of seeing the entire fashion cycle—from buying the merchandise in the market through promotion and advertising to the floor level, where the sale to the customer takes place. Such people enjoy the satisfaction of having control of the entire process. The danger, minor at best, is that that person may tend to favor one category of merchandise. It is said, "Once a blouse buyer, always a blouse buyer." Such a person will tend to fall back on his or her expert knowledge of the blouse department if a problem of sales, profit, or operation crops up.

When the owner of the store serves as the fashion authority, the buying, merchandising, and advertising is under the control of one person, so there is no need for liaison or coordination. The result: complete dependence on vendors and sales reps for fashion information, reinforcing the fashion image already established through the limited merchandise presentations. One-person operations rarely use outside sources for fashion or advertising help; they rely on seat-of-the-pants opinions and impressions.

Occasionally the trade press or some fashion magazine will take an interest in small-store retailing and will run feature articles and highlight unique operations, but the bigger stores, being bigger spenders, are better prospects for the media. It has been noted that big stores can often learn from the successes of small operations. But many independent operators fail to take advantage of the successes of large stores. There is learning to be done on both sides.

FASHION PROMOTION IN CHAIN STORES

Fashion chains, the stores you find in every major shopping center, are spread out all over the country. Some are national chains, some regional, some confined to major cities and suburbs. Wherever they are, the same promotional calendar is followed. Local area needs are considered, and most companies allow for some discretionary advertising spending under specified conditions.

Local knowledge is important in satisfying the fashion needs of an area. Information garnered at the local level can be passed on to headquarters rapidly with the efficient electronic data-processing systems most major chains have now or will be installing soon. When certain areas report activity in a brand, category, or item, some headquarters have the flexibility to move fast, to reorder quantities of the wanted items and gear up for advertising and promotion at the same time. National chains sometimes cannot move as rapidly as the regional chains. It takes more time for the information to reach the decision-making level, and consequently longer to get to the merchandise and promotion levels.

The national chains must have greater expertise. Since their buying decisions involve tremendous amounts of merchandise with heavy financial commitments, mistakes are costly. As a result, chain store fashion promotion is built on styles and items that are proven winners. They must be "right" from several standpoints— quality, selection, availability, and price. Chains look for items with wide appeal that can be offered to the buying public at modest prices. The "exclusive" lines they carry are usually merchandise produced under the chain's private brand names by selected manufacturers. Private labels carried by national chains become national brands by their very existence, not by the process of being advertised nationally by manufacturers in national magazines, in newspapers, or on television.

The fashion direction in chain stores is basically one of coordination, established through regularly distributed sales promotion brochures, bulletins, reports, and other communications (Figure 11.5). Some chains employ fashion directors who travel to foreign and domestic markets seeking styles that will have mass appeal for their clientele. One technique involves the purchase of high-priced originals of new styles which are sent to contracted manufacturers for adaptation or copying. They are then produced in quantity for distribution to the stores, to be sold at popular prices.

Personal contact between stores and national chain headquarters is limited because of distance, time, and cost factors. Heavy emphasis is placed on paperwork for detailed and accurate communication among all units of the store network. The sales promotion department must develop systems and procedures for disseminating required information in a clear, understandable manner. The absence of personal contact is filled by detailed, minutely spelled out instructions sent to regional supervisors, store managers, or whichever executives assume the responsibility for advertising and promotion (Figure 11.6).

The advertising function may be as simple as calling the local newspaper to buy space for a finished ad supplied by the home office. It may mean calling the local radio station to buy a schedule to announce a traveling fashion show. It may mean arranging a press party to introduce a visiting fashion designer. Or it may mean producing complete ads specifically for one store running a special promotion not involving any other stores in the chain. In almost all cases, the advertising and promotion budgets are controlled at company headquarters, and sales promotion expenditures and materials are determined and produced there too.

A typical monthly sales promotion package could include the

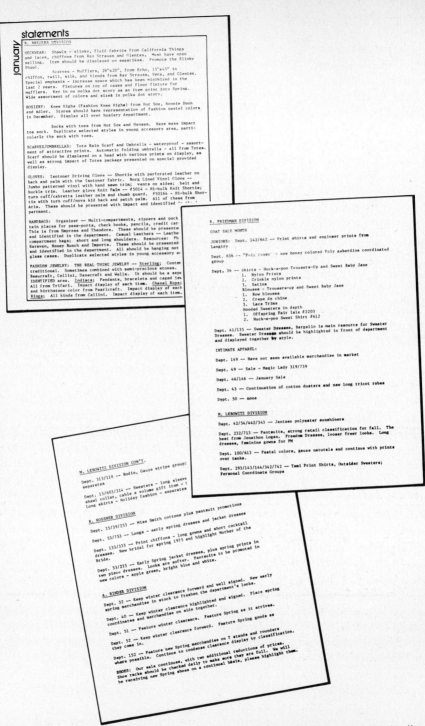

statements

january

R. BREUERS DIVISION

NECKWEAR: Shawls - slinky, fluid fabrics from California Things and laces, chiffons from Ray Strauss and Glentex. Must have open selling. Item should be displayed on swastikas. Promote the Slinky Shawl.

Scarves - Mufflers, 28"x28", from Echo, 15"x45" in chiffon, twill, silk, and blends from Ray Strauss, Vera, and Glentex. Special emphasis - increase space which has been minimized in the last 2 years. Fixtures on top of cases and floor fixture for mufflers. Key in on polka dot story as an item going into Spring. Wide assortment of colors and sizes in polka dot story.

HOSIERY: Knee Highs (Fashion Knee Highs) from Hot Sox, Ronnie Doon and Adler. Stores should have representation of fashion pastel colors in December. Display all over hosiery department.

Socks with toes from Hot Sox and Hansen. Have mass impact toe sock. Duplicate selected styles in young accessory area, particularly the sock with toes.

SCARVES/UMBRELLAS: Tote Rain Scarf and Umbrella - waterproof - assortment of attractive prints. Automatic folding umbrella - all from Totes. Scarf should be displayed on a head with various prints on display, as well as strong impact of Totes package presented on special provided display.

GLOVES: Isotoner Driving Glove -- Shortie with perforated leather on back and palm with the Isotoner fabric. Borg Lined Vinyl Glove -- Jumbo patterned vinyl with hand sewn trim; vents on sides; belt and buckle trim. Leather glove Knit Palm -- #5014 - Hi-bulk Knit Shortie; turn cuff/cabretta leather palm and thumb guard, #50164 - Hi-bulk Shortie with turn cuff/nova kid back and patch palm. All of these from Aris. These should be presented with impact and identified in the department.

HANDBAGS: Organizer -- Multi-compartments, zippers and pock tain places for pass-ports, check books, pencils, credit car This is from Empress and Theodore. These should be presente and identified in the department. Casual Leathers -- Leather compartment bags; short and long shoulders. Resources: Ph Karavan, Honey Bunch and Imports. These should be presented and identified in the department. All should be hanging not glass cases. Duplicate selected styles in young accessory a

FASHION JEWELRY: THE REAL THING JEWELRY -- Sterling; Conte traditional. Sometimes combined with semi-precious stones. Beaucraft, Cellini, Danecraft and Wells. It should be a sepa IDENTIFIED area. Zodiacs; Pendants, bracelets and caged je All from Trifari. Impact display of each item. Chanel Rope: and birthstone color from Pearlcraft. Impact display of each Rings; All kinds from Cellini. Impact display of each item.

R. FRIEDMAN DIVISION

COAT SALE MONTH

JUNIORS: Dept. 142/642 -- Print shirts and engineer prints from Langtry

Dept. 636 -- "Poly Power" - new honey colored Poly gaberdine coordinated group

Dept. 36 -- Shirts - Huck-a-poo Trousers-Up and Sweet Baby Jane
1. Nylon Prints
2. Crinkle nylon prints
3. Satins
Blouses - Trousers-up and Sweet Baby Jane
1. Bow blouses
2. Crepe de chine
3. Lace Trims
Hooded Sweaters in depth
1. Offspring Fair Isle #2203
2. Huck-a-poo Sweat Shirt #612

Dept. 41/135 -- Sweater Dresses, Bargello is main resource for Sweater Dresses. Sweater Dresses should be highlighted in front of department and displayed together by style.

INTIMATE APPAREL:

Dept. 149 -- Have not seen available merchandise in market

Dept. 49 -- Sale - Magic Lady 319/739

Dept. 46/146 -- January Sale

Dept. 43 -- Continuation of cotton dusters and new long tricot robes

Dept. 50 -- none

M. LEBOWITZ DIVISION

Dept. 42/54/442/343 -- Jantzen polyester sunshiners

Dept. 232/713 -- Pantsuits, strong retail classification for fall. The best from Jonathon Logan. Freedom Dresses, looser freer looks. Long dresses, feminine gowns for PM

Dept. 100/613 -- Pastel colors, gauze naturals and continue with prints over tanks.

Dept. 293/143/144/342/742 -- Tami Print Shirts, Outsider Sweaters; Personal Coordinate Groups

---

M. LEBOWITZ DIVISION CON'T.

Dept. 313/118 -- Bodin, Gauze stripe group; separates

Dept. 13/603/314 -- Sweaters - long sleeve shawl collar, cable a volume gift item - I Long shirts - Holiday fashion - separates

R. ROSSNER DIVISION

Dept. 35/39/253 -- Miss Smith cottons plus pantsuit promotions

Dept. 53/753 -- Longs - early spring dresses and jacket dresses

Dept. 133/333 -- Print chiffons - long gowns and short cocktail dresses. New bridal for spring 1975 and highlight Mother of the Bride.

Dept. 33/233 -- Early Spring jacket dresses, plus spring prints in two piece dresses. Looks are softer. Pantsuits to be promoted in new colors - apple green, bright blue and white.

A. BINDER DIVISION

Dept. 32 -- Keep winter clearance forward and well signed. New early spring merchandise in stock to freshen the department's looks. Place spring

Dept. 40 -- Keep winter clearance highlighted and signed. Place spring coordinates and merchandise on side together.

Dept. 51 -- Feature winter clearance. Feature Spring as it arrives.

Dept. 52 -- Keep winter clearance forward. Feature Spring goods as they come in.

Dept. 152 -- Feature new Spring merchandise on T stands and rounders where possible. Continue to condense clearance display by classification.

SHOES: Our sale continues, with two additional reductions of prices. Shoe racks should be checked daily to make sure they are full. We will be receiving new Spring shoes on a continual basis, please highlight them.

Figure 11.5   Specific information for each merchandise division is disseminated to each branch store, department by department.

direct mail & inserts

JANUARY EVENTS BOOKLET (incl. Sneak Preview Rug & Drapery Sale) --
Effective December 31st, mailed 320M - Washington and
180M - Baltimore

HALF YEARLY FURNITURE SALE -- January 5th, Washington
470M - Washington

WHITE SALE -- mails 200M in Baltimore on January 16th, inserts 470M
in Washington on January 19th

PRIVATE SALES - TC/MH/LOM -- January 17th, Washington only, 490M

PRIVATE SALES - RE/NO/ED -- January 17th and 18th, Baltimore only,
150M

MONTGOMERY MALL MEN'S SALE -- January 22nd, Washington only - 20M

LAUREL CARPET EVENT -- January 22nd, Washington only - 9.2M

F STREET PRIVATE SALE -- January 23rd, Washington only - 175M

showcase

January 10th -- Salisbury Bridal Show at the Asbury Methodist Church

January 15th -- Washington, D. C. Bridal Show at the Mayflower Hotel

January 21st -- Scholastic Art Awards...Entries begin to arrive at
F Street Store.

January 22nd -- Baltimore Bridal Show at the Martin's West.

January 20th through January 23rd -- SmokEnders Open Meetings begin:
SS...Cafeteria...Monday at 7:30PM
PK...Training Room...Wednesday at 7:30PM
MH...Restaurant...Thursday at 7:30PM

January 27th through January 31st -- SmokEnders Classes begin

B

(B) Direct mail, newspaper insert schedule, with dates for special merchandise showings.

merchandise presentation

The mini seasons of Spring...all communicated by the pageantry of earthtoned banners sparked by the color of the event. January Events, Half Yearly, Spring Banners, Pastel Pales.

Kickoff January 6th, Spring Banners, 4'x8' panels, posters, Statements.

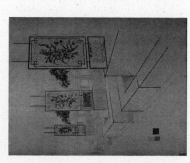

WINDOWS AND INTERIORS

January 1st through January 15th -- PALES -- new whitened pales...
all in advanced spring fabrics and silhouettes...monochromatic
dressing.

January 15th through January 31st -- THE BIG STORY -- soft easy
dressing...fluid fabric...soft shaping...the loosened-up silhouette.

shops

THE GOOD EARTH -- new naturals, updated gauze shops with the
addition of poplin, denim and chino.

A

(A) Merchandise presentation instructions.

Figure 11.6 (A) Merchandise presentation instructions.

following types of information:

- A list of special promotions and holidays for the month or period covered by the bulletin (Figure 11.7)
- An introduction detailing the merchandising strategy for the month written by the merchandise manager
- The fashion advertising copy theme for the month
- Sample newspaper ad layouts and copy
- Floor plan for in-store display and signs
- Promotion and publicity suggestions
- Letters of invitation to selected customers
- Guidelines for informal modeling in the store
- Suggestions for internal communications

Despite the frenzied pace of the retail world, the fashion director or fashion authority must exercise ultimate control over the fashion image. Regardless of pressures from buyers and merchandise managers, and sometimes from management itself, the fashion director must reject anything that deviates from the store's image.

Remember, you do not have to look like Bloomingdale's. In fact, if you are not Bloomingdale's, trying to look like the great New York store can lead to disaster. Even Bloomingdale's is not the same in Washington, D.C., as it is in New York, simply because the customers in the two cities are different. Sure, there are many similarities in the stores, but the needs and desires of the store's audiences are not the same. Smart management sees to it that the stores cater to the customers' preferences, not the company's way of doing things.

Fashions, customer wants, and life-styles change constantly; knowing what's happening, and what's right for the customers in each market, is the primary job of the fashion director. The right information, and research from the customers themselves, disseminated throughout the organization, will result in the buying and promoting of the merchandise customers want. In that direction lies success in fashion retailing.

FASHION PUBLICITY AND PUBLIC RELATIONS

A strong weapon in the sales promotion arsenal of the retail store is its public relations department. Sometimes it is set up as a separate function of the sales promotion department, sometimes as an additional responsibility of the fashion director. In the large retail establishment, public relations could be a four- or five-person department; in the independent store it could be the owner or local manager.

broadcast

RADIO: WASHINGTON

DATE	EVENT
1/8/75	Alex Coleman & Heather Coordinates
1/8-10/75	Major Pre-Inventory China & Glass Clearance JOINT
1/8-10/75	Pre-Inventory Sale JOINT
1/10/75	50% Off Antique Satin JOINT
1/11/75	Oriental Rug Sale
1/12-13/75	Serta All Size Bedding Sale
1/14-15/75	Bridal Show
1/15-16/75	TC/MH/LO Men's Clothing Sale
1/16-17/75	F Street Fur Sale
1/21-22/75	F Street Men's Warehouse Sale
1/24-25/75	Golden Opportunity Day
1/31/75	20% Off Ready Made Curtains JOINT
1/31-2/1/75	Serta All Size Bedding Sale

RADIO: BALTIMORE

1/8-10/75	Major Pre-Inventory China & Glass Clearance JOINT
1/8-10/75	Pre-Inventory Sale JOINT
1/10/75	50% Off Antique Satin JOINT
1/16-17/75	ED/NO/REIS Fur Sale
1/21-22/75	Bridal Show
1/24-25/75	Golden Opportunity Day
1/26/75	GR Oriental Rug Sale
1/31/75	20% Off Ready Made Curtains JOINT

A

Figure 11.7 (A) Radio broadcast schedule.

enclosures

BALTIMORE

REMITTANCE ENVELOPE: Queen Casuals...Dept. 13

January 6th - 10th
Cannon Sheets.....................Dept. 6
4 Seasons Casuals..Miss Smith.....Dept. 39
Rochas Parfums....................Dept. 11

January 13th - 17th
Holly Hill........................Dept. 39
Rochas Parfums....................Dept. 11
Pollenex Back Massager............Dept. 127

January 20th - 24th
Pollenex Foot Massager............Dept. 127
Kay Windsor Dresses...............Dept. 753
Country Miss......................Dept. 34

January 27th - February 1st
Kay Windsor Dresses...............Dept. 753
Country Miss......................Dept. 34

WASHINGTON

REMITTANCE ENVELOPE: Queen Casuals...Dept. 13

January 6th - 10th
Cannon Sheets.....................Dept. 6
4 Seasons Casuals..Miss Smith.....Dept. 39
Rochas Parfums....................Dept. 11

January 13th - 17th
Rochas Parfums....................Dept. 11
4 Seasons Casuals..Miss Smith.....Dept. 39
Pollenex Back Massager............Dept. 127

January 20th - 24th
Pollenex Foot Massager............Dept. 127
Country Miss Dresses..............Dept. 34
Kay Windsor Dresses...............Dept. 753

January 27th - 31st
Country Miss Dresses..............Dept. 34
Kay Windsor Dresses...............Dept. 753

B

(B) Statement enclosure schedule.

First, let us clarify terms. *Public relations* is the development and maintenance of interaction between your store and your "public." *Publicity* is one aspect of public relations. Publicity is free space or air time secured by the store in newspapers, magazines, trade publications, or on radio or television. Press publicity is more easily obtained by the stores that make fashion news. The visit of a fashion designer; the charity show introducing the new season's styles; the opening of a new boutique for career women; the announcement of a new store site—all these are legitimate news items of interest to the community and relatively certain of some coverage by the local press. If the event is big enough, radio and television news coverage is possible.

The amount of coverage, and whether the event gets reported at all, depends on the space available to the editorial department when it comes time to make up the paper for the day. Although there may be justification for your story running, the decision of the editors is final. In most newspapers and news media, there is a definite separation between the editorial and advertising departments. Even the largest advertiser has no assurance of publicity. The newsworthiness of every item is judged by the editors, and your most important announcement may never get into the news columns if other items are deemed of more interest to the reading public. Trying to push a story into the paper because you are a big spender with the advertising side could doom your big story to obscurity. It may seem that the big store gets much more space in the paper, but that may be because the big store is doing many more newsworthy and interesting things.

Public Relations as a Total Store Function

In the final analysis, your public image is what the public thinks you are, not necessarily what you say you are. All statements and promises that emanate from a store—in advertising, in publicity, and by word of mouth—are promises that must be fulfilled when the customer visits your place of business.

- If your ads say you give prompt service, it had better be true.
- If you claim to have friendly salespeople, keep the grouches off the sales floor.
- If you advertise the newest fashions, don't mix in older merchandise on the sales floor.
- If you promise a courteous return policy, don't let your people cross-examine the customer.

All these items are not under the jurisdiction of the sales promotion manager, but that executive, knowing that everything that happens in the store affects the results of advertising and sales promotion, should exert some pressure to create the positive mood in which stores operate best.

The importance of the way the public perceives your store has a marked effect on the total sales promotion program. If you have presented a constant diet of sales and off-price merchandise promotion in your advertising, you will not get good response to a regular-priced fashion ad. If you have trained the public to see you as a moderate-to-low-priced operation, the introduction of higher-priced designer fashions may not have immediate acceptance. An occasional participation in a community event may not have the same effect as a continuing program of civic involvement.

People like to shop in stores that are considered part of the community. Many chain store operations, aware of the need to establish good community relations, insist that their store managers and junior executives involve themselves in civic, church, and educational activities in their communities. It's good "press" when the store manager heads up the local United Way drive, or is president of the PTA. The public feels more comfortable shopping in stores if they know the people as individuals. The friendliness and involvement of the store's management rubs off on the lower-echelon personnel and encourages them to follow suit.

We know of a major department store that insisted that its executives be involved in their communities to the point where semi-annual reports on outside activities were required and time off, even during work days, was permitted in the name of community involvement. At Rich's in Atlanta, the store motto, "You are Rich's," was a slogan to live by. There was no public relations department, because every employee was a public relations representative of that store whenever he or she stepped outside the four walls of the company. That attitude was reflected in the demeanor of the people who worked in the store and their pride in being part of the organization. Rich's *esprit de corps* was envied by every other retailer in town.

As noted previously, it is a law of chemistry that nothing ever filters up. This is also true in retailing. The attitudes—and actions—of top management filter down to the selling floor. The friendly, we-care-for-you pledges given so freely in newspaper, radio, and television announcements are often just slogans. If management insists on sincerely caring for its clientele, and shows it by a similar attitude toward its employees, the public will soon know it is genuine store policy. The feeling permeates from senior management to the divisional level, to the relationships between buyers and their assistants, and from the junior executives to the salespeople on the all-important selling floor.

Great store slogans like "Give the lady what she wants" or "The customer is always right" would not have survived all these years if the words were not implemented with pride and devotion throughout the stores. Stores of any size can become household names, but slogans alone don't do it. A store's way of life does.

The recent growth of the consumer movement reaffirmed the need for constantly maintaining good relations with the many publics with which a store deals. In addition to the buying public, a store must establish good relations with the media, with competitors, with manufacturers, with government and with labor. Retailers must establish confidence and credibility with the consuming public in order to ensure future growth. In dealing with suppliers and manufacturers, the stores must provide the quality and value their customers expect and demand.

Working with the media can be tricky, but it is important. The skepticism of newswriters and reporters regarding business, especially retailing and advertising, is well known. This tendency to hold business in low regard is unfortunate, but true. The cliché of the peddler and the swift-moving merchant, out to fleece the unsuspecting public, has been perpetuated and exaggerated in song and story for decades. The percentage of unethical merchants to the total number of honest and law-abiding storekeepers and store managers throughout history is microscopic, yet the bad image persists in many quarters.

Working with the Media

A good rule of thumb to follow in working with the media is to screen the stories you send out. Not every event in a retail fashion store is of intense interest to the readers of the local newspaper. It may be the major happening in the life of your fashion buyer, who wants to see the story of the fashion show in print, but judgment must be exercised by the fashion publicity person. If the paper is receiving a weekly flow of press releases from your store, announcing every event, large and small, the editor may ignore them because of the sheer regularity of their arrival. If, however, you select only the most important, most newsworthy stories, send them by special messenger, then call the editor and explain why this event is special, you might stand a better chance.

On the other hand, some papers are always looking for material. They need filler for their fashion and women's interest pages. If you can establish personal contacts and good personal relations with the press in your community, you have a much better chance for success in publicizing your fashion activities. Invite them to your special occasions, fashion shows, store openings, parties. They may not come, but they will appreciate the invitation. Many will cover the event in person. Take the fashion writers to lunch, if you can. Let them know far in advance about coming events. If you can, promise them exclusives or first information on happenings. It may help you get publicity if the paper knows competitive media will not be duplicating the story. At all costs, be honest in your relations with the press. Once a promise is broken, or an "exclusive" leaked to another paper, your credibility is destroyed, and it will take some time before the breach can be healed. Giving an "exclusive" to several media hoping for better total coverage could backfire and cost you much grief in your attempts to get publicity in the future.

It is a natural tendency to steer your story to the biggest news source in your city. The leading paper, with the biggest circulation, may be where you want your story to run. But it may be harder to get space in that paper because of its dominant position. The paper's staff may also be less cooperative because of the dominance, and limited in space. The number two paper, trying harder, may be more eager to run your fashion stories. If the objective is to get publicity to improve your store's relations with a visiting manufacturer or designer, getting into print may be more important than getting into the bigger paper. The visitors are interested in seeing their brand names or designer names in print, and being in the second paper for sure may be a wiser decision than trying for the bigger paper and striking out.

Preparing your material to make it easy for the publication or station to use can help you get publicity. When preparing news releases for newspapers, be sure your writers know how to write "newspaper style." Journalists know that editors look for the who-what-where-and-when in a good newspaper lead—so your story should be written so it can be used by the paper with a minimum of trouble. It is easy to toss your press release into the wastebasket if it is badly written, confusing, and obviously "plugging" a store event.

When a charitable or civic organization is benefitting from your fashion show, don't start your story: "Blank's Department Store will present a fashion show for the benefit of St. Mary's Hospital." A better, more acceptable lead would be: "The St. Mary's Hospital Annual Benefit Event will take place Sunday night at the Blah Blah Hotel." Then, at the end or middle of the release include: ". . . The special show, Highlights of Things to Come, will feature fashions from Blank's Department Store." This way, the charity aspect of the story will get the editor's attention, the story may run, and the name of the store must be included as one of the details.

The same approach can be used in writing announcements for radio. Instead of expecting the station personnel to rewrite your press release, write it for radio in the first place. Check with the station's public service or news department to find out what kind of announcements they prefer—30 or 60 seconds in length, live or on tape, full information or fact sheet—then deliver it accordingly. As noted earlier, a 60-second spot runs 150 to 160 words, a 30-second spot approximately 75 words—enough to get your special event or fashion story across. Remember, lead with the event and keep the sponsor credit line or location at the end.

Preparing for the Press Interview

It is important to prepare for an interview with a reporter as carefully as you would prepare for any other promotional event. Each interview, each conversation with newspaper or broadcast people, is an opportunity to improve the fashion image of the store. You can communicate the store's story to thousands of people who are potential customers and others who may become customers. By giving the reporter the information easily and swiftly, with a minimum of fuss, you are setting the stage for future news stories.

When you have the opportunity for a full-scale interview of a store executive or visiting fashion person, don't mess up the chance. Once a reporter experiences difficulty in developing a story from your company, the paper may be reluctant to respond to your next request for coverage. Most retailers appreciate the value of publicity, so getting cooperation from buyers and merchandisers should be no problem.

There are several basic rules for planning and handling press interviews that will apply, with variations, to most situations.

1. Make sure the right person is interviewed. Don't let the reporter interview the fashion director or the buyer when the fashion designer is the real story. If the store president insists on being the spokesperson for the store at all times, you may have a problem. Sometimes you can set up the interview with the paper so that only the visiting personality is "news." In the long run it pays to avoid situations that may backfire and ruin your good relations with the media.

2. Try to avoid setting up interviews when there is no real news to deliver. A routine show or a run-of-the-mill announcement of an executive promotion isn't always worth the reporter's time. Sometimes it is better to pass up a publicity request from store man-

agement and save your limited opportunity for free space for really important stories.

3. Plan the time and place of the interview carefully. If it is going to be a personality piece, plan the interview around lunch. If it is to present a new fashion line or designer clothes, the best place for the meeting is in the store.

4. Do your homework. Prepare a fact sheet of all the pertinent facts you want covered in the interview. Think of the questions that might be asked and have the answers ready. Don't prepare a press release for an interview. The reporter may resent being told what to write.

5. As fashion director, you might have to step in and save the interview if the reporter isn't as knowledgeable and fashion-minded as you would like. Often neophyte reporters are "broken in" on retail accounts. In these instances you may have to lead the interview, suggest questions—and answers—and provide the story line. Again, if you've done your homework, you'll be ready for any contingency.

6. Be ready to sell your story to the interviewer. You must be able to convince this person of the importance of the story, because your story will be up against competition for space when it gets to the editor's desk. Having a thorough knowledge of the publication doing the interview will help you slant the conversation in the direction of the paper's audience. Being familiar with the writer's work will flatter and impress the reporter. It is also an excellent way of opening the interview on a friendly note.

Other publics to be dealt with are vendors, competitors, and community groups. Good relations with manufacturers includes smoothness in the buying of merchandise and payment for that merchandise according to contract terms. Problems that arise in the shipping, handling, and distribution of merchandise can make for sticky situations with vendors. It is usually a buyer problem, but it could affect the fashion picture somewhere along the line.

Retailers try to retain friendly relations with their competition, often joining forces for the mutual benefit of the industry. Most belong to trade associations organized to work for the general good.

From an individual store standpoint, the world of public relations and publicity is mostly limited to relations with the buying public, the people with which the store does business, and of course the media. Some stores buy advertising space and time to reach the public with specific information they want to be sure is disseminated. These are usually store-oriented announcements— store openings, visiting celebrities, special events, and activities. The high cost of newsprint and the limits of broadcast time make it unreasonable to expect that all important stories get the coverage the store wishes. The problem is universal: Major corporations spend big money on radio and television to influence the way people think about them.

THE ROLE OF SPECIAL EVENTS[1]

Many stores have made a commitment to their communities that is expressed in the presentation of special events in the stores. A department store is part of the basic fabric of a community—perhaps not in the same sense as churches, schools, and hospitals, but certainly in the same way as the industries, clubs, restaurants, theaters, museums, and parks that give each community its unique identity.

Department store management that recognizes its place in the community as something more than a business involves itself in the social and civic life of the community. It does this through special events that are, to a great extent, altruistic. Such a department store makes a commitment to the cultural and educational needs of consumers, while catering to their physical needs for clothing, furnishings, and utensils. To some degree, specialty stores, chain store branches, and individual store owners can also participate in the lives of their communities—limited, of course, by financial and personnel capabilities.

A special event is something that will bring people to a store, or a shopping center, whether they are shopping or not. It is an added attraction to bring shoppers to your store to make their purchases, and to draw them away from their normal shopping habits. Special events are also used to draw people from department to department within the store. Special events can include fashion shows, craft fairs, cooking demonstrations and classes, decorating workshops, cosmetic clinics and seminars of many kinds, from how to knit to how to change and repair a tire. Personal appearances by artists, craftspeople, authors, movie stars, sports personalities are all special events. Exhibits of art, science, antiques, and costumes are other opportunities to enrich the lives of the shoppers in the community.

Measuring the results of special events is difficult. Unless store management understands that certain events—exhibits, workshops, some fashion shows—are designed to attract people, not necessarily customers, your special events program may be in trou-

[1] The last section of this chapter under the heading "The Role of Special Events" has been adapted from a presentation by Peck Klose, senior vice-president, sales promotion, Frederick Atkins, Inc., New York.

ble. Some special events—housewares shows and demonstrations, trunk showings—can be judged on the yardstick of sales. Despite controversy regarding the value of special events, they should be an integral part of the store's sales promotion program, part of the overall marketing strategy along with the merchandise mix, merchandise presentation, and advertising. If planned and executed as carefully and skillfully as the rest of the promotional program, special events can add a valuable dimension to the total store personality and provide that something special that all stores seek to set themselves apart from their competitors.

Once established as a continuing element in the program, a similar procedure of budgeting, planning, scheduling, developing themes, and communicating the news to the store's public follows. Whether the special events job is part of the ad manager's function or the fashion director's, or the sole task of a special events coordinator, it ultimately becomes the responsibility of the entire store. Everyone gets involved in special events, since they touch all aspects of a store's operation. Every event, whether it is an import fair, a fashion extravaganza, or a salute to the Mother of the Year, takes planning and integration into the total marketing strategy of the store. A community-involved store involves all its people in varying degrees. That store operates at many levels to achieve its marketing goals. Special events could be part of the mortar that holds the whole structure together.

QUESTIONS FOR DISCUSSION AND CLASS ASSIGNMENTS

1. Explain the differences among fashion advertising, fashion promotion, and fashion publicity.
2. Describe the qualifications of the fashion director in a major fashion-oriented department store.
3. What are the responsibilities of the fashion director? Interview the fashion director in your local department store. Compare his or her duties with those included in this chapter.
4. As the fashion authority of the store, how does the fashion director exert influence on the merchandising and sales promotion departments?
5. Describe how fashion shows could serve as sales training for salespeople in the fashion departments.
6. Visit your local fashion store and observe the presentation of a fashion show. Discuss the procedure with the fashion people and compare it with the checklist in this chapter.
7. List the problems of putting on a fashion show for your local women's club, especially when the club wants to use members as models.

8. Compare the procedures for staging fashion shows in a major specialty store with the problems of putting on a show in a local branch store.
9. Describe the fashion director's role in establishing and maintaining good public relations for the retail store.
10. Explain the statement that public relations is a total store function.
11. Discuss the special events program as a function of sales promotion and public relations in a department store.

Chapter 12
Developing the Sales Promotion Team

It may seem anachronistic to speak of team and teamwork on the heels of the "Me generation." So much has been written and broadcast about self-image, looking out for number one, self-gratification, and personal fulfillment that the word "teamwork" may sound like something from a foreign language. The seventies saw the phenomenon of the single household, the single parent, and living alone and liking it. So why should we expect teamwork in advertising and sales promotion?

Not too long ago, Vince Lombardi, when coach of the champion Green Bay Packers, was for many years held up to business executives as the classic example of the take-charge leader. He taught his players the fundamentals of how to win football games and drilled them, trained them, and led them to many professional football championships. He is credited with slogans like "Winning isn't the most important thing. Winning is the *only* thing." He expected and demanded 110 percent effort—perfect execution by every player on every play in every game. His players respected him—many loved him—and his techniques of leadership were lauded and emulated throughout the land.

But he failed to develop an organization, for when he left Green Bay to assume a similar, more lucrative post in Washington, D.C., the team foundered and had mediocre success. Initially, problems were caused by the lack of high draft choices (caused by the inverted selection system of the National Football League, which allows the poorer teams to choose college players first), but more probably because the success was a one-man achievement. The Green Bay Packers have failed to attain their former level of accomplishment to this day.

It is interesting to note that the name of Vince Lombardi is not invoked as it once was as the epitome of leadership style. His domineering technique is still around, but the collapse of the team without his presence was an indictment of his real management ability. Also, it is doubtful if he could control a team like that today. This generation would rebel against such authoritarian methods and would not subordinate their needs as readily to the team's goals. Superstars, with superstar salaries, have often forced the firing of the coach when the team loses. The contemporary coach, like the contemporary manager, must primarily be concerned with developing the ability of the staff to be flexible and adaptable, to understand and solve their personal problems themselves. In sports today, when one team triumphs over another, it is usually announced that the winners were more highly motivated. Winners in business are also highly motivated.

This statement is especially true in advertising and sales promotion, because there is rarely a successful newspaper ad, radio or television commercial, or fashion show conceived, planned, and produced by one person. There are and have been many great advertising ideas, but no one person did the entire job of bringing it to light. If the great idea was a copy story, it took the addition of layout, headline, artwork, and production to complete the idea and make it happen. If the hot idea was visual, the copy and headline story had to finish communicating the thought to the prospect. Many advertising people carry samples of ads they have worked on, to be presented as "my ads" when seeking employment. A wise interviewer pins down the claim to the exact portion of the ad that was created by the interviewee.

Each member of the team contributes to the success of advertising, and each should take a portion of the credit. The idea itself ranks high in importance, because nothing happens without the idea. But without the execution, the idea flounders. It takes teamwork to complete the thought and make something happen.

ORGANIZING AN EFFECTIVE
ADVERTISING DEPARTMENT

Putting together an effective team for any purpose requires understanding that people are different. You can publish rules and regulations, but no two people will interpret and react to them in exactly the same way. Someone once said that some people are like wheelbarrows—they have to be pushed. Others are like kites—you must keep a string on them or they fly off in all directions. Some are like footballs—you don't know which way they will bounce. Still others are like balloons—always ready to blow up. And some are like neon lights—fragile and temperamental. The blending of diverse personalities into a working group is the challenge all managers face.

Think of it as a symphony conductor trying to get the best results from a group of highly trained, talented musicians. The conductor must not only *make* them play together; he or she must make them *want* to play. They must be convinced that the conductor's goals are the same as theirs.

Draw that same parallel in an advertising office. There must be pride in the creation of an interesting, effective ad. Each individual must be happy to share in the credit for a successful promotion, a smooth-running fashion show. The copywriter, the layout designer, the art director, the typesetter, even the proofreader must be made to feel part of the team. The less creative jobholders—secretaries, clerks, bookkeepers—should be aware of the importance of their roles. Keeping every member of the staff involved and functioning at a high level of performance is the job of the manager. Achieving this goal will spell the difference between harmony or discord.

SELECTING THE ADVERTISING MANAGER

The supreme test of a manager is finding out whether or not that manager is an effective teacher. Many people are administrators, others are budget controllers. Creative people can often create but cannot teach. Basically, if you are not a good teacher, you are not a good manager, and vice versa. It is not enough, in the helter-skelter pace of the retail advertising world, to issue directives in the belief that the troops will follow unquestioningly. It may not happen if you decide to lead by example and expect the group to follow along.

Different kinds of teaching are required, each technique tailored to the individuals in your department. The manager must be able to answer the staff's questions, should welcome and encourage

EXHIBIT 12.1

BEHAVIORAL CHARACTERISTICS OF EFFECTIVE MANAGERS

All managers are not born with natural talent. But good managers can be taught and trained. Retail stores have been notoriously weak in personnel training. Good managers can overcome the lack of formal training by learning on the job and emulating the best managerial experiences possible. Here is one version of how an experienced sales training executive describes effective managing.

1. Accepts full responsibility for performance
2. Works to build the team
3. Establishes high standards of performance
4. Evaluates performance fairly and objectively
5. Requires good technical skills specific to functional area
6. Inspires success patterns in work unit
7. Is honest with subordinates
8. Delegates challenging work (you don't lose authority, you are still responsible)
9. Assigns goals in assignments with consideration for individual talent and capabilities
10. Accepts feedback from subordinates at conclusion of assignment
11. Keeps subordinates informed of organizational changes that affect them
12. Evaluates training needs and frequently provides discussion opportunities

SOURCE: Leslie J. Ades, Executive Director, Ades Marketing Consortium, Los Angeles. Leadership Effectiveness Seminar, unpublished manuscript, 1978. By permission.

them, and should spend as much time as necessary explaining, clarifying, and justifying the reasons why certain decisions are made. One of the major frustrations of rank-and-file employees or members of large staffs is not knowing why things are happening—why certain ads are run certain ways, why headlines are changed, why artwork has to be redone.

Team leaders must have people around with whom they are comfortable. This does not mean sycophants or people who always say "yes" to whatever the boss suggests. It means people who can be depended upon to do the job the way the director and the store see it. There must be an attitude of professionalism, one that says the project, no matter how big or how difficult, will be finished on time and to the best of the department's ability.

To foster this type of attitude, communications channels must be open and their use encouraged. The manager must inform the staff of the store's goals and the status of ongoing projects. It is especially important that department heads—art directors, copy chiefs— feel free to contribute to the formulation of plans and projects. In addition, they must be kept abreast of all departmental projects so they can feed the director accurate status reports on a regular basis.

Department heads must have a sense of mutual confidence in their relationship with the sales promotion director so that they can discuss problems and possible solutions openly or ask for guidance without fear of criticism. This atmosphere of open communication builds a solid, well-meshed team that produces up to potential. This is preferable to an organization, intimidated by or fearful of its leader, that staggers and stumbles through a project.

The teaching role of the manager also reveals the strengths and weaknesses of the staff—who is dependable, who needs watching, where additional training is needed, and who is ready for promotion to a more responsible position. Teaching includes training, and the more people who can be developed within the ranks of the staff, the better. Nothing disrupts the harmony of an ad department as much as the sudden arrival from the outside of a new person in a key, higher-paying job to which several staff members aspired.

Leaders in all fields have always had certain characteristics in common, personality traits that add up to success (Exhibit 12.1). These are the kinds of traits that are looked for when it is time to choose the person ready to move up in management:

Hard, Steady Worker. Without dedication to the work ethic, results just do not happen. Most things can be accomplished through hard work, and very little of value happens easily. As the discouraged neophyte is often told, "No one promised it would be easy."

Optimism. All leaders have that positive approach, the belief in ultimate success even when things are rough. It is the conviction that the glass is half full, not half empty.

Enthusiasm. Some people believe that nothing can be done without enthusiasm. It fuels creative, innovative action, indispensable in advertising and promotion people. And it generates both the desire and the energy to get things done.

Individualism. Every true leader is a distinct individual. This characteristic may have to be controlled and exhibited sparingly on the way up the ladder, but people look for it in leaders.

Imagination. Leaders have the capacity to visualize the results they want and the steps required to reach those results. Organizational ability helps make the idea happen.

Cordiality. The ability to get along with people, showing a fair and friendly attitude toward subordinates as well as superiors.

"Listen-ability." Must be able to ask cogent questions, then sit back and listen with great concentration. The "open door" policy must also include an open mind.

Trust. The leader must be blessed with true respect, confidence, and mutual trust in other workers. Honesty in all dealings goes along with this trait.

Flexibility. The manager must combine strength and pliability, and be open and adaptable to constantly changing situations and conditions.

Judgment. The successful leader can be depended on to balance the facts, size up conflicting opinions and information, and come up with the right rational decisions.

Finding and selecting an advertising manager with this "laundry list" of personal qualifications may seem an impossible task, for you must add to that list technical skills and experience in marketing, advertising, and promotion. No company expects to hire anyone with all these abilities, but endeavors to find people that most closely fill the bill.

Problems the advertising manager must face and cope with include the supposed temperamental attitudes of creative members of the staff. Young, idealistic artists and writers are notoriously anti-organization-minded. Their training rarely includes information or understanding of how the business world works. The ad manager must overcome these inhibiting factors in developing his advertising team. The changing attitudes of young people can make the manager's job more difficult. The desire to "do one's own thing" can destroy attempts to coordinate the group's activities. The need to motivate all members of the team, knowing that each individual requires special treatment, uses up a great deal of managerial time and effort. Dealing with your staff at their varying levels of competency is probably the toughest challenge of management.

The advertising manager can make it to the top from many pathways. In an era of cost control, the production person may look most attractive to management. When creativity or a new image is sought by store executives, they search the ranks of art directors to spearhead a new visual appearance for the store's promotion image. Often overlooked is the strong copywriter, who can work well with the buying staff to develop merchandise copy themes that sell. Marketing-oriented people are growing in popularity with retail organizations. If there is sufficient practical advertising and promotion background to go with it, that combination will produce a surefire candidate for top executive in the sales promotion office.

Good managers strike a balance between the authoritative dictatorial figure issuing commands and the benign, understanding father (or mother) figure getting results through reason and persuasion. Tommy Lasorda, the successful manager of the Los Angeles Dodgers baseball team, compared leadership to holding a dove in your hands. If you hold the dove too tightly, you'll kill it. If you hold it too lightly, it will fly away. In the same context, if you hold down creative people, you destroy their initiative. If you give them too much leeway, they fly out of control in all directions. Managerial talent consists of knowing when to do something and when to do nothing, and still get the job done.

STAFFING THE ADVERTISING AND PROMOTION OFFICE

Every advertising and promotion manager would like to have the best person possible in every part of the department. With talent and experience comes high salaries, and that factor alone limits the number of "superstars" an advertising department can afford. A basic plan for a medium-size operation would include paying good money for those in key positions and doing the best you can with the balance of the budget. Key positions include a competent layout artist or art director, a strong, merchandise-oriented copy person, and a production person to pull together the technical and budgetary areas. Additional personnel are then added as needed, with outside services and media assistance filling the gaps until the budget can afford more staff.

In any given group, staff, office, or organization there is a mix of good and average performers. There is no room for bad performers, although fast footwork and a glib tongue can mask the subpar person for a period of time. Rarely do all members of the group deliver top performances consistently, day after day. Yet there are some who achieve a high level of production most of the time. There are specific characteristics most achievers possess. The top performers have developed them to a higher degree than the rest. Many of these characteristics were noted as leadership qualities, and they are. The following list is somewhat different and applies more specifically to rank-and-file people—the workers the ad manager depends on to get the job done:

- Successful people have a good opinion of themselves, of their self-worth. They relish challenge and know they can do whatever they set out to do.
- Responsible people are an asset to the operation of an advertising office. They are sought out by management and given added duties, because management knows the job will be done. Trust is a valuable attribute.
- Optimism is inherent in achievers. They know they are capable and they are sure of success. What better trait for people whose results will be measured in the public's response to promises they make in ads?
- Goal-oriented people have direction. They know where they are heading. Integrating their goals into the broad plan of the department's interests involves them and brings greater results.
- Without imagination, the advertising person is lost. One of the problems the ad person must overcome is the inability of others to visualize. The advertiser must imagine how the message will be received by the listener or reader in order to present it in the best way. If you can create images in the minds of the public, you can produce convincing advertising.
- Good advertising people are well aware of the world around them—of trends, of life-style changes, of public attitudes and problems. The signals you receive from everything around you help you to be a better person and a better performer.
- Creativity is the name of the game. Always seeking a new or better way to present a well-known piece of merchandise is an everyday problem in retail advertising. High performers spew forth new ideas without effort. Their minds are constantly digging, probing, thinking of how to do it better, quicker, smoother, neater.
- Good advertising people are communicators. They get their ideas across clearly and directly. They empathize with audiences so they can understand their needs and present problem-solving ideas through their ads.

Staff your department with people you can trust, who work well under pressure, who enjoy work and have the potential for growth. Select people who can be trained and train them. You may see them hired away for more money than you can pay them, but you'll find you wouldn't want it any other way. It is far better to have good people for a shorter period of time than to hire poor performers because they are cheaper and easier to hang on to. The higher the level of performance you achieve from your advertising staff, the more your competition may lure your people away with promises of higher pay. Your reputation as a trainer and teacher will offset the loss because you will attract a steady stream of job seekers who will fill the gap. You will also enhance your reputation as an effective leader and manager. The better the department, the greater the esteem of its director.

This sounds like a grim prospect of a continuous training program—and this is especially true in the larger department store organization—but it seems to work out that way. Once reconciled to the role, the advertising and promotion manager gets added satisfaction from watching new people come, learn, grow, and move on. Every top ad manager in every major city has an "alumni club" of former staff members working throughout the city in bigger and better jobs, thanks to the learning and training received on the job. Major department stores find this a mixed blessing, for they become the training ground for the rest of the city's retailers.

The pace and pressure of the daily activities of a retail store ad department will prepare the average newcomer for a good career in advertising. Many a retail ad person has made the transition from retail store to advertising agency. It is much more difficult to move from agency to retail advertising. The pace is much quicker, the pressure greater, the work harder and longer. But retail ad people have one great satisfaction—or curse: They know almost immediately whether the ad was successful. National ad people can't do that, and many wouldn't want to. But the retail ad job, closely linked to the direct sale of merchandise, gives the ad person an added dimension of actual achievement other advertising jobs do not.

In staffing advertising and promotion departments, managers tend to recruit people they know or people they have worked with before. The new manager wants to be sure of the loyalty and support of the staff and wonders about residual fidelity to the previous boss. Management birds of a feather also flock together. Advertising managers have a certain attraction for certain types of people. Creative types attract creative types. Serious, no-fooling-around types attract their counterparts. Innovators attract innovators. Unfortunately, losers tend to attract losers. They may feel comfortable working together, but like types don't always make good teams.

Management sometimes select people who have worked at

stores they respect, assuming they must be good if they worked at good stores. This is not always true. Many inefficient advertising people escape management scrutiny for a length of time, then hang on a little longer while the ad manager procrastinates about making a change. The search for the replacement takes more time, so when the worker is finally dismissed, a year or more may have passed. This year appears on the person's track record and looks good on a résumé when prospective employers see it. But it could be a misleading piece of information. Good interviewers are aware of this and check credentials by phone or mail to ensure the accuracy of reports of experience and ability.

BLENDING THE ACTIVITIES OF THE SALES PROMOTION TEAM

The management skills required to operate a smoothly functioning sales promotion team have been outlined. A clearly defined plan of operation, specific job assignments leaving no room for confusion, and open lines of communication make the machine roll without friction. There are enough things that can go wrong in the ordinary day-to-day operation of a retail store without compounding the situation with personnel problems in the advertising department.

A manager with a facility for leadership uses mastery of the art of decision making to blend the different personalities of fashion director, advertising manager, visual merchandising (display) director, and art director into a working team. This manager clearly defines the problem, collects the necessary data, and develops and selects alternatives before making the correct decision and following through.

The better listener you are, the more you are tuned in to your department heads and their subordinates, the more likelihood there is that they may be able to solve many of their own problems. Instilling the team concept into their thinking at all times helps. You gain staff members' respect by showing them that using their management skills within their own areas of responsibility will not antagonize the people working under them.

The display director who develops a window or interior display theme uncoordinated with the advertising and fashion divisions weakens the store's total impact. The advertising campaign that ignores the fashion image of the store fails to enhance the public's impression of the store's personality. The fashion director who operates in a vacuum, producing fashion shows for the sake of producing fashion shows as "showbiz," is equally at fault.

The sales promotion manager's responsibility is clear. It is the coordination of all facets of the promotion effort. Everything must work together in order to present the store's personality to the buying public in the best way possible. A staff that is highly motivated, with good morale, produces advertising and promotion much more effectively than a staff working under an autocratic leader who deals in half-truths, partial information, and the belief that people work best under pressure. That may be true of some people, but as we have indicated, people are individuals and must be treated as individuals. Like most good management practices, building morale does not start at the bottom of the organization—it comes down through the framework of the company from the top.

The troublesome grapevine, the source of all rumors that exist in most organizations, can only be overcome by openly providing information to all those concerned. Advertising staffs, window trimmers, fashion show fitters, and others at that level of employment often are kept in the dark about too many things. Supervisors who hold back information about long-range promotion plans prevent interested staff people from feeling they are part of the team and from understanding where they fit in the scheme of things.

People want to "belong." Even in the age of "me," a key to people "finding themselves" fits very closely with the desire of workers to "position" themselves within the organization. The clerk on the selling floor will feel more a part of the store family if kept informed about matters of personal concern by the floor supervisor. The advertising copywriter will tackle a tough selling story after learning how important that fashion show is in securing the department's sales figures for the month. The seamstress in the fashion workroom will feel more involved if invited to see the rehearsals of the super fashion show during the production schedule.

It's called involvement. Unfortunately, too many times and in too many stores, executives fail to recognize the importance of involving everyone in the organization. The problem is particularly acute in large retail establishments with many layers of authority and slow, antiquated communications systems. The independent retailer does not have as much of a problem, since the sales staff is right there in the store. All it requires to bring them up to date on the next event planned is to talk to them during the preopening morning meetings.

It is really not that difficult to maintain communications in large stores if the systems are there and they operate efficiently. Bulletins from headquarters to branch stores do not mean much if they are not read at store level. Area supervisors can hold in-person meetings on their swings through the territories. Ad managers can hold meetings every week, or daily if necessary, to keep the advertising and promotion people informed and involved in the store's activities. General meetings, involving all departments of the sales promotion division, should be held periodically, with follow-up meetings scheduled by department heads to discuss and outline each area's role in producing the final product. Meetings where various members of the advertising and sales promotion team share in the presentation are vital and productive. It gives each of the department heads the opportunity to "shine" in front of peers and store executives. It is also a great way to keep everyone posted, up-to-date, and on the same track.

Scheduled gatherings to inform, instruct, and educate members of the organization are indispensable to business success. The other side of the coin—following up and determining that plans are carried out to successful conclusions—is equally important. Blending the efforts of skilled advertising and promotion people into forward-moving, efficient teamwork shows results in the successful advertising campaign, the sparkling fashion show, and the award-winning window display. The team functions more successfully than any of its parts operating independently.

TRAINING THE PROMOTION STAFF

If you accept the premise that all growth after age 21 is optional, the question is this: Who will pay for this added education and training, and how does the person in the sales promotion organization add information and expertise while working?

Good stores have on-the-job training programs and offer opportunities for advancement to ambitious employees. Many stores will underwrite the cost of employees' going to school at night on their own time. Night schools, junior colleges, community colleges, and extension divisions of universities schedule classes, many taught by professionals in their fields. Retail classes in marketing, buying, and administration are available in most cities. Advertising and sales promotion classes are sometimes harder to find, but staff people who seek out courses conducted by practitioners in the various phases of advertising will find it rewarding. Specialized classes in newspaper, radio, television, and direct mail, presented by working professionals, provide people in the field the rare opportunity of asking questions they cannot (or would be embarrassed to) ask on the job. Learning from professionals is an accepted practice throughout the business world and is recommended for people willing to learn after their formal schooling ends.

Although retailing has always been an industry where women have been able to rise through the ranks on merit without being handicapped because they were women, opportunities for advancement to higher management are now greater than ever. Books and seminars aimed at the growing number of working women focus on the problems of women managers working in what was once strictly a man's world. Some of these efforts are humorous or facetious, but the problem is real. The double standard still exists in many businesses. In a majority of companies men are judged and compensated on a different scale than women. Women holding the same jobs as men are often paid lower salaries. This situation, fortunately, is changing rapidly. Pressure from government agencies, the women's movement, and other sources is helping. And the retailing and advertising industries have been fairer to the woman worker than most other businesses. Training and growth opportunities for women increase constantly. As competition for promotions continues, women may have to seek outside sources to increase their knowledge and skills. They cannot expect that the men they seek to compete with, or replace, will offer the kind of training and education they need.

Advertising executives, when surveyed, indicated that courses in writing, marketing, economics, psychology, sociology, and literature are most useful for the beginning advertising person. Specialization in any or several of these areas may make the neophyte more marketable. Many college graduates are disappointed when their diplomas do not automatically qualify them for high-paying top-echelon jobs upon graduation. Most college educations are not job-oriented, especially those outside the professions—law, medicine, architecture. The existence of professional courses in advertising, art, photography, radio, and television are there for the people with the will and motivation to learn a profession. The college degree may not mean all it should at the outset, but down the line, when promotion is in the balance, the college degree will help tilt the scales in favor of that person.

Relatively few schools offer courses in retailing in sufficient depth to graduate people fully prepared for jobs in the retail world. With the exception of executive training programs offered to college graduates by major department stores and limited internship programs available in other retail organizations, most people in retailing learn the business from the people who are working in the stores. In the climb up the ladder from salesperson to head of stock to assistant buyer to buyer to merchandise manager, the individual learns the position from the person just ahead in the pecking order. This accounts to some degree for the repetitive nature of most retail activities. Promotions and special events occur at the same time in the same month year after year because "that's the way it is." The sales promotion calendar is highly predictable because each succeeding planner follows the course set down by the preceding administration. The pattern is set, established over the years, and probably will resist change for years to come. As long as the primary school for training retailers is the retail arena itself, the likelihood of major change is limited.

Many retail fortunes and dynasties began with men who boosted themselves by their own genius. They were not, for the most part, school-educated men. This is not to underplay their intelligence or wisdom. Their success speaks for itself. But in current times, as these family traditions have passed or are fading, with conglomerates and major retailing and merchandising firms spreading throughout the land as giant chains serving the needs of their communities, innovations are on the horizon.

The retail establishments of the 1970s were a far cry from those of the 1920s, 1930s, and 1940s. The 1980s will see more change. The entrance into the retail picture of marketing people, of economic and financial experts, is giving retailing a new look. The development of the shopping center as the new "downtown" in many communities has changed the face of major cities. And the search for talented people who can cope with the marketing, retailing, and sales promotion problems of the future will turn more and more to educated, trained, people-oriented individuals to operate the stores of tomorrow. And as the world of retailing changes, the creative, enthusiastic, and imaginative people of the advertising and sales promotion world will be there to communicate with the buying public. That will be a great, new retail advertising experience.

QUESTIONS FOR DISCUSSION AND CLASS ASSIGNMENTS

1. Describe how managing an advertising office requires the ability to motivate different types of people into becoming a smooth-working creative team.
2. List the personality traits usually associated with good leadership and discuss how they apply to the management of an advertising and sales promotion office.
3. Good team workers can accomplish their personal goals, use their creativity, and still accept direction and responsibility in the performance of their duties. What personality traits do these people usually possess?
4. Describe how the sales promotion manager encourages coordination and cooperation through long-range planning and continuous update meetings.
5. Discuss the necessity of on-the-job training in a retail sales promotion

office. What kinds of training can the manager arrange for to develop and motivate team effort?

6. Discuss the difficulty in developing creative sales promotion teamwork in today's atmosphere of narcissism and "me-first" attitudes.
7. Recruiting promising talent to fill the many positions to keep the sales promotion office functioning is a constant problem. What sources of new talent should retail stores be developing?

Appendixes

Appendix 1
Glossary of Terms: How to Talk Like a Retailer

Ad Requisition (Ad Request Form).   Information sheets filled out by store buyers to tell the advertising department the facts about merchandise to be advertised. Requisitions should ask pertinent questions that make the buyer reveal the main selling points of the merchandise. Copywriters write ad copy after reading the ad requisition and checking the actual merchandise.

Advertising Manager.   Administers the ad office. Many larger stores have two ad managers, one for creative and production functions and one for business and operations. May be head of sales promotion or may report to the sales promotion manager. In some stores, the ad manager supervises print ads while the broadcast ad manager handles radio and TV, with both supervised by the sales promotion director.

Anniversary Sale.   A store's "Anniversary" sale is not necessarily the store's real birthday. The date is selected as an appropriate time to promote a storewide or chainwide sale. Many stores have anniversary sales in October, a "quiet" period between the heavy fall promotions and the beginning of Christmas activity.

Art.   Also called artwork. The illustrations for print ads. Could be photography if the store uses photos. Smaller stores use manufacturers' mats or photos or artwork. Larger stores create their own art.

Assistant Buyer. The buyer's first assistant. Acts as buyer in the buyer's absence. This job is either the first step on the road to promotion for an executive trainee in a department store or a dead end, depending largely on the assistant's aptitude and aggressiveness and the buyer's training ability.

Bait and Switch. An illegal retail practice where merchandise is advertised at an attractive price in order to lure the customer into the store without having the item available to the customer. Instead, the customer is discouraged from buying the advertised item and is "stepped up" to higher-priced merchandise in the same category. In some cases the salesperson is penalized by the store if the advertised item is sold. Illegal by FTC rulings and punishable by heavy fines.

Bank. Each day a salesperson is issued a "bank" of money by the accounting department in order to make change for customers. Each salesperson handles all cash transactions from an assigned cash drawer. Banks are picked up each morning and returned at the end of the day with tallies accounting for the day's business.

BBB—Better Business Bureau. Organization sponsored and supported by business in the area to police retail policies, practices, and advertising. Guards against extravagant claims and misleading ad copy. Has no enforcement power, except publicity releases and pressure from consumer groups. Relies on self-enforcement by business.

Boutique. A small shop specializing in the newest fashions for trendy men and women. Often a shop within a large store. Fashion-conscious specialty chains have grown using this concept.

Branches. Suburban locations developed from downtown-based stores. Great growth after World War II with population shift to the suburbs. Central buying and management from downtown or headquarters store controls merchandising and operations. General manager of branch store is key executive responsible for sales and profit.

Branch Store Coordinator. Somewhere between buyer and assistant buyer in the pecking order. Responsible for flow of merchandise and information between branches and main store. May be merchandise manager of branch store with general manager of branch limited to physical operation responsibilities.

Budget. Detailed outline of a store's plan of spending for merchandise, operation expenses, and sales promotion to achieve a predetermined profit goal.

Build-up Layout. Designing a partial page of newspaper advertising from several small ads to achieve a larger look on a page. Grouping several small ads, stacking them to dominate part or all of a page.

Busy. As in "This ad looks too busy." Means there are too many things going on in the ad, with no single focal point. Ads should be designed to catch the eye and lead it through the ad to the store name. Used by executives who don't like the look of an ad but don't know why.

Buyer. Key executive in a department store's chain of command. Buyers plan and buy the merchandise, operate to create a profit, supervise salespeople, work with sales supporting personnel, travel to markets to buy merchandise, write advertising information copy, work with advertising and sales promotion personnel. Report to divisional merchandise manager. Specific duties vary by size of store, experience of buyer, or store policy. Influential in many nonbuying decisions.

Buying Office. Organizations in key buying cities (New York, Los Angeles, Dallas) that assist the store's buying staff in the market when the buyers are at home base. Independent stores pay a professional buying office to service their needs. Major stores establish their own buying offices.

Catalog Showroom Store. Retail operation that displays samples of merchandise, sells from warehouse stock, fills orders from catalog, with discounted prices indicated by printed formula. Merchandise is picked up at store by customer after filling out order slip. Low overhead operation, best for hard lines, nationally advertised merchandise.

Charge Accounts. A store's life blood—credit! Almost every store has some kind of credit; even discounters take Bankamericard and MasterCard. Stores with their own charge account systems have a built-in customer list available for special mailings. Three types usually available: regular charge, payment due in 30 days without carrying charge; permanent budget, minimum payment monthly, with legal limit carrying charges; time payment, set amount of monthly payments until merchandise is paid off.

Charge Back. Bill that store issues to vendors to collect money owed for co-op advertising or merchandise rebates. In advertising control, each ad is charged back to its department to keep budgets in balance.

Christmas Season. Biggest retail season of the year. Begins as soon after Labor Day as the retailer dares. Most stores aim for November as target date for installation or expansion of all "Christmas" departments. Trim-the-tree and toy departments get ready first. Christmas decor should be installed no later than November 15. Christmas shopping starts the day after Thanksgiving and runs through Christmas Eve. Stores do 25 to 45 percent of annual sales volume during this period, with some, such as jewelry and furs, grossing even more. The number of Christmas shopping days varies depending on where Thanksgiving falls in the calendar.

Circular. Special printed advertising supplement inserted and delivered with the newspaper or mailed directly to the consumer. Can be printed in tabloid or full newspaper size as desired, using color and paper better than regular newsprint to call attention to a special event or storewide sale. Occupant or resident mailing lists can be purchased for distribution of circulars.

Comparison Shopper. Store employee who shops the competition for price and quality comparison. Reports to merchandise manager and/or sales promotion manager. Prevents ads running at prices higher than competition's; discovers new or "hot" items at other stores; reports on traffic and sales activities of competitors' ads.

Competition. Any other retailer in competition for the customer's dollar. Many stores limit their competitive targets to same-category merchandisers. Others consider all retail, regular priced or discount, as competition. Danger in overemphasis on competition—may influence too many decisions. Best to do one's own thing.

Co-op. Cooperative funds available from manufacturers for advertising. Co-op contracts offer to share costs of advertising in amounts based on purchases of merchandise (e.g. 50/50 up to 3 percent of purchases). Money is set aside in escrow by vendor and refunded to store upon receipt of proof of performance as specified in co-op contract.

Copy. Usually refers to the text portion of an ad, but essentially is the idea of the ad. Consists of the headline, the copy block (the selling portion of the ad—words to induce customer action), price, store identification, and department location. In retail ads, there is always a price; in national ads, rarely.

Courtesy Days. The first days of a sale when charge or special list customers are invited to shop ahead of the rush. Usually lasts two or three days, after which regular advertising is launched.

Customer. The person to whom all retailers cater. Any person with spendable income, the person to whom all sales efforts are directed.

Cut. A metal, composition, or plastic engraving made by an acid etching process from artwork or photograph to illustrate a newspaper ad. A newspaper picture can be produced by a cut or from a mat. Duplicate cuts can be rolled from mats.

Discontinued. A style or item removed from the production line for any of several reasons: end of season, slow selling, and so on. Offered to retailers at reduced prices, enabling store to offer "current" merchandise at sale prices.

Discounter. Low-overhead, mass-merchandise retail operation, generally self-service, with extended store hours and few customer services. Usually operates at lower markup than traditional department or fashion store.

Display Department. The part of the store's sales promotion department that plans and executes in-store and window promotion of merchandise. Often encompasses sign department. Display manager reports to sales promotion manager. In some high-fashion operations, called visual merchandise director and reports to store president.

Divisional Merchandise Manager. Top executive of a store division.

Division (Merchandise). Large related groups of merchandise departments headed by a divisional merchandise manager. In soft lines: women's and misses' apparel; men and boys' wear; children's wear; intimate apparel; fashion accessories. In hard lines: home furnishings, furniture, housewares, gifts, linens, accessories; major appliances, carpeting, and rugs.

Dog. Merchandise that doesn't sell.

Domestics. Merchandise category that includes sheets, blankets, pillows, comforters, pillowcases. Originally made only of "white" fabrics, hence the department's traditional "white sale."

Downstairs Store. Euphemism for bargain basement. Also called budget store. In metropolitan cities, department stores carried their cheaper goods in the downstairs area, below street level. As stores located certain regular-price departments, like housewares, furniture, or carpeting in basement areas, the name was changed to reflect the new arrangement.

Downtown. The central business district where most stores are located. Usually the base or "flagship" store in department store chains, headquarters for the suburban stores.

EDP—Electronic Data Processing. Computerized information on inventory, open to buy, personnel, charge accounts—any store function the store puts into the computer bank for later retrieval.

Event. A happening. A special promotion, off-price sale, fashion show, storewide sale, or merchandise import fair.

Exclusive. Merchandise available at one store only. Some national brands will grant exclusivity to key stores, if prestige and sales volume warrant, on certain merchandise. A store could be chosen to introduce a new line or item and be "the only place in town" for a limited time. Stores develop private brand programs to compete with national brands and other stores' exclusives. Applies mainly to high-fashion and couture items where mass distribution is not a factor.

Eyeball Control. Personal inventory control system, where the retailer can judge inventories on sight, through personal knowledge of what was bought, what was sold, and what remains in stock. Obsolete since advent of multiunit stores and computer controls.

Fashion Director. The store person who is the arbiter of taste in fashion, coordinating the activities of the merchandising and advertising staffs. Travels to market with buyers or to fashion centers to report on and interpret trends to merchandising and store executives. Carries responsibility for store's fashion image.

Fashion Seasons. Do not follow normal calendar. Seasons are designated by the store and indicated on every piece of merchandise to show when it was taken into stock. The "age" of the merchandise can determine when markdowns will be taken. Store knows which fashions are current—the ticket will show the season letter. Basic fashion seasons are fall, holiday, cruise (early spring), winter, easter, spring, summer.

FTC—Federal Trade Commission. The government regulatory body vitally interested in business practices, cooperative advertising, and related subjects. Rules on deceptive and unfair advertising. Has power to levy fines, publicize deceptive advertising, or penalize store executives for major infractions.

Figures. The arithmetic of the retail business.

Floor Line. Location of department by floor or branch, listed at end of copy block in print ad; in close of broadcast commercial.

Foreign Office. Resident buying office for a store or a group of stores located in cities outside the United States.

Full Line. Refers to a store that carries both soft-line and hard-line merchandise.

Furniture Warehouse Store. High-volume retail operation conducting business in "warehouse" atmosphere, with merchandise stacked by category and sold directly to customer, who takes furniture home. Delivery, credit, and other services are available and are added to the basic low selling price.

General Merchandise Manager.   Usually No. 2 or No. 3 executive responsible for overall merchandise operation. Divisionals report to GMM. Responsibilities include merchandising, sales promotion, gross margin profit planning, and store profits.

Gift Certificate.   A voucher for merchandise sold to shopper at gift buying time who can't decide what gift to buy. Redeemable in merchandise or credit on account, never in cash.

Hang-Tags.   Tickets attached to merchandise that tell customer price and size. Also includes, for store purposes, codes that tell vendor, style, department, season letter. Portion of hang-tag stays with garment, portion is registered for control. Hang-tags often activate alarm systems if not removed—a shoplifter deterrent. Also lists garment care instructions.

Hard Lines.   Merchandise categories including home furnishings, toys, sporting goods, appliances, and other nonfashion groups such as curtains, draperies, carpeting, bedspreads.

Hot Item.   Merchandise that is selling well. The type of item that brings maximum results when advertised.

Image.   The store's personality is its image—the picture it reflects to its buying public and to the community. There can be a difference between the image the store thinks it is projecting and the way the community perceives it. Most stores have ongoing programs to change, enhance, or better their image.

Import.   Merchandise produced in foreign countries and brought to the United States for sale. A high percentage of imports can be found in most stores. The growing emphasis on import merchandise has become a serious problem for American industry and labor.

Import Fair.   Special promotion of import merchandise, often produced with cooperation of the foreign tourist and commerce departments. Includes visits by the country's celebrities and dignitaries and tie-ins with airlines, historical tourist spots, and so on.

In the Market.   A buyer's visit to manufacturers. Buyers travel periodically to the centers of merchandise to buy, to keep up with trends and maintain contacts with manufacturers, their representatives, and with their stores' resident buying offices.

Inventory.   Book inventory is a written or computerized record of what there is to sell—merchandise on hand in the stores or warehouse. The inventory figure is arrived at by unit control people who add the merchandise on hand at the beginning of the period to merchandise received, then subtract merchandise sold. Physical inventory, a check on the book inventory, is an actual count of merchandise taken twice a year. The difference between the book and physical inventories is called overage or shrinkage, and is a cause of concern to all retailers.

Island.   A table or flat store fixture placed in traffic spots on the floor for display of special merchandise.

Item.   An individual piece of merchandise.

Item Advertising. Advertising of specific items, rather than categories of merchandise. Price is always a featured part of this advertising.

Kill (an ad). Cancel a scheduled ad because of nonarrival of merchandise, price cut by competitor, or change of mind by the buyer.

Knockoff. A cheaper copy of a popular item. A prevalent procedure in the fashion business. During any season many fashions are driven out of favor by knockoffs which cheapen the appeal of the original in the minds of fashion customers. Even jewelry items can be knocked off in cheaper metals and fake stones.

Layaway. A deferred payment system where the customer selects the merchandise, and it is held in storage while regular weekly payments are made. By an agreed-upon date, the customer pays the outstanding balance and takes the merchandise home. Still popular in low-end retail operations.

Layout. The design or plan of a print ad, done in pencil or ink and reproduced in quantity for store distribution. The layout indicates the position and sizes of the various elements of the ad—the headline, art, copy, signature, and floor line. Layouts are distributed to copywriters, artists, typesetters, buyers, and merchandise managers.

Linage. Measurement of newspaper space. Space is usually measured by the number of agate lines multiplied by the number of newspaper columns wide. There are 14 agate lines to an inch. Some papers still measure in column-inches rather than lines. There are 300 lines to a column, so that an 8-column page has 2400 lines (8 × 300). A tabloid page is 1000 lines.

Line. (1) All the merchandise shown by one manufacturer or designed in one season. (2) Newspaper space, as noted. (3) Used plurally, lines can be the whole store inventory, as in "full-line" store. (4) Hard-line or soft-line merchandise.

Logo. A store's or manufacturer's signature or design, also called a sig cut, printed in a unique way for easy and quick identification.

Loss Leader. An item advertised at an exceptionally low price to bring in customer traffic. A nonprofit item, often below cost. Illegal to sell below cost in some states. As a promotional device, the store attempts to "trade up" the customer to a higher priced item.

Markdowns. Reduction of price from original ticketed price because merchandise is not selling fast enough. Unsold merchandise is marked down periodically until sold, on a pattern established by store policy.

Markup. The difference between the cost price of the merchandise and the retail price. Markup is added to cost price to cover operating expenses (salaries, overhead, promotion) and produce a profit. Usually expressed as a percentage when discussing how much merchandise has been marked up. Maintained markup is a measure of a buyer's performance over a period of time.

Merchandise. Whatever a store has to sell, its stock.

Night Openings. The night or nights stores are open. Varies from city to city. Many parts of the country have night openings every weekday. Most shopping centers encourage night shopping.

NRMA—National Retail Merchants Association. National trade association of department stores and specialty stores that provides member stores with management, merchandising, and sales promotion guidance.

Off-Price. A promotional price, less than regular price.

On the Floor. Where the action takes place. At key times, the place the alert buyer wants to be, to keep up with customer activity.

Open-to-Buy. The amount of money a buyer has to spend for a given period. Represents a figure computed from the stock on hand at the start of period, adding in merchandise received and sales registered, and checked against the planned sales and planned stock on hand at end of the period.

Order Board. Special switchboard designed to receive and handle phone orders from customers. Operators have copies of all ads to answer customer questions. Order boards are often open while the store is closed.

Outpost. Branch of a department in another part of the same store. Frequently outposts stock merchandise from several departments to help customers buy related fashion items in one convenient place.

Overbought. The condition of a department when the buyer has too much merchandise on hand that is not selling and no open-to-buy with which to bring in new merchandise and attract business.

Personal Shopper. A specialized store employee who shops for customers to their exact specifications. A great special service where affordable.

Pickup. Advertising terminology for an ad that runs in a metropolitan newspaper and is then "picked up" and rerun in a suburban paper for branch stores. Also applies to ads, artwork, or copy "picked up" or repeated when a successful promotion is repeated.

Pieces. Refers to the quantity of merchandise on hand. A prescribed amount of pieces should be on hand to cover an ad when it runs.

Profit. The reason why any business is run—to show a return on the investment of time and money by the people involved.

Promotion. (1) An event designed to promote store traffic. (2) A specially priced merchandise offering. (3) Something a buyer purchases to promote—special merchandise. (4) Advancement in position or job.

Promotion Plan. A written outline of the sales objectives of a department or division for any given period, including methods the buyer plans to use to accomplish the plan. Usually based on past performance, last year's sales, plus a percentage of increase for the planned period.

Promotional Store. Classification of store that runs mostly off-price ads and applies short markups to most regular merchandise. Their ads are usually called "borax" ads, perhaps unfairly. Promotional stores consistently undersell their competition and work on smaller profit margins.

Proof. Impression of a print ad submitted by newspaper or magazine to advertiser for approval prior to publication. The proof shows the ad as it is planned to look, with copy set in type, reproductions of the artwork, engravings, and the store's logo placed within the space the ad will run. The advertising department submits proof for buyer and/or merchandise manager okay, corrects inaccuracies in copy information or art production, sends proof back to paper with release (okay) to print, or asks for revised proof for further checking.

Protection. The security system set up by the store to protect its merchandise from shoplifters and employee thefts, and for general safety. Store detectives are used for deterrent as well as apprehension purposes. Protection, in the advertising sense, means separation in the advertising medium from competing items or stores.

Receiving. The division of the store that accepts merchandise coming into the store. Receiving occurs in warehouses or directly into stores. Merchandise moves from the receiving dock to the receiving room for ticketing and distribution.

Release. The final approval form attached to proofs sent to a newspaper indicating that all changes have been made and the ad is cleared to run as is or with changes shown. The publication assumes responsibility for making all changes indicated on release proof.

Resource. Manufacturer or vendor. Buyers seek to maintain good resource relationships to assure service and competitive advantages.

Returns. Merchandise returned to store by customers. The store's return policy affects its image and should be clear to customers to avoid trouble on the floor. Loose enforcement of return policy can affect profits. Returns to vendors are merchandise the manufacturer will take back for various reasons—poor workmanship, helping the buyer in an overstock situation, ability to transship the merchandise to another store.

Runner. A best-selling item, high on the customer "want" list.

Sales Promotion. The store division responsible for the store's sales activities—advertising, promotion, display, signs.

Schlock. Merchandise of poor quality, cheaply made and low-priced.

Season Letter. Coded alphabet letters on price tickets that tell when the merchandise came into the store and how old it is. Serves as an indication of merchandise selling trends.

Service Desk. Where customer goes to return merchandise, register complaints, buy gift wraps. These functions often handled at combination cash/wrap stands.

Services. Extras offered by stores to make shopping more pleasant. Include free parking, credit, snack and restaurant facilities, gift wrap, post office, night openings, delivery, and other "fringe" benefits that discount retailers do not always offer.

Shop. Special selling area organized around seasons or specific categories of merchandise—ski shops, swimsuit shops, fashion accessories, boutique, Mother's Day gifts.

Shrinkage. Merchandise that disappears through carelessness, bookkeeping errors, shoplifting, and so on, from one inventory to the next.

Soft Lines. Merchandise not included in home furnishings, toys, sporting goods, housewares. All fashion apparel for men, women, and children, plus infants' wear.

Specialty Shop. A retail store that concentrates on one aspect of men's, women's, or children's fashions or activities. Includes sex groups (men or women only), age groups (infants' or children's wear), sports (ski shop).

Spot. Commercial on radio or television. Spot announcements are mostly 30 or 60 seconds long and highlight a single, or at most, two items. Spot illustration in a print ad is a detailed sketch showing a special feature not obvious in the main illustration.

Statement Enclosure. Ads that are placed in customers' charge statements each month. Colorful and well designed, they are usually furnished free of charge by vendors. A form of direct mail not always popular with customers. Package stuffers are similar types of printed advertising except that they are placed directly into customer's packages by the cashiers or package wrappers.

Store Hours. The hours the store is open.

Store Money. Gift certificates or credit slips for returned merchandise. Not redeemable for cash.

Suggestion Selling. Suggesting the purchase of related items in addition to the original purchases, like a tie with a shirt, blouses to go with skirts, hats with jackets, and so on.

Sunday Openings. Rapidly growing trend in retailing to keep stores open on Sunday for customer and family shopping convenience. "Blue" laws in many Eastern and Midwest cities prohibit Sunday shopping; many Western cities have had Sunday openings for years.

Systems. The procedures that must be followed in order for a store to operate in a systematic and organized manner. Everything is spelled out, from how to write a salescheck and how to register a sale, to handling will call and layaway transactions.

Take-Withs. Purchases the customer takes home; encouraged in stores where delivery costs are high.

Tearsheet. An ad torn from the publication in which it ran. This is considered proof that the ad ran on the day it was supposed to and represents proof of performance for collecting co-op money.

Tie-In. An ad sponsored by more than one advertiser, such as a magazine ad in which a store, an airline, and a luggage manufacturer participate, with costs shared. A tie-in might feature an airline in a store's advertising in exchange for the airline offering a free trip in a drawing held for store customers.

Topper. Signs placed on top of merchandise display signs indicating something special, like "Anniversary Sale" or "As Advertised."

Trading up. Selling the customer something more expensive than the item he or she came in to buy. High-pressure methods can convert this accepted practice into the illegal "bait and switch" technique.

Traffic. The ebb and flow of people into a store. Much effort is expended to ensure constant traffic under the theory that if there are enough people in the store, sales will result.

Training Squad. Specially selected college graduates picked to undergo executive training. These are expected to be the store's future executives.

Transaction. For record purposes, a single sale completed by a single salesperson. Total transactions, and the size of the average transaction, are indicators of retail success.

Turnover. The velocity with which merchandise passes from the merchant to the customer and new merchandise is ordered to replace the merchandise sold. The faster the turnover, the more profitable the business, since the faster flow of money, reusing the same merchandise investment over and over again without seeking new financing, adds up to greater earnings.

Unit Control. The organization responsible for book inventory. The stubs pulled when merchandise is sold are counted and subtracted from the on-hand number of pieces in the unit control book so the buyer can tell what is selling and what needs reordering.

UPS—United Parcel Service. A private nationwide delivery service catering to retail stores, making direct deliveries to branches all over the country. UPS also delivers mail in many cities.

Vendor Money. Money made available by manufacturers to retailers for running ads using the vendor's merchandise. The costs of the ad are shared between the retailer and the vendor.

Vendors. Manufacturers or suppliers of merchandise and service.

Volume. The gross amount of business a store does in a period of time. The difference between volume and the cost of doing business is profit.

White Goods. Merchandise carried in the linens and domestics departments. White sales are held in January, May, and August. In the appliance industry, white goods are washers, dryers, refrigerators, and stoves. Radios, stereos, and TVs are brown goods.

White Space. The open space in an ad that frames and focuses attention on the main elements. White space can be used to lead the eye of the reader through the ad. Many retailers consider white space as wasted space and fill every nook and cranny of every ad with something.

Will Call. Merchandise that will be picked up at a later time. Applies to layaway purchases, phone purchases to be picked up in person, and so on.

Window Display. Using the windows of the store to attract attention from passing traffic by displaying merchandise attractively, in use or in stylized settings to lure passers-by into the store.

Wanted. "Most popular," as in "this is what the customers want." Indicated by the rapid sale of the item in the store.

SOURCES: Compiled from personal experience of the authors and a variety of other sources, especially from the Southern California Broadcasting Association.

Appendix 2
Glossary of Terms—Radio:
How to Talk Like a
Radio Person

Across the Board. Spots scheduled during the same time period daily.

Adjacency. A position (time) next to a certain program.

Affidavit. A certified statement (notarized if required), of exact dates and times when announcements were broadcast.

Agency Commission. A percentage (normally 15 percent) of gross billing allowed the advertising agency of record on a given account.

Aircheck. Tape made of commercial or program at time of airing.

AM or Amplitude Modulation. The audio signal for AM radio.

Announcement. Commercial or spot; an ad of 60, 30, 20, or 10 seconds.

ARB or Arbitron. Research service using diary method, selecting homes from telephone directories.

Audience Survey. A sampling of the population over a given period of time to determine radio listening. Sampling results are projected into estimates for the entire population, showing distribution by dayparts and by listeners' age and sex among stations to which a certain minimum of listening was found in the sample.

Average Quarter Hour Audience. The average number of listeners tuned into a station during a daypart.

Availabilities. Unsold time slots where commercials can be placed.

BTA. Best time available; same as run of schedule.

Call Letters. Station identification. Most stations west of the Mississippi River have call letters preceded by a K; stations to the east use W.

Campaign. Planned radio advertising schedule of specific length.

Commercial Protection. Minimum time span between commercials for competitive advertisers established by station policy.

Contemporary Music. Pop, also called Top 40, Rock and Roll.

Continuity. Script for radio commercial.

Contract Year. Twelve-month period beginning with date of first broadcast.

Commercial. A paid announcement.

Communicator. Radio conversation personality on talk station who interviews personalities, talks with listeners and newsmakers.

Co-op or Cooperative Advertising. Sharing of ad costs between manufacturer and retailer.

Cost-per-Thousand or CPM. The ratio of the cost to reach 1000 listeners. If a station delivers 50,000 listeners for $50, the CPM is $1.

Country-Western. Station format featuring country-western music.

Coverage Area. The geographical area reached by a station, based on the station's physical facilities and pattern of signal. Also service area.

Cumulative Audience or Cume. The number of different people listening to a station over a given period of time. The net or unduplicated audience. Also called the "reach" of the station.

Dayparts. Division of radio day: drive time, midday, night time, post-midnight. Station rates vary by dayparts and audience listening during those periods.

Daytimer. Radio station licensed by FCC to operate only from sunup to sundown.

Demographics. Data relative to age, sex, income, and so on for a given audience. Stations sell time by offering specific audiences to potential advertisers.

Disc Jockey or Deejay. Radio personality who hosts a recorded-music show.

Direct Response Announcements. Commercials announcing telephone numbers and/or addresses to promote direct product sales or inquiries.

Donut. Kind of commercial with live copy between the musical or prerecorded open and close.

Drive Time. Radio dayparts in morning and afternoon when commuters are driving to and from work. Usually 6 A.M. to 10 A.M. and 3 P.M. to 7 P.M.

End Rate. The lowest rate at which a station offers commercial time to advertisers, usually based on total number of spots purchased within a predetermined period.

ET—Electrical Transcription. Commercial copy, played on a turntable. Rare today, since most prerecorded copy is played from a tape cartridge.

Ethnic Programming. A station format devoted to one or more ethnic groups.

FCC—Federal Communications Commission. Federal agency that regulates number of stations, power, broadcast hours, (and communications throughout America). Authorized by Federal Communications Act of 1934, as amended.

Fixed Position. A guaranteed specific time slot for a commercial announcement.

Flight. The period of time covered by a radio schedule. Term refers to one period in a series of nonconsecutive periods.

FM or Frequency Modulation. The audio signal for FM radio; also audio signal for television.

Format. Kind of programming a station presents; middle-of-the-road music, contemporary, all news, talk, country-western and others.

Four-Book Average. Average of consecutive rating reports (Arbitron), providing more reliable estimates of specific groups, age, sex, income than a single report can.

Frequency. Average number of times an individual is exposed to a given advertiser's message over a specified length of time. Also applies to the number of cycles per second at which a station transmits its signal. Measured in kilohertz and megahertz.

Frequency Discount. Rate reduction for specified number of announcements during a given span of time. Also called quantity discount. Standard media practice—quantity purchase means lower cost per spot.

GRP or Gross Rating Points. The sum of all average quarter-hour ratings in a schedule; also the total of *reach* multiplied by *frequency*. Represents the total audience reached, including duplications. A rating point is a number based on the audience compared to all the potential listeners in that demographic.

Horizontal Buy. Scheduling of spots over several consecutive days, usually a full week.

Housewife Time. Radio daypart (usually between 10 A.M. and 3 P.M.), when housewives are readily reached by radio. Now known as "midday."

ID—Identification. Ten-second commercial that keeps an advertiser's name before the public. Also station break or station ID.

Image or Institutional Ads. Commercials emphasizing the personality or business concept of the advertiser rather than promoting a specific product.

Independent. A station not affiliated with a network.

In-Home Audience. Total audience listening to radio in and around the home.

Jingle. Musical signature or logo used to identify advertiser on the air.

Live Copy. Ad copy read by station announcer or personality, instead of being prerecorded.

Live Tag. Message added live by announcer to recorded commercial (for local address, price).

Log. Station record of times programs and commercials were on the air. Recorded by hour, minute, seconds.

Logo. Musical or sound-effects "signature."

Make Good. An announcement run in place of a regularly scheduled spot that did not run as scheduled due to error, technical difficulty, and so on.

Metro Rating Area. Central market area; includes city and its Standard Metropolitan Statistical Area (SMSA).

Middle-of-the-Road. Station format featuring popular music, personalities, news, sports.

Minute. 60-second commercial; 140–160 word script.

Morning Man. Station personality hosting A.M. drive time show.

NAB—National Association of Broadcasters. Association of radio and TV stations established to maintain industry standards and work with government.

National Rate. Rate for national advertisers on station offering both local and national rates.

Network. A group of affiliated stations which have contracted to carry certain programming of American Broadcasting Company, Columbia Broadcasting System, Mutual Broadcasting System, National Broadcasting Company, or other (regional) program originators.

Open End. Recorded commercial that provides room at the end for a live tag.

Out of Home Audience. Radio listeners to auto and portable radios outside the home.

O&O—Owned and Operated. A station owned and managed directly by a network.

Package Plan. Combination of spots offered to advertisers at a special price.

Participation. A spot announcement appearing during a program; several sponsors share cost of show.

Premium Rate. Extra charge for valuable time (fixed position, station breaks, news).

Preempt. To replace a scheduled program or commercial with something of greater immediate interest, often unexpected, like special news coverage.

Rate Card. Published list of costs of airtime issued by radio stations.

Rate Holder. Minimum schedule to preserve rate advantages during a hiatus in regular schedule.

Rates. A station's charges for commercial time.

Rate Protection. The guarantee of a certain rate for an established length of time.

Rating. The estimated size of the audience of an average 15-minute time segment expressed as a percentage of total persons in a demographic segment of the population.

Rating Service. A company that surveys a sample of the population and projects estimates of listeners to radio stations.

Reach. The number of different individuals a given station, program, or ad campaign reaches over a given span of time.

Rebate. An amount paid back or credited to an advertiser whose earned rate falls below that originally contracted for because more spots ran than were scheduled, thereby reducing individual spot cost.

Remote. Broadcast from place other than station's own studio. Remotes are often done from stores for special events.

Rock 'n Roll. A station format featuring strictly contemporary, heavy-beat music. Also called contemporary or Top 40.

Run of Schedule—ROS. Same as best time available (BTA). Quantity buy of spots to be run where they can best fit into schedule. Usually immediately preemptible, low cost per spot.

Saturation. Using a heavy schedule of commercials to get message across to as many listeners as quickly as possible. Used to build quick audience for sale event, new product, or special promotion.

Scatter Plan. See run of schedule; also called rotation.

Schedule. Times of day and dates an advertiser's commercials are to run.

Script. Radio copy, also called continuity.

Separation. Time between competitive commercials.

Sets in Use. The number of radios turned on at any given time.

Share of Audience. Percentage of total tuned-in audience listening to a given station during specific time period.

Simulcast. The simultaneous broadcast of the same program on AM and FM or TV and radio.

Single Rate. Local and national rates are identical.

Sponsor. Radio advertiser.

Spot. Commercial or announcement.

Station Break. An announcement of station's identification.

Strip Programming. Spots scheduled for the same time slot every day.

Tag. Announcement at end of recorded commercial with added information.

Talent. On-air radio performer.

Talk. Station format with telephone interviews, conversations with celebrities, listeners, and so on.

TF—Til Forbid. Advertising schedule without fixed expiration date.

Time Classifications. Dayparts, time segments during broadcast day priced differently and denoted by letter symbols—AAA time, B time, and so on.

Total Audience Plan or TAP Plan. Spot package consisting of a combination of spots in more than one time classification, usually a mix of prime time and other dayparts to cover station's entire audience.

Traffic. Department that processes orders and handles the commercial scheduling of announcements.

Vertical Saturation. Scheduling of spots densely (from "top" to "bottom" of the day) over a limited number of days to reach largest number of listeners during a concentrated period of time.

SOURCE: Adapted from Radio Advertising Bureau and augmented from authors' personal experience.

Appendix 3
Glossary of Terms—TV:
Common Television Terms

A.D. Associate or assistant director.

ADI—Area of Dominant Influence. An exclusive geographic area of counties in which the home market television stations hold a dominance of total hours viewed. ADI is a term used by the American Research Bureau and is similar to DMA, designated marketing area, used by the A.C. Nielsen Company.

AFTRA. American Federation of Television and Radio Artists, the union to which artists performing on tape belong.

ARB—American Research Bureau. A research company specializing in local, individual, market television and radio rating reports.

Aberration. Image distortion because of electrical interference.

Abstract Set. A neutral background for TV sets, programs.

Academy Leader. A specially marked "lead" into a film's start for cuing seconds of time, for feeding film into projector, for film alignment.

Acetate. Also called "cell," a transparent sheet to make graphics, change lighting colors.

Acoustics. Sound resonance of studio.

Across-the-Board. Advertising or programming scheduled at the same time Monday through Friday or Monday through Sunday, a "board" being a week.

Additive Primary Colors.   Color television's primaries are green, blue and red, combined to produce white.

Adjacencies.   Two television programs scheduled one after the other on the same station.

Affiliate.   Station with a contractual relationship with one or more networks to carry the network(s) originated programs and announcements.

Agency Commission.   Percentage of advertiser billing paid station to agency of record for purchase of time.

Air-Check.   Videotape made of what's telecast at time it's aired.

Allocation.   The frequency and power assigned a broadcaster by the Federal Communications Commission.

Amplifier.   Instrument that strengthens an electronic signal, boosts sound.

Animation.   Action is still artwork shot frame by frame in film cameras or electronically edited on videotape.

Announcement.   A message from an advertiser, station, public service organization within or between programs.

Announcer's Booth.   Soundproof room used by off-camera announcer.

Answer Print.   First composite film print struck from negative. Shows if color, quality are acceptable, need corrections. First acceptable answer print becomes release print.

Audience Composition.   The number or percentage of homes or people described by age group, sex, or other characteristics.

Audience Flow.   Movement of homes or people from program to program, or from nonviewing to program viewing or program viewing to off.

Audimeter.   A. C. Nielsen Company's automatic mechanical recording device which produces minute-by-minute TV tuning records. It's attached to a TV set, results transmitted by wire to a central tabulating station.

Audio.   The sounds of television.

Availability.   Air time available to be bought.

Average Audience (AA).   Percentage of TV households tuned to a program during an average minute.

BAR.   Broadcast Advertisers Reports, a firm that measures television advertiser activity in 75 markets to give estimates of commercial use and expenditures.

BTA.   Best times available, and the same as ROS, run of schedule. Announcements scheduled in a station's available time.

Background projection.   Same as rear projection, where a visual is projected behind a translucent screen to make a background for a telecast.

Balance.   The right proportions of sound, gray scale, and color mix of audio, even spreading of light.

Basic Set.   Empty set before props are added.

Bat Blacks.   Turning a picture to black to show darkness or to super over the picture.

Beep (or Blip).   A quick sound at the start of a videotape's cue track, to help editing or telecasting.

Billboard.   Credits at the start of a program or at closing, giving sponsor, list of characters and stars, directors, and so on.

Blackout. When the market where a sporting event takes place is excluded from TV coverage to boost paying attendance at the event.

Black Velour. Nonreflective, black velvet drapes.

Blasting. Too much sound through a microphone.

Bleed. Edge allowed around what's transmitted that can be lost by the home set without spoiling reception.

Block. String of consecutive time periods on one station.

Block Programming. Usually when a network strings similar-appeal shows together in a row to pull a continuing audience.

Board. Control panel in the control room or a week—either Monday through Friday or Monday through Sunday (as in "Across the Board").

Board Fade. Slow diminishing of sound by operator of control panel.

Boom. Cranelike device suspending microphone or camera in midair out of viewing range.

Booth. Soundproof room from which off-camera announcer speaks or for voice recording of audio tracks for film, videotape.

Break. A stopping point in studio work or a point within or between programming where a message is inserted.

Bridge. Short visual or audio sequence that connects commercial to program, or one part of a program to another.

Brightness Control. Instrument to measure and vary amount of light of a projected image.

Bring It Up. Asking the sound engineer to increase volume.

Broadcasting. Radio and television. Also, transmitting a signal that can be received by a radio or TV set.

Bust Shot or Chest Shot. A camera shot showing a person from the chest up.

CAB Rating. Cooperative Analysis of Broadcasting, a figure that measures popularity, gathered by telephone interviews.

CATV. Community Antenna Television, television by cable versus television by antenna. CATV is received on a subscription basis, whereas commercial television is free.

CCTV. Closed-circuit television.

CPM. Cost per thousand.

Call Letters. The name of a station. Call letters are assigned by the Federal Communications Commission, and in general those stations east of the Mississippi River begin theirs with W, and west of it they begin them with K.

Camera. Instrument that transforms a visual image to electrical impulses through an optical system and a light-sensitive pickup tube.

Camera Cards. Also called flip cards, they usually show titles and credits to be picked up by the camera.

Camera Cue Light or Tally Light. A red light on the camera to show it's the one in use.

Campaign. An advertising effort.

Cans. Taken from the can containers that hold film, it can mean a completed film. It can also stand for earphones.

Carrier Wave. Transmission of TV impulses by electronic wave.

Cathode Ray Tube. Tube containing an electron gun that directs a regulated beam of electrons on a fluorescent screen.

Cell. A transparent acetate sheet.

Centering Control. A horizontal and vertical control to frame a TV picture properly.

Channel. A frequency band assigned to a television station for its telecasting.

Cheat. Varying the positions of actors on a TV set to get a better picture. An example would be two people supposedly facing each other, but each facing out toward the camera—a position not noticed by the viewer.

Chroma Key. A videotape effect where an image is inserted against a different background. Similar to blue matting in film production.

Chrominance Channels. Channels in a color camera that send blue, green, and red signals.

Circulation. In television, it's called audience. The total number of people or homes that actually tune to a network or a station in a period of time—generally measured as a week or a month.

Client. In television, the agency or advertiser buying time.

Clip. A portion of film, sometimes film footage, shot for other use or general use, and inserted into a film under production.

Close-up. A very close—sometimes called "tight"—camera shot on a person or subject to show details.

Closed Circuit. Television that goes from camera to monitor(s) but is not telecast over the air.

Coaxial Cable. The cable that carries network or CATV programming from station to station or into subscribers' homes.

Coincidental Survey. Survey where people are questioned about their TV viewing at the moment they were interrupted by the interviewer.

Colorburst or Color Bars. A standard for color transmission set by the Society for Motion Picture and Television Engineers. Color bars are a check for correct setting levels and phasing when fed to monitors.

Color Correction. A skill that produces tonal qualities of colors by using shades, filters, lights.

Color Tape. A videotape that has already been recorded with color programming or commercials with appropriate audio. A videotape can record either color or black and white, according to the choice of the producers.

Commercial. Announcement, message, spot, but differing from these synonyms in that it is paid for by an advertiser versus free public service messages stations carry.

Commercial Impressions. The sum of the audiences to each message in a schedule. Members of the audience can be included more than once because a person or home is counted for each message viewed.

Commercial Protection. The minimum time on a station an advertiser wants to elapse between the telecasting of his commercials and one of his competitors.

Compatible Color System. A TV set that can receive either color or black and white.

Composite Master.   Final, end product on videotape or film that includes all regular elements and special effects.

Confirmation.   An acceptance of a commercial announcement schedule, either verbal or written, by the telecaster.

Continuity.   An audio-video script; a smoothly achieved production attributed to thorough scripting; a show emceed by an announcer with a fully prepared script.

Contrast.   Ratio of light and dark on a TV screen.

Control Room.   Enclosed area where TV production is controlled.

Co-op.   Contributions in time costs or production help by a manufacturer to the advertiser of the manufacturer's product.

Copy.   The words of a commercial.

Cost per Thousand.   CPM, the cost of television to reach 1000 homes or people; divide the audience by the announcement's or schedule's cost.

Countdown.   Usually ten seconds at the start of a tape or film as a cue to telecasting exactly on time.

Counterprogramming.   A program of specific audience appeal scheduled in competition with other programs of highly different audience appeal.

Coverage.   The homes which can be reached by a television station's signal.

Coverage Area.   The geographic area that takes in all the homes covered by the station's signal.

Cover Shot.   Also insurance or protection shot, it's a safeguard: a wide-angle picture that can be switched to quickly. An example is football programming, where camera on a player may switch suddenly to camera on broad stadium.

Crane.   A dolly that moves the camera up or down and sideways.

Crawl.   A visual, usually words but sometimes artwork, that moves up or down or side to side across the TV screen. Most often used to superimpose titles against a background, the crawl is two rollers, feed and take-up, with camera picking up what's shown.

Credits.   A list of the people who produced and starred in a show, usually at the end.

Crop.   The right picture composition by a camera.

Cue.   The signal to begin.

Cue Card.   Off-camera card with words an on-camera performer speaks.

Cue Marks.   Small holes in a film frame's corner to guide production.

Cue Sheet.   A complete list of production cues for one program or commercial.

Cumulative Audience (Cume).   Net, unduplicated number of homes or people reached by a TV advertising schedule over a specific period of time. Cumes are usually based on four weeks and they measure reach —how many people—as well as frequency—how often the same people are re-reached.

Cushion.   Parts of a program that can be removed without spoiling its flow to cut it to an exact TV time length.

Cut.   Either a direction to stop production or a production technique where one visual or picture changes abruptly to another. A popular use is "quick cuts," many fast picture changes.

Cut-In.   A message that cuts into a program. Local or regional messages in a network show, a news bulletin.

Cutting.   Editing film.

DMA—Designated Marketing Area.   An exclusive geographic area of counties in which the home market television stations are estimated to have the largest quarter-hour audience share. DMA is a term used by the A. C. Nielsen Company and it is similar to ADI, area of dominant influence, used by the American Research Bureau.

Dayparts.   Times of telecast; generally morning, afternoon, early evening, night and late night.

Decibel.   A unit of measurement for the loudness of sounds. Equal to about the smallest difference of loudness normally detectable to the human ear, whose ranges include about 130 decibels on a scale—starting point at 1 for the least audible sound.

Definition.   Amount of detail in the reproduction of a television picture.

Delayed broadcast (DB).   TV station's transmission of a network program at different times or days of the national telecast. Can also happen weeks after the first broadcast. Delays usually happen in one- or two-station markets, where all networks cannot "clear" simultaneously.

Demographic Characteristics (Demographics).   The various sex, age, family, educational, and economic characteristics of the TV audience.

Diary.   A questionnaire in which a person records his or her (and other family members') daily television viewing.

Dimmer.   Control for intensity of light.

Direct Response Advertisers.   Advertiser commercials that ask for prompt response from viewer. Advertisers' commercials show telephone numbers and box numbers to order or inquire about products or services.

Director.   Person in charge of coordinating a production before and during the telecast.

Dishpan.   A large circular antenna or transmitter.

Dissolve.   A fading out of pictures or words while other pictures or words appear. This may be done slowly or rapidly.

Distortion.   (1) Audio: Abnormal altering of sound. (2) Video: far objects appear small; near objects appear large. (3) Electronic: exaggeration of width or height of picture.

Dolly.   The movement of camera toward or away from objects. Direction to dolly-in, dolly-back.

Dolly Camera.   A movable camera on wheels.

Down-and-Under.   Directions to a musician or sound effects person to decrease volume and allow for speech to be heard. The opposite is up-and-over where music is raised as speech ends.

Downstage.   Area closest to the audience. "Move downstage" directs movement to be toward the camera.

Drape.   Backdrop of special surroundings needed for production of show.

Drop.   Backgrounds of scenery painted on canvas.

Dropout. Horizontal white dots on a TV screen caused by spots on a videotape.

Dry Run. Rehearsal before actual production.

Dub. Often called "dupe," a copy made from an original tape. A videotape or film release print.

Dubbing. Transcribing sound from one recording medium to another.

Dupe. Film or tape which has been printed from original.

Duplication. Reaching the same people more than once with an advertiser schedule.

ECU. Extreme close-up, generally a head shot.

ETV. Educational television.

Edit. To change from one scene or shot to another electronically or by splicing.

Effects. Visual effects, created electronically or optically.

Eightball. Nondirectional round microphone.

Electronic Editing. Process achieved electronically of putting picture and sound together without cutting tape.

Electron Gun. Device which throws electrons into a narrowly focused beam.

Emulsion. Photosensitive layer of film.

Erase. Electronically wiping clean the picture and sound on a tape; tape can then be used again.

Establishing Shot. Establishment of a general scene.

FM. Frequency modulation, audio signal for television.

Fact Sheet. Checklist of what's to be covered during telecast.

Fade. Slowly appearing visual from black (fade in) or in reverse visual slowly disappearing to black (fade to black).

Faking. Editing in film work to give appearance of authenticity.

Feed. Program fed by network to a local station; remote telecast microwave feed.

Feedback. Improper microphone hookup causing the accidental closing of inbound and outbound ends of a circuit which causes a squeal or howl.

Fidelity. Capacity for reproduction of original signal.

Field Intensity Contour Map. Map of the reception; intensity of television.

Field Mounted Tripod Camera. Camera mounted on a three-legged stand.

Field Pickup. Camera transmission to a studio.

Fill. Program material used if a regular program runs short.

Fill Light. Extra light to brighten shadowy light.

Film Chain. Film projector system; its camera, cables, monitor, controls and power supply.

Film Clip. Piece of film inserted into another film or run as part of a show.

Film Loop. Clipped film with spliced ends used for special effects.

Film Pickup. Transfer of film information to electronic information.

Film Strip. Two or more 35 mm film frames shown in order.

Film Transfer. Copy on film of a television production either live, video-tape or on film; also called a "kine" from the term kinescope.

Film Transmission. Transmission of a motion picture on television.

Filters. Usually video lens filters to diffuse light and reduce glare.

Filter Hike. Special voice effects microphone.

First Generation. Either the first print from the original or a magnetic tape original.

Fixed Focus. Setting the lens to hold the focus at a set distance.

Fixed Installation. Permanent installation.

Fixed Rate. Station's price for a time slot which guarantees that the advertiser's announcement will run in that position without preemption.

Fixed Service. Closed circuit television transmission, usually short-range.

Flagship Station. Network's main station.

Flare. Light reflections from shiny objects causing dark flashes.

Flash. A short explanatory sequence in a television production.

Flashback or Cutback. Return to scene shown before.

Flat. Painted props that act as scenery. Or in lighting, improper highlights and contrasts in a picture. Or in video, improper definition of a picture.

Flighting. Scheduling a heavy advertising schedule for a period of time, then stopping advertising altogether only to come back later with another heavy schedule. Used to build strong impact to support sales goals, seasonal selling, new product introduction.

Flip. (1) To change flipcard visually. (2) To change lens on camera.

Flip Stand. Device holding flipcards that can be flipped so rapidly that the change is not apparent.

Floodlight. Bank of nondirectional lights capable of lighting a specific area without glare or shadow.

Floor Manager. Person in charge of the studio during production.

Fly. Scenery suspended by ropes or wires.

Focus. Adjustment of camera lens guaranteeing perfect registration and definition of picture projected on monitor and home receiver.

Follow Shot. Following an action with a stationary camera.

Footage. A way to measure film length, or a piece of film shot for multiple uses.

Format. Programming a station does. Also the script or program outline for a production.

Frame. Single picture: $\frac{1}{30}$ second in television, $\frac{1}{24}$ second on film, or one picture of a storyboard. Can also be cameraman command to establish composition.

Frame Frequency. Number of times per second a picture passes through film gate.

Freeze Frame. To stop a film projector on one film frame or to reprint a single frame to give appearance of stopped motion.

Freeze It. To make an exact guide in which to televise a show, or a command to hold a shot.

Frequency. Average number of times an unduplicated audience viewed a television schedule.

Fringe Area. The farthest edges of a TV signal's reach.

Fringe Time. The dayparts immediately preceding and following nighttime; early evening fringe comes before, and late night fringe after, nighttime.

Gain. How strong an audio or video signal is.

Generation. The copy of a tape or film: Copies from the master are second generation; a copy from a second generation becomes a third generation.

Ghost. A double image.

Glitch. A noise on videotape.

Go to Black. Slow visual fade to black.

Gooseneck. Microphone on a stand that bends in any direction.

Gray Scale. Difference between black and white determined by ten shades used in camera adjustment.

Gross Audience. The sum of the audiences to each message in a schedule.

Gross Rating Points (GRPs). The sum of the audiences to each message in a schedule. Example: ten announcements, each with a 10 rating, would give a total of 100 GRPs.

Halo Effect or Halation. Dark area around a bright object.

Head. Device that records video or audio on magnetic tape and has capacity for playback.

Hiatus. The off-the-air time of an advertiser. Example: Advertiser has heavy schedule one month and follows with a week's hiatus.

Highlights. Brightness areas.

Homes. Homes owning one or more sets. The basic measurement for television. Does not include sets viewed in public or any place other than the private household.

Homes Using TV (HUT). The percentage of homes viewing during a given time period.

Horizontal Saturation. Heavy announcement schedule placed at the same time for several days, usually to target a specific audience that views at that time of day.

Households. A synonym for "homes," the number that have one or more TV sets.

ID. Station identification; also, name for an announcement which is not more than 10 seconds long.

Idiot Cards. Cards with script written on them for performers.

Image or Institutional Ads. Commercials that sell an advertiser's concept of doing business or personality rather than individual products.

Independent Station. Stations not affiliated with any network.

Insert. Also called key. Replacing part of one picture signal with the signal of another.

Instant Replay. The immediate playback of a videotaped action.

In Sync. When the audio portion matches the video.

Integrated Commercials. Commercials designed to fit the format of the program they are aired in. Also a commercial where more than one product is advertised but appears to the viewer as a single announcement.

Interference. Disturbance of the television signal between the time it is transmitted and the time it is received.

In the Can. A finished filmed or taped show.

Iris. Controls the amount of light that passes through a lens in a given time period.

Island Position. Commercial time within a program where only one product or company announcement is telecast; a commercial surrounded by programming.

Jack. A plug, female (jack field).

Jingle. Identifying music and/or lyrics.

Jitter. Jumping of a television picture.

Key. Main source of light.

Key Numbers. Identifying numbers marked along the edge of film.

Kicker Light. Light from behind and to the side of a subject.

Kill. To take out of operation.

Kine. Pronounced "kinny," it is the shortened version of kinescope; filming of a television program from a monitor.

LS. Long Shot.

Lapel Microphone. Microphone attached to lapel.

Lavaliere. Microphone worn on string around the neck.

Leader. Portion of film, blank, that allows for threading and cuing.

Lens. Glass ground and shaped to arrange and direct light rays.

Lens Turret. A rotating disk mounted on the front of a camera with two or more lenses attached. Lens can be changed by rotating the disk.

Level. The intensity of an audio or video signal.

Limbo. Camera shot where subject has no frame of reference.

Lip Sync. When the spoken word and lip action agree, or moving lips coincide with prerecorded sound track.

Live. Transmission of program at the time of shooting.

Live Copy. Copy read by announcer at time it is aired.

Live Feed. A network feeding its affiliates a program while it is being aired.

Live Tag. Short message added to commercial at time of broadcast by announcer.

Local Advertiser. Advertiser whose business and advertising are on television in only one market.

Log. Breakdown of the day's broadcasting into seconds.

Logo. Identifying symbol.

MNA Ratings. A. C. Nielsen's Multi-Network Area Ratings based on a sample of audimeter homes in 70 markets for evening periods and 62 markets for daytime periods where all three networks have facilities.

MOS. From "mitout sound." Silent.

MS. Medium shot.

Magnetic Tape. A plastic tape coated with iron oxide. These particles can be arranged in different patterns by an electromagnetic head. The particles will remain in that pattern until rearranged by another electromagnet. As the tape passes over a pickup head, they are transformed into an electronic signal which can reproduce either audio or video or both.

Make-Good.   A time slot filled with a commercial previously scheduled to run earlier but through the fault of a station or network the announcement was partially or not at all aired.

Masking.   Hiding a part of the set by covering it.

Master.   The original finished production either on tape or film.

Master Control.   Control center for production and transmission of programming.

Matte.   Overlaying words or a scene on another scene on film.

Megacycle.   A wave pattern having one million complete cycles every second.

Microwave.   Frequency range between infrared and shortwave radio. It can be used to carry TV signals through the air for long distances.

Mix.   Combining and blending audio sources.

Mobile Unit.   A small television studio on wheels used to cover action away from the studio. Signal can be microwaved back to the studio for broadcast or recorded on videotape for later broadcast.

Modeling Light.   A light that dramatizes depth of three dimensional objects.

Modulation.   The variance in a wave pattern, in frequency or amplitude, frequency being the number of complete cycles in a second and amplitude the height of a wave from peak to trough.

Monitor.   The gathering of television research information through electronic equipment. Also a TV receiver in a control room.

Montage.   Combining several pictures together to make one.

Moviola.   An instrument used to view film while being edited.

NAB Code.   A set of rules creating programming and advertising standards for the television and radio industries developed by the National Association of Broadcasters.

NSI (Nielsen Station Index).   Abbreviation of title for A. C. Nielsen's local market service or rating reports.

NTI (Nielsen Television Index).   Abbreviation of title for A. C. Nielsen's national network service or rating reports.

Network.   A linkup of many stations by cable and/or microwave to allow simultaneous broadcast on all stations from one originating point.

Network Feed.   The sending of program material over network lines to affiliates around the country. Feed may be aired live or taped and broadcast later.

Nielsen.   The A. C. Nielsen Company. A market research firm engaged in national and local market measurement of television audiences.

O&O Stations.   Stations owned and operated by a national network. FCC restrictions limit corporate ownership to seven TV and seven radio stations. Only five of the TV stations may be VHF.

OTO.   One time only.

Off Camera.   Action not visible on camera.

On the Air.   Broadcasting.

Open End. A program or commercial with no set ending. End may be different each time the show or commercial is aired.

Operating Sheet. A written guide for the day's programming.

Optical Sound Track. A visible track that runs along the side of film. The sound and the picture are recorded at the same time. Sound is produced in projection when the jagged lines of the track pass between a light source and a photosensitive sound-producing device.

Original. The first recording on videotape before any postproduction work is done.

Out of Sync. When the audio does not match the video. Also when the TV picture rolls, the receiver is out of sync with the broadcast signal.

Outtake. Filmed or taped scenes not shown in final program.

PD. Program director, responsible for what the station broadcasts.

Package. A complete program sold as a unit.

Package Plan. A combination of availabilities offered to an advertiser by a station.

Pan. Rotating a camera around its axis from side to side, or up and down.

Participations. Commercials aired in a program which is not sponsored by the advertiser.

Patching. Combining two or more audio and/or video sources into a single circuit.

Pedestal. Camera base that may be raised or lowered.

Piggyback. A company's long commercial made up of two individual announcements for different brands or products placed back to back.

Pilot. A single episode of a TV series produced especially to show advertisers how the series will look.

Playback. Replay of a recorded program.

Plug. To promote a product or advertiser on a program.

Power. The amount of electricity, in watts, a station operates on.

Preemptible Spots. Commercials sold at reduced rates with the station having the option to sell that same time slot to an advertiser willing to pay the full rate.

Preemption. Replacing a scheduled program with one of more immediate interest, on a one-time-only basis.

Prescoring. Recording the sound for a program before recording the picture.

Prime Time. The hours between 7:30 P.M. to 11:00 P.M. in Eastern, Mountain and Pacific time zones and 6:30 P.M. to 10:00 P.M. in the Central time zone.

Producer. The creator and organizer of television shows, usually in charge of all financial matters.

Profile Piece. A dimensional piece of landscape terrain used as background.

Public Domain. Property belonging to the public, subject to appropriation by anyone.

Public TV. Television programming supported by the public through government funds and direct donations without benefit of advertiser's funds.

ROS—Run of station. Run of schedule. Commercials bought to be run any available times at the station's discretion.

RP. Rear screen or background projection.

Rate Card. A station's or network's price list.

Rate Holder. Broadcast time bought as part of a package plan for a discount rather than for its audience value.

Rate Protection. The length of time an advertiser is guaranteed a certain rate.

Rating. A research-based estimate of a program's audience size expressed as a percentage of the total sample.

Reach. The number or percent of audience exposed to one or more announcements or programs.

Reaction Shot. A shot showing the emotional response of a person.

Rebroadcast. A program that is aired more than once.

Recall. The ability of viewers to remember an advertiser's name and/or products after being exposed to his commercials, as measured by research.

Recording. Registering light and sound waves to be re-created at any time.

Regional. The use of television to cover a geographical section of the country instead of the total country or just one market.

Release Print. The final videotape or film approved for on-air use.

Remote. A telecast from outside the studio. An example would be a sports event.

Remote Control. The technical operation of broadcasting from outside a studio.

Renewal. Renewing an existing advertiser's contract before it expires and extending it.

Repeat. A rebroadcast.

Rerun. A rebroadcast.

Resolution. The amount of resolution determines the detail and clarity of a TV picture.

Retail Rate. A lower station rate for commercials carried by local or single-market advertisers.

Reverb. Also called reverberation; echo effects added to sound.

Rewind. Reversing a film or videotape that has been run to put it back to its starting point.

Rights. What the station pays for the right to broadcast a program or special event, usually a sports event. If the program is sponsored, this is generally charged to the sponsor.

Riser. A small platform.

Rollout. An advertising/marketing technique where advertising is expanded to cover more and more markets as sales of a product also expand.

Rough Cut. The first steps of film editing, where film segments are spliced together prior to adding special optical effects.

Running Part. An actor's continuous role in a television serial.

Running Shot. When a cameraman follows the action with a dollied camera.

Rushes. Film quickly processed for evaluation.

SAG. The union to which actors performing on film belong.

SI. Sponsor identification.

SOF. Sound on film.

SOT. Sound on videotape.

Sandwich. Commercial with a set open and close and a live-copy middle.

Saturation. A heavy use of commercials in a short period of time to get the message to a lot of people in a short period of time or reach the same people many times.

Scanning. The movement of the electron beam from left to right and down the TV screen.

Schedule. Time of day and dates an advertiser's commercials or a station's or network's programs are planned to run.

Second Generation. A second copy of film or tape.

Sets in Use. See Homes Using Television (HUT).

Shading. Adjusting the white and black levels of a TV picture.

Share of Audience. The percentage of the total TV viewing audience tuned to a particular program in a given time period.

Shot. A picture produced by a TV camera.

Signature. The video and/or audio symbol used to identify a program.

Sign Off. An announcement made at the end of a broadcast day.

Sign On. An announcement made at the beginning of the broadcast day.

Simulcast. Broadcasting of the same program on TV and radio at the same time.

Single System. Film with sound on film. Picture and sound recorded on the same film at the same time.

Skewing. A zigzag pattern in a videotape playback resulting from improper adjustment of playback mechanism.

Skip Frame. Printing on alternate frames to speed up action.

Slate. A board or card which describes the program and those responsible for it.

Slide. A single frame film transparency.

Snap. Perfect registration of a TV picture.

Snow. Weak video signal; looks like snow on the TV screen.

Solid State. A system that uses transistors instead of vacuum tubes.

Sound Effects. Studio-created sounds to give the illusion of real life sounds.

Sound Track. A strip that runs down the side of film that carries sound, either magnetic or optical. On videotape, magnetic only.

Special Effects. Mechanically or electronically produced visuals for enhancement of the TV picture.

Splice. The joining of two pieces of film to form one continuous piece.

Split Screen. TV screen electronically divided to show two or more pictures at once.

Sponsor. An advertiser who buys all or part of a program. He is entitled to all of the commercial time in the portion(s) he buys.

Spot. Sometimes used as a synonym for announcement, spot is technically television time bought market by market if an advertiser wants to promote his company or brand in more than one market.

Spotlight. A concentrated beam of light.

Standby. The command to be ready for action.

Station Break. Time—on or about the hour or half-hour—during which the station identifies itself; station may also run commercials.

Station Identification. An announcement in which a station identified itself according to FCC requirements.

Station Lineup. The number of TV stations broadcasting a network program.

Still. A stop-motion photograph.

Stock Shot. Photographic materials used in many different programs.

Stop Action. Stopping a subject in motion. In film, by repeating the same frame; in tape, by electronically holding the image.

Stop Leader. A blank piece of film between two shows on the same reel. It indicates to the projectionist when to stop the film.

Storyboards. Artwork which shows the sequence of a TV commercial with all its major visual changes.

Stretch. A command to slow down the pace to fill the allotted time.

Strike. Breaking down a set after the production.

Superimpose. Overlapping two or more video sources to create one picture. Parts of one picture can be seen through the other.

Sustaining Show. An unsponsored network or local program.

Sync. Matching of sound to picture.

Sync Pulse. An electronic signal sent to TV receiver to tell it when to scan so the picture on the receiver matches the signal broadcast.

T. Abbreviation for time. The number of times an advertisement is aired.

TBA. To be announced.

TD. Technical director.

TF. Til forbid; advertising schedule with no fixed expiration date. It runs until the advertiser terminates it.

Tag. Information added to complete a commercial: usually a retailer name where advertised merchandise can be bought.

Take-up Reel. Reel on tape machine or film projector that receives used tape or film.

Tally Light. The red light on a camera indicating when the camera's output is being aired or recorded.

Tape. Magnetic tape.

Target. Light-sensitive front plate of the TV camera's pickup tube on which the lens focuses.

Telecast. Television broadcasting.

Telephoto Lens. A lens used to make far-away objects appear closer.

Teleprompter. A device that rolls a script across a magnified screen and placed on the front of the camera so the performer can refer to it without losing much eye contact.

Television.   The transmission or reproduction of a screen or view by converting light rays to electrical waves back to light rays.

Test Pattern.   A geometrical design with vertical and horizontal lines used to align a TV camera's picture.

Title Card.   A card with credits and title printed on it, to be used with a camera.

Title Drum.   A large wheel around which is attached a long piece of paper with credits and titles. The wheel revolves, giving the titles the appearance of a smooth crawl up the screen.

Total Audience Rating.   A. C. Nielsen's TA Rating, the percentage of national audimeter homes tuned to a program for six or more consecutive minutes.

Traffic.   Departments in stations and ad agencies that ensure broadcasting of scheduled commercials.

Transcription.   A recorded announcement.

Transistor.   A small electronic instrument that replaces the vacuum tube.

Transition.   Changing from one program mood to another.

Treatment.   How a topic, theme, or show should be handled.

Turnover.   The ratio of people who view a program only once over several time periods to the average number viewing in one period. Continued use of low turnover programs lets advertiser reach same viewer over and over.

TV Satellite.   A station whose only purpose is to increase the broadcast range of a "mother" station. It receives the TV signal and retransmits it.

UHF.   Ultra High Frequency; channels 14 to 83.

Unduplicated Audience.   The number of viewers reached only once by a television schedule.

VHF.   Very High Frequency; channels 2 to 13.

VTR.   Videotape recording; magnetic tape recording of sight and sound.

Vertical Saturation.   One of the choices an advertiser has when he buys time.

Video.   The visual portion of a television broadcast.

Video Engineer.   Ensures proper adjustment of video signal before and during broadcast.

Video Signal.   The electrical impulses sent by a TV station's transmitter, received by a TV set and transformed into a picture on the screen.

Videotape.   Magnetic tape that records sound and picture at the same time. There are many different sizes, but most stations use 2″ right now.

Voiceover.   Any time an announcer's voice is broadcast but announcer is not shown. Most often refers to commercials with film or slides as video.

WFM—Wave Form Monitor (Oscilloscope).   A piece of test equipment to measure audio or video signals. It allows video engineer to adjust levels to ensure a good signal is being broadcast.

Wipe.   Visual effect where one video signal replaces another, gradually across the screen. One appears to be wiped off to reveal a second picture.

Woof.   Engineering term for stop.

Workprint.   An edited version of film usually in black and white.

Zoom.   To make the camera's subject appear to move closer or away from the camera by moving elements in the lens.

Zoom Lens.   A lens that changes smoothly from a wide-angle to a closeup without moving the camera.

SOURCE: By permission of Television Bureau of Advertising.

Appendix 4
Glossary of Terms—
Newspaper Jargon
Translated

ABC. The Audit Bureau of Circulations. Organization comprised of publishers, advertisers and agencies. Its purpose is to provide accurate, verified circulation figures.

Agate Line. There are 14 agate lines to the column inch. Thus, an agate line is a space one column wide by $\frac{1}{14}$ inch deep.

Ampersand. The sign &.

Artwork. Anything prepared for reproduction by an artist, designer, photographer, and so on.

Assembly. All the elements of an advertisement, in position and ready for photography for reproduction.

Asterisk. The sign *.

Basis Weight. The weight in pounds of a ream (500 sheets) of paper in a given standard size for that grade.

Bleed Page. Page on which illustrations or other elements are printed out to the page edge, leaving no margin.

Body Type. Used to set descriptive prose, or story, all in one type face.

Boldface. A type that is thicker and prints blacker.

CAM. Classified advertising manager.

Cast (verb). Pouring molten metal into a mat, making an image of the mat in metal.

Closing Date. The last minute a publication will accept copy, cuts, or corrections for a particular issue.

Column Inch. A space one column wide by one inch deep—14 agate lines.

Composing Room. Where type is set and combined with engravings or casts for stereotyping.

Compositor. One who sets type by hand or machine.

Copy. Typewritten words submitted to the printer; art in an engraving shop.

Crop. To cut off undesired areas of photo or art work; to bring the engraving to the desired proportions.

Cutoff Rule. A line separating one ad from the next, at least a full column wide.

Display Advertising. Advertising that appears in any part of the publication except the classified section.

Display Type. The larger size types used in headlines and sometimes subheads, as opposed to body types.

Double Truck. An advertisement which occupies two facing pages including the margin between them, commonly known as the gutter.

Earlug. Upper right or left hand corners of the front page of a section above the regular type area.

Edition. That part of the press run completed before or between any regular changes in news content.

Em. Same as a pica.

Filling In. The disappearance of the small spaces in letters like e and a, caused by excessive ink or a defective mat.

Flop. To reverse photo or art work when making an engraving.

Folio Line. A line at the top or bottom of a newspaper page giving the newspaper name, the page number and publication date.

Font. A complete case or set of matrices for one size of one typeface, including capitals and lower-case letters, numerals, and so on.

Glossy (Glossy Print). Shiny finished photo print, better for newspaper reproduction because of sharper contrasts compared with softer matte-finish papers.

Gutter. The innermost margins between two facing pages.

Halftone. An engraved reproduction of any artwork that has a gradation of tones.

Hi-Fi Color. Process for preprinting rolls of high-quality color advertisements which appear in continuous wallpaper pattern bleeding off top and bottom of newspaper page (see SpectaColor).

Kill. Cancel or destroy ad.

Layout. The design for the advertisement showing the positions of various elements (heading, body copy, illustration, signature).

Lead. A space band of metal less than type height to introduce white space between lines of type.

Leader. A line of dots, dashes or stars intended to lead the eye to important facts or figures.

Line Engraving. An engraving made from a drawing, reproduction proof, or other copy in black and white devoid of intermediate tones of gray.

Linotype. A typesetting machine that is similar to a typewriter in its keyboard but casts in metal a complete line at a time.

Logo (Logotype). Signature cut (either original artwork or specially set or matted type.)

Ludlow. A machine for casting small quantities of type for handset matrices. Used only when smaller Linotype faces are not suitable, as handsetting is a slow process.

Makeup. The placement of advertising and news on the page.

Mat (Matrix). A sheet of papier-maché which bears a clear, exact impression of an engraving and/or type. It is produced by placing a blank sheet in the metal and submitting it to pressure. Molten metal may then be poured into this mold, called a mat, to make a single unit replica of the original elements. Also: A metal mold of a single letter used in a Linotype machine.

Overprinting. Printing one color of ink on top of another, such as a black headline on a red tint block. This also is the method by which delicate skin tones are achieved in process color.

Overrun. Copies printed in excess of circulation requirements.

Pica. A printers' measure equal to $\frac{1}{6}$ inch.

Point. The basic unit of measurement of type size, 8 point, 10 point, and so on. There are 72 points to the inch.

Process Color. Full color. Normally produced by superimposing the primary colors and black on each other.

Progressives. A set of proofs for each color used in a color ad. They show each color separately and also in successive combinations in the order in which the color will be printed.

Proof. A reproduction made prior to the mat of an ad or other printed material. It is used for marking corrections.

Proofreader. Person who scans proofs in search of errors.

Register. Alignment of printing elements so that all elements will fall precisely into their intended area, particularly relevant to process color.

Register Marks. The dots or cross marks placed on photos, artwork, or engravings to ensure proper register.

Repro Proof. An engraver's proof on very white, enamel finish, glossy paper.

Reverse. In practice, considered to be white printing on a black background.

ROP. Run of paper, as distinguished from specific positions.

Serif. The short cross-line at the terminals of the main stroke in some typefaces. Sans-serif: Type having no serif. Example: SERIF, SANS-SERIF.

Show-through. An undesirable condition in which printing on the reverse side of a sheet can be seen through the sheet.

SpectaColor. Printing process similar to Hi-Fi, but with margins top and bottom (see Hi-Fi).

Stereotype.   Process of casting a type metal impression of a matrix.
Typeface.   Design of type (Gothic, Roman); not to be confused with size.
Widow.   A word on a line by itself at the end of a paragraph.

SOURCE: "Retail Street," *The Toronto Star.* By permission.

Appendix 5
Essentials of a Good Ad—
Newspaper

The increasing complexity of retailing—such as the rapid growth and diversity of competition, changing customer shopping habits, and the continuing squeeze on profits—has made it vitally important that merchants get full value from their advertising investments.

The newspaper ad is the retailer's best store window and salesperson. Nearly everyone reads a daily newspaper, and readers shop the newspaper for good values. Yet the effectiveness of advertising varies widely. In terms of readership and sales results. Some ads are far more successful than others. Here, then, are some of the basic factors and rules to consider in transforming newspaper white space into ads that sell.

The most important single factor determining how many people will read any newspaper ad is the skill and technique used in preparing the ad. Readership studies have generally indicated that:

• Ad noting increases with the size of the ad.
• People note more ads directed at their own sex.

- Color, particularly for illustrations, increases the number of readers.
- Tie-ins with local and/or special news events are effective in attracting readership.

The following suggestions for copy and layout are drawn from several studies. When effectively used, these techniques and rules generally increase readership.

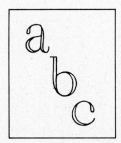

1. MAKE YOUR ADS EASILY RECOGNIZABLE

Studies have shown that advertisements which are distinctive in their use of art, layout techniques and typefaces usually enjoy a higher readership than run-of-the-mill advertising. Try to make your ads distinctively different in appearance from the advertising of your competitors—and then keep your ads' appearance consistent. This way, readers will recognize your ads even before they read them.

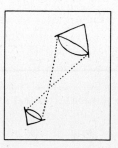

2. USE A SIMPLE LAYOUT

Ads should not be crossword puzzles. The layout should carry the reader's eye through the message easily and in proper sequence: from headline to illustration to explanatory copy to price to your store's name. Avoid the use of too many different typefaces, overly decorative borders, and reverse plates. All these devices are distracting and will reduce the number of readers who receive your entire message.

3. USE A DOMINANT ELEMENT

A large picture or headline can ensure quick visibility. Photographs and realistic drawings have about equal attention-getting value, but photographs of real people win more readership. So do action pictures. Photographs of local people or places also have high attention value. Use good artwork. It will pay off in extra readership.

4. USE A PROMINENT BENEFIT HEADLINE

The first question a reader asks of an ad is: "What's in it for me?" Select the main benefit which your merchandise offers and feature it in a compelling headline. Amplify this message in subheads. Remember that label headlines do little selling and always try to appeal to one or more of the basic desires of your readers: safety, fun, leisure, health, beauty, thrift, popularity. "How to" headlines encourage full copy readership, as do headlines that include specific information or helpful suggestions. Avoid generalized quality claims. Your headline will be easier to read if it is black-on-white and is not surprinted on part of the illustration.

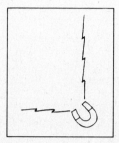

5. LET YOUR WHITE SPACE WORK FOR YOU

Don't overcrowd your ad. White space is an important layout element in newspaper advertising because the average page is so heavy with small type. White space focuses the reader's attention on your ad and will make your headline and illustration stand out. When a crowded ad is necessary, such as for a sale, departmentalize your items so that the reader can find his way through them easily.

6. MAKE YOUR COPY COMPLETE

Know all there is to know about the merchandise you sell and select the benefits most appealing to your customers. These benefits might have to do with fashion, design, performance, or the construction of your merchandise. Sizes and colors available are important, pertinent information. Your copy should be enthusiastic, sincere. A block of copy written in complete sentences is easier to read than one composed of phrases and random words. In designing the layout of a copy block, use a boldface lead-in. Small pictures in sequence will often help readership.

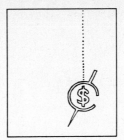

7. STATE PRICE OR RANGE OF PRICES

Dollar figures have good attention value. Don't be afraid to quote your price, even if it's high. Readers often will overestimate omitted prices. If the advertised price is high, explain why the item represents a good value—perhaps because of superior materials or workmanship, or extra luxury features. If the price is low, support it with factual statements which create belief, such as information on your close-out sale, special purchase, or clearance. Point out the actual saving to the reader and spell out your credit and layaway plans. If the item is not immediately available, state when delivery can be made.

8. SPECIFY BRANDED MERCHANDISE

If the item is a known brand, say so in your advertising. Manufacturers spend large sums to sell their goods, and you can capitalize on their advertising while enhancing the reputation of your store by featuring branded items.

9. INCLUDE RELATED ITEMS

Make two sales instead of one by offering related items along with a featured one. For instance, when a dishwasher is advertised, also show a disposer.

10. URGE YOUR READERS TO BUY NOW

Ask for the sale. You can stimulate prompt action by using such phrases as "limited supply" or "this week only." If mail-order coupons are included in your ads, provide spaces large enough for customers to fill them in easily.

DON'T FORGET YOUR STORE NAME AND ADDRESS

Check every ad to be certain you have included your store name, address, telephone number and store hours. Even if yours is a long-established store, this is important. According to U.S. government statistics, one out of every 10 families in your town probably moves each year. Don't overemphasize your signature, but make it plain. In a large ad, mention the store name several times in the copy.

DON'T BE TOO CLEVER

Many people distrust cleverness in advertising, just as they distrust salesmen who are too glib. Headlines and copy generally are far more effective when they are straightforward than when they are tricky. Clever or tricky headlines and copy often are misunderstood.

DON'T USE UNUSUAL OR DIFFICULT WORDS

Many of your customers may not understand words which are familiar to you. Words like "couturier," "gourmet," "coiffure," as well as trade and technical terms, may be confusing and misunderstood. Everybody understands simple language. Nobody resents it. Use it.

DON'T GENERALIZE

Be specific at all times. Shoppers want all the facts before they buy. Facts sell more.

DON'T MAKE EXCESSIVE CLAIMS

The surest way to lose customers is to make claims in your advertising that you can't back up in your store. Go easy with superlatives and unbelievable values. Remember: If you claim your prices are unbelievable, your readers are likely to agree.

SOURCE: By permission of the Newspaper Advertising Bureau.

Appendix 6
Dos and Don'ts for Writing
Retail Copy—Television

DO

1. Rely on supers to indicate mandatory copy (e.g., 19" measured diagonally).
2. Keep the theme of the institutional campaign in all spots (jingle, tag line, and so on).
3. For a sale spot, mention sale price and amount of savings rather than regular and sale prices.
4. Make sure pictures and words have equal strength.
5. Keep copy simple; use uncomplicated sentences, preferably short.
6. Let copy *supplement* what's seen on the screen rather than describe what the viewer sees. (Exception: audio which underscores supers that drive home an important point—price, unique feature of item or service, time limit of offer.)
7. Provide facts: advantages of item, fabric, brand name, range of sizes, colors.
8. Strive for copy that reflects the personality of the store.

Hard sell is inappropriate for a "status" store, elegance and sophistication is wrong for a discounter.

9. Avoid overdoing words like "sensational," "terrific," "fantastic," "once-in-a-lifetime."
10. Avoid clichés, flowery adjectives, assumptions such as "you've never seen anything like it."
11. Write to a specific objective.
12. Write to a specific audience.
13. Remember your commercial will appear in a highly competitive environment—try to in some way be distinctive.
14. Prerecord where possible.
15. Know what vendors are doing and relate store spots to their themes.
16. Establish a store image and be sure the image is in your commercials.
17. Use a store's slogan, worked into a meaningful summation line, if possible.
18. Broaden copy to include not just the desirability of the item(s) or event, but the advantages of shopping at the store as well. In other words, whenever possible sell the "house" as well as the item or event.
19. Relate copy to what the store is saying in newspapers or radio. But not word-for-word . . . the message must be adapted to the medium. Thus, each of the media reinforces the other but each in the way most effective for each.
20. Strive for consistency of copy style, so that the store does not sound like a different store from commercial to commercial.
21. Within the limits of consistent store personality, write with appropriate language to the audience. Masculine words for men's wear, breezy current idioms for junior items. In other words, write "people talk," not "ad" language.
22. Think twice about on-camera spokespersons. They often distract.
23. Stay tight—television is an intimate medium and at its best when you are close up.
24. Use music where possible; it can unify the spot as well as cover the sound problems encountered in many studios.
25. Time your copy by reading it aloud, the way it will be delivered on the air.
26. Use supers as sparingly as possible.
27. Presume nothing—if it can go wrong it probably will.
28. Devote great emphasis to preproduction.
29. Preplan your goals.

30. Prepare your merchandise and make sure you have plenty of back-up merchandise where needed.
31. Watch commercials from other stores.

DON'T

1. Cram too many words or items into the time slot . . . vocal delivery is rushed, the viewer gets confused, very little audio is retained.
2. Bombard the viewer with a number of different ideas or prices or benefits; concentrate on just the one or two most important features.
3. Write television copy as you would print, or even radio. It's a whole 'nother thing. Visualize what's happening on the screen as you are writing.
4. Make abrupt jumps in copy from one thing to another. Use a "bridge" phrase.
5. Strive for "cute" copy unless it's deliberate "camp."
6. Write to your own cultural/social level, but to the audience you're attempting to reach for the store and the item. This does not mean talking down (which is rightfully perceived as insulting) or multisyllabic "snob" style (which is rightfully perceived as an affectation.)
7. Rely on supers to show the type of information which belongs in audio. If necessary eliminate even the cleverest line of copy (no matter how much it hurts) to allow time for important information.
8. Forget to include or conclude with "viewer-take-action" copy. Words like "come," "see the whole selection," "save while the sale is on," "don't miss it," "this week only," "just once a year, and the time is now."
9. "Oversuper" the commercial.
10. "Overproduce" it—simplicity is the key.
11. "Overprop" it—particularly with props that might distract, or be more attractive than the merchandise itself.
12. Try to be all things to all people.
13. Write an illustrated radio commercial. If it doesn't really need video to be effective—start again.
14. Pay any attention to any of the above if you get a sensational idea that breaks the rules.

SOURCE: By permission of Television Bureau of Advertising.

Appendix 7
Co-op Advertising Control Sheet (Retailer)

Retailer _____ Manufacturer _____ Sales contact _____

name and/or number _____ Phone number _____

Co-op terms _____ Accrual period _____

Reimbursement requirements _____ Send invoices to _____

Accrued merchandise purchased ($)	Co-op $ accrued	Radio ADS w/dates	Radio costs	Newspaper ADS w/dates	Newspaper ad cost	TV ads w/dates	TV costs	Date invoice submitted	Co-op $ balance	Co-op payment received

Appendix 8
Advertising Copy Form:
Request for Run-of-Paper Ad

	Newspaper

TO: Sales Promotion Manager
Advertising Manager

Instructions:
Prepare in quadruplicate
(Div. Mdse. Mgr. retain trip.)
(Buyer retain quad.)

Date request submitted	Preferred date for ad	Ad copy and merchandise ready for advertising department	In color

Position request (if available)	Amount Vendor	Opening stock in units		Reorders	
		Floor	Mail order	Period	Available quantity

Dept.	Space	Manufacturer and item(s)	Retail	Estimated ten days sales in number of pieces

Total unit sales _____

Total dollar sales $ _____

Remarks or comments (include quantity sold in previous similar promotion):

_____

_____

_____

_____

_____

Initiated by (buyer):	Dept.	Reviewed & approved by (div. mdse. mgr.):

ORIGINAL—To Advertising Department

Department _____

Notice of Paid Advertising

Manufacturer's name _____

Attention of _____

Manufacturer's address _____

_____

Newspaper date _____ Name _____

_____ date _____ Name _____

Describe merchandise _____

Advertising Agreement

Manufacturer agrees to pay:

Indicate below:

☐ 1. Full charge   4. Your share as agreed _____

☐ 2. One half charge   5. Up to amount of _____

☐ 3. _____ charge   6. Other _____

Person with whom agreement made _____ Date _____

Special billing instructions _____

_____

Buyer's signature _____

To be filled out by the advertising department

Linage, total ad _____ Rate $ _____

Cost, Total ad $ _____ Amount to be billed $ _____

Treasurer's bill no. _____

SOURCE: By permission of Budd Gore, Inc.

Appendix 9
Retail Copy Information Form

Store Heidi's Fashion Corner   Department Sportswear

Scheduled for   Running Dates May 22 to 30

What is the merchandise?   Orlon Acrylic Sweaters

What is the single most important selling point the
commercial should stress (value, price, comfort,
fashion, prestige)?
                    Popular Spring Colors

                    Machine washable

                    Soft, cashmere look

List other selling points in order of importance.
(benefits to the customer)
          Full fashioned for better fit

          3 styles-cardigan, pullover, turtleneck

          Lightweight for spring wear

          Wear with pants or skirt

Specifications or materials (sizes, colors, materials)
          Choice of 4 colors — White, royal blue

                              Green, yellow

          Sizes 34 to 40

List customer conveniences (credit, parking, special
hours)
          Bankamericard, Mastercharge

          Plenty of free parking

          4 convenient locations

Who is the prospective buyer of this item?

          Women and teens

Selling price

          7.98

Comparative (if any)

Type of merchandise

[x] Regular price

[ ] Special price

[x] New item

[ ] Prestige

Mail or phone orders

[ ] Yes   [x] No

Brand name (if any)
          Cataline

Phone No. 782-2222

Store address:

          Topanga, Ventura,
          Cerritos and DelAmo
          Shopping Centers

Store hours:

          10 to 9 daily

          10 to 6 Sunday

Appendix 10
Advertising Copy
Information Form:
Storewide Clearance

Storewide clearance			Date _____		
Date(s) _____ Merchandise manager _____					
Please submit listings for the _____ store to be used in the _____					
newspaper. You are requested to turn in lists to advertising office in triplicate on this form.					

Dept.	Quantity	Item description	Merchandise in all stores	Comparative price	Sales price

SOURCE: By permission of Budd Gore, Inc.

Appendix 11
Advertising Results Survey

NOTE: *We must get accurate measurements of the results of our advertising campaigns. If you complete this form carefully and objectively, it will help us invest advertising dollars more effectively.*

Inventory the advertised item each day for six days after the ad or commercials run. Complete the form. Turn it in as directed.

Item advertised: _____

Type of ad:　Sale _____ Regular price _____ Special event: _____

Day/date ad(s) ran:　_____ _____　　Department: _____

Medium:　Radio _____　　Newspaper _____　　Television _____

Daily Report

Weather:　Day 1 _____ Day 2 _____ Day 3 _____ Day 4 _____ Day 5 _____ Day 6 _____

Identify:　CLE (clear)　　CL (cloudy)　　R (rain)　　S (snow)　　W (warm)　　C (cold)

Units in stock before ad campaign: _____

Units sold:　Day 1 _____ Day 2 _____ Day 3 _____ Day 4 _____ Day 5 _____ Day 6 _____

Units remaining after 6 days: _____ Retail price each unit $ _____

Summary

Did this promotion generate traffic for your department?　　　☐ Yes　　☐ No

Did this promotion generate sales of other items?　　　☐ Yes　　☐ No

In your opinion was this promotion successful?　　　☐ Yes　　☐ No

Do you have suggestions for ways to improve this promotion? _____

_____

_____

_____

_____

Submitted by: _____

Department: _____

SOURCE: The Webster Group, New York. Copyright 1977, The Webster Group.

Appendix 12
Retail Accounting Calendar

1981 Spring Season

FEBRUARY

S	M	T	W	T	F	S
4	5	6	7	8	9	10
11	12	13	14	15	16	17
18	19	20	21	22	23	24
25	26	27	28	1	2	3

MARCH

S	M	T	W	T	F	S
4	5	6	7	8	9	10
11	12	13	14	15	16	17
18	19	20	21	22	23	24
25	26	27	28	29	30	31
1	2	3	4	5	6	7

APRIL

S	M	T	W	T	F	S
8	9	10	11	12	13	14
15	16	17	18	19	20	21
22	23	24	25	26	27	28
29	30	31	1	2	3	4
5						

MAY

S	M	T	W	T	F	S
6	7	8	9	10	11	12
13	14	15	16	17	18	19
20	21	22	23	24	25	26
27	28	29	30	31	1	2

JUNE

S	M	T	W	T	F	S
3	4	5	6	7	8	9
10	11	12	13	14	15	16
17	18	19	20	21	22	23
24	25	26	27	28	29	30
1	2	3	4	5	6	7

JULY

S	M	T	W	T	F	S
8	9	10	11	12	13	14
15	16	17	18	19	20	21
22	23	24	25	26	27	28
29	30	31	1	2	3	4

1981 Fall Season

AUGUST

S	M	T	W	T	F	S
5	6	7	8	9	10	11
12	13	14	15	16	17	18
19	20	21	22	23	24	25
26	27	28	29	30	31	1

SEPTEMBER

S	M	T	W	T	F	S
2	3	4	5	6	7	8
9	10	11	12	13	14	15
16	17	18	19	20	21	22
23	24	25	26	27	28	29
30	1	2	3	4	5	6

OCTOBER

S	M	T	W	T	F	S
7	8	9	10	11	12	13
14	15	16	17	18	19	20
21	22	23	24	25	26	27
28	29	30	31	1	2	3

NOVEMBER

S	M	T	W	T	F	S
4	5	6	7	8	9	10
11	12	13	14	15	16	17
18	19	20	21	22	23	24
25	26	27	28	29	30	1

DECEMBER

S	M	T	W	T	F	S
2	3	4	5	6	7	8
9	10	11	12	13	14	15
16	17	18	19	20	21	22
23	24	25	26	27	28	29
30	31	1	2	3	4	5

JANUARY

S	M	T	W	T	F	S
6	7	8	9	10	11	12
13	14	15	16	17	18	19
20	21	22	23	24	25	26
27	28	29	30	31	1	2

Holidays, Holy Days, and Commemorative Days

Feb. 12 Lincoln's Birthday
14 St. Valentine's Day
19 Washington's Birthday
28 Ash Wednesday

Mar. 17 St. Patrick's Day

Apr. 8 Palm Sunday
12 Jewish Passover
13 Good Friday
15 Easter Sunday

May 13 Mother's Day
19 Armed Forces Day
28 Memorial Day

June 10 Children's Day
14 Flag Day
17 Father's Day

July 4 Independence Day

Sept. 3 Labor Day
22 Jewish New Year

Oct. 1 Jewish Yom Kippur
8 Columbus Day
22 Veterans Day
31 Halloween

Nov. 6 Election Day
22 Thanksgiving Day

Dec. 25 Christmas Day

Jan. 1 New Year's Day

SOURCE: Standard Retail Accounting Calendar. Used by permission.

Appendix 13
Better Business Bureau Bulletin: Comparative Price Terminology

The following guides are intended to serve as a reference for advertisers who wish to maintain the highest standards in their advertising. Advertisers observing these guides will be well within the limits imposed by the Federal Trade Commission's "Guides Against Deceptive Pricing."

1. Regular:
   Usually:
   Our regular:

   A temporary markdown from your own regular price. Goods return to regular price at expiration of offer.

2. Formerly:
   Was:
   Were:

   A permanent markdown from your own price in the recent regular course of business.

3. Originally:

   A permanent markdown from your original price, not necessarily recent. Show intermediate markdowns if taken—originally $10, was $7.50, now $5.

4. List:
   Suggested list:
   Mfg.'s list:
   Suggested retail:
   Preticketed:

Used only if actually your own regular selling price, or is price at which the merchandise is generally sold in your trade area.

5. Size price ($1.49 size):

Same requirement as "list price" above.

6. Comparable value:
   Compare at:

Comparable item must be of like grade and quality, and must be generally available in the trading area at the stated comparable price.

7. Save $15:
   Save 50%:

Savings from your own regular selling price.

8. Save up to _____%:

The minimum and maximum savings should be stated when a range of savings is advertised— save 10% to 40%.

9. Special purchases:

Exercise extreme care when stating comparative prices of special purchases. Make clear whether the special is in relation to your own prices or to those in the trading area.

10. Introductory offers:

A comparative price if used should be the one at which you actually expect to offer the item in the regular course of business.

11. Free offers:
    2 for 1 sales:

All the terms and conditions must be plainly disclosed. You may not increase the regular price, or decrease the quality or quantity of the article to be purchased in order to offer the free item.

12. Wholesale or factory prices:

A retailer selling to the general public shall not imply that he is a wholesaler or that he sells at wholesale prices.

13. Seconds:
    Imperfects:

Advertising should specify whenever other than perfect goods are

Irregulars: offered. Price comparisons should show that imperfects are being compared to the price if perfect, when such is the case.

The California Business and Professions Code, Section 17501 states:

For the purpose of this article the worth or value of any thing advertised is the prevailing market price, wholesale if the offer is at wholesale, retail if the offer is at retail, at the time of publication of such advertisement in the locality wherein the advertisement is published.

No price shall be advertised as a former price of any advertised thing, unless the alleged former price was the prevailing market price as above defined within three months next immediately preceding the publication of the advertisement or unless the date when the alleged former price did prevail is clearly, exactly and conspicuously stated in the advertisement.

Appendix 14
Long-Range Planning System: How to Plan and Execute an Efficient Advertising Program

A. Research your sales history
1. Compare sales and advertising trends—national, regional, local.
2. Check your advertising timing versus seasonal sales trends.
3. Compare against competition—major events, promotional emphasis.
4. Sources for economic statistics—recent information aids.
5. Look at yesterday but plan for tomorrow.
B. Planning the advertising program
1. Sales goals must be established first.
2. Plan your advertising investment—choice of methods; influence of co-op advertising.
3. Decide what merchandise to advertise—fulfilling customer needs.
4. Decide when to advertise—the importance of timing.
5. Prepare a detailed schedule of major and seasonal

events including (a) "natural" selling events, (b) seasonal events, (c) calendar of holidays, (d) special events.

C. How to prepare your advertising
1. Select the product or service.
2. Write your selling story—list benefits and product points.
3. Design the layout of print ad, storyboard for TV or radio.
4. Secure professional talent as needed.
5. Media, ad agencies, freelancers offer advertising help.
6. Check your ad proofs and radio/TV scripts carefully—errors cost.

D. Decide where to advertise
1. Know your potential market—demographics, location, life-styles.
2. Reach your potential market—available media, costs, effectiveness.
3. Working with advertising media—service before and after the buy.
4. Is newspaper the retailer's best friend? or direct mail? or broadcast?

E. Types of advertising
1. Product advertising—the merchandise/ advertising cycle.
2. Institutional advertising—selling the store at all times.
3. Public relations advertising—special events, community activities.

F. What to do after the ad runs
1. Sales meetings—informed salespeople help advertising results.
2. Displays, signs—windows, department presentations.
3. Internal advertising—maximizing store traffic.
4. Customer relations—developing a climate for effective selling.

Appendix 15
Long-Range Planning System: Outline of Department Store Six-Month Planning Procedure

STAGE I

The initial meeting for the fall season takes place in early March. Spring planning starts in early September. In attendance will be all divisional merchandise managers and sales supporting department heads. At this meeting overall projections and plans for the fall season will be outlined by the store president and other major executives, and should include:

- Broad statements of policy
- Economic forecasts and trends, regional and local
- Planned major changes and scheduled store improvements

Sales goals for the fall season are established at this meeting. This will be a closed meeting, consuming at least half a day.

STAGE II (NEXT SIX WEEKS)

Each divisional head will begin planning the six-month program for his or her division—building up the divisional program from the individual departments' needs and plans. Each divisional manager will talk with buyers, study past performances and sales trends, make suggestions and recommendations for improved performance for the fall season. The sum of the individual meetings with each buyer add up to a composite picture of the division and its sales goals.

STAGE III (NEXT SIX WEEKS)

The sales supporting divisions, including the sales promotion group, are following the same procedure. The sales promotion and advertising managers communicate with the divisional managers periodically as they develop their merchandise programs.

Early May

The sales promotion division's role in the planning procedure encompasses the promotional needs of the various divisions of the store. Through a series of conferences with divisional heads, the ad executives receive and digest the various requirements of the merchandise divisions to incorporate into the total store fall program.

STAGE IV (MID-MAY)

Individual presentation of divisional plans to the executive committee for approval or amendment. Joint presentation by divisional merchandise managers and sales promotion manager. Adjustments made as needed.

STAGE V

The storewide reporting meeting for fall will be held in late May, before May 30, at which time each manager and divisional head, merchandising and sales supporting, will present their plans, in talks of 20 to 30 minutes each, to the assembled management group. The meeting is held outside the store, taking the entire day if necessary. At the end of each presentation, the executive making the talk handles the discussion and questions and answers about the division's plans. By the end of the day, an overall picture of the store's plans for fall will have emerged at a level where all participants will be aware of what is expected of them, and their peers, for the coming season.

STAGE VI (STOREWIDE REPORTING MEETING)

The sales promotion division presents to the group the promotional themes for seasonal and sales events in conjunction with and separate from the merchandise activities for fall. Budgets, advertising emphases, and newsmaking events add sparkle and enthusiasm to the anticipated fall season. Sales promotion adds the showmanship without which the all-day meeting would probably be dull and boring.

STAGE VII

The completed plan for fall is printed and distributed to the management and executives of the store.

Appendix 16
Printing Processes

Printing is basically the action of reproducing an image in quantity —the transferring of an image from one surface to another through the medium of ink. This printing action can be accomplished through a number of different processes, but in commercial use, four major processes are employed: relief (letterpress), planographic (offset-lithography), intaglio (gravure), and stencil (screen printing). Each process has its advantages and limitations related to different printing requirements. In addition to the major processes, there are others for specialized or limited usage.

All printed materials, regardless of the type process used, are produced in three distinct operations: pre-press, on-press and post-press. Pre-press operations include preparation of all copy, design, art, photos, typography, halftone screening, color separations, stripping and assembly, proofing and platemaking. On-press is where the actual transfer of the image to paper occurs, and on-press operations are concerned with precise positioning of plates for register, control of ink coverage, and speed of impression. Post-press operations cover all finishing work, such as folding, trimming, binding, stacking, and packaging for shipment.

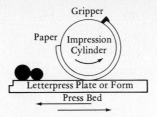

LETTERPRESS (RELIEF)

This is the oldest printing process. All image areas are raised in relief above the nonimage areas. This process uses metal type, engravings, forms combining both, or duplicate plates to carry the image. Ink is applied by rollers to the raised surfaces, then transferred directly onto paper. Impression is sharp and clear but can vary with the smoothness and texture of paper.

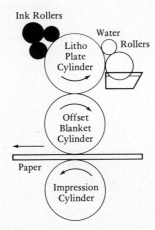

OFFSET-LITHOGRAPHY (PLANOGRAPHIC)

Litho plates carry both the image and nonimage areas on the same plane or level. Ink receptivity and transfer is controlled by the natural principle that water and oil do not mix. Image areas are photoprinted onto a thin metal plate that has been chemically sensitized to accept ink and repel water in the image areas. Nonimage areas accept water and repel ink. In offset-lithography, the plate first contacts rollers of water or dampening solution, then the inked rollers. The inked image is then transferred or offset from the plate onto a rubber blanket cylinder, then onto paper. The resilience of the rubber blanket permits offset-lithography on a wide range of surface textures.

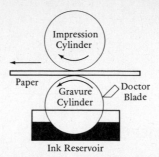

GRAVURE (INTAGLIO)

Gravure is the opposite of relief printing. Etched image areas are recessed into a metal plate to form reservoirs or wells for ink. The total image area is screened with depths of the wells controlling the amount of ink transferred and the density of tone on paper. The etched cylinder rotates in a fountain of ink, filling the wells. A doctor blade then wipes all ink from the nonrecessed, nonimage areas of the plate. The image is then transferred directly from the plate onto paper by the impression cylinder. Gravure provides quality reproduction on both smooth and textured surfaces.

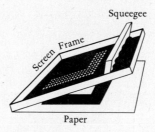

SCREEN PROCESS (STENCIL)

Screen printing is achieved by use of a hand-cut or photographically prepared stencil which covers the nonimage areas. The screen material can be silk, nylon, or stainless-steel mesh. Printing is done in a frame by forcing transfer of ink through the screen area with a rubber squeegee. Heavy ink consistency and coarse halftone screen limitations restrict reproduction quality of halftones, but the process offers high opacity and brilliance. Virtually any surface, shape, size, or thickness can be screen-printed.

SOURCE: Reprinted from *Graphics Master 2* with permission from the publisher: Dean Lem Associates, Inc., P. O. Box 46086, Los Angeles, CA 90046

Appendix 17
Sign Requisition Form

		DATE SUBMITTED SIGN DEPT. USE ONLY

CENTRAL SIGN DEPT. (ext. 4540, 4551)

	DEPT.	PHONE EXT.	SPECIAL EVENT	AD DATE	DATE NEEDED ASAP NOT ACCEPTABLE
DATE ORDERED _____ / _____				/	
ORDERED BY _____					/

QUANTITY NEEDED				All Stores
Downtown	1	Carlsbad	17	
Wilshire	2	Oxnard	18	
Crenshaw	3	El Cajon	19	
Lakewood	4	Riverside	20	
Laurel Plaza	5	Eagle Rock	21	
Eastland	6	The City	22	
South Bay	7	Westminster	23	
San Diego	8	Fox Hills	24	
Buena Park	9	Brea	25	
Topanga Pl.	10	1000 Oaks	26	
West L.A.	11	Miss. Viejo	27	
Whittier	12	La Jolla	28	
Costa Mesa	13	Cerritos	34	
Arcadia	14	Los Altos	35	
S. Bern	15			
Montclair	16	**TOTAL**		

CHECK SIZE (one size per requisition)

☐ Horizontal 7 x 11   ☐ Horizontal 5½ x 7   ☐ Horizontal 3½ x 5½

☐ Vertical 7 x 11   ☐ Vertical 5½ x 7   ☐ Vertical 11 x 14

☐ FULL SHEET
Event begins: _____ /
Event ends: _____ /
Gen. mgr. or DMM approval: _____
List copy on back

REQUISITION DEADLINES
- 2 weeks for regular merchandise signs
- 4 weeks for storewide sale, i.e., spring sale
- 3 weeks for full sheet signs

Validate both copies in the sign dept. with date and time.
Retain buyer's copy.
Submit sign requisitions to the sign dept. store 1

LATE REQUISITION APPROVAL

DMM _____ Sign Dept. _____
DMM _____ Sign Dept. _____
DMM _____ Sign Dept. _____

PLEASE PRINT
HEADLINE: Identify merchandise

SELLING FEATURES: List 4 good reasons for the customer to buy

CURRENT SELLING PRICE $

COMPARATIVE SELLING PRICE:
All comparative prices must be **substantiated:** "I assume full responsibility for insuring that a G–131 (authority for use of a price valuation) is on file in the Comparison Shopper's Office for this specific item."
Buyer's signature: _____

Regularly $ _____ (Temporary markdown returning to regular price)
If perfect $ _____ (Imperfects compared to perfect price)
Value $ _____ (Selling price of identical merchandise in competitive sotre.)
Comparable value $ _____ (Selling price of similar merchandise in competitive sotre)
Was $ _____ (Permanent markdown) (single units)
Were $ _____ (Permanent markdown) (pairs/multiples)

CENTRAL SIGN DEPT. USE ONLY

EDITED	TYPESET	SENT

SOURCE: By permission of May Company, Los Angeles.

Appendix 18
Sign Requisition
Instructions

1. Print your name, department, and extension clearly so that you can be notified of any problem.
2. Name any special event *specifically* (fall, Christmas, month-end).
3. Order *only* two signs for each store. Every sign must have a backer. The number listed should be the number of individual signs desired, not pairs.
4. *Headline:* the merchandise should be named *specifically*. This line will appear on your sign in **bold** print. Do not list as merely "sportswear."
5. Two *bullet lines only.*
6. *Selling features:* If you wish, a manufacturer's name may appear on this line.
7. *Selling features:* Information which helps to sell the merchandise and is not obvious to the customer. Stress quality, utility, ease of care, fashion, value, and selection.
8. *Selling features:* Sizes should appear on the last line when listed.

9. *Selling price:* This is the price at which the merchandise will be sold. It should always be listed and will appear in **bold** type on the printed sign.
10. *Comparative pricing:* List for reduced merchandise or special values; must be listed for any merchandise which is on sale, imperfect, or of special value.

SOURCE: By permission of May Company, Los Angeles.

Appendix 19
Merchandise Sign Policy

1. Merchandise signs are used only for the following purposes:
   - *Trend merchandise:* New, innovative, trend-setting. There must be a selection large enough to fill a rack.
   - *New merchandise:* Received recently and has unusual selling features not readily apparent to the customer (stain resistant, water repellent, and so on).
   - *Unmarked merchandise:* Has not been ticketed. Sold entirely by the price on the sign.
   - *Own brand merchandise:* Produced by the company. The brand name should appear on the sign.
2. Merchandise signs are printed in the following sizes: $5\frac{1}{2}'' \times 7''$ horizontal. *Note:* Budget stores: $7'' \times 11''$ horizontal.
3. All merchandise signs are printed in brown optima typeface on beige sisal paper by the Sign Department.
4. Designed trademarks of manufacturers may NOT be used on merchandise signs.

5. Manufacturer-prepared signs may *NOT* be on display, walls, fixtures, or counters unless submitted to the Sign Department for approval.
6. Sign holders must be used for all signs. They must *never* be taped or stapled to walls, fixtures, or counters.
7. Signs may *not* be altered. Nothing should be taped or stapled to them, including words or prices. If the sign is incorrect, it should be reordered. Branch stores should notify the buyer and the Sign Department.
8. Merchandise signs must be in good condition. Dirty, faded, or worn-out signs must be taken down and reordered.
9. Merchandise signs must be currently approved for use. They should be printed in the proper format, typeface, and design. *All outdated signs should be discarded.*
10. All requisitions for merchandise signs must be submitted to the Sign Department for copy approval, printing, and distribution.

SOURCE: By permission of May Company, Los Angeles.

Appendix 20
Merchandise Sign Sample

GIFTS TO GO

gifts from arizona naturals

- hand painted paper mache boxes
- filled with scents of potpourri florals in large and small sizes

8.00-12.00

136

SOURCE: By permission of May Company, Los Angeles.

Bibliography

The Arbitron Company. *New Season for Arbitron Television.* April 1980.

The Arbitron Company. *Quick Reference Guide to Arbitron Radio Market Report.* September 1977.

Barmash, Isadore. *The Self-Made Man.* New York: Macmillan, 1969.

Bedell, Clyde. *How to Write Advertising That Sells.* New York: McGraw-Hill, 1940.

Edwards, Charles M., Jr., and Russell A. Brown. *Retail Advertising and Sales Promotion.* Englewood Cliffs, N.J.: Prentice-Hall, 1959.

Facts About Newspapers. American Newspaper Publishers Association, 1980.

Heighton, Elizabeth J., and Don R. Cunningham. *Advertising in the Broadcast Media.* Belmont, Calif.: Wadsworth, 1976.

Jarnow, Jeannette A., and Beatrice Judelle. *Inside the Fashion Business,* 2nd ed. New York: Wiley, 1974.

Kleppner, Otto. *Advertising Procedure,* 6th ed. Englewood Cliffs, N.J.: Prentice-Hall, 1973.

Lem, Dean Phillip. *Graphic Master,* 2nd ed. Los Angeles, Calif.: Dean Lem Associates, 1977.

Newspaper Advertising Bureau. *Advertising Planbook, 1980.*

National Retail Merchants Association. *Advertising, Sales Promotion Planbook, 1980.*

National Retail Merchants Association, New York. *The Buyer's Manual, 1979.*

Ocko, Judy Young, and M. L. Rosenblum. *How To Be a Retail Advertising Pro.* New York: Sales Promotion Division, National Retail Merchants Association, 1977.

Osborn, Alex F. *Applied Imagination.* New York: Scribner's, 1957.

Radio Advertising Bureau. *Advertising Planbook, 1980.*

Radio Advertising Bureau. *Radio Facts, 1980.*

"Retail Street." *The Toronto Star.* Toronto, 1980.

Rosenblum, M. L. *How To Design Effective Store Advertising.* New York: Sales Promotion Division, National Retail Merchants Association, 1961.

Seklemian, M. *Sek Says.* New York: Milton B. Conhaim, Inc., 1979.

Television Bureau of Advertising. *TV Basics 24,* 1981.

Index

82 83 84 85 86 9 8 7 6 5 4 3 2 1